hands-on
english language learning
Middle Years

Project Editor
Jennifer E. Lawson

Contributing Authors
Trish Hamlin
Jennifer E. Lawson
Daria Orloff
Clea Schmidt

Project Reviewers
Joanna Bates
Caroline Lai
Miles MacFarlane
Anita Riedl
Barbara Thomson

PORTAGE & MAIN PRESS
Winnipeg • Manitoba • Canada

© 2011 by Jennifer Lawson

Pages of this publication designated as reproducible with the following icon may be reproduced under licence from Access Copyright. All other pages may only be reproduced with the express written permission of Portage & Main Press, or as permitted by law.

All rights are otherwise reserved and no part of this publication may be reproduced, stored in a retrieval system, or transmitted in any form or by any means, electronic, mechanic, photocopying, scanning, recording or otherwise, except as specifically authorized.

Portage & Main Press gratefully acknowledges the financial support of the Province of Manitoba through the Department of Culture, Heritage, Tourism & Sport and the Manitoba Book Publishing Tax Credit, and the Government of Canada through the Canada Book Fund (CBF) for our publishing activities.

Hands-On English Language Learning Middle Years
ISBN: 978-1-55379-260-4
Printed and bound in Canada by Prolific

Series Editor:
Leslie Malkin

Book and Cover Design:
Relish Design Studio

Cover Photo Credits:
©iStockphoto.com

Illustrations:
Jess Dixon
Lisa Rae

PORTAGE & MAIN PRESS

100 – 318 McDermot Ave.
Winnipeg, MB Canada R3A 0A2
Email: books@portageandmainpress.com
Tel: 204-987-3500
Toll-free fax: 1-866-734-8477
Toll-free: 1-800-667-9673

www.pandmpress.com

Contents

Introduction to *Hands-On English Language Learning* ... 1

Program Introduction ... 1
Who Are English Language Learners (ELLs)? ... 1
Stages of Language Acquisition ... 1
Program Principles ... 2
The Middle-Years Learner ... 4
Topics of Study ... 4
Program Implementation ... 5
Tips for Teachers ... 7
Classroom Environment ... 7
Timelines ... 8
Classroom Management ... 8
Cooperative Learning Activities ... 8
Peer Helpers ... 9
Important Notes About Terminology ... 9
Using Care and Sensitivity ... 10
Scope and Sequence Charts for *Hands-On English Language Learning* ... 11
Subject-Area Correlation ... 20

Hands-On English Language Learning Assessment Plan ... 32

Introduction ... 32
Cultural Knowledge ... 32
Cultural Competency ... 32
Purposes of Classroom-Based Assessment for Language Learning and Use ... 33
Assessment Tasks Appropriate for Middle-Years English Language Learners ... 33
Teacher Considerations When Assessing Middle-Years English Language Learners ... 34
Assessment Tools ... 34
Assessment Blackline Masters ... 37
References ... 41

Module 1 ... 43

Introduction ... 44
Books for Students ... 48
Websites ... 50
  1 Greetings/Social Communication ... 51
  2 The Classroom ... 58
  3 The School ... 65
  4 School Activities ... 71
  5 The Alphabet ... 76
  6 Colours ... 83
  7 Numbers, Counting, and Math ... 88
  8 The Calendar – Days of the Week ... 99
  9 The Calendar – Months of the Year ... 104
  10 Personal Information ... 109
  11 Culminating Activity: Creating A Board Game ... 117
References for Teachers ... 121

Module 2 ... 123

Introduction ... 124
Books for Students ... 128
Websites ... 130
  1 Emotions ... 132
  2 Clothing ... 139
  3 Food ... 147
  4 Body Parts and Health ... 159
  5 Physical Activities ... 168
  6 Hobbies and Interests ... 175
  7 Music and Instruments ... 181
  8 Homes ... 189
  9 The Community ... 196
  10 Ordering Food ... 203
  11 Technology ... 211
  12 Culminating Activity: Creating an "All About Me" Electronic Portfolio ... 216
References for Teachers ... 220

Module 3 — 223
Introduction — 224
Books for Students — 228
Websites — 230
  1 Canadian Geography — 232
  2 Canadian Symbols — 242
  3 Celebrations and Holidays — 248
  4 Relationships — 257
  5 Rules, Laws, and Responsibility — 262
  6 Government — 268
  7 World Geography — 277
  8 North America — 283
  9 Cultural Diversity — 288
  10 Our World Community — 295
  11 Basic Human Needs — 299
  12 Human Rights — 307
  13 The Media — 313
  14 Culminating Activity: Designing a Newspaper — 319
References for Teachers — 323

Module 4 — 325
Introduction — 326
Books for Students — 330
Websites — 332
  1 Nature — 336
  2 Weather and Seasons — 343
  3 Animals of Canada — 352
  4 Plants of Canada — 363
  5 Natural Habitats — 372
  6 Importance of the Environment — 379
  7 Human Impact on the Environment — 384
  8 Air Pollution — 389
  9 Water — 395
  10 Reduce, Reuse, Recycle — 401
  11 Saving Energy — 406
  12 Culminating Activity: Sustainability Life Practices — 410
References for Teachers — 414

Module 5 — 415
Introduction — 416
Step 1: Assessment for Learning — 416
Step 2: Curriculum Review — 417
Step 3: Instructional Strategies — 418
Making Connections to Prior Knowledge — 418
Building Vocabulary — 420
Conceptual Understanding — 421
Conducting Research — 422
The Language-Rich Classroom — 424
Other Things to Consider for Unit Planning — 425
Concluding Note to Teachers — 426
Unit Planning Blackline Masters — 427
References — 430

Introduction to
Hands-On English Language Learning

Important Note About Blackline Masters

A series of blackline masters accompanies each lesson of *Hands-On English Language Learning*, comprising content such as Vocabulary Cards, Activity Sheets, Glossary sheets, and so on. Each blackline master (BLM) has a sequential reference number: For example, BLM 3.6.2 is the second BLM from module 3, lesson 6. All BLMs are found on the CD that accompanies *Hands-On English Language Learning*, and each BLM is easily located on the CD via its reference number. You will find snapshots of these BLMs at the end of each lesson in the *Hands-On English Language Learning* book (four BLMs per page).

Program Introduction

The *Hands-On English Language Learning* program focuses on developing students' English language skills through listening, speaking, reading, writing, viewing, and representing. In keeping with the philosophy of the *Hands-On* series of books, activities presented herein are student-centered and use authentic, hands-on experiences to support and encourage English language learning.

The *Hands-On English Language Learning* program is designed to be a resource for classroom teachers, specialist teachers working with English language learners, and other educational professionals who support these students.

Who Are English Language Learners (ELLs)?

Students may be learning English as an additional language for a variety of reasons. English language learners include

- Students new to Canada whose first language is not English, and who may already have received age-appropriate schooling, may have had periods of interrupted schooling, or may have had no previous schooling;

- Students new to Canada who have experienced living in refugee camps for all or part of their lives. These children may have limited or no school experience, and may also have experienced traumatic events in their lives;

- Students born in Canada and who have been raised and/or educated in a language other than English, such as children from German-speaking Hutterite colonies;

- Aboriginal students who come to school speaking one or more Aboriginal languages or who speak a dialect of English that has been strongly influenced by Aboriginal languages.

The background and experiences of English language learners vary from student to student; this must be carefully considered when planning their education, and instruction should be differentiated to meet the needs of individual students. This will ensure that instruction is appropriate for each English language learner. It is critically important to take into consideration the individual language profiles of each learner when planning programming for them.

Stages of Language Acquisition

Current research on language acquisition indicates that language learners progress through various stages of proficiency in

▶

listening, speaking, reading, writing, viewing, and representing. Provincial policy documents related to English language learning in Canada and abroad reflect this premise by identifying the characteristics of learners in the different stages of language acquisition. The following outlines some of these characteristics using one common structure:

Stage 1 – These students use English for essential daily purposes and are becoming familiar with English language patterns. They try to make sense of messages and show some limited understanding of shorter passages of language. Their comprehension often relies on visual cues or gestures. Students frequently respond non-verbally (for example, by nodding their heads for "yes") or with single words or short phrases.

Stage 2 – These students use English in supported and familiar activities and contexts. They listen with greater understanding and use everyday expressions independently. They demonstrate growing confidence and use personally relevant language appropriately.

Stage 3 – These students use English independently in most contexts. They speak with less hesitation and demonstrate increasing understanding. They produce more complex phrases and sentences and participate more fully in activities related to academic content areas. They use newly acquired vocabulary to retell, describe, explain, and compare.

Stage 4 – These students use English with proficiency that enables them to interact effectively in a wide range of personal and academic contexts. Stage 4 is often the longest in the language-acquisition process. There may be significant differences between the ability of students at the beginning of this stage and those at the end of this stage. Students use more extensive vocabulary with greater accuracy and correctness. They use reading and writing skills to explore concepts in greater depth, even though their proficiency is still developing in language that is specific to academic program areas (Adapted from the *Ontario Curriculum, Grades 1–8: English as a Second Language and English Literacy Development,* 2001).

The four-stage developmental continuum described above reflects the approach used by several educational jurisdictions to identify language levels of middle-years students. It is important to note that these descriptions are summative in nature and do not replace the guidelines presented in provincial policy documents related to English language learners. Teachers are encouraged to review the guidelines presented in such documents and then use the ***Hands-On English Language Learning*** program to support local mandates.

The ***Hands-On English Language Learning*** program has been designed to accommodate this four-stage continuum. The modules have been developed with a developmental progression: module 1 is for beginning English language learners, while modules 2, 3, and 4 offer progressively more challenging language learning opportunities for students (module 5 has a different format altogether, guiding teachers in developing their own curriculum-specific unit plans). However, it is also important to note that each module offers a variety of suggestions for differentiation, and also provides numerous opportunities for whole-class integrated learning experiences. As such, the lessons in modules 2, 3, and 4 can be used at varying middle-years grades, with students of diverse language abilities.

Program Principles

The themes and activities presented in the ***Hands-On English Language Learning*** program are based on the following guiding principles:

1. Activities and resources recognize, validate, encourage, and build on students' background knowledge and experiences;

2. Activities and resources promote the development of bilingual skills, by encouraging connections between students' first language and English;

3. Essential language skills and knowledge form the basis of preliminary activities;

4. Subject-area content is used as a vehicle for English-language instruction/learning;

5. Activities highlight the different ways in which language is used in various subject areas;

6. A variety of concrete and visual supports are used frequently throughout the program;

7. Activities are designed to enable students in the different stages of learning English and/or at varying stages of development in English literacy to be successful;

8. Listening, speaking, reading, writing, viewing, and representing tasks form the basis of lesson activities, to encompass the wide range of English language skills and concepts.

9. Language skills should be integrated and embedded in meaningful contexts to maximize learning.

10. Students require explicit instruction in learning about and engaging with different aspects of diversity, including linguistic, cultural, socio-economic, age, and gender diversity.

11. Activities are designed to integrate concepts and skills from all subject areas. This thematic approach allows ELL students to make connections between new ideas, vocabulary, and language structures (Freeman and Freeman 2007).

12. Emphasis is placed on teaching skills and concepts that exist across all subject areas. This includes research skills, problem solving, decision-making, and critical thinking.

13. Students benefit from developing an understanding of their own metacognitive processes. In the middle years, students should be encouraged to think about their thinking related to their own learning, reflect on what they know and what they do not know.

14. The role of parents is significant for all students, but the academic stakes are much higher for the middle-years learner than for younger children. Therefore, parental support and involvement in student learning is essential.

Note: It is crucial to understand that parental involvement, while important, may be challenging. Some parents arriving in Canada may be limited in their knowledge of English. Others may also have limited literacy skills in their first language. As such, cultural liaisons and community translators will be an asset. For more information about refugee students, please refer to the publication *Students from Refugee Backgrounds: A Guide for Teachers and Schools* found on the British Columbia Ministry of Education website (see <www.bced.gov.bc.ca/esl/refugees_teachers_guide.pdf>).

15. In order to address the diverse needs of English language learners, differentiated instruction is requisite. Some ELL students will have school experience and reading/writing skills in their first language. Other students may have limited school experience and may therefore be emergent readers and writers. Teachers must consider these diverse needs and adapt each student's program accordingly, including activities, activity sheets, and assessment techniques. Suggestions for adaptations are made throughout the ***Hands-On English Language Learning*** book, but teachers are also encouraged to base differentiated

▶

instruction strategies on the individual skills and strengths of each student.

The Middle-Years Learner

In the Canadian school system, "middle years" usually refers to grades 5 to 8 students between the ages of 10 and 14 years. Children in this age range have distinct developmental needs, and they require a unique learning environment that meets their specific requirements and which may differ from those of students in early-years and senior-years classrooms. The middle years are a time of transition from concrete, emergent learning experiences toward more abstract contexts. Although every child is unique, middle years students tend to share some common traits.

Note: The following description is of the typical middle-years learner, regardless of whether or not he or she is an English language learner.

Middle years students:

- Demonstrate a wide range of development in the transition between concrete and abstract thinking;
- Prefer active learning experiences to conventional academics;
- Prefer interaction with peers during learning experiences;
- Respond positively to real-life contexts and situations;
- May show a strong need for approval from both peers and adults;
- Demonstrate an interest in social and environmental issues;
- Value democratic practices in the classroom;
- Are influenced by adult role models who listen to personal concerns;
- Demonstrate a more sophisticated sense of humour.

In responding to these traits, the following strategies will benefit the middle-years English language learner and serve the middle-years teacher well:

- Use a wide variety of methodologies to differentiate instruction.
- Communicate clear expectations.
- Use student curiosity and interests to focus classroom inquiry.
- Plan for and implement a variety of learning experiences, including independent, collaborative, and cooperative learning.
- Give specific feedback, and celebrate student achievements.
- Embed instruction in meaningful activities.
- Model effective interpersonal communication skills.
- Get to know students by gaining an understanding of their background and academic strengths and challenges.
- Value and validate students' concerns and ideas.
- Promote a democratic classroom to encourage students to take increasing responsibility.
- Display a sense of humour and an element of fun in the classroom setting.

(Adapted from *Grades 5 to 8 English Language Arts: A Foundation for Implementation*, Manitoba Education and Training, 1998.)

Topics of Study

The ***Hands-On English Language Learning*** program includes topics of study that will assist students in developing language skills as well as experiential knowledge related to their school, their community, and the world around them. Consideration has been given to essential language skills and knowledge required by Canadian students.

▶

Module 1 focuses on basic language skills, with topics such as the classroom, the school, numbers, colours, letters, and calendars. These lessons are intended to give students essential language skills required to communicate and participate in their classroom and school.

Modules 2, 3, and 4 focus on the following themes:

Module 2: Environmental Issues

Module 3: Cultural Diversity

Module 4: Global Citizenship

Themes and activities are age-appropriate and of high interest to middle-years students, and have been created to foster the development of essential English-language vocabulary and skills in listening, speaking, reading, writing, viewing, and representing. Consideration has also been given to current curricular documents (see subject-area correlation charts on pages 20–31) as well as to research in acquisition of English as an additional language.

Module 5 provides guidance for teachers for developing their own curriculum-specific unit plans to meet the needs of English-language learners within an inclusive learning environment.

Program Implementation

Hands-On English Language Learning is arranged in a format that makes it easy for teachers to plan and implement. All modules in ***Hands-On English Language Learning*** are organized as follows:

Introduction: This section introduces the overall topic of study for the module. It provides a general outline, background information for teachers, and planning notes.

Books for Students and **Websites:** This section offers a list of children's books and several annotated websites that relate to lesson topics. Resources incorporate a variety of diverse authors, topics, and viewpoints.

Lessons: Each module is organized into lessons, and each lesson includes the following:

Curricular Connections: All lessons provide information on how topics align with subject-area curricula in language arts, mathematics, science, social studies, physical education/health, and the arts.

Background Information for Teachers: Some lessons provide teachers with content knowledge required to present the lesson, or other important related information teachers might need to help them lead the lesson. This information is offered in a clear, concise format and focuses specifically on the topic of study.

Vocabulary: New vocabulary introduced in the lesson is listed at the beginning of each lesson. Vocabulary cards with the lesson's new vocabulary are also included at the end of the lesson to support students in learning (and teachers in defining) new vocabulary.

Note: For most vocabulary cards, a picture is included with the new word. Some particularly abstract vocabulary, however, such as *effect(s)* and *book review* (see module 4, lesson 7), are difficult to illustrate. For this vocabulary, only the word is included on the card. Teachers should introduce such vocabulary in context to ensure understanding. For example, the term *book review* can be introduced after reading a book with the class and conducting a book review with teacher guidance. Then, students and teachers can explore and discuss ways of illustrating the vocabulary card to reflect students' understanding of the term.

Materials: A complete list of materials required to conduct the lesson's main activities is provided. The quantity of materials necessary will depend on how the activities are conducted. If students are working individually, teachers will need enough materials for each student. If

▶

Introduction

students are working in groups, the materials required will be significantly reduced. Many of the items are for teachers to use for display or demonstration purposes, or to make charts for recording students' ideas. In some cases, visual materials (for example, large pictures, sample charts) have been included with the activity to assist teachers in presenting ideas and questions and encouraging discussion.

Activities: A variety of task types need to be practised in a range of communicative contexts to support learners in reaching their language-learning goals. Accordingly, the main activity within each lesson is divided into five parts:

Integrated Class Activities: To create meaningful links to the rest of the classroom community as well as to academic content areas, these activities are intended for the whole class. They focus on curricular topics and/or academic skills, and enable students to participate in meaningful and contextual learning experiences.

Whole-Class Career Connections: Middle-years students are progressively more interested in exploring their future life plans and benefit from opportunities to learn about career choices, future educational opportunities, and employability skills. Each lesson in the *Hands-On English Language Learning* program includes suggestions for engaging students in activities related to career education; specifically, career topics are connected to the topic of each lesson. These activities will benefit all students in an inclusive classroom setting, and it is suggested that they be considered whole-class learning experiences.

Note: Both the integrated class activities and the whole-class career connections can be implemented at various times during the lesson. For example, doing an integrated class activity as a springboard to other instruction allows for the introduction of academic content and language that will benefit all students while supporting ELLs through scaffolding. Alternatively, doing whole-class career connections activities following instructional, peer, and independent activities provides another context for ELLs to use and review vocabulary and concepts just learned. As such, teachers will make these decisions according to the needs of their students, while understanding the benefits to varying the sequencing of lessons and maintaining flexibility in planning.

Instructional Activities: Intended to be led by a teacher or other qualified adult, these activities are designed to introduce new language and teach new concepts. Each activity comprises a step-by-step procedure with higher-level questioning techniques and suggestions to encourage discussion, inquiry, decision making, and problem solving.

Peer Activities: These cooperative learning activities, designed for small, combined groups or pairs of both English language learners and peer helpers, foster student relations and classroom community (see page 9 for more about peer helpers).

Independent Activities: Designed for use by individual students, these include activity sheets, practice tasks, and solitary games.

Activity Sheets: Most lessons include (a) reproducible activity sheet(s), which is (are) designed to correlate with the lesson's instruction and new concepts. Students will use some of these activity sheets to record ideas during instructional activities, and others as independent follow-up activities to instructional and peer activities. Depending on their students' needs, teachers may choose to have students work on these activity sheets independently, in pairs, or in small groups. Alternatively, teachers may choose to read through the activity sheets aloud and complete them together as a group; or, they may transform the activity sheets into overheads, PowerPoints, or other technologically generated images. Since it is also important for students to learn to create their own charts and recording formats, teachers can use the activity sheets as examples of ways to record and communicate ideas about an activity. Students can then create their own sheets rather than use the ones provided.

Next Steps: Some lessons include this section, which guides teachers through a subsequent activity or sequence of activities to carry out with students, following developmentally from the preceding activity or activities. For example, the instructional activity for a lesson on numbers and counting may include a detailed description of activities using numbers from 0 to 10. The next step would be to move to using numbers and counting to 20, then to 30, and so on.

Extensions: Most lessons include optional extension activities to extend, enrich, and reinforce the lesson's vocabulary and concepts.

Assessment Suggestions: Throughout each module, several suggestions are made for assessing student learning. Assessment is addressed in detail in the next section of *Hands-On English Language Learning.* These strategies focus specifically on assessment *for,* assessment *as,* and assessment *of* learning (please refer to pages 35–36 within the *Hands-On English Language Learning* Assessment Plan for more information on this approach). Keep in mind that the suggestions are merely ideas to consider; for any lesson, you are also encouraged to refer to the other assessment strategies described in the next section or to use your own assessment practices.

Tips for Teachers

When implementing lessons for English-language learners, consider the following best practices:

- Simplify vocabulary and sentence structure to encourage comprehension, but use a natural voice and pace.
- Give instructions and ask questions in clear, simple English.
- Use many verbal and nonverbal cues throughout activities. Nonverbal cues include visuals, gestures, and concrete materials.
- Allow learners sufficient response time for oral answers.
- Review vocabulary and concepts regularly to check for learner comprehension.
- Emphasize a gradual release of responsibility of learning and performing tasks. Move students from dependence on the teachers or peer helpers through increasing degrees of independence to self reliance and full independence.
- Use graphic organizers to assist English-language learners in learning and recording vocabulary and concepts. A variety of graphic organizers is used throughout the *Hands-On English Language Learning* program.
- Remember that learner "errors" are typically part of the early stage of language acquisition as ELLs attempt to communicate. Mispronunciations, inappropriate word choices, and grammatical errors are part of this process and are to be expected. During this process, it is important for teachers to encourage communication and language usage in terms of listening, speaking, reading, writing, viewing, and representing, as these practices are the avenue to refining students' language skills.

Classroom Environment

The classroom environment is an important component of the learning process. An active environment—one that gently hums with the purposeful conversations and activities of students—indicates that meaningful learning is taking place.

Note: It is important to understand that, in the beginning stages of English-language learning, students will most often experience a silent period during which the emphasis will be on observation and a processing of the new language, which is done non-verbally.

While studying a specific topic, the classroom should display related objects and materials, student work, pictures and posters, maps, graphs, and charts made during activities, and summary charts of important concepts taught and learned. These visuals reinforce concepts and skills that have been emphasized during lessons, and can be used by students as an ongoing part of their learning resources.

Timelines

No two groups of learners will cover topics at the same rate, and so planning the duration of each module is left up to the teacher. In some cases, the lesson activities described will not be completed during one block of time and will have to be carried over. In other cases, students may be especially interested in one topic, and teachers may decide to expand upon it. It is also important to use ongoing assessment to determine and track student progress and plan appropriately. The individual needs of students should be considered—there are no strict timelines involved in the ***Hands-On English Language Learning*** program.

Classroom Management

Although active learning is emphasized throughout this program, the manner in which the activities are implemented depends upon individual circumstances. As in every classroom, there is a diversity of needs to be met. Teachers are adept at planning to meet these needs through differentiated instruction and thorough planning. How teachers support the progress of English language learners will depend on several factors, including the number of English language learners in the class and the stage of language acquisition for each one, the needs of other students in the class, and the additional supports available. In some cases, for instance, educational or teacher assistants may be provided for English language learners. This added support can be used in many ways: for example, the assistant can work with individual or small groups of English language learners who are at the same stage of language acquisition. Alternatively, the assistant can work with other students in the classroom, giving the teacher time to focus on the English language learners.

In some instances, teachers may have English language learners working with materials and resources individually; in others, teachers may choose to use small group settings. Small groups encourage the development of language and social skills, enable all students to be active in the learning process, and mean less cost in terms of materials and equipment. Again, classroom organization is up to the teacher who, ultimately, determines how the students in his or her care function best in the learning environment.

Note: All learners, and ELLs in particular, will need support in developing the group work skills necessary to complete cooperative learning tasks. Again, depending on prior learning experiences, learners may be unfamiliar with this process.

Cooperative Learning Activities

Throughout each module of ***Hands-On English Language Learning*** you will find several activities with a cooperative learning component. Cooperative learning is an educational approach that encourages students to work together to complete learning tasks. The optimal group size is four students, and active participation and responsibility to the group are key characteristics of this approach.

Cooperative learning activities can help English language learners' language development for a number of reasons:

- The speaking is natural, authentic communication.
- There is a positive interdependence as learners rely on all group members.
- Students work with a group of supportive peers, which makes it easier to take risks with the language.
- This type of activity maximizes output; output with peers can be more meaningful than with a teacher/adult.
- When English-speaking students understand their ELL peers better, they gain an understanding of diverse backgrounds, and they become accustomed to different accents (Coelho, 2004).

Peer Helpers

All lessons presented in each module of **Hands-On English Language Learning** require the support of peer helpers. It is essential to identify students who are both willing and able to support English language learners for this role. At the beginning of the school year, or prior to the arrival of a new ELL student, the teacher should identify a pool of potential peer helpers. Students who make good peer helpers are responsible, reliable, keen, friendly, and good-natured; it is not always necessary to choose the top students. Before any peer activities with ELL students, the teacher and peer helpers should discuss what being an ELL peer helper involves and the benefits to both the ELL student and the peer helper.

Note: It is important for students working together in a peer setting to focus on English language usage. However, it is also helpful, when possible, for ELL students to work with others who speak the same first language. This allows ELLs access to translation and interpretation, validates their first language, and builds on their background experiences.

Other students, for whom English is an additional language but who do not share the same first language as the new English language learner, may act as peer helpers. This allows the former to refine their English skills and acknowledges their contributions to the classroom community. Therefore, peer helpers may include both students for whom English is their first language and students for whom English is an additional language.

It is also important to note that there may be some classroom contexts with a very high percentage of beginning English language learners with various first languages. In this case, it may be necessary to include students from outside the classroom as peer helpers. However, many of the peer activities may also be done using various groupings of students, including strategic pairing or heterogeneous grouping.

Important Notes About Terminology

Throughout **Hands-On English Language Learning**, the authors and editors have made choices about terminology and the best ways to articulate specific concepts and terms. The goals are always to be as inclusive, politically correct, succinct, and current as possible. Here are some of the terminology choices we have made, with details about our rationale, when appropriate:

English language learner (learning)/ELL: There are many ways to refer to students who are learning English (as well as to the discipline of teaching English to non-English speakers). For many years, the term *English-as-a-second-language* has been used in reference to these

▶

students. More recently, the phrase *English-as-an-additional-language* has been used, to account for the fact that for many students English may well be a third or fourth language. We have chosen to use the term *English language learning* and, as such, we refer to students as *English language learners*, because it conveys the essence of the concept on which this book is based—learning to speak the English language.

English-speaking student is the term we use to refer to students for whom English is a first language and to distinguish these students from their English-language-learner classmates. We recognize that the term *English-speaking student* is not completely accurate, since ELL students are also English-speaking students— though their language use is still developing. The rationale for use of this term is simply one of space.

Aboriginal: We use the term *Aboriginal* to refer collectively to students (or other people) of First Nations, Inuit, and Métis descent.

First language: We use this term to refer to a students' home or primary language—that is, the first language that the student learned to speak (and read/write, if the student is literate) from parents, family members, and other members of the community; the language that is spoken in the students' home or in the country from which the student originated.

Country of origin: We use this term to refer to a students' home country—that is, the country from which the student originated (though not necessarily the *last* country in which the student lived or stayed before coming to Canada) or from which his or her parents (and/or family) originated.

Using Care and Sensitivity

It is important to be cautious and sensitive when asking students to share information about past experiences. Some ELL students will have gone through traumatic events, and sharing information about these events may be difficult. This is also true when having students share information about their homes. Some ELL students will have lived in refugee camps or other places where homes were less than comfortable. Allow students to choose whether or not to share information. Seek advice from the school guidance counselor about this, and consider the needs and expectations of each ELL student on an individual basis.

Scope and Sequence Charts for *Hands-On English Language Learning*

The ***Hands-On English Language Learning*** program is based on topics and outcomes/expectations commonly found in Canadian curriculum documents, and has been designed to reflect Canadian policy guidelines related to English language learners. The documents listed below were considered in the development of this resource.*

Note: Although program terminology may vary from province/territory to province/territory (for example, *English language learning, English as a second language, English as an additional language*), the pedagogy underlying the programs has a common framework.

The Scope and Sequence charts on the following pages identify target behaviours for students that correlate with many of the themes found in these Canadian subject-area curriculum documents for middle-years education (see subject-area correlation charts on pages 20-31).

Each module builds and reviews academic concepts, language structures, and vocabulary students will need across the curriculum. The lessons and activities within each module are not necessarily intended to be used in sequential order; teachers are encouraged to determine the order that works best for their class based on the needs and interests of students and the topics on which they are focusing. At the same time, lesson topics focus on basic language skills, subject-area themes, and common life skills that will support language learners as they develop competence and proficiency in English.

Note: *Hands On English Language Learning* also includes a universal design template, offering planning guidelines, teaching strategies, and blackline masters for use with specific topics not covered in modules 1 to 4. See module 5 on page 415.

*ELL Policy Documents

Alberta Education. *English as a Second Language: Guide to Implementation – Kindergarten to Grade 9.* Edmonton: Alberta Education, Learning and Teaching Resources Branch, 2007.

British Columbia Ministry of Education. *English as a Second Language Policy and Guidelines.* Victoria: British Columbia Ministry of Education, 2009.

_____. *English as a Second Language: Standards.* Victoria: British Columbia Ministry of Education Special Programs Branch, 2001.

_____. *English as a Second Language Learners: A Guide for Classroom Teachers.* Victoria: British Columbia Ministry of Education Special Programs Branch, 1999.

British Columbia Ministry of Education. *English as a Second Language Learners: A Guide for ESL Specialists.* Victoria: British Columbia Ministry of Education Special Programs Branch, 1999.

Government of Prince Edward Island. English as an Additional Language (EAL)/French as an Additional Language (FAL) Reception Centre. Government of Prince Edward Island. <www.gov.pe.ca/eal>

Manitoba Education. *English as an Additional Language (EAL) and Literacy, Academics, and Language (LAL), Kindergarten to Grade 12, Manitoba Curriculum Framework of Outcomes.* Winnipeg: Manitoba Education, September 2010 (draft).

Introduction

New Brunswick Department of Education. *A Resource Guide for Educators of English Second Language Learners.* Fredericton: New Brunswick Educational Services Branch, Department of Education, 1996.

Newfoundland and Labrador Department of Education. *English Second Language Learners: A Handbook for Educators.* St. John's, NL: Department of Education (Newfoundland and Labrador), 2001.

Nova Scotia Department of Education. *Guidelines for English as a Second Language (ESL) Programming and Services.* Halifax: Nova Scotia Department of Education, 2003.

Ontario Ministry of Education. *Supporting English Language Learners: A Practical Guide for Ontario Educators, Grades 1 to 8.* Toronto: Queen's Printer for Ontario, 2008.

Ontario Ministry of Education. *The Ontario Curriculum Grades 1-8 English as a Second Language and English Literacy Development – A Resource Guide.* Toronto: Queen's Printer for Ontario, 2001.

Scope and Sequence

Module 1

Lesson	Topic	Target Language Outcomes
		Students will:
1	Greetings/Social Communication	■ Express meaning in English using common greetings ■ Use different communication patterns and language when interacting with a friend versus a teacher/other adult ■ Use appropriate social behaviour during classroom discussions versus social settings
2	The Classroom	■ Demonstrate understanding of key classroom vocabulary and simple commands/one-step directions (for example, *line up, sit down, open your book,* and so on) ■ Follow some classroom rules and routines
3	The School	■ Demonstrate understanding of key school-related vocabulary ■ Seek information about the school using short patterned questions (for example, *Where is the gym?*) ■ Follow some school routines and schedules
4	School Activities	■ Identify and use vocabulary related to school classes, schedules, and extra-curricular activities ■ Develop organizational skills related to school responsibilities ■ Develop time-management skills related to school responsibilities and activities
5	The Alphabet	■ Recognize and print the Roman alphabet (upper and lowercase) ■ Use letters to represent words
6	Colours	■ Replace nouns with pronouns in an exchange (for example, *What colour is the apple? It is red.*) ■ Provide one-word responses to prompts using colour vocabulary
7	Numbers and Counting	■ Receptively recognize and understand number words ■ Count orally to a specified number (depending on the grade level of the student)
8	The Calendar: Days of the Week	■ Name the days of the week ■ Sequence the days of the week ■ Use weekly calendars to plan and follow personal activities
9	The Calendar: Months of the Year	■ Name the months of the year ■ Place appropriate information on a calendar
10	Personal Information	■ Use vocabulary to convey personal information ■ Use illustrations to express ideas ■ Articulate personal information in appropriate settings ■ Understand safety issues related to sharing personal information
11	Culminating Activity: Creating a Board Game	■ Use design skills based on a model ■ Follow directions and rules of games ■ Use simple instructions to teach a game to others

Module 2

Lesson	Topic	Target Language Outcomes
		Students will:
1	Emotions	■ Write or draw appropriately to the task (for example, use letters and words from a wordlist to label pictures) ■ Use illustrations to accompany a written text
2	Clothing	■ Demonstrate understanding using verbal responses ■ Describe and compare descriptions of self and others ■ Use a combination of drawings and letters/words to convey meaning ■ Begin to compose independently with prompting ■ Use adjectives for purposes of description or adding emphasis
3	Food	■ Engage in a range of activities such as identifying different types of food, discussing likes and dislikes, and categorizing types of food ■ Ask clarifying questions or make comments using short phrases and simple sentences ■ Copy single words or phrases
4	Body Parts and Health	■ Give a short series of instructions or ask questions of a friend ■ Use verbal and non-verbal cues to respond ■ Use a picture dictionary ■ Dictate labels, phrases, and sentences to a scribe
5	Physical Activities	■ Show willingness to listen to others ■ Initiate, respond in, or lead conversations involving a group of peers ■ Follow directions with two or three steps ■ Show willingness to speak and share work with others
6	Hobbies and Interests	■ Engage in cooperative learning ■ Listen and compare descriptions of self and others ■ Read/view description of self and others ■ Use more open-ended sentences with less prompting
7	Music	■ Identify musical instruments and equipment ■ Express likes and dislikes, and provide reasoning ■ Use listening skills to respond to music ■ Communicate ideas through visual representations ■ Explore music related to various cultures
8	Homes	■ Identify different types of homes ■ Identify rooms, furniture, and other features of homes ■ Use design skills to create floor plans ■ Express opinions, and justify decisions
9	The Community	■ Identify various components of a community ■ Use maps to identify local places in the community ■ Draw routes within the local community ■ Describe and follow safety rules for travel within the local community
10	Ordering Food	■ Respond to unseen speakers (for example, on the telephone) ■ Understand some common phrases in both their full and contracted forms (for example, *I would/I'd, that is/that's…*) ■ Ask for clarification (for example, *please repeat, what does this word mean?*) ■ Use a framework to write a particular text type

| 11 | Technology | ■ Identify vocabulary related to technology
■ Describe and follow rules for internet and cell phone safety |
| 12 | Culminating Activity: Creating an "All About Me" Electronic Portfolio | ■ Reflect on their own work to make selections
■ Use time-management skills to track project work
■ Work independently to complete a task
■ Develop public presentation skills to share academic work |

Module 3

Lesson	Topic	Target Language Outcomes Students will:
1	Canadian Geography	■ Speak more frequently in complete sentences ■ Demonstrate an ability to form sentences (that will likely reflect an inconsistent use of standard English grammatical forms and sounds) ■ Listen for the main points of a story ■ Engage in a cooperative learning activity ■ Understand pictures and some words in an age-appropriate story book
2	Canadian Symbols	■ Compose short letters, stories, posters, and so on ■ Show awareness of capitalization (and when to use it), punctuation, and spelling, but apply the rules irregularly ■ Represent words using more than a single letter
3	Celebrations and Holidays	■ Identify key points of information from an authentic text ■ Identify recurring common words in a text ■ Recognize different text formats (for example, book versus newspaper)
4	Relationships	■ Use vocabulary related to friendship, personality traits, teamwork, and conflict ■ Describe positive and negative personality traits ■ Identify ways to solve conflicts
5	Rules, Laws, and Responsibility	■ Follow instructions and rules to play games ■ Explain the importance of rules ■ Explain the consequences of breaking rules ■ Discuss the responsibilities of citizens ■ Identify people and services intended to protect citizens and maintain the law
6	Government	■ Identify the meaning of *government* ■ Classify services based on levels of government ■ Identify government leaders
7	World Geography	■ Practise language or tasks that are difficult (for example, identifying and printing specific target vocabulary onto a map) ■ Match a range of familiar spoken words with written words ■ Recognize the difference between upper and lowercase letters
8	North America	■ Use a text type appropriate to the purpose (for example, use of abbreviations when writing notes or filling in maps) ■ Follow a sequence of two or three instructions related to mapping vocabulary ■ Engage in activities with peers inside and outside the classroom ■ Attend to capitalization, punctuation, and spelling in writing
9	Cultural Diversity	■ Describe, in their own words, the meaning of *culture* ■ Share language and stories from their own culture ■ Identify cultural groups within the class, school, and community ■ Use oral and written language to conduct and record results of a survey
10	Our World Community	■ Identify similarities and differences between various countries (climate, flora, fauna, geography, language, currency, food, and so on) ■ Conduct research and present findings visually and with text
11	Basic Human Needs	■ Identify key points of information from an authentic text ■ Identify recurring common words in a text ■ Recognize different text formats (for example, book versus newspaper)

12	Human Rights	■ Identify basic human rights and the rights of children ■ Read poetry, and explore the meaning of verse ■ Read poetry aloud in public venues
13	The Media	■ Express understanding and lack of understanding through comprehension questions ■ Repeat to make oneself understood
14	Culminating Activity: Designing a Newspaper	■ Explore and identify the parts of a newspaper ■ Follow given structures to format text ■ Gather information from various sources ■ Write from various points of view ■ Use visuals to support text

Module 4

Lesson	Topic	Target Language Outcomes Students will:
1	Nature	■ Participate, without prompting, in academic discussions ■ Produce texts in different genres relevant to various academic content areas (for example, graphic organizers, diagrams)
2	Weather and Seasons	■ Practise reading based on models provided ■ Complete sentences with more than one-word responses, though sentences may be incomplete and have some letters/words missing ■ Show willingness to speak and share work with others
3	Animals of Canada	■ Work with peers who are similar as well as different ■ Engage in a range of activities to develop speaking, listening, reading, writing, viewing, and representing skills
4	Plants of Canada	■ Locate and identify local plants ■ Use representation skills, including illustrations and words, to describe objects
5	Natural Habitats	■ Demonstrate understanding using verbal responses ■ Describe and compare descriptions of the natural environment ■ Use a combination of drawings and letters/words to convey meaning ■ Use adjectives for describing or to add emphasis ■ Use nouns, adjectives, verbs, and adverbs to describe the natural environment
6	Importance of the Environment	■ Classify and compare objects made by humans and those found in the natural environment ■ Identify components of the natural environment ■ Describe the ways humans use the natural environment ■ Develop questioning skills by conducting interviews
7	Human Impact on the Environment	■ Use listening and speaking skills to respond to literature ■ Respond to illustrations to predict and describe story events ■ Use writing skills to complete book reviews ■ Explain cause, effect, and solutions to given environmental problems
8	Air Pollution	■ Listen and respond to literature ■ Identify events in a story ■ Retell a story in one's own words ■ Sequence events in a story ■ Identify facts in non-fiction text
9	Water	■ Follow directions to perform a hands-on investigation ■ Predict, observe, and describe results ■ Suggest actions to reduce water pollution and conserve water ■ Use writing and representing to convey a convincing message
10	Reduce, Reuse, Recycle	■ Speak more frequently in complete sentences ■ Listen for and identify main points in non-fiction text ■ Engage in a cooperative-learning activity ■ Gather and record information through the use of surveys ■ Draw conclusions from results
11	Saving Energy	■ Describe and compare similar objects ■ Work cooperatively on a group task ■ Convey ideas using pictures and words

12	Culminating Activity: Sustainability Life Practices	<ul><li>Make decisions based on personal interests and opinions</li><li>Design a plan of action</li><li>Share plan of action orally and in writing</li><li>Express ideas, share opinions, and provide reasons for choices</li><li>Take action to follow through on plans</li></ul>

Subject-Area Correlation

Hands-On English Language Learning is intended for integrated use in the mainstream classroom setting. Although there are many opportunities for individual-student, paired-student, and small-group learning, the focus of the program is to support students' language learning along with their classmates. As such, the topics of lessons developed in this resource have been chosen specifically to correlate with curricular topics taught in Canadian schools.

On the following pages, correlation charts are provided to indicate how lessons are connected to subject-area concepts and skills. Separate correlation charts have been developed for Western/Northern Canada, Ontario, and Atlantic Canada and identify grade-level correlations for Language Arts, Mathematics, Science, Social Studies, the Arts, and Physical Education/Health.

Western/Northern Canada Curricular Correlations: Module 1

Lesson	Topic	Subject and Grade-Level Correlations					
		Language Arts	Math	Science	Social Studies	Arts	Physical Education/ Health
1	Greetings/Social Communication	5, 6, 7, 8			5, 6, 7, 8	5, 6, 7, 8	5, 6, 7, 8
2	The Classroom	5, 6, 7, 8			5, 6, 7, 8	5, 6, 7, 8	
3	The School	5, 6, 7, 8			5, 6, 7, 8	5, 6, 7, 8	
4	School Activities		5, 6, 7, 8	5, 6, 7, 8	5, 6, 7, 8	5, 6, 7, 8	5, 6, 7, 8
5	The Alphabet	5, 6, 7, 8				5, 6, 7, 8	
6	Colours	5, 6, 7, 8				5, 6, 7, 8	
7	Numbers and Counting	5, 6, 7, 8	5, 6, 7, 8			5, 6, 7, 8	
8	The Calendar: Days of the Week	5, 6, 7, 8	5, 6, 7, 8			5, 6, 7, 8	5, 6, 7, 8
9	The Calendar: Months of the Year	5, 6, 7, 8	5, 6, 7, 8			5, 6, 7, 8	5, 6, 7, 8
10	Personal Information	5, 6, 7, 8	5, 6, 7, 8			5, 6, 7, 8	5, 6, 7, 8
11	Culminating Activity: Creating a Board Game	5, 6, 7, 8	5, 6, 7, 8			5, 6, 7, 8	5, 6, 7, 8

▶

Western/Northern Canada Curricular Correlations: Module 2

Lesson	Topic	Subject and Grade-Level Correlations					
		Language Arts	Math	Science	Social Studies	Arts	Physical Education/ Health
1	Emotions	5, 6, 7, 8			5, 6, 7, 8	5, 6, 7, 8	5, 6, 7, 8
2	Clothing	5, 6, 7, 8		5, 6, 7, 8	5, 6, 7, 8	5, 6, 7, 8	5, 6, 7, 8
3	Food	5, 6, 7, 8	5, 6, 7, 8	5, 6, 7, 8	5, 6, 7, 8	5, 6, 7, 8	5, 6, 7, 8
4	Body Parts and Health	5, 6, 7, 8		5, 8	5, 6, 7, 8	5, 6, 7, 8	5, 6, 7, 8
5	Physical Activities	5, 6, 7, 8		5, 8		5, 6, 7, 8	5, 6, 7, 8
6	Hobbies and Interests	5, 6, 7, 8		5, 8		5, 6, 7, 8	5, 6, 7, 8
7	Music	5, 6, 7, 8				5, 6, 7, 8	5, 6, 7, 8
8	Homes	5, 6, 7, 8			5, 6, 7, 8	5, 6, 7, 8	5, 6, 7, 8
9	The Community	5, 6, 7, 8			5, 6, 7, 8	5, 6, 7, 8	5, 6, 7, 8
10	Ordering Food	5, 6, 7, 8	5, 6, 7, 8	5, 8		5, 6, 7, 8	5, 6, 7, 8
11	Technology	5, 6, 7, 8		5, 6, 7, 8	5, 6, 7, 8	5, 6, 7, 8	5, 6, 7, 8
12	Culminating Activity: Creating an "All About Me" Electronic Portfolio	5, 6, 7, 8				5, 6, 7, 8	5, 6, 7, 8

▶

Western/Northern Canada Curricular Correlations: Module 3

Lesson	Topic	Subject and Grade-Level Correlations					
		Language Arts	Math	Science	Social Studies	Arts	Physical Education/ Health
1	Canadian Geography	5, 6, 7, 8			5, 6, 7, 8	5, 6, 7, 8	
2	Canadian Symbols	5, 6, 7, 8			5, 6, 7, 8	5, 6, 7, 8	5, 6, 7, 8
3	Celebrations and Holidays	5, 6, 7, 8			5, 6, 7, 8	5, 6, 7, 8	5, 6, 7, 8
4	Relationships	5, 6, 7, 8			5, 6, 7, 8	5, 6, 7, 8	5, 6, 7, 8
5	Rules, Laws, and Responsibility	5, 6, 7, 8			5, 6, 7, 8	5, 6, 7, 8	5, 6, 7, 8
6	Governments	5, 6, 7, 8			5, 6, 7, 8	5, 6, 7, 8	5, 6, 7, 8
7	World Geography	5, 6, 7, 8			5, 6, 7, 8	5, 6, 7, 8	
8	North America	5, 6, 7, 8			5, 6, 7, 8	5, 6, 7, 8	
9	Cultural Diversity	5, 6, 7, 8			5, 6, 7, 8	5, 6, 7, 8	5, 6, 7, 8
10	Our World Community	5, 6, 7, 8			5, 6, 7, 8	5, 6, 7, 8	5, 6, 7, 8
11	Basic Human Needs	5, 6, 7, 8			5, 6, 7, 8	5, 6, 7, 8	5, 6, 7, 8
12	Human Rights	5, 6, 7, 8			5, 6, 7, 8	5, 6, 7, 8	5, 6, 7, 8
13	The Media	5, 6, 7, 8			5, 6, 7, 8	5, 6, 7, 8	5, 6, 7, 8
14	Culminating Activity: Designing a Newspaper	5, 6, 7, 8			5, 6, 7, 8	5, 6, 7, 8	5, 6, 7, 8

▶

Western/Northern Canada Curricular Correlations: Module 4

Lesson	Topic	Subject and Grade-Level Correlations					
		Language Arts	Math	Science	Social Studies	Arts	Physical Education/ Health
1	Nature	5, 6, 7, 8		5, 6, 7, 8	5, 6, 7, 8	5, 6, 7, 8	
2	Weather and Seasons	5, 6, 7, 8	5, 6, 7, 8	5, 6, 7, 8	5, 6, 7, 8	5, 6, 7, 8	5, 6, 7, 8
3	Animals of Canada	5, 6, 7, 8		5, 6, 7, 8		5, 6, 7, 8	
4	Plants of Canada	5, 6, 7, 8		5, 6, 7, 8		5, 6, 7, 8	
5	Natural Habitats	5, 6, 7, 8		5, 6, 7, 8		5, 6, 7, 8	5, 6, 7, 8
6	Importance of the Environment	5, 6, 7, 8		5, 6, 7, 8	5, 6, 7, 8	5, 6, 7, 8	5, 6, 7, 8
7	Human Impact on the Environment	5, 6, 7, 8		5, 6, 7, 8	5, 6, 7, 8	5, 6, 7, 8	5, 6, 7, 8
8	Air Pollution	5, 6, 7, 8		5, 6, 7, 8	5, 6, 7, 8	5, 6, 7, 8	5, 6, 7, 8
9	Water	5, 6, 7, 8		5, 6, 7, 8	5, 6, 7, 8	5, 6, 7, 8	5, 6, 7, 8
10	Reduce, Reuse, Recycle	5, 6, 7, 8		5, 6, 7, 8	5, 6, 7, 8	5, 6, 7, 8	5, 6, 7, 8
11	Saving Energy	5, 6, 7, 8	5, 6, 7, 8	5, 6, 7, 8	5, 6, 7, 8	5, 6, 7, 8	5, 6, 7, 8
12	Culminating Activity: Sustainability Life Practices	5, 6, 7, 8	5, 6, 7, 8	5, 6, 7, 8	5, 6, 7, 8	5, 6, 7, 8	5, 6, 7, 8

Ontario Curricular Correlations: Module 1

Lesson	Topic	Subject and Grade-Level Correlations					
		Language Arts	Math	Science	Social Studies	Arts	Physical Education/ Health
1	Greetings/Social Communication	5, 6, 7, 8			5, 6, 7, 8	5, 6, 7, 8	5, 6, 7, 8
2	The Classroom	5, 6, 7, 8			5, 6, 7, 8	5, 6, 7, 8	
3	The School	5, 6, 7, 8			5, 6, 7, 8	5, 6, 7, 8	
4	School Activities		5, 6, 7, 8	5, 6, 7, 8	5, 6, 7, 8	5, 6, 7, 8	5, 6, 7, 8
5	The Alphabet	5, 6, 7, 8				5, 6, 7, 8	
6	Colours	5, 6, 7, 8				5, 6, 7, 8	
7	Numbers and Counting	5, 6, 7, 8	5, 6, 7, 8			5, 6, 7, 8	
8	The Calendar: Days of the Week	5, 6, 7, 8	5, 6, 7, 8			5, 6, 7, 8	5, 6, 7, 8
9	The Calendar: Months of the Year	5, 6, 7, 8	5, 6, 7, 8			5, 6, 7, 8	5, 6, 7, 8
10	Personal Information	5, 6, 7, 8	5, 6, 7, 8			5, 6, 7, 8	5, 6, 7, 8
11	Culminating Activity: Creating a Board Game	5, 6, 7, 8	5, 6, 7, 8			5, 6, 7, 8	5, 6, 7, 8

Ontario Curricular Correlations: Module 2

Lesson	Topic	Subject and Grade-Level Correlations					
		Language Arts	Math	Science	Social Studies	Arts	Physical Education/ Health
1	Emotions	5, 6, 7, 8			5, 6, 7, 8	5, 6, 7, 8	5, 6, 7, 8
2	Clothing	5, 6, 7, 8		5, 6, 7, 8	5, 6, 7, 8	5, 6, 7, 8	5, 6, 7, 8
3	Food	5, 6, 7, 8	5, 6, 7, 8	5, 6, 7, 8	5, 6, 7, 8	5, 6, 7, 8	5, 6, 7, 8
4	Body Parts and Health	5, 6, 7, 8		5, 8	5, 6, 7, 8	5, 6, 7, 8	5, 6, 7, 8
5	Physical Activities	5, 6, 7, 8		5, 8		5, 6, 7, 8	5, 6, 7, 8
6	Hobbies and Interests	5, 6, 7, 8		5, 8		5, 6, 7, 8	5, 6, 7, 8
7	Music	5, 6, 7, 8				5, 6, 7, 8	5, 6, 7, 8
8	Homes	5, 6, 7, 8			5, 6, 7, 8	5, 6, 7, 8	5, 6, 7, 8
9	The Community	5, 6, 7, 8			5, 6, 7, 8	5, 6, 7, 8	5, 6, 7, 8
10	Ordering Food	5, 6, 7, 8	5, 6, 7, 8	5, 8		5, 6, 7, 8	5, 6, 7, 8
11	Technology	5, 6, 7, 8		5, 6, 7, 8	5, 6, 7, 8	5, 6, 7, 8	5, 6, 7, 8
12	Culminating Activity: Creating an "All About Me" Electronic Portfolio	5, 6, 7, 8				5, 6, 7, 8	5, 6, 7, 8

Ontario Curricular Correlations: Module 3

Lesson	Topic	Subject and Grade-Level Correlations					
		Language Arts	Math	Science	Social Studies	Arts	Physical Education/ Health
1	Canadian Geography	5, 6, 7, 8			5, 6, 7, 8	5, 6, 7, 8	
2	Canadian Symbols	5, 6, 7, 8			5, 6, 7, 8	5, 6, 7, 8	5, 6, 7, 8
3	Celebrations and Holidays	5, 6, 7, 8			5, 6, 7, 8	5, 6, 7, 8	5, 6, 7, 8
4	Relationships	5, 6, 7, 8			5, 6, 7, 8	5, 6, 7, 8	5, 6, 7, 8
5	Rules, Laws, and Responsibility	5, 6, 7, 8			5, 6, 7, 8	5, 6, 7, 8	5, 6, 7, 8
6	Governments	5, 6, 7, 8			5, 6, 7, 8	5, 6, 7, 8	5, 6, 7, 8
7	World Geography	5, 6, 7, 8			5, 6, 7, 8	5, 6, 7, 8	
8	North America	5, 6, 7, 8			5, 6, 7, 8	5, 6, 7, 8	
9	Cultural Diversity	5, 6, 7, 8			5, 6, 7, 8	5, 6, 7, 8	5, 6, 7, 8
10	Our World Community	5, 6, 7, 8			5, 6, 7, 8	5, 6, 7, 8	5, 6, 7, 8
11	Basic Human Needs	5, 6, 7, 8			5, 6, 7, 8	5, 6, 7, 8	5, 6, 7, 8
12	Human Rights	5, 6, 7, 8			5, 6, 7, 8	5, 6, 7, 8	5, 6, 7, 8
13	The Media	5, 6, 7, 8			5, 6, 7, 8	5, 6, 7, 8	5, 6, 7, 8
14	Culminating Activity: Designing a Newspaper	5, 6, 7, 8			5, 6, 7, 8	5, 6, 7, 8	5, 6, 7, 8

▶

Ontario Curricular Correlations: Module 4

Lesson	Topic	Subject and Grade-Level Correlations					
		Language Arts	Math	Science	Social Studies	Arts	Physical Education/ Health
1	Nature	5, 6, 7, 8		5, 6, 7, 8	5, 6, 7, 8	5, 6, 7, 8	
2	Weather and Seasons	5, 6, 7, 8	5, 6, 7, 8	5, 6, 7, 8	5, 6, 7, 8	5, 6, 7, 8	5, 6, 7, 8
3	Animals of Canada	5, 6, 7, 8		5, 6, 7, 8		5, 6, 7, 8	
4	Plants of Canada	5, 6, 7, 8		5, 6, 7, 8		5, 6, 7, 8	
5	Natural Habitats	5, 6, 7, 8		5, 6, 7, 8		5, 6, 7, 8	5, 6, 7, 8
6	Importance of the Environment	5, 6, 7, 8		5, 6, 7, 8	5, 6, 7, 8	5, 6, 7, 8	5, 6, 7, 8
7	Human Impact on the Environment	5, 6, 7, 8		5, 6, 7, 8	5, 6, 7, 8	5, 6, 7, 8	5, 6, 7, 8
8	Air Pollution	5, 6, 7, 8		5, 6, 7, 8	5, 6, 7, 8	5, 6, 7, 8	5, 6, 7, 8
9	Water	5, 6, 7, 8		5, 6, 7, 8	5, 6, 7, 8	5, 6, 7, 8	5, 6, 7, 8
10	Reduce, Reuse, Recycle	5, 6, 7, 8		5, 6, 7, 8	5, 6, 7, 8	5, 6, 7, 8	5, 6, 7, 8
11	Saving Energy	5, 6, 7, 8	5, 6, 7, 8	5, 6, 7, 8	5, 6, 7, 8	5, 6, 7, 8	5, 6, 7, 8
12	Culminating Activity: Sustainability Life Practices	5, 6, 7, 8	5, 6, 7, 8	5, 6, 7, 8	5, 6, 7, 8	5, 6, 7, 8	5, 6, 7, 8

▶

Atlantic Canada Curricular Correlations: Module 1

Lesson	Topic	Subject and Grade-Level Correlations					
		Language Arts	Math	Science	Social Studies	Arts	Physical Education/ Health
1	Greetings/Social Communication	5, 6, 7, 8			5, 6, 7, 8	5, 6, 7, 8	5, 6, 7, 8
2	The Classroom	5, 6, 7, 8			5, 6, 7, 8	5, 6, 7, 8	
3	The School	5, 6, 7, 8			5, 6, 7, 8	5, 6, 7, 8	
4	School Activities		5, 6, 7, 8	5, 6, 7, 8	5, 6, 7, 8	5, 6, 7, 8	5, 6, 7, 8
5	The Alphabet	5, 6, 7, 8				5, 6, 7, 8	
6	Colours	5, 6, 7, 8				5, 6, 7, 8	
7	Numbers and Counting	5, 6, 7, 8	5, 6, 7, 8			5, 6, 7, 8	
8	The Calendar: Days of the Week	5, 6, 7, 8	5, 6, 7, 8			5, 6, 7, 8	5, 6, 7, 8
9	The Calendar: Months of the Year	5, 6, 7, 8	5, 6, 7, 8			5, 6, 7, 8	5, 6, 7, 8
10	Personal Information	5, 6, 7, 8	5, 6, 7, 8			5, 6, 7, 8	5, 6, 7, 8
11	Culminating Activity: Creating a Board Game	5, 6, 7, 8	5, 6, 7, 8			5, 6, 7, 8	5, 6, 7, 8

▶

Atlantic Canada Curricular Correlations: Module 2

Lesson	Topic	Subject and Grade-Level Correlations					
		Language Arts	Math	Science	Social Studies	Arts	Physical Education/ Health
1	Emotions	5, 6, 7, 8			5, 6, 7, 8	5, 6, 7, 8	5, 6, 7, 8
2	Clothing	5, 6, 7, 8		5, 6, 7, 8	5, 6, 7, 8	5, 6, 7, 8	5, 6, 7, 8
3	Food	5, 6, 7, 8	5, 6, 7, 8	5, 6, 7, 8	5, 6, 7, 8	5, 6, 7, 8	5, 6, 7, 8
4	Body Parts and Health	5, 6, 7, 8		5, 8	5, 6, 7, 8	5, 6, 7, 8	5, 6, 7, 8
5	Physical Activities	5, 6, 7, 8		5, 8		5, 6, 7, 8	5, 6, 7, 8
6	Hobbies and Interests	5, 6, 7, 8		5, 8		5, 6, 7, 8	5, 6, 7, 8
7	Music	5, 6, 7, 8				5, 6, 7, 8	5, 6, 7, 8
8	Homes	5, 6, 7, 8			5, 6, 7, 8	5, 6, 7, 8	5, 6, 7, 8
9	The Community	5, 6, 7, 8			5, 6, 7, 8	5, 6, 7, 8	5, 6, 7, 8
10	Ordering Food	5, 6, 7, 8	5, 6, 7, 8	5, 8		5, 6, 7, 8	5, 6, 7, 8
11	Technology	5, 6, 7, 8		5, 6, 7, 8	5, 6, 7, 8	5, 6, 7, 8	5, 6, 7, 8
12	Culminating Activity: Creating an "All About Me" Electronic Portfolio	5, 6, 7, 8				5, 6, 7, 8	5, 6, 7, 8

Atlantic Canada Curricular Correlations: Module 3

Lesson	Topic	Subject and Grade-Level Correlations					
		Language Arts	Math	Science	Social Studies	Arts	Physical Education/ Health
1	Canadian Geography	5, 6, 7, 8			5, 6, 7, 8	5, 6, 7, 8	
2	Canadian Symbols	5, 6, 7, 8			5, 6, 7, 8	5, 6, 7, 8	5, 6, 7, 8
3	Celebrations and Holidays	5, 6, 7, 8			5, 6, 7, 8	5, 6, 7, 8	5, 6, 7, 8
4	Relationships	5, 6, 7, 8			5, 6, 7, 8	5, 6, 7, 8	5, 6, 7, 8
5	Rules, Laws, and Responsibility	5, 6, 7, 8			5, 6, 7, 8	5, 6, 7, 8	5, 6, 7, 8
6	Governments	5, 6, 7, 8			5, 6, 7, 8	5, 6, 7, 8	5, 6, 7, 8
7	World Geography	5, 6, 7, 8			5, 6, 7, 8	5, 6, 7, 8	
8	North America	5, 6, 7, 8			5, 6, 7, 8	5, 6, 7, 8	
9	Cultural Diversity	5, 6, 7, 8			5, 6, 7, 8	5, 6, 7, 8	5, 6, 7, 8
10	Our World Community	5, 6, 7, 8			5, 6, 7, 8	5, 6, 7, 8	5, 6, 7, 8
11	Basic Human Needs	5, 6, 7, 8			5, 6, 7, 8	5, 6, 7, 8	5, 6, 7, 8
12	Human Rights	5, 6, 7, 8			5, 6, 7, 8	5, 6, 7, 8	5, 6, 7, 8
13	The Media	5, 6, 7, 8			5, 6, 7, 8	5, 6, 7, 8	5, 6, 7, 8
14	Culminating Activity: Designing a Newspaper	5, 6, 7, 8			5, 6, 7, 8	5, 6, 7, 8	5, 6, 7, 8

Atlantic Canada Curricular Correlations: Module 4

Lesson	Topic	Subject and Grade-Level Correlations					
		Language Arts	Math	Science	Social Studies	Arts	Physical Education/ Health
1	Nature	5, 6, 7, 8		5, 6, 7, 8	5, 6, 7, 8	5, 6, 7, 8	
2	Weather and Seasons	5, 6, 7, 8	5, 6, 7, 8	5, 6, 7, 8	5, 6, 7, 8	5, 6, 7, 8	5, 6, 7, 8
3	Animals of Canada	5, 6, 7, 8		5, 6, 7, 8		5, 6, 7, 8	
4	Plants of Canada	5, 6, 7, 8		5, 6, 7, 8		5, 6, 7, 8	
5	Natural Habitats	5, 6, 7, 8		5, 6, 7, 8		5, 6, 7, 8	5, 6, 7, 8
6	Importance of the Environment	5, 6, 7, 8		5, 6, 7, 8	5, 6, 7, 8	5, 6, 7, 8	5, 6, 7, 8
7	Human Impact on the Environment	5, 6, 7, 8		5, 6, 7, 8	5, 6, 7, 8	5, 6, 7, 8	5, 6, 7, 8
8	Air Pollution	5, 6, 7, 8		5, 6, 7, 8	5, 6, 7, 8	5, 6, 7, 8	5, 6, 7, 8
9	Water	5, 6, 7, 8		5, 6, 7, 8	5, 6, 7, 8	5, 6, 7, 8	5, 6, 7, 8
10	Reduce, Reuse, Recycle	5, 6, 7, 8		5, 6, 7, 8	5, 6, 7, 8	5, 6, 7, 8	5, 6, 7, 8
11	Saving Energy	5, 6, 7, 8	5, 6, 7, 8	5, 6, 7, 8	5, 6, 7, 8	5, 6, 7, 8	5, 6, 7, 8
12	Culminating Activity: Sustainability Life Practices	5, 6, 7, 8	5, 6, 7, 8	5, 6, 7, 8	5, 6, 7, 8	5, 6, 7, 8	5, 6, 7, 8

Hands-On English Language Learning Assessment Plan

Introduction

Assessing the progress of English language learners involves selecting assessment techniques that are both valid—in other words, that "measure what they are supposed to measure"—and fair—that is, they "provide meaningful and appropriate information about a child's language-use ability and avoid bias against any child because of that child's characteristics (first language and cultural background, age, gender, and so on)" (McKay 2006). In addition to assessing learners in ways that are culturally, linguistically, and developmentally appropriate, assessment techniques should encourage students to demonstrate their language abilities and knowledge through meaningful tasks and activities that align with the current educational focus on assessment *for* learning, assessment *as* learning, and assessment *of* learning (Earl and Katz 2006).

Recent literature on supporting English language learners (for example, *Instruction and Assessment of ESL Learners: Promoting Success in your Classroom*, by Faye Brownlie, Catherine Feniak, and Vicki McCarthy; *Assessment and ESL: An Alternative Approach*, by Barbara Law and Mary Eckes) provide insight into the various functions of classroom-based assessment for language learning and offer teacher-friendly approaches to conducting authentic and relevant assessment. This section provides an overview of assessment purposes and tasks, followed by considerations teachers should take into account when assessing middle-years English language learners. The following is not an exhaustive overview of assessment purposes, strategies, and considerations but is intended to add some English language learner-specific ideas to teachers' existing assessment repertoires.

Cultural Knowledge

It is important that teachers working with students of various cultures develop an understanding of cultural identities. Knowledge of students' background and culture will enable teachers to make stronger connections with their students and their students' families. As such, it will be beneficial to connect with community liaisons representing various cultures, and to access resources on cultural identities. One valuable website that offers cultural information on all countries is the Centre for Intercultural Learning (Foreign Affairs and International Trade Canada) "Country Insights": <www.intercultures.ca/cil-cai/countryinsights-apercuspays-eng.asp>.

Note: Keep in mind that resources such as the Country Insights website can only ever provide a partial view of certain cultural characteristics. Also, remember that students and their families provide the best source of information about their own lives and cultures.

Cultural Competency

Cultural competency refers to an ability to interact effectively with people of different cultures. Cultural competence encompasses four components: (a) Awareness of one's own cultural worldview, (b) Attitude towards cultural differences, (c) Knowledge of different cultural practices and worldviews, and (d) cross-cultural skills. Developing cultural competence results in an ability to understand, communicate with, and effectively interact with people across cultures (Mercedes and Vaughn 2007).

To reflect on your own level of cultural competency, consider completing the **Cultural Competency Checklist** (I.1) shown on page 37.

Purposes of Classroom-Based Assessment for Language Learning and Use

In addition to some of the classroom assessments that teachers may use with other students, certain assessments may be particularly appropriate for use with English language learners. For example, assessment for placement purposes might involve administering an interview, a short reading session, and a writing task to a language learner to determine the appropriate stage of language development (ELL students may well be at different stages with different language skills) (McKay). Assessing a learner for placement purposes should allow the learner to demonstrate knowledge and abilities across different language skill areas and tasks.

Another key assessment purpose is assessment to encourage and motivate, in which language learners are shown "what they have learned and [given] positive feedback, motivating them to succeed" (McKay). This type of assessment, while useful for all learners, is particularly relevant for English language learners in light of the vulnerability that accompanies learning another language (McKay) and the demands of learning the curriculum content at the same time as they are learning to speak English.

Assessment Tasks Appropriate for Middle-Years English Language Learners

Teachers of middle-years learners often embed at least a component of their assessment in the daily routines of the class. These familiar assessment techniques, including anecdotal records, individual student observations, rubrics, and portfolios, may also be used appropriately with English language learners.

When assessing language learners, teachers should use activities across a range of contexts and tasks to obtain a more accurate picture of students' understanding and progress. For example, rather than relying on written tasks, the following approaches can also be useful (adapted from Schmidt and Tavares 2006):

- Observe and note how students perform specific tasks or activities.

- Ask questions, preferably while students are engaged in a relevant task, as this provides contextual support.

- Ask students to show their understanding visually; for example, through hands-on demonstration or drawing.

- Ensure that tasks, activities, and criteria are appropriate for students' stage(s) of English language development.

- Adapt tasks as appropriate. English language learners' difficulties with the English language can mask their true understanding and abilities. Therefore, teachers may allow more time, use shorter extracts of texts, or ask for shorter responses. Increase the language component of the tasks as students become more proficient.

- Where appropriate, ensure that tasks are graded in terms of language demands such that while the rest of the class may attempt all questions or tasks, there will be some more accessible ones that English language learners can also perform successfully.

- Refer to appropriate ELL frameworks to find outcomes more appropriate for English language learners. Where English language learners have insufficient English to achieve the grade-level outcomes for a specific subject at the appropriate level, ELL outcomes will be more appropriate than outcomes at lower levels of the subject area.

- Explicitly outline the assessment criteria when setting formal assessment tasks.

- Provide a clear outline of what is expected and valued in a good response for those English language learners who may be accustomed to more traditional assessment processes. This strategy particularly applies to more open-ended tasks where a degree of analysis or reflection is required. Teachers should also give explicit feedback in terms of the assessment criteria.

- Clearly model the expectations of written and spoken tasks, and provide some guidance on how the task is to be presented.

- For presentations or longer assignments such as a portfolio, model a sample structure of what each section might contain, and, where appropriate, model some language support. This strategy may involve providing sentence starters for each section or recording examples of the kind of language required on the board or chart paper.

Teacher Considerations When Assessing Middle-Years English Language Learners

The following points offer considerations for teachers as they approach classroom assessment involving English language learners:

- Once English language learners have received initial assessment and placement, ongoing assessment is required to make teaching-related decisions, to inform students and parents about learners' progress, to collect evidence of progress for reporting purposes, and to complete summative evaluations (McKay).

- Most English language learners will continue to need support and instruction for at least five to seven years after arrival, even though they are fluent in everyday English (Coelho 2004). Ongoing support with academic content and language is extremely important as learners progress through the middle-years grades and academic demands increase.

- Classroom teachers, subject-area teachers, and ELL-specialists have a role to play in supporting and assessing English language learners.

- English language learners should not be compared to students whose first language is English; they should be assessed according to standards of ELL proficiency.

- Assessment of oral language (for example, pronunciation) should focus on clarity and comprehensibility, not on eliminating accents. ELL teaching should be additive in nature and should not focus on replacing students' first languages with English.

Assessment Tools

The *Hands-On English Language Learning* program provides a variety of assessment tools that enable teachers to build a comprehensive and authentic assessment plan for students. When ELL students first arrive, it is important for classroom teachers to conduct informal observations in order to determine the abilities and needs of each student. The **Entry Observation** form (I.2), shown on page 37, may be used to record anecdotal observations, comments, and recommendations. The anecdotal data will also assist the teacher in determining educational programming for the student. As well, combined with other information about the student's background, this information will enable the teacher to respond holistically—or meet the needs of the whole student.

In keeping with current education research, authentic and effective assessment includes three different kinds of assessment: assessment *for* learning, assessment *as* learning, and assessment *of* learning. Teachers can use these assessment tools to help identify students' language skills, stages, and progress.

Assessment for *learning* refers to the use of assessment tools for formative assessment to identify a student's current stage of English language acquisition, for the purpose of program planning. *Assessment* as *learning* refers to the use of assessment tools for encouraging student reflection and self-assessment. *Assessment* of *learning* refers to the use of assessment strategies for summative assessment, for reporting purposes, or for placement purposes (Earl and Katz 2006).

Assessment for Learning
To assess students as they work, use the assessment for learning suggestions and questions provided with many lessons/activities. Questions focus on the lesson outcomes, language skills, and active inquiry.

While observing and conversing with students, use the **Anecdotal Record** sheet (I.3) and the **Individual Student Observations** sheet (I.4) to record assessment-for-learning data.

Anecdotal Record (I.3): For an authentic view of a student's progress in acquiring English language skills, recording observations during activities is critical. The Anecdotal Record sheet, shown on page 37, provides the teacher with a format for recording individual or group observations.

Individual Student Observations (I.4): During activities when teachers wish to focus more on individual students, the Individual Student Observations sheet, also shown on page 37, may be useful. This blackline master provides more space for comments and is especially useful during conferencing, interviews, or individual student presentations.

Data collected from Anecdotal Record sheets and Individual Student Observations sheets can help teachers identify the language development of students according to their performance on given tasks.

Assessment as Learning
It is important to encourage students to reflect on their own learning and progress in acquiring English language skills. For this purpose, teachers will find an **Entrance Autobiography** sheet (I.5), a **Student Self-Assessment** sheet (I.6), and a **Cooperative Skills Self-Assessment** sheet (I.7), all shown on page 38.

Note that the Entrance Autobiography sheet (I.6) should be completed by ELL students with support from family members and/or a translator (if available). The activity provides an opportunity for students to share their background experience in terms of family, culture, and past schooling.

Other effective strategies for student self-assessment include the use of student illustrations, audio recordings, and journal writing. A blackline master for **Journal Writing** (I.8) is shown on page 38.

Note: It is important to keep in mind that students with limited English language skills may not be able to fully articulate self-assessment. For this reason, self-assessment should be limited in the early stages of language acquisition, or, alternatively, and if there are bilingual peers with whom the ELL student can work, conducted in their first language. As students develop greater skills in English, they will be more confident and capable of demonstrating their ability to reflect on their own learning.

Assessment of Learning

Assessment of learning provides a summary of student progress at a particular point in time related to the accomplishment of the curricular outcomes/expectations. Assessment of learning suggestions are provided throughout each module of the *Hands-On English Language Learning* program. To record student results, use the **Anecdotal Record** sheet (I.3), shown on page 37, the **Individual Student Observations** sheet (I.4), also shown on page 37, and the **Vocabulary Tracking Checklist** (I.9), shown on page 39.

During and after lessons, it is important to determine the degree to which students are able to use new vocabulary. The Vocabulary Tracking Checklist (I.9) is for recording observations in this area. Teachers can record vocabulary from a specific lesson or select and record vocabulary from a series of lessons/modules on the tracking sheet; then, they can assess students during lessons or through individual conferences. The Vocabulary Tracking sheet can be used for both assessment *for* learning and assessment *of* learning.

To assess students' abilities to work effectively in a group, a **Cooperative Skills Teacher Assessment** sheet (I.10) is shown on page 39 for use while observing the interaction within the groups.

Performance Assessment

Assessment *of* learning also includes *performance assessment,* which is planned, systematic observation and assessment of students for a specific activity. Teacher- or teacher/student-created Rubrics can be used to assess student performance.

A sample **Rubric** (I.11) and a **Rubric** blackline master for teacher use (I.12) are both shown on page 39. For any given activity, select four language criteria that relate to the learning outcomes. Students receive a checkmark for each criterion accomplished for a possible total rubric score of four. Teachers may then transfer the rubric scores onto the **Rubric Class Record** sheet (I.13), shown on page 40.

Note: Performance tasks can be used for both assessment *of* learning and assessment *for* learning.

Portfolios

With student input, teachers may select student work to include in an English language portfolio or in a section of a multi-subject portfolio. This can include activity sheets, illustrations, photographs, as well as other written material. Teachers may use the portfolio to reflect on the student's progress over the course of the school year. Blackline masters are included to organize the portfolio: both the **Portfolio Table of Contents** sheet (I.14) and the **Portfolio Entry Record** sheet (I.15) are shown on page 40.

Note: In each module of the *Hands-On English Language Learning* program, assessment suggestions are provided for several lessons. It is important to keep in mind that these are merely suggestions. Teachers are encouraged to use the assessment strategies in a wide variety of ways, to use these assessment ideas to build an effective assessment plan, and to rely on their own valuable experiences as educators.

I.1

Date: _____

Cultural Competency Checklist

Circle the number that best describes your response to the statements below.
Use the following descriptors:

1. Disagree   2. Neutral/Unsure   3. Agree

I have high expectations of all students.	1	2	3
My classroom curriculum reflects the experiences, cultures and perspectives of a range of cultural and ethnic groups.	1	2	3
Classroom materials and resources reflect cultural diversity and specifically reflect the cultures represented in my classroom.	1	2	3
Classroom displays reflect cultural diversity.	1	2	3
Student reading materials available in the classroom and school library reflect the cultures represented in my classroom.	1	2	3
The teaching styles I use address and support the learning styles of students.	1	2	3
The assessment and testing procedures I use are culturally sensitive.	1	2	3
The classroom culture reflects a sense of community and respect for diversity.	1	2	3
Students show respect for other students' first language(s) and dialect(s).	1	2	3
I have an effective plan for the involvement of parents/family in the classroom program.	1	2	3
I make an effort to research and learn about the cultural identities of my students.	1	2	3
I have adequate knowledge of other cultures to be able to work in a diverse setting.	1	2	3
I have sufficient training in the recognition of stereotyping, prejudices, and bias.	1	2	3
The school I work in adequately represents cultural groups in pictures and displays.	1	2	3

I.2

Date: _____

Entry Observation

Student Information

Student Name _____ Age _____

First Language _____

Country of Origin _____

Past School Experience _____

Initial Observations

Interactions with other students:

Response to teacher(s):

Activities/tools that engage the student:

Comments/Recommendations

_____
_____
_____
_____

I.3

Date: _____

Anecdotal Record

Purpose of Observation: _____

Student/Group	Student/Group
Comments	Comments
Student/Group	Student/Group
Comments	Comments
Student/Group	Student/Group
Comments	Comments

I.4

Date: _____

Individual Student Observations

Purpose of Observation: _____

Student: _____
Observations

Student: _____
Observations

Student: _____
Observations

Blackline Masters

Blackline Masters

I.5 — Entrance Autobiography

Date: _____ Name: _____

My Family	My Languages
Past School Experience	Coming to Canada
My Favourite Things	Other Important Information

I.6 — Student Self-Assessment

Date: _____ Name: _____

Looking At My Learning

1. Topic: _____
2. Activity: _____
3. What I learned: _____
4. Diagrams or Pictures:

[ ]

5. I would like to learn more about: _____
6. I would like to improve in: _____

I.7 — Cooperative Skills Self-Assessment

Date: _____ Name: _____

Students in my group:
_____ _____
_____ _____

Group Work – How Did I Do Today?

Group Work	How I Did (✓)		
	Very Good	Satisfactory	Needs Improvement
I shared ideas.			
I listened to others.			
I asked questions.			
I encouraged others.			
I helped with the work.			
I stayed on task.			

I did very well in _____

Next time I would like to improve in _____

I.8 — My Journal

My Journal

Name: _____ Date: _____

[ ]

Today, I _____ (describe activity)

I learned _____

I would like to learn more about _____

My Journal

Name: _____ Date: _____

[ ]

Today, I _____ (describe activity)

I learned _____

I would like to learn more about _____

Blackline Masters

Vocabulary Tracking Checklist

Student: _____

Vocabulary Words	Date
	✓ Achieved or NY – Not Yet

Cooperative Skills Teacher Assessment

Date: _____
Task: _____

Group Member	Cooperative Skills				
	Contributes ideas and questions	Respects and accepts contributions of others	Negotiates roles and responsibilities of each group member	Remains focused and encourages others to stay on task	Completes individual commitment to the group

Comments: _____

Sample Rubric

Activity: Clothing
Module: Middle Years, module 2
Date: October 12

4 – Full Accomplishment
3 – Substantial Accomplishment
2 – Partial Accomplishment
1 – Little Accomplishment

Student	Criteria			Rubric Score /4
	Identifies personal clothing by name	Uses present continuous to describe what he or she is wearing ("I am wearing…")	Identifies clothing appropriate to seasonal changes	Uses writing to describe favourite clothing and accessories
Jessie	✓	✓	✓		3
Sion	✓	✓	✓	✓	4

SAMPLE

Rubric

Activity: _____
Module: _____
Date: _____

4 – Full Accomplishment
3 – Substantial Accomplishment
2 – Partial Accomplishment
1 – Little Accomplishment

Student	Criteria				Rubric Score /4

Blackline Masters

I.13

Teacher: _____

Rubric Class Record

Student	Module/Activity/Date
	Rubric Scores /4

Scores on Specific Tasks	Assessment
1	Little Accomplishment
2	Partial Accomplishment
3	Substantial Accomplishment
4	Full Accomplishment

I.14

Date: _____   Name: _____

English Language Learning Portfolio Table of Contents

Entry	Date	Selection
1.		
2.		
3.		
4.		
5.		
6.		
7.		
8.		
9.		
10.		
11.		
12.		
13.		
14.		
15.		
16.		
17.		
18.		
19.		
20.		

I.15

Date: _____   Name: _____

English Language Learning Portfolio Entry Record

This work was chosen by _____

This work is _____

I chose this work because _____

Date: _____   Name: _____

English Language Learning Portfolio Entry Record

This work was chosen by _____

This work is _____

I chose this work because _____

References

Banks, James, and Cherry McGee Banks (Eds). *Multicultural Education: Issues and Perspectives,* 4th edition. New York: Wiley, 2001.

Banks, James et al. *Democracy and Diversity: Principles and Concepts for Educating Citizens in a Global Age.* Seattle: Center for Multicultural Education, College of Education, University of Washington, 2005.

Bigelow, Bill, and Bob Peterson. *Rethinking Globalization: Teaching for Justice in an Unjust World.* Milwaukee, WI: Rethinking Schools Ltd., 2002.

British Columbia Ministry of Education. "Students from Refugee Backgrounds: A Guide for Teachers and Schools." Victoria: Queen's Printer for British Columbia, 2009, <www.bced.gov.bc.ca/esl/refugees_teachers_guide.pdf>.

Brownlie, Faye, Catherine Feniak, and Vicki McCarthy. *Instruction and Assessment of ESL Learners: Promoting Success in Your Classroom.* Winnipeg: Portage & Main Press, 2004.

Coelho, Elizabeth. *Adding English: A Guide to Teaching in Multilingual Classrooms.* Toronto: Pippin Publishing, 2004.

Drum, Jan, Steve Hughes, and George Otero. *Global Winners: 74 Learning Activities for Inside and Outside the Classroom.* Yarmouth, ME: Intercultural Press, 1994.

Earl, Lorna M., Steven Katz, and Manitoba Education, Citizenship and Youth. *Rethinking Classroom Assessment with Purpose in Mind: Assessment for Learning, Assessment as Learning, Assessment of Learning.* Winnipeg: Western and Northern Canadian Protocol for Collaboration in Education (WNCP), 2006.

Freeman, David, and Yvonne Freeman. *English Language Learners: The Essential Guide.* New York: Scholastic Teaching Resources, 2007.

Law, Barbara, and Mary Eckes. *Assessment and ESL: An Alternative Approach.* Winnipeg: Portage & Main Press, 2007.

Lawson, Jennifer et al. *Hands-On Social Studies, Grade 1* (Manitoba edition). Winnipeg: Portage & Main Press, 2003.

Lawson, Jennifer et al. *Hands-On Social Studies, Grade 2* (Manitoba edition). Winnipeg: Portage & Main Press, 2003.

Lawson, Jennifer, et al. *Hands-On Social Studies, Grade 3* (Manitoba edition). Winnipeg: Portage & Main Press, 2003.

Lawson, Jennifer, et al. *Hands-On Social Studies, Grade 4* (Manitoba edition). Winnipeg: Portage & Main Press, 2003.

Manitoba Education and Training. *Grades 5 to 8 English Language Arts: A Foundation for Implementation.* Winnipeg, MB: Manitoba Education and Training, 1998.

Martin, Mercedes, and Billy Vaughn. "Cultural Competence: The Nuts & Bolts of Diversity & Inclusion." *Strategic Diversity & Inclusion Management* (now *Diversity Officer* magazine) v1 n1 (spring 2007): 31–38 <http://diversityofficermagazine.com/cultural-competence/cultural-competence-the-nuts-bolts-of-diversity-inclusion>, accessed January 2011).

McKay, Penny. *Assessing Young Language Learners.* Cambridge, UK: Cambridge University Press, 2006.

Schmidt, Clea, and Tony Tavares. *English as an Additional Language (EAL) and Literacy, Academics, and Language (LAL), Kindergarten to Grade 12, Manitoba Curriculum Framework of Outcomes.* Winnipeg: Manitoba Education, 2010 (draft).

Middle Years
Module 1

Introduction

This module of **Hands-On English Language Learning** is designed for use with students in grades 5 to 8 who are at a beginning stage of English language acquisition (see Stages of Language Acquisition on page 1 of the Introduction to **Hands-On English Language Learning**). Students at this stage use English for survival purposes and are becoming familiar with English language patterns. They try to make sense of messages and show some limited understanding of shorter passages of language. Their comprehension often relies on visual cues or gestures. These students frequently respond non-verbally (for example, by nodding their heads for "yes") or with single words, short phrases, or responses in their first languages.

Accordingly, the lessons in this module focus on survival language, everyday English, and basic concepts needed in the classroom and school settings. At the same time, the lessons focus on extending students' language development and understanding of basic concepts through hands-on activities and real-life applications.

Effective Teaching Strategies for English Language Learners

While teaching the lessons in this module, be sure to consider the following:

- Students learn language through interaction with others. Create a learning environment that encourages and provides opportunities for rich dialogue and social communication.
- Use many verbal and non-verbal cues throughout activities. Non-verbal cues include visuals, gestures, and concrete materials.
- Simplify vocabulary and sentence structure to encourage comprehension.
- Give instructions, and ask questions in clear, simple English. Paraphrase regularly, using other words to restate and to simplify communication.
- Allow learners sufficient response time for oral responses.
- Provide opportunity for students to use patterned language, in which certain language structures are repeated in various contexts or with different vocabulary.
- Review vocabulary and concepts regularly to provide reinforcement and to check for learner comprehension.
- Encourage, where appropriate, the strategic use of students' first languages.
- Determine prior knowledge, and build a bridge between it and new learning.

Reinforcing Vocabulary

Students should learn to recognize and understand the vocabulary presented in this module. At the same time, they should be encouraged to make connections between their first languages and the English language. To reinforce vocabulary, consider creating a multilingual word wall for the classroom, personal subject/topic-specific bilingual picture dictionaries, and individual vocabulary folders for students.

Multilingual Word Wall

Dedicate a classroom bulletin board to your multilingual word wall, and display the letters of the English alphabet along the top. Use index cards to record English vocabulary introduced in each lesson, tacking these to the board under the appropriate letter. Also include vocabulary in students' first languages (use students' prior knowledge, bilingual dictionaries, other students, staff, parents, and bilingual members of the community as sources of vocabulary). This contributes to the world/classroom-as-a-global-village message, validates first languages/cultures, and creates an atmosphere of inclusiveness. It also establishes an environment in which knowledge about other languages, and the merits of multilingualism are highlighted and celebrated. Along with vocabulary, also include picture and phrase cues, as appropriate. Encourage students to refer to the word wall during activities and assignments.

Vocabulary Folders

If it is not feasible to dedicate classroom wall space to a word wall, use open legal-size folders to make multilingual vocabulary folders for students. Open each folder, and divide it into 26 sections on the inside, one section for each letter of the alphabet, filling up the entire inside area (as in the illustration below). There are two ways students can collect and record vocabulary—they can glue small envelopes to each lettered section and then record vocabulary on small cards to be housed in the envelopes, or they can record new vocabulary on sticky notes and attach the notes directly to the appropriate lettered sections. Either way, be sure students also include illustrations, usage examples, as well as related vocabulary from their first language with their recorded English vocabulary. Students can close the folder again for storage (for this reason, do not have letter boxes directly on the folder crease).

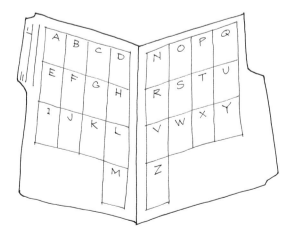

Personal Dictionaries

It can also benefit students to create their own personal English language dictionaries for reference during lessons. Use one of the blackline masters included with lesson 1 (1.1.6, 1.1.7). Or, have students use notebooks with sticky notes to indicate alphabetization.

Note: There are two blackline masters provided for the personal dictionary. The first provides a column for English words and a column for pictures/descriptors (1.1.6). The second may be beneficial for students who are literate in their first language, since another column is provided to record both English and first-language translations (1.1.7). Teachers may choose the template that best meets the needs of individual students.

Note: In addition to recording English words in their personal dictionaries, also have students record words in their first languages where appropriate. This helps them make bilingual connections and extends meaning. It will therefore benefit ELL students if bilingual dictionaries are available in English and their first languages (see Books for Students on page 48 and References for Teachers on page 121).

Differentiating Instruction

A number of English language learners will have been in school prior to their arrival at your school and, as a result, will have literacy skills that are on par with their same-age peers. Other students may have little or no previous school experience and may not be literate in their first languages. Consequently, the lessons in this module of *Hands-On English Language Learning* offer many opportunities to help students develop their reading and writing skills while learning English. Visual cues, concrete manipulatives, and cooperative learning are needed to support students as they learn all aspects of the English language.

However, teachers will still need to differentiate instruction and adapt both activities and activity sheets to meet the needs of individual learners. For example, a student with limited skills in reading and writing might work with a peer to complete activity sheets or use drawings instead of words. As another example, personal dictionaries may be essential for ELL students but can be equally beneficial for all students in the class through differentiation. More academically advanced students might collect descriptive words for use in personal writing, while students requiring additional support in spelling might collect challenging words for use in writing activities while, at the same time, ELL students would collect target vocabulary with pictures to reinforce recognition. Suggestions for adapting programs are made throughout the module, but teachers are also encouraged to use their own experience, techniques, and personal knowledge of students to differentiate instruction.

Peer Helpers

Many of the lessons presented in this module require the support of peer helpers to work in partnership with ELL students. Developing a classroom culture of inclusion and acceptance will be enhanced by working with the class to develop criteria for helpers, and to discuss why it is important to work together in the spirit of collaboration and community.

Every student in the class should have the opportunity to help and interact with the ELL students in their class; it is not always necessary to choose the top academic students. Before any peer activity with ELL students, the teacher and peer helpers should discuss the specific task, and the benefits to both the ELL student and the peer helper.

Note: It is important that students working together in a peer-helper setting focus on English language usage. However, it is also helpful for ELL students, when possible, to have contact with others who speak the same first language. This allows them access to translation and interpretation, and also validates their first languages and builds on prior experiences.

Note: Throughout *Hands-On English Language Learning*, we use the term *English-speaking student* (rather than the more cumbersome *students for whom English is a first language*) to distinguish these students from their English-language-learner classmates. We recognize that the term *English-speaking student* is not completely accurate, since ELL students are also English-speaking students—though their language use is still developing. The rationale for use of this term is simply one of space.

Assessing Students' Prior Knowledge – Assessment for Learning

Before beginning this module, it is beneficial to determine students' prior knowledge of lesson concepts and which of the target vocabulary students already know. This provides information that allows teachers to develop lessons and instructional activities to capitalize on students' strengths and address their needs. As a pre-module assessment strategy, consider using the Vocabulary Tracking Checklist (I.9; shown on page 39 in the Introduction to *Hands-On English Language Learning*) along with all vocabulary cards provided in the module. Conference with ELL students individually, and review the target vocabulary with them to determine the vocabulary with which they are familiar. Also, discuss concepts related to the vocabulary in order to reveal prior knowledge, and address gaps.

Note: This assessment activity also serves as an activating strategy that introduces students to the language, visuals, and concepts focused on throughout the module.

Career Connections

All modules in the *Hands On English Language Learning* program for middle years include a focus on career education for students. These activities are intended for use with the whole class, in an integrated setting, since career education is an important topic for all students. For ELL students specifically, such activities will offer them insight into the possibilities for their future, since some of the careers available to them may not be a part of the job market in their countries of origin. Learning about careers offers students a closer look at one aspect of Canadian culture, so students acquire essential understanding and knowledge while developing language skills.

It is important to note that some of the language used during career connection activities might be quite challenging for ELL students. For example, there is a focus on employability skills, and their importance in the workplace. Although some of the vocabulary used in describing these skills is at a more advanced language level, the activities themselves are well-suited to both ELL students and their English-speaking peers. Career connection activities focus on class discussion, guest presentations, role playing, and so on, and ELL students will be able to participate in this immersive environment.

Books for Students

Avant-Cooke, Karen. *The Colorguardians and the Magic Books of Color.* Bloomington, IN: Xlibris, 2005.

Frasier, Debra. *A Birthday Cake Is No Ordinary Cake.* Orlando, FL: Harcourt, 2006.

_____. *On the Day You Were Born.* San Diego, CA: Harcourt, 1991.

Gonyea, Mark. *A Book About Color: A Clear and Simple Guide for Young Artists.* New York: Henry Holt, 2010.

Herzog, Brad. *A Is for Amazing Moments – A Sports Alphabet.* Chelsea, MI: Sleeping Bear Press, 2008.

_____. *K Is for Kick – A Soccer Alphabet.* Chelsea, MI: Sleeping Bear Press, 2007.

_____. *T Is for Touchdown – A Football Alphabet.* Chelsea, MI: Sleeping Bear Press, 2007.

_____. *H Is for Home Run – A Baseball Alphabet.* Chelsea, MI: Sleeping Bear Press, 2004.

_____. *E Is for Extreme – An Extreme Sports Alphabet.* Chelsea, MI: Sleeping Bear Press, 2003.

Napier, Matt. *Z Is for Zamboni – A Hockey Alphabet.* Chelsea, MI: Sleeping Bear Press, 2006.

Thong, Roseanne. *One Is a Drummer: A Book of Numbers.* San Francisco: Chronicle Books, 2004.

_____. *Red Is a Dragon: A Book of Colors.* San Francisco: Chronicle Books, 2001.

Ulmer, Michael. *J Is for Jump Shot – A Basketball Alphabet.* Chelsea, MI: Sleeping Bear Press, 2007.

Young, Judy. *H Is for Hook – A Fishing Alphabet.* Chelsea, MI: Sleeping Bear Press, 2008.

Multicultural Books

Aboff, Marcie. *Guatemala ABCs: A Book About the People and Places of Guatemala.* Minneapolis, MN: Picture Window Books, 2006.

Aliki. *Painted Words and Spoken Memories.* New York: Greenwillow Books, 1998.

Berge, Ann. *Russia ABCs: A Book About the People and Places of Russia.* Minneapolis, MN: Picture Window Books, 2004.

Blackstone, Stella. *My Granny Went to Market: A Round-the World Counting Rhyme.* Cambridge MA: Barefoot Books, 2005.

Cheung, Hyechong, and Prodeepta Das. *K Is for Korea.* London, UK: Frances Lincoln Children's Books, 2008.

Cooper, Sharon Katz. *Venezuela ABCs: A Book About the People and Places of Venezuela.* Minneapolis, MN: Picture Window Books, 2007.

_____. *Italy ABCs: A Book About the People and Places of Italy.* Minneapolis, MN: Picture Window Books, 2006.

Cordero, Flor de Maria. *M Is for Mexico.* London, UK: Frances Lincoln Children's Books, 2008.

Das, Prodeepta. *I Is for India.* London, UK: Frances Lincoln Children's Books, 2004.

Gorman, Lovenia. *A Is for Algonquin: An Ontario Alphabet.* Chelsea, MI: Sleeping Bear Press, 2005.

Heiman, Sarah. *Australia ABCs: A Book About the People and Places of Australia.* Minneapolis, MN: Picture Window Books, 2003.

_____. *Egypt ABCs: A Book About the People and Places of Egypt.* Minneapolis, MN: Picture Window Books, 2003.

Heiman, Sarah. *Germany ABCs: A Book About the People and Places of Germany*. Minneapolis, MN: Picture Window Books, 2003.

____. *Kenya ABCs: A Book About the People and Places of Kenya*. Minneapolis, MN: Picture Window Books, 2003.

Krach, Maywan Shen. *D Is for Doufu: An Alphabet Book of Chinese Culture*. Arcadia, CA: Shen's Books, 1997.

Nishiyama, Akira, and Yoshio Komatsu. *Wonderful Houses Around the World*. Bolinas, CA: Shelter Publications, 2004.

Sanders, Nancy I. *D Is for Drinking Gourd: An African American Alphabet*: Chelsea, MI: Sleeping Bear Press, 2007.

Schroeder, Holly. *Israel ABCs: A Book About the People and Places of Israel*. Minneapolis, MN: Picture Window Books, 2004.

____. *New Zealand ABCs: A Book About the People and Places of New Zealand*. Minneapolis, MN: Picture Window Books, 2004.

Seidman, David. *Brazil ABCs: A Book About the People and Places of Brazil*. Minneapolis, MN: Picture Window Books, 2007.

Shoulders, Michael, and Debbie Shoulders. *D Is for Drum: A Native American Alphabet*. Chelsea, MI: Sleeping Bear Press, 2006.

Various authors. Countries of the World series. Mankato, MN: Capstone Press, 1997–2003 (39 titles).

Wells, Ruth. *A to Zen: A Book of Japanese Culture*. Saxonville, MA: Picture Books Studio, 1992.

Language Resources

Adelson-Goldstein, Jayme, and Norma Shapiro. *Oxford Picture Dictionary* series[*], New York: Oxford University Press, 2008.

Cleary, Brian P. *Hairy, Scary, Ordinary: What Is an Adjective?* Minneapolis: Carolrhoda Books, 2000.

Hill, L.A., and Charles Innes. *Oxford Children's Picture Dictionary*. London, UK: Oxford University Press, 1997.

Mantra Lingua. *My Talking Dictionary: Book and CD Rom*. London, UK: TalkingPen Publications, 2005 (48 dual-language editions).

Ross Keyes, Joan. *The Oxford Picture Dictionary for Kids*. New York: Oxford University Press, 1998.

Walker, Michael. *Amazing English Buddy Book*. Lebanon, Indiana: Addison-Wesley, 1995.

____. *Amazing English Buddy Book: Newcomer Level*. Lebanon, Indiana: Addison-Wesley, 1995.

---

[*]Bilingual versions of the *Oxford Picture Dictionary* are available for English and the following: Arabic, Brazilian-Portuguese, Chinese, French, Japanese, Korean, Russian, Spanish, Thai, Urdu, and Vietnamese.

Websites

- <www.ed.gov/pubs/CompactforReading/index.html>

    A Compact for Reading & School-Home Links: This site offers a number of activities to support emerging readers. While not specifically intended for ELL instruction, it has value for ELL teachers.

- <www.intercultures.ca/cil-cai/countryinsights-apercuspays-eng.asp>

    Country Insights: This site provides information about different cultures and includes advice on cultural "do's" and "don'ts."

- <www.eslcafe.com>

    Dave's ESL Cafe: A popular ELL site, Dave's ESL Cafe targets both teachers and students. For a wide range of activities and games focusing on teaching young learners, go to "stuff for teachers," click on "idea cookbook," and go to "kids."

- <www.edu.gov.mb.ca/k12/cur/diversity/eal/index.html>

    Diversity and Equity in Education – English as an Additional Language: This site provides provincial ELL information and is a great searchable database of educational sites including ELL sites.

- <www.englishclub.com/younglearners/index.htm>

    EnglishClub.com: Geared to learners and teachers of English, featured activities cover topics such as numbers, rhyming words, colours, shapes, animals, and the alphabet, as well as some short stories. Additional young learner links are provided at the bottom of the page.

- <www.esl-lounge.com>

    ESL-Lounge.com: This site offers free ELL lesson materials and plans with an emphasis on communication; most of the resources are geared to getting students talking. Included are printable grammar worksheets, surveys, flashcards, and reading comprehension and communication activities for each level. The site also provides board games and song lyrics for teachers as well as a section devoted to phonetics and improving English pronunciation.

- <www.mes-english.com>

    MES-English: This site offers free ELL resources for teachers of young learners. The resources are versatile and useful in many K–6 classrooms. The site provides free flashcards, handouts to match, phonics cards, and ELL games.

- <www.onestopenglish.com>

    OneStopEnglish: This site offers numerous free resources and lesson-plan ideas. The following links are particularly helpful when planning lessons for young ELL learners: "young learners," "flashcards," and "games and activities."

- <www.songsforteaching.com/esleflesol.htm>

    Songs for Teaching: Using music to promote learning, this site provides a number of song lyrics accompanied by sound clips that teach conversational English and vocabulary.

1 Greetings/Social Communication

Curricular Connections

- Language Arts: speaking, listening, reading, writing, viewing, representing
- Social Studies: cultural diversity
- Health: social communication
- Drama: role play

Background Information for Teachers

Many language learners (especially children and adolescents) undergo a silent period during which they delay attempts to speak in the new language. They may be more intent on listening to and observing their new surroundings, language, and peers. However, they may also engage in private speech (talking out loud to themselves) in preparation for social speech.

It is important not to force students to speak in the additional language before they are ready. Teachers who are working with beginners may want to start with a receptive (listening) activity before leading into an expressive (speaking) one.

Vocabulary – Greetings/Social Communication

- Hello
- Hi
- Goodbye
- Bye
- Good morning
- Goodnight
- Mr.
- Miss
- Ms.
- Mrs.
- teacher
- friend

Materials

- "Greetings" sheet (included. Photocopy sheet for each ELL student and one more for demonstration purposes.) (1.1.1)
- "First Day of School" sheet (included. Photocopy sheet for each ELL student and one more for demonstration purposes.) (1.1.2)
- whiteboard
- dry-erase markers
- vocabulary cards – *Greetings/Social Communication* (included. Photocopy two sets of cards onto sturdy tagboard, and cut apart.) (1.1.3)
- role play cards (included. Photocopy one set of cards for each ELL student.) (1.1.4)
- Employability Skills Checklist (included. Copy onto a large sheet of experience chart paper, and display in the classroom for ongoing reference, or make an overhead or PowerPoint copy of checklist.) (1.1.8)
- poster paper

Integrated Class Activities

- When introducing ELL students to greetings terminology and concepts, it is important to emphasize the oral language of the classroom environment. Students will acquire this type of language naturally; presentation should be done orally first, and then as follow-up with instructional activities suggested below.

- Discuss how we greet and refer to different people by formal and informal names; for example, we use *Mr., Mrs., Ms.*, and *Dr.* in formal settings and first names for informal settings and with peers.

▶

- Have students share different greetings in their first languages, discussing how different people are greeted (elders, parents, friends, and so on). Many languages, for example, add endings to words to indicate politeness or formality.

- Consider including students' first-language greetings and salutations in everyday classroom routines. This emphasis on the multilingual classroom celebrates diversity and acknowledges the value of learning other languages.

- As a class, create a multilingual "Welcome" poster for the classroom door. Have students record greetings terms (*hello*, *hi*, *welcome*, and so on) in English and in languages that reflect the school community.

- To expand recognition of the school's global context and to encourage and foster a whole-school atmosphere that is inclusive, use students' first-language greetings and salutations in morning announcements for the entire school.

- Discuss social skills related to greeting people (for example, shaking hands, making eye contact). Also discuss how acceptable social skills vary from culture to culture. Encourage students to share examples from their own cultures.

Whole-Class Career Connections

- Discuss the importance of social communication skills in the workplace for dealing with colleagues, customers, and the general public.

- Brainstorm a list of jobs that require strong skills in greeting and social communication — for example, people who work in telecommunications (telephone operators, telemarketers, and others who communicate by telephone), receptionists, store greeters.

- Have students role play employees with strong and weak social communication skills, for example:
  - A school secretary answering the telephone
  - An order-taker at a drive-through fastfood restaurant
  - A salesperson trying to sell a pair of running shoes

- Introduce students to the Employability Skills Checklist (included, 1.1.8). Explain that this list of skills was developed by employers and government representatives and is used across Canada to identify the skills employees need in all workplaces. Discuss the various skills, and have students identify unfamiliar terms. Use dictionaries to clarify terminology.

Note: The Employability Skills Checklist may be challenging for new ELL students. Nonetheless, they will benefit from the informal class discussion related to these skills and will gain language and conceptual knowledge within this integrated setting. Have ELL students who are more literate in their own languages use bilingual dictionaries to enhance understanding of the Employability Skills Checklist.

- Have students identify which of the employability skills relate to social communication.

Instructional Activity: Part One

Distribute the "Greetings" sheet (1.1.1) to students, and use it to introduce the topic of greetings/social communication. Have students look at the picture in each frame as you point to and read the words. Repeat this procedure a second time, encouraging students to say the words and phrases with you. As various target vocabulary comes up during this activity record it on the whiteboard.

Note: This is a good opportunity for students to share greetings in their first languages.

Now, distribute the "First Day of School" sheet (1.1.2), and read it aloud, pointing to the pictures and phrases as you read. Read through the sheet again, and have students say the words and phrases with you. Record target vocabulary on the whiteboard as it comes up.

Note: Choral repetition activities are generally less intimidating for learners and are effective at this beginning stage of language acquisition.

Instructional Activity: Part Two

Use the vocabulary cards – *Greetings/Social Communication* (1.1.3) to introduce students to the target vocabulary. Place the cards face up on a table. Have a student select a card and pass it to you. Display the card for all students to see as you say the word aloud. Say the word aloud again as you pass the card to a student, and have the student repeat the word. Continue this pass-and-repeat activity for all vocabulary cards.

Note: This would be a good time to discuss the different ways to greet a person, depending on who the person is. For example, to a friend, you might say, "Hey, (Keiko)!" To a teacher, you would say, "Hello, (Mrs. Parker)."

Next, spread out the vocabulary cards face up on a table, and ask an ELL student to identify each different expression or term. For example:

- Teacher: Good night. Can you point to the card that shows "good night"?
- Student: (points to or picks up card).
- Teacher: Great! That is the "good night" card. Now, please show me the card for "Mr."

Note: Although it may seem repetitive, it is important to use the target vocabulary as much as possible with students. Build in as many receptive activities as you can until the student is more comfortable expressing the language.

Finally, review the vocabulary cards again, and invite students to share similar expressions or terms from their first languages.

Peer Activities

- Have two English-speaking peer helpers work with each ELL student and use the role play cards (1.1.4). Ask one peer helper to choose one of the cards with only two characters in the frame (third, fourth, or fifth card) and read it to the second peer helper; then, have the two peer helpers role play the situation. As the ELL student becomes comfortable with the activity, the three-character cards may be used with the ELL student taking over one of the roles. Students can also trade roles and use each card again.

Note: At the beginning of language acquisition, some ELL students may not speak at all and may initially simply watch the interactive role play between peers. Allow students plenty of time to develop receptive language acquisition.

- Have an ELL student and a peer helper use two sets of vocabulary cards – *Greetings/Social Communication* (1.1.3) to play the game Concentration. Ask players to shuffle the deck of cards and spread them out facedown on a table. Then, tell players to take turns flipping over two cards, trying to make a match. Each time a card is flipped over, have the player say the term on the card. Play continues until all cards are matched.

Independent Activity: Activity Sheet A

Note: If ELL students have limited reading/writing skills, have them work with peer helpers or adults to complete this activity sheet.

Directions to students:

Read the words and phrases at the top of the first page. Print or write each word/phrase into the correct speech bubble (1.1.5).

Extensions

- Begin a multilingual word wall (see page 44) for new vocabulary. Add new vocabulary – *Greetings/Social Communication* to the language word wall. Also add the vocabulary in students' first languages, as well as illustrations and other visuals related to the vocabulary.

- If it is not feasible to dedicate classroom wall space to a word wall, use open legal-size folders to make multilingual vocabulary folders for students. Open each folder, and divide it into 26 sections on the inside, one section for each letter of the alphabet, filling up the entire inside area (see page 45). Have students record new vocabulary on sticky notes, including illustrations, usage examples, and related vocabulary from their first language(s), and attach the stickies to the inside of the folder under the appropriate letter. Students can close the folder again for storage (for this reason, do not have letter boxes directly on the folder crease).

- Have students use notebooks, index cards, or the personal dictionary blackline masters included (1.1.6, 1.1.7) to create personal dictionaries in which they can record new words and expressions that they learn in each lesson. Have students add new vocabulary – *Greetings/Social Communication* to their personal dictionaries. Encourage them to use pictures, their emerging English language, and/or their first language(s) to represent the new terms.

Note: There are two blackline masters provided for the personal dictionary. The first provides a column for English words and a column for pictures/descriptors (1.1.6). The second may be beneficial for students who are literate in their first language, since another column is provided to record both English and first-language translations (1.1.7). Teachers may choose the template that best meets the needs of individual students.

1.1.1

1.1.2

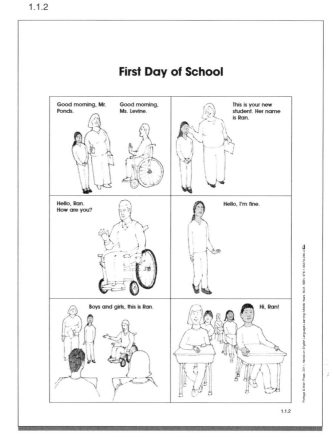

1.1.3

1.1.3

Vocabulary Cards – Greetings/Social Communication

| teacher | friend |

Employability Skills Checklist: Skills You Need in the World of Work

1. Main Skills

- **Communication skills**
  - read and understand different kinds of information (e.g., words, graphs, charts, drawings);
  - write and speak so that others pay attention and understand what you say;
  - listen to others, and ask questions to understand what others are thinking;
  - use different types of technology (e.g., e-mail, voicemail) to share information;
  - use what you already know about science, technology, and math to help you clearly explain your ideas to others.

- **Information skills**
  - use technology to find information, sort it out, consider all information found, and use what is helpful;
  - describe or explain the skills that you need for each subject (e.g., the arts, languages, science, technology, mathematics, social sciences, and the humanities).

- **Skills With Numbers**
  - decide what you need to measure or calculate;
  - observe and record information using suitable tools (e.g., pencil and paper, marker and chart paper) and technology (computer, whiteboard).

- **Thinking and problem-solving skills**
  - look at a situation, and decide if there is a problem and what it could be;
  - use information to consider what different people think about something;
  - understand what the main cause of a problem is;
  - understand all parts of a problem, including difficulties with individual people or between people and difficulties because of technology, science, or math;
  - look at and consider possible solutions to a problem creatively;
  - use science, technology, and mathematics to help you think and learn;
  - use science, technology, and mathematics to help you share what you learn or know, solve problems, and make decisions;
  - look at different solutions, and make suggestions or decisions to deal with problems;
  - carry out solutions to problems;
  - look at solutions to see if they are working, and try to improve solutions, where possible.

2. Teamwork Skills

These are the skills and qualities you need to be a helpful and valuable member of a team. You will have more success working on any project or team when you can:

- **Work well with others**
  - understand *how* groups or teams work so you can help contribute to the group;
  - make sure that a team's plans are clear;
  - listen to, respect, accept, and encourage others' thoughts, beliefs, and help;
  - recognize and respect that different people have different ideas and beliefs;
  - accept and offer advice in a helpful and polite way;
  - help a team by sharing information and what you know;
  - lead or help the group, and encourage other group members to work hard;
  - understand that disagreement in a group is okay and can help lead to solutions;
  - understand disagreements, and help to settle them, when this makes sense.

3. Personal Management Skills

These are the skills, thoughts, and behaviours that can help a person to do well in his or her work. You will have more opportunities to do well when you:

- **Help with projects and other responsibilities**
  - plan, create, or complete a project or other job from start to finish, knowing how you will do it, and how it will look when you are done;
  - create a plan, ask others what they think of it, test your plan, improve it if possible or if needed, and then do it;
  - work hard on a project or job so that the result is what you planned and hoped for;
  - use tools and technology that will help you to work on the project or job;
  - accept any needed changes in plans or new information about the project;
  - keep track of a project or job, noticing what worked well, and finding ways to improve.

- **Think and behave positively**
  - feel good about yourself and what you do;
  - are honest, dependable, and you make good choices while working with people, problems, and situations;
  - see your own hard work and success, as well as others' hard work and success;
  - take care of your personal health;
  - are interested in a project and in working hard and creatively to do it.

- **Adapt to a situation easily**
  - can work either on your own or as a part of a team;
  - can work on more than one job or project at the same time;
  - are creative, act wisely, and can suggest other ways to get the job done;
  - accept change, and adjust to it in a cooperative and positive way;
  - learn from your mistakes, and accept others' thoughts and ideas about your work;
  - accept that you may have questions that may not have simple answers.

- **Continue learning**
  - are willing to grow by learning more and getting more skills;
  - look at your skills and what you already know, and decide which skills you need to work on more, and what things you still need to learn;
  - find new ways, reasons, and opportunities to learn;
  - decide what you want and need to learn;
  - plan how you will learn, what you want or need to learn, and then do it.

- **Work safely**
  - know how to stay healthy and safe on your own and as part of a group;
  - act in ways that keep you and the group healthy and safe.

Adapted from *Employability Skills 2000+* brochure, The Conference Board of Canada (2000), <www.conferenceboard.ca/Libraries/EDUC_PUBLIC/esp2000.sflb>

2 The Classroom

Curricular Connections

- Language Arts: speaking, listening, reading, writing, viewing, representing
- Mathematics: tallies, graphs
- Social Studies: rules and responsibilities, cultural diversity
- Art: drawing, photography
- Drama: acting, role play

Background Information for Teachers

Prior to beginning activities related to the classroom and school, it would be appropriate to provide students with some simplified information about basic classroom and school rules and expected behaviours. It may be beneficial to further reinforce these with help from a student or volunteer translator, if available. This will help to familiarize learners with school and classroom routines, facilitate their understanding of differences in expectations that may be evident in different schooling contexts, and help to ensure the safety of all students. It is also recommended that important school rules and safety precautions be provided in writing in the student's first language for students to take home and share with family members.

Note: Basic classroom information, school rules, and expected behaviours may need to be reviewed frequently throughout the school year, especially for students and families with limited school experience.

Vocabulary – The Classroom

There is a great deal of vocabulary introduced in this lesson. Students will acquire these words incidentally, through informal exposure in the integrated classroom setting. Nonetheless, they may be more successful acquiring the new vocabulary if you break up this lesson into several sessions and limit the number of words introduced per session. In addition to using the multilingual word wall or personal vocabulary folders, label items around the classroom so students begin to associate words with particular things.

Note: Be sure to include multilingual labels on the classroom objects as well.

The Classroom

- paper
- pencil
- pen
- eraser
- notebook
- book
- whiteboard
- marker
- coloured pencil
- timetable
- agenda
- binder
- loose-leaf paper
- divider
- report cover
- file folder
- tape
- highlighter
- backpack
- computer
- calculator
- chair
- desk
- table
- pencil sharpener
- paint
- paintbrush
- student
- teacher
- floor
- door
- window

2

- scissors
- ruler
- glue
- clock

Related Actions

- read
- write
- print
- pay attention
- listen
- look/watch
- study
- draw
- colour
- sit down
- stand up
- open
- close
- walk
- line up
- look here

Add to the target vocabulary lists any other words or phrases that you feel are appropriate. Use index cards to make additional vocabulary cards.

Materials

- Classroom Objects sheet (included. Make a copy for each ELL student as well as one for demonstration purposes.) (1.2.1)
- blank index cards
- markers
- tape
- vocabulary cards – *The Classroom* (included. Photocopy three sets onto sturdy tagboard, and cut apart cards.) (1.2.2)
- vocabulary cards – *Related Actions* (included. Photocopy one set onto sturdy tagboard, and cut apart cards.) (1.2.3)
- digital camera(s)
- scissors
- glue

Integrated Class Activities

- Use the set of vocabulary cards – *Related Actions* (1.2.3) to play a version of the game Simon Says as a class. (You may wish to use different names from students' cultures [or use students' own names] instead of the name Simon. For example, "Abed says, pretend to open a door.") Display the vocabulary cards – *Related Actions* to support ELL students as they participate in this activity. To play, have students follow directions the caller gives but only when he or she says "Simon says" before the rest of the directions. For example, if the caller says, "Simon says, sit down," students should sit down. However, if the caller says, simply, "Stand up," students should not respond to the command and should remain sitting (or in whatever position they were in prior to the direction "stand up"). If students choose to add more actions to the game (other than those introduced in the lesson), record and illustrate these on blank index cards, and add them to the vocabulary cards on display. Be sure to incorporate ELL students' culture(s) into the game by including one or two actions that the entire class must learn in ELL students' first language(s).

Note: If you have not already labelled classroom items (see previous page), you may choose to do one of the following two activities.

- Use one set of vocabulary cards – *The Classroom* (1.2.2) to label items throughout the classroom. This will help ELL students with language acquisition and usage, and may also support other students in their reading, writing, and spelling.
- Have students use blank index cards to create multilingual labels for classroom items, reflecting all of their first languages.
- Use the vocabulary cards – *The Classroom* (1.2.2) to inform students of the classroom

supplies they will need for a given class activity. For example, prior to a lesson, display the cards showing scissors, ruler, pencil, and eraser. Have students use the cards to prepare for the activity and have the supplies ready for use. This routine helps students to develop organizational skills and learning preparedness.

- Have students work in groups to create tallies for classroom supplies they have collectively. For example, have them count and tally the number of coloured pencils and regular pencils they have. They can then use the tallies to create bar graphs. ELL students can use the vocabulary cards – *The Classroom* to support them during this activity.

Whole-Class Career Connections

- Have various school staff members (teachers, paraprofessionals, custodial staff, administration, secretarial staff, bus drivers, special itinerants) discuss their careers with students, focusing on training required for the job, rewards, and challenges.

- Invite a representative from a publisher of educational books to discuss the publisher's role in schools. This is also an excellent opportunity for students to learn about how educational books are published.

- Invite a local school board trustee to talk to students about the election process and a trustee's role in the school division/district.

Instructional Activity: Part One

Distribute copies of the Classroom Objects sheet (1.2.1) to students, and begin by pointing to various items on the demonstration copy. Say each word, and encourage students to repeat it. At this stage, do not focus too heavily on pronunciation. Walk around the classroom with students, identifying these objects in their environment.

As English vocabulary is introduced, have ELL students share corresponding terminology from their first languages. Record terminology (in English as well as in students' first language[s]) on blank index cards, and use tape to affix the cards to the classroom objects.

Now, display one set of vocabulary cards – *The Classroom*. Have students match objects on the cards to those on the classroom objects sheet. Then, ask students to identify these objects in the classroom.

Instructional Activity: Part Two

Note: This activity employs a language-learning strategy called Total Physical Response (TPR). Developed by Dr. James Asher in 1977, TPR relies on the use of commands that require physical movement, which is a simple way to encourage learners to move about and loosen up. TPR allows learners to do a lot of listening accompanied by physical responses (reaching, grabbing, moving, looking) before they are required to speak; for example: *Stand up; Sit down; Open the door; Close the window.* Initially, no verbal response is necessary. Eventually, however, students will become comfortable enough to verbally respond to questions and to ask questions themselves.

Display the vocabulary cards – *Related Actions* (1.2.3). Present each card, read it aloud, and act out the action. Then, pass the card to a student, and have him or her say the word and act out the action. Repeat this for all cards.

Next, show one card at a time to students, read the action aloud, and have them follow the command. Use a digital camera to take pictures of each student following each command.

Note: These photographs can be placed in ELL students' personal dictionaries along with related vocabulary.

Peer Activity

Have each ELL student work with a peer helper and use two sets of vocabulary cards – *The Classroom* (1.2.2) to play a modified version of the card game Go Fish. First, teach students the following sentence stems to use during the game:

- Player 1: Do you have a (pen)?
- Player 2: Yes (hands over card).

OR

- No, I do not have a (pen), go fish (player 1 picks up a card from the pile).

Independent Activity: Activity Sheet A

Note: If students have limited reading/writing skills, have them work with a peer helper or adult to complete this sheet. Bilingual dictionaries can also be used to support students.

Directions to students:

Look at the words at the top of the sheet. Match these words to the pictures of classroom objects. Print or write the words under the correct pictures. Use the vocabulary cards – *The Classroom* to help you (1.2.4).

Extensions

- Add new vocabulary to the multilingual word wall.
- Have students add new vocabulary to their personal vocabulary folders or personal dictionaries.
- Provide students with (a) digital camera(s). Have them plan, stage, and take pictures of classroom items being used by classmates (in a whole-class setting). Print enlargements of these photos, and display them along with the vocabulary cards; use yarn or string to connect the cards to the items in the photo.
- Play a hands-on memory game with students. Display several classroom objects on a table, and cover them with a sheet. Remove the sheet, and have students examine the objects. Model pronunciation of the word for each object as you point to it. Then, cover the objects with the sheet again, and have students name or draw each object that they can remember.
- Have students play a more challenging memory game, which involves remembering the item and its location. Place 10 classroom items on a 2 x 5 grid drawn on paper (as below):

Memory-Game Grid

Give students 30 seconds to review the items and their positions on the grid. Then, cover the items with a second piece of paper. Provide students with the vocabulary cards – *The Classroom* and a second identical 2 x 5 grid. Have students try to place the vocabulary cards on the grid in the same positions as the items.

Assessment of Learning

Once all the classroom vocabulary has been thoroughly reviewed, gather as many of the actual objects as possible (pencils, erasers, paper, and so on). Name each item one at a time, and ask the student to retrieve it. Use the Vocabulary Tracking Checklist (I.9), shown in the Introduction to **Hands-On English Language Learning** on page 39, to record vocabulary that the student knows, as well as those words still to be mastered.

Blackline Masters

1.2.1

Classroom Objects

1. pen
2. notebook
3. pencil
4. teacher
5. window
6. glue
7. book
8. desk
9. whiteboard
10. door
11. ruler
12. eraser
13. paper
14. coloured pencils
15. marker
16. table
17. pencil sharpener
18. floor
19. clock
20. student
21. chair
22. scissors
23. timetable
24. agenda
25. binder
26. loose-leaf paper
27. divider
28. report cover
29. file folder
30. tape
31. highlighter
32. backpack
33. computer
34. calculator
35. paint
36. paint brush

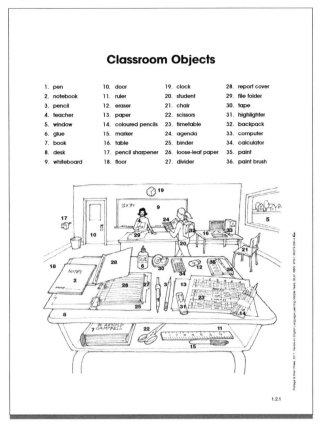

1.2.2

Vocabulary Cards - The Classroom

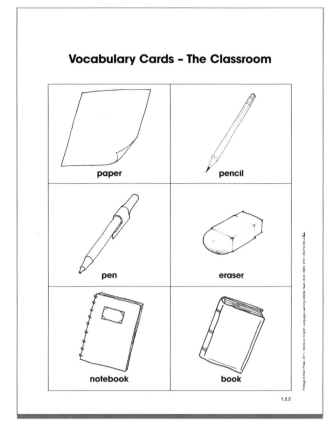

paper | pencil
pen | eraser
notebook | book

1.2.2

Vocabulary Cards - The Classroom

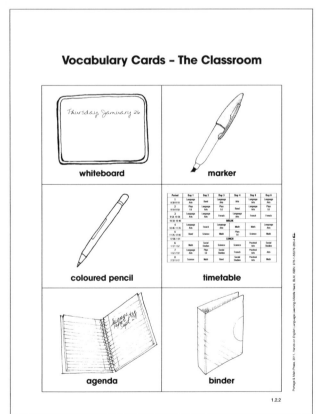

whiteboard | marker
coloured pencil | timetable
agenda | binder

1.2.2

Vocabulary Cards - The Classroom

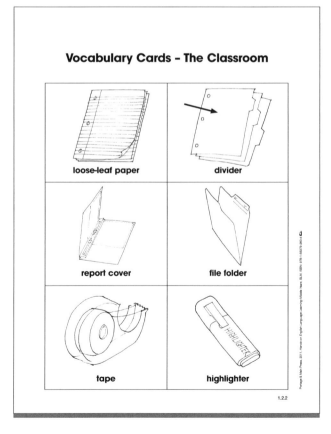

loose-leaf paper | divider
report cover | file folder
tape | highlighter

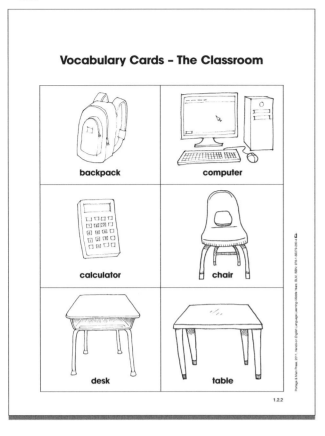
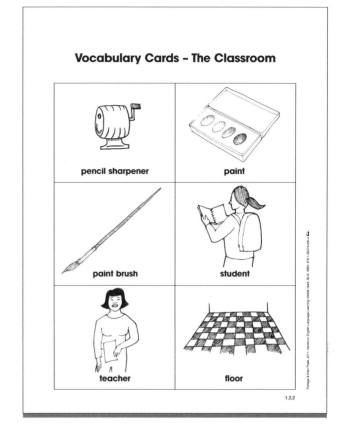
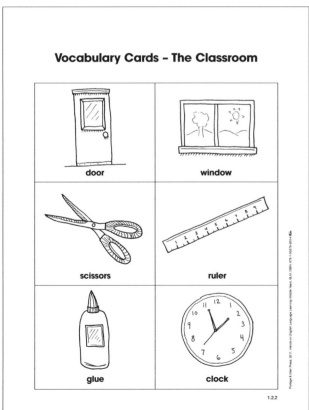
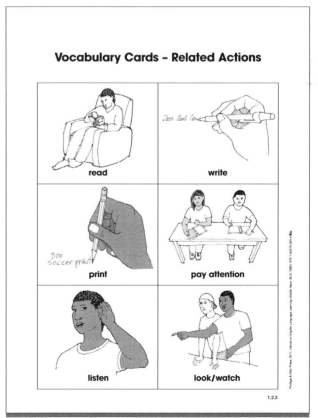

Blackline Masters

1.2.3

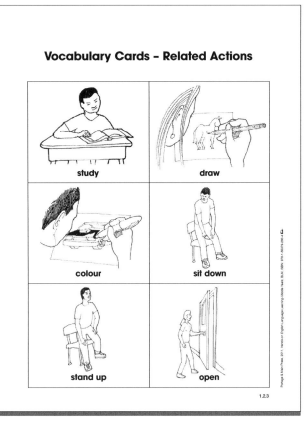

1.2.3

1.2.4

Date: _____ Name: _____

Classroom Objects

notebook	desk	coloured pencils	clock	file folder
teacher	whiteboard	marker	agenda	tape
window	door	pencil sharpener	binder	calculator
glue	ruler	floor	report cover	paint brush

2A

1.2.4

1.2.4

Date: _____ Name: _____

pen	paper	scissors	highlighter
pencil	table	timetable	backpack
book	student	loose-leaf paper	computer
eraser	chair	divider	paint

2A

1.2.4

64 – 1.2.3 – 1.2.4

3 The School

Curricular Connections

- Language Arts: speaking, listening, reading, writing, viewing, representing
- Mathematics: tallies, graphs, scale, proportion
- Social Studies: mapping skills, cardinal directions
- Art: drawing, photography

Background Information for Teachers

Similar to the previous lesson, there is a great deal of vocabulary introduced in this lesson. It is important to note that vocabulary should be taught over time. It is also good practice to review and use any previously learned vocabulary whenever possible. This is called "recycling." It is best to use words from previous lessons by including them in some of the activities from the new lesson. Another option is to include a warm-up activity at the beginning of each new lesson during which previously learned words are revisited. Warm-up activities should be very simple and should not last longer than about five minutes. Some examples include:

- Match the picture to the word.
- Act out/mime the words while giving directions/commands. For example, "Show me (a pen)"; "Point to (the clock)"; "Go to (the whiteboard)."
- Look at a picture, and say/read the word.
- Use the vocabulary cards – The School (1.3.1) to play a variation of the game Pictionary. Have one student select a card and illustrate it on the whiteboard. Ask the other students to guess the identity of the word.
- Do chain drills with students. A chain drill, which focuses on the use of patterned language, begins with the teacher and is then passed off from one student to the next. Any drill used for ELL instruction should focus on only one or two language forms at a time (grammatical or phonological structures) through some sort of repetition. For example:

- Teacher: I have a pencil. What do you have?
- Student 1: I have a book. What do you have?
- Student 2: I have scissors. What do you have?

OR

- Teacher: I am going to the classroom. Where are you going?
- Student 1: I am going to the gym. Where are you going?
- Student 2: I am going to the office. Where are you going?

OR

- Teacher: I like apples. What do you like?
- Student 1: I like pears. What do you like?
- Student 2: I like grapes. What do you like?
- Student 3: I like bananas. What do you like?

Vocabulary – The School

- school
- classroom
- hallway
- washroom/bathroom
- library
- gym
- office
- principal
- vice-principal
- computer lab
- art room
- lockers

3

- cafeteria
- canteen
- music room
- band room
- human ecology – foods room
- human ecology – sewing room
- woodworking shop
- science lab
- staff room
- bus
- fire alarm
- field
- water fountain
- secretary

Materials

- vocabulary cards – *The School* (included. Photocopy two sets onto sturdy tagboard, and cut apart cards.) (1.3.1)
- whiteboard
- chart paper
- markers
- file folder
- masking tape or sticky tack
- digital camera(s)
- tagboard
- binder rings
- hole punch
- scissors
- paper
- coloured pencils
- index cards
- "treasure" treat (for example, fresh fruit or muffins)
- box decorated like a treasure chest (optional)
- simple map of the school (make this yourself, or use a student-created map from the first integrated class activity to the right)
- mural paper

Integrated Class Activities

- Mapping skills are necessary for all students to develop, as they are an important part of the social studies curriculum and have practical applications in everyday life. One beneficial activity to do with all students is to have all them create maps or floor plans of their classroom and school. Be sure to explain that maps are like "bird's-eye" pictures, meaning that students must imagine themselves looking down on the area. Begin by having students create maps of the classroom, and have them progress to mapping a wing, a floor, or a section of the school, working towards eventually mapping the entire school and grounds. Display the vocabulary cards – *The School* (1.3.1) during this activity to support ELL students in their language acquisition and to support all students in tracking the locations and labels they should include on their maps.

Note: To differentiate instruction and correlate with math content, you may choose to have some students draw their maps to a specific scale.

- Create a treasure hunt for students. On a map of the school, use coloured dots or stars to mark various locations. At each location, tape an index card with a two-digit number on it. Have students read the map to find those locations, and then record, on a blank sheet of paper, the number on the index card they find there, as well as what the location is.

For example, you might identify the principal's office with a star on the school map. Next to the principal's office, you would then hang an index card with the number 25 (for instance). On their sheets of paper, students would record "25: principal's office."

66   Hands-On English Language Learning • Middle Years

3

Once students have located and identified all index cards, share a celebratory "treasure" treat, such as fresh fruit or muffins. For added excitement, place the treat inside a box decorated like a treasure chest.

- Have students collect data on the number of students in each of the school's classes. Divide the class into pairs or small groups of students. Give each pair or group a map of the school with a few classes/classrooms highlighted, and have them tally the number of students in those classes. Each pair or group should have a different set of classes to tally, and all classes in the school should be included in the overall activity. Later, create a large map of the school on mural paper, and record the class tallies on it. This data can then be used to create pictographs or bar graphs.

- Encourage all students to share past school experiences (if applicable) by drawing pictures of their former schools, bringing photos, and telling about their other schooling experiences. Students can also write about these experiences in their writing journals or create a graphic organizer, such as a Venn diagram, that compares similarities and differences between the school in their country of origin and their school in Canada.

Whole-Class Career Connections

- Take a tour of the school to identify various people who work at the school. Have students observe and identify the tasks being done by these personnel.

- Brainstorm, and record on chart paper, a list of the various jobs done by personnel in the school. Discuss how each of these people helps the students and the school to function.

- Have school employees present to students about their training, skills, and job descriptions.

Note: Prior to guests' presentations, make sure students identify questions that they would like to ask regarding each person's career. Although it is not appropriate for students to ask about a presenter's salary (this is generally confidential), it is reasonable for them to research this information for themselves (or with your help). The following three websites present average salaries/wages for various jobs in Canada:

<www.livingin-canada.com/wages-for-social-education-jobs-canada.html>

<www.payscale.com/research/CA/Employer_Type=School_%2f_School_District/Salary>

<http://resource.educationcanada.com/salaries.html>

Note: Teach students appropriate ways to thank guest speakers and other visitors. Have the designated thanker practise the expression of thanks ahead of time.

- Have students refer to the Employability Skills Checklist included with lesson 1 (1.1.8) and identify skills that they observe school employees using. For example, have students identify the skills that their teacher, school custodian, and computer technologist uses.

Instructional Activity

Use one set of vocabulary cards – *The School* (1.3.1) to introduce the target vocabulary to students. Use masking tape or sticky tack to attach the cards to the inside of a file folder. This allows easy access to the cards and visibility during a walk around the school.

Take students on a tour around the school, using the school map as a guide. Identify each location, person, and item shown on the cards. Also, encourage ELL students to share terminology from their first language(s).

▶

During the tour, use various sentence patterns to review the target vocabulary with students. For example:

- Teacher: Where are we?
- Student: We are in the library.
- Teacher: Who is this?
- Student: This is the principal.
- Teacher: Where is the fire alarm?
- Student: The fire alarm is over there (or, in the hall).

Peer Activity

- Have each ELL student work one-on-one with a peer helper. Provide the pair with one set of vocabulary cards – *The School* (1.3.1) and a digital camera. Send students on a mission to take pictures of each place, person, or item in the set of cards.

Note: Be sure to inform school staff that students will be taking pictures. As well, have students ask permission prior to taking a photograph of each person. This is an excellent opportunity to practise essential communication, such as, "May I please take your picture?"

As students locate and photograph each place, person, or item, ask the peer helper to read aloud the word on the corresponding card, point to the picture, and encourage the ELL student to repeat the word. Also, have the ELL student say the name of the place, person, or item in his or her first language. Have the pair repeat this procedure as they locate and photograph each place, person, or item.

Note: Make a small copy or print of each photo students take. Mount each photo onto sturdy tagboard, punch a hole in the top, and use a binder ring to attach all photos together. Photo booklets can then be used as a communication tool for referring to places, people, and items throughout the school.

Independent Activity: Activity Sheet A

Note: Have students with limited reading/writing abilities work with a peer helper or adult to complete this sheet.

Directions to students:

Write about and draw pictures of the people and places in your school. Try to record both the names of people and where in the school they work. Use the vocabulary cards to help you. See the example below (1.3.2):

People	Place
Mr. Barrack – gym teacher (draw picture of Mr. Barrack)	Gym (draw picture of gym)
Ms. Singh – grade 5 teacher (draw picture of Ms. Singh)	Room 103 (draw picture of room 103)

Extensions

- Add new vocabulary to the multilingual word wall.
- Have students add new vocabulary to their personal vocabulary folders or personal dictionaries.

Assessment of Learning

Once students have had a lot of exposure to new vocabulary introduced in lessons 2 and 3, take them on a classroom/school walk. Bring along vocabulary cards from both lessons 2 and 3 (1.2.2, 1.3.1). Have students identify the vocabulary in the appropriate location. To track student progress use the Vocabulary Tracking Checklist (I.9), shown in the introduction to *Hands-On English Language Learning* on page 39.

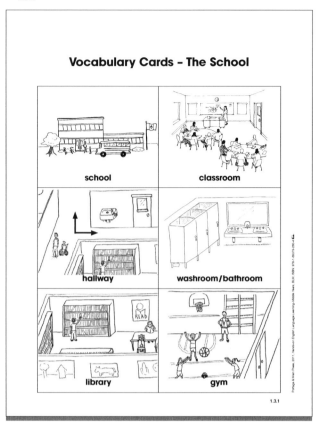
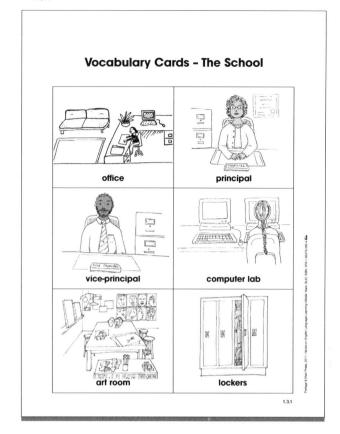
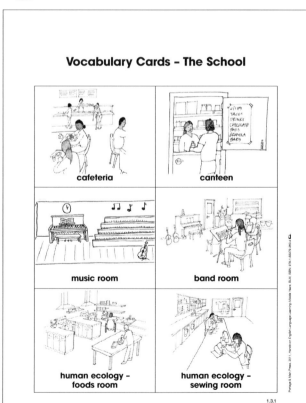
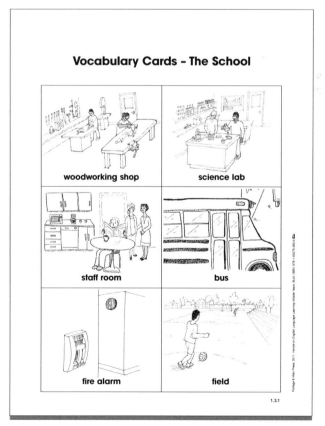

Blackline Masters

1.3.1

Vocabulary Cards - The School

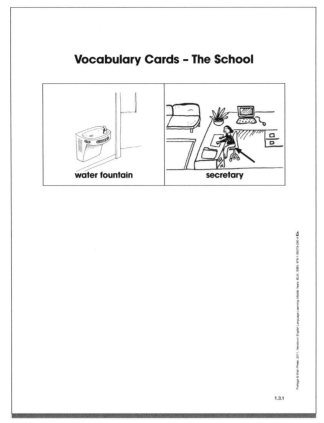

water fountain | secretary

1.3.2

Date: _____ Name: _____

My School

People	Places

3A

4 | School Activities

Curricular Connections

- Language Arts: speaking, listening, reading, writing, viewing, representing
- Mathematics: tallies, graphs, scale, proportion, telling time
- Social Studies: mapping skills, cardinal directions
- Physical Education: sports teams and extracurricular sports, physical activity clubs
- Art: drawing, photography

Background Information for Teachers

This lesson helps ELL students learn about the many activities that take place within the school, including both core subjects and extracurricular activities. The lesson also offers an opportunity to focus on learning to use a timetable and agenda and on developing time-management skills.

Vocabulary – School Activities

- timetable
- agenda
- Language Arts
- Mathematics
- Science
- Social studies
- French
- Art
- Music
- Band
- Library
- Physical Education
- Health
- Human Ecology – Foods
- Human Ecology – Sewing
- Woodworking
- Technology
- Drama
- sports teams
- Choir
- book club
- student council

Note: Use index cards to make additional vocabulary cards to represent other courses and/or extracurricular activities offered in your school but not mentioned in the preceding list.

Materials

- vocabulary cards – *School Activities* (included. Photocopy two sets onto sturdy tagboard, and cut apart cards. Also photocopy one set for each ELL-student/peer-helper pair.) (1.4.1)
- index cards
- masking tape or sticky tack
- collection of supplies/equipment/materials used for various school subjects (textbooks, novels, dictionaries, geometry set, art supplies, soccer ball/volley ball, and so on)
- classroom timetable (Make one photocopy for each student, and make a display copy on chart paper or on an overhead transparency for use on the overhead projector.)
- school schedule (including school start, opening exercises, class start, breaks, lunch, school end, each with corresponding times)
- teaching clock (with moveable hands)
- chart paper
- metre stick
- mural paper
- markers
- sticky notes
- list of your school's extracurricular activities

Integrated Class Activities

- All students will benefit from regular reviews of classroom timetables and the school schedule. Display a copy of the school schedule first. Discuss the times that are listed, and have students use the teaching

▶

4

clock to replicate those times. This is an excellent opportunity to discuss the importance of punctuality for school and for classes.

- Display the classroom timetable. Discuss the times and courses listed for each school day. Use the teaching clock to identify the times.

On chart paper, list each subject included on the timetable. Have students brainstorm a list of supplies/things they must bring with them to each class. For example:

- Physical Education: shorts, t-shirt, runners
- Math: textbook, coil-bound notebook, calculator, pencils, erasers, ruler
- Band: instrument, music folder

Discuss the importance of being properly prepared for classes.

- As a class, brainstorm a list of the school's extracurricular activities. Include sports, clubs, and interest groups. Draw a two-column table on chart paper, and record these activities in the left column of the chart.

Note: Some newcomers may not be familiar with specific extracurricular activities and the required equipment or supplies. Accommodations for these students may include using vocabulary cards and visiting various classrooms or programs to see first-hand what is involved and required.

Next, provide each student with several sticky notes. Have students record their names on several notes and then stick one note to the chart in the right-hand column next to each activity they have already participated in or plan to participate in. For example, if a student was on the volleyball team, is a member of the chess club, and plans to audition for the upcoming school musical, he or she would put a sticky with his or her name on it in the right column next to each of these activities.

Discuss students' interests in these activities, and have them share what each of the various activities involve. This is an excellent opportunity for students to learn about activities in which they may not otherwise have participated. Students are sometimes hesitant to join a group without knowing details, so this discussion may offer some valuable information that may encourage students to try out new activities. It is also a great opportunity for students to share activities in which they participated prior to their present school experience.

- Most middle-years schools encourage the use of student agendas to record information and to offer better communication between home and school. If your class does not use agendas, consider starting this practice. As a class, discuss the importance of using the agendas, and review the kind of information that students should record in them (homework, special events, tests, field trips, library book due dates, and so on). Encourage all students to take time at the end of each class to record important information in their agendas.

Note: Also encourage students to record this information in their first languages, to offer better communication with family members.

Instructional Activity

Provide each student with a copy of the classroom timetable. Display the vocabulary cards – *School Activities* (1.4.1). Introduce the cards, and have students identify each word on their timetables.

Display the collection of supplies/equipment/materials used in the various school subjects. Together with students, peruse textbooks used in various subjects as well as other equipment and supplies.

4

Then, use the teaching clock to identify each of the times listed on the timetable. Say each time aloud, and have students repeat it.

Note: Depending on students' reading and time-telling abilities, you may wish to have them create more user-friendly timetables, with illustrations for subjects (perhaps simplified variations of those found on the vocabulary cards) and small clock faces with times recorded.

Peer Activities

- Provide ELL-student/peer-helper pairs with mural paper, markers, a copy of the school map from lesson 3 (see page 66), and a set of vocabulary cards – *School Activities.* Have each pair of students create a large-scale map of the school on mural paper and then use masking tape or sticky tack to attach each vocabulary card to the map in the location where that school activity is held.

Note: Students will not use the vocabulary cards for *timetable* or *agenda* for this activity.

- Have each ELL student pair up with a peer helper to participate in a variety of extracurricular school activities.

Note: Joining new activities together with a peer will be helpful for most new students.

Independent Activity: Part One: Activity Sheet A

Note: Depending on the level of ELL students' reading, writing, and speaking skills, you may wish to have peer helpers support ELL students in completing the survey on the activity sheet.

Directions to students:

Survey students in your class to see what their favourite school subject is. Record your results as a tally. Answer the questions at the bottom of the sheet (1.4.2).

Independent Activity: Part Two: Activity Sheet B

Note: Depending on the level of ELL students' reading, writing, and speaking skills, you may wish to have peer helpers support ELL students in completing the survey on the activity sheet.

Directions to students:

Survey students in your class to see what their favourite extracurricular school activity is. Record your results as a tally. Answer the questions at the bottom of the sheet (1.4.3).

Extensions

- Add new vocabulary to the multilingual word wall.

- Have students add new vocabulary to their personal vocabulary folders or personal dictionaries.

- Consider initiating new extracurricular school activities that are reflective of ELL students' cultures. For example, start a language class or a cultural dance group. Invite ELL students, their family members, and community members to participate in these groups.

- Use survey results from Activity Sheet A (1.4.2) and Activity Sheet B (1.4.3) to create bar graphs with students, indicating their favourite school subjects, and extracurricular activities. You can also create double bar graphs by having students gather data for girls and boys separately.

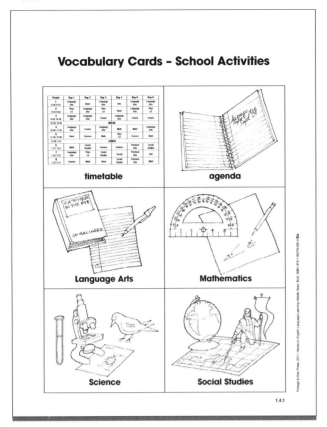

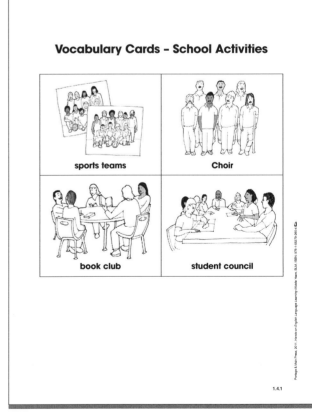

Class Survey 1

Date: _____ Name: _____

Question: What is your favourite school subject?

Results

Subject	Tally

What subject is the favourite for the most students? _____

What is *your* favourite school subject? _____

4A

Class Survey 2

Date: _____ Name: _____

Question: What is your favourite school activity outside of class (extracurricular activity)?

Results

Activity	Tally

Which activity is the favourite for the most students? _____

What is *your* favourite activity? _____

4B

Blackline Masters

5 The Alphabet

Curricular Connections

- Language Arts: speaking, listening, reading, writing, viewing, representing
- Mathematics: tallies, graphs
- Social Studies: cultural diversity
- Art: drawing

Background Information for Teachers

This lesson provides activities for instruction on and assessment of students' competence with the Roman alphabet, as well as manuscript printing and cursive writing. Many ELL students will be familiar with this written symbolic form and will not require instruction on this topic. Others, whose first languages do not use the Roman alphabet, may have limited exposure to these English-language symbols. For these students, the activities in this lesson will prove beneficial.

Note: It is important to ensure that middle-years students do not perceive activities and teaching materials as being too juvenile, as this may embarrass adolescents. Be sure to select resources appropriate to middle-years students. For example, select alphabet books with a multicultural or special-interest focus such as sports (see the Books for Students list at the end of the introduction to module 1, on page 48).

In most middle-years classrooms the printed or written alphabet will not be displayed on the wall (unless it is a classroom geared to ELL students). For students who require access to the printed or written alphabet while doing daily work, consider gluing a set of Roman alphabet letter cards (included with this lesson, 1.5.1) inside a file folder. You can also include a manuscript printing and cursive writing strip (included with this lesson, 1.5.4, 1.5.5) to support handwriting. Students can access the folder as needed.

Depending on the literacy level of your ELL students, you may choose to focus on manuscript printing or cursive writing. Resources for both are included in this lesson.

Materials

- alphabet books (see Books for Students list, page 48)
- Roman alphabet letter cards (Photocopy one set onto sturdy tagboard, and cut out cards.) (1.5.1)
- uppercase alphabet inventory sheet (included. Make one copy for each ELL student.) (1.5.2)
- lowercase alphabet inventory sheet (included. Make one copy for each ELL student.) (1.5.3)
- poster paper (one piece for each ELL student)
- classroom alphabet chart
- manuscript printing alphabet strip (included. Make one copy for each ELL student. Cut apart the three sections, and tape them together into one long strip.) (1.5.4)
- cursive writing alphabet strip (included. Make one copy for each ELL student. Cut apart the three sections, and tape them together into one long strip.) (1.5.5)
- glue
- scissors
- magazines, catalogues, flyers, and clip-art pictures
- pencils
- markers or coloured pencils
- whiteboards (one for each ELL student)
- dry-erase markers (one for each ELL student)
- erasers (one for each ELL student)
- cashier tape
- drawing paper
- chart paper

Integrated Class Activities

Alphabetization is an important concept for all students, as it helps to develop spelling and sequencing skills required for dictionary usage. Consider the following activities for focusing on these skills:

▶

5

- Have students use cashier tape to create their own alphabet strips (with manuscript printing or cursive writing) depicting words and objects from their countries of origin or that reflect their individual interests. They can then share their alphabet strips with classmates to acknowledge and build upon all students' background experiences, interests, and cultures.

- Emphasize the letters in students' names as a springboard to reading, writing, and to English proficiency. Have each student print his or her first name vertically on a piece of drawing paper and then record and illustrate familiar words that begin with each letter. ELL students might include new English words that they have learned, as in the following example:

    Jacket
    out
    sun
    eat
    friend

    Students may also choose to record words that reflect their interests, hobbies, skills, and personality traits. In both cases, have students include illustrations where appropriate.

- Record all students' first names on a piece of chart paper. Make a tally of the number of times each letter of the alphabet is used in the total list of names. Then, use the data to create a bar graph with students. Encourage students to read and interpret the graph. Which letter of the alphabet is used most often in their names? Which letter is used least often? To extend this activity, gather data for girls' and boys' names separately in order to create double bar graphs.

- Play the game I Spy as a class, focusing on the alphabet as well as on classroom objects. For example, one student might say, "I spy, with my little eye, something in the classroom that starts with the letter *B*" (book). As an added challenge, you can modify the game to focus on *ending* letters of classroom objects (for example, "I spy, with my little eye, something in the classroom that ends with the letter *k*."

- Research alphabets from around the world (other than Roman). Have students, family members, and community members teach the class some of the letters or words from various alphabets. Have students learn to record their names in various alphabets.

Note: It is important for teachers to understand students' backgrounds when conducting this activity, as some languages do not have alphabets (Chinese, Korean) but, rather, logographic characters. In this case, students could learn some of these characters. In other cases, students and family members may not be literate in their first language(s), and it is important to be sensitive in these situations.

Instructional Activity: Part One: Alphabet Inventory

Read aloud a book that focuses on the alphabet. While reading, discuss the pictures by pointing to, and identifying, the objects shown and the corresponding alphabet letters.

Have students select special interest alphabet books to read, and have them identify letters, sounds, and words while reading.

Assessment for Learning

Use the Roman alphabet letter cards (1.5.1) to assess students' alphabet skills in order to plan further instruction. Hold up a card, and ask the ELL student to identify the letter and its sound. Use the uppercase alphabet inventory sheet (1.5.2) to keep track of the student's progress.

▶

Variation: As the student's vocabulary bank increases, challenge him or her to complete this activity by naming the letter and then saying a word that represents (starts with) that letter (for example, *P* is for pencil).

Next Step

Use the Roman alphabet letter cards to review and assess students' recognition of lowercase letters. Hold up a card, and ask the student to identify the letter and its sound. Use a copy of the lowercase alphabet inventory sheet (1.5.3) to keep track of the student's progress.

Note: This is a good opportunity for students to share information about other alphabets or characters (for example, from their countries of origin), noting how letters and symbols are written or pronounced in other languages.

Instructional Activity: Part Two

Provide each ELL student with a manuscript printing alphabet strip (1.5.4) and a cursive writing alphabet strip (1.5.5). Have students line up the printing and cursive writing strips, one above the other, so that the letters correlate.

Then, provide ELL students with whiteboards, dry erase markers, and erasers. Have them practise using cursive script to write the letters of the alphabet.

Note: Provide plenty of opportunities for students to practise cursive writing. This is a skill from which many students in the class will benefit, so you can also do the activity with the whole class.

Peer Activity

Note: Before beginning this activity, divide large sheets of poster paper into 26 sections by drawing grid lines.

Have a peer helper work one-on-one with each ELL student. Provide each pair of students with a piece of poster paper with grid lines marked and a cursive writing alphabet strip. Have students use the alphabet strip as a guide to write the sequence of letters on the poster paper, one letter per section.

Note: Encourage students to write the letters large, but at the top of each section. They will need room to glue a picture below each letter.

Next, have each pair of students select a theme for an alphabet poster they will create. Encourage them to consider special interests such as sports, rock bands, fashion, books, and song titles. Provide students with magazines, flyers, catalogues, and clip-art pictures as well as glue and scissors. Have the pairs find a picture for each letter of the alphabet (keeping the theme for their poster in mind) and glue the pictures under the correct letters.

Note: Choose one or both of the activity sheets below—for manuscript printing and cursive writing—depending on the needs of your ELL students.

Independent Activity: Part One: Activity Sheet A

Directions to students:

Practise printing each letter on the activity sheet. Draw a picture that represents each letter (1.5.6).

Independent Activity: Part Two: Activity Sheet B

Directions to students:

Practise using cursive writing to record each letter on the activity sheet. Draw a picture that represents each letter (1.5.7).

5

Extensions

- Add new vocabulary to the multilingual word wall.

- Have students add new vocabulary to their personal vocabulary folders or personal dictionaries.

- Copy and cut apart one set of Roman alphabet letter cards (1.5.1). Have students cut each card in half to separate the letter from the pictures. Ask them to mix up the cards. Have students match each letter to its corresponding picture and then sequence the cards from *A* to *Z*.

- Cut apart a cursive writing alphabet strip (1.5.5) into individual letters. Use the picture-only sections of the Roman alphabet letter cards (1.5.1) cut apart in the previous extension activity, and have students match the pictures to the written letters.

Blackline Masters

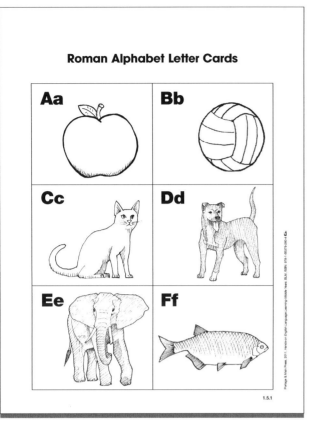

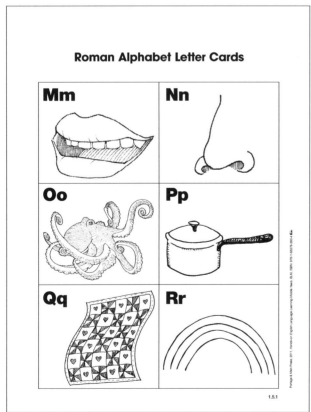

Roman Alphabet Letter Cards

Ss	Tt
Uu	Vv
Ww	Xx

80 – 1.5.1

1.5.1

Roman Alphabet Letter Cards

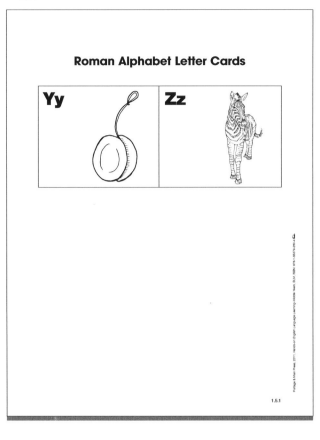

1.5.1

1.5.2

Date: _____   Name: _____

Uppercase Alphabet Inventory

Letter	Reads	Prints	Represents Letter With Example
A			
B			
C			
D			
E			
F			
G			
H			
I			
J			
K			
L			
M			
N			
O			
P			
Q			
R			
S			
T			
U			
V			
W			
X			
Y			
Z			

1.5.2

Blackline Masters

1.5.3

Date: _____   Name: _____

Lowercase Alphabet Inventory

Letter	Reads	Prints	Represents Letter With Example
a			
b			
c			
d			
e			
f			
g			
h			
i			
j			
k			
l			
m			
n			
o			
p			
q			
r			
s			
t			
u			
v			
w			
x			
y			
z			

1.5.3

1.5.4

Manuscript Printing Alphabet Strip

Aa Bb Cc Dd Ee Ff Gg Hh

Ii Jj Kk Ll Mm Nn Oo Pp Qq

Rr Ss Tt Uu Vv Ww Xx Yy Zz

1.5.4

Blackline Masters

1.5.5

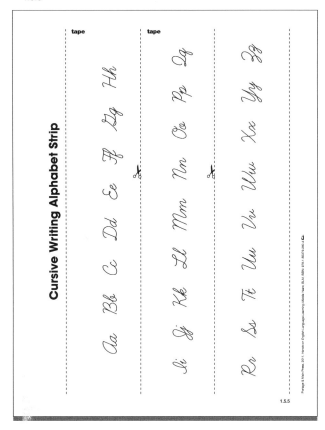

1.5.6

Date: _____ Name: _____

The Alphabet

Aa ___	Bb ___	Cc ___	Dd ___
Ee ___	Ff ___	Gg ___	Hh ___
Ii ___	Jj ___	Kk ___	Ll ___
Mm ___	Nn ___	Oo ___	Pp ___
Qq ___	Rr ___	Ss ___	Tt ___
Uu ___	Vv ___	Ww ___	Xx ___
Yy ___	Zz ___		

5A

1.5.7

Date: _____ Name: _____

The Alphabet

Aa ___	Bb ___	Cc ___	Dd ___
Ee ___	Ff ___	Gg ___	Hh ___
Ii ___	Jj ___	Kk ___	Ll ___
Mm ___	Nn ___	Oo ___	Pp ___
Qq ___	Rr ___	Ss ___	Tt ___
Uu ___	Vv ___	Ww ___	Xx ___
Yy ___	Zz ___		

5B

6 Colours

Curricular Connections

- Language Arts: speaking, listening, reading, writing, viewing, representing
- Mathematics: surveys, tallies, graphs
- Science: light spectrums, rainbows
- Art: primary and secondary colours, colour mixing, art production

Vocabulary – Colours

Colours

- red
- orange
- yellow
- green
- blue
- purple
- pink
- brown
- black
- white
- grey

Colour Objects

- apple
- carrot
- banana
- grass
- sky
- grapes
- flamingo
- bear
- panther
- clouds
- elephant

Note: Some of the colour objects presented in this lesson might be unfamiliar to some ELL students. Use blank index cards to make vocabulary cards for objects from ELL students' countries of origin. Include objects with which students can make an immediate connection such as cultural foods (for example, yellow: curry; orange: mango), animals, plants, and so on.

Materials

- books that focus on colours

Note: Select books for older students, such as *The Colorguardians and the Magic Books of Colour* by Karen Avant-Cooke, or *A Book About Color: A Clear and Simple Guide for Young Artists* by Mark Gonyea)

- vocabulary cards – Colours (included. Photocopy onto sturdy tagboard, cut apart cards, and colour the pictures in the appropriate colours.) (1.6.1)
- blank index cards
- markers or coloured pencils
- small pieces of drawing paper (cut 8½" x 11" sheets into four pieces)
- poster paper
- various art materials (yarn, paper, paint, fabric, magazine pictures, coloured foil, tissue, cellophane, and so on)
- magazines
- scissors
- glue
- classroom object to represent each colour (for example, brown: desk; red: fire-alarm bell)
- various colours of Plasticine, play dough, or modelling clay
- painting supplies (paper, paint, paintbrushes, containers for water)
- coloured blocks
- coloured stickers

▶

6

Integrated Class Activities

- Have students explore primary and secondary colours, the colour wheel, and colour mixing through art activities. Painting is especially effective for observing the results of mixing colours. Encourage dialogue among students as they explore, and display vocabulary cards – *colours* to support ELL students.

- Use various colours of playdough, Plasticine, or modelling clay to have students explore colour mixing kinaesthetically.

- Explore the spectrum of colours in the rainbow with students, teaching them the range and order of the colours. Encourage students to create acronyms or funny sentences to help them remember the order. For example, one way to remember the order red, orange, yellow, green, blue, indigo, violet is with the name Roy G. Biv. Another way is with the sentence "Reading on your green bench is voluntary."

- Survey students to determine their favourite colours. Create a tally, and then transfer this information onto a bar graph. To make double or triple bar graphs, survey students from more than one grade, and organize the data into these groups.

Whole-Class Career Connections

- Brainstorm a list of careers that would use or be focused on colour. This might include:
  - Artist
  - House painter
  - Interior decorator
  - Interior designer
  - Fashion designer
  - Hardware store worker (paint mixing)

- Refer to the Employability Skills Checklist included with lesson 1 (1.1.8), and determine how each of these skills relates to tasks undertaken by individuals in the careers students identified in the preceding activity. For example, discuss how a house painter might select and use appropriate tools and technology for a task or project.

Instructional Activity: Part One

Read aloud the books that focus on colour. While reading, discuss the pictures by pointing to and identifying each object and its corresponding colour.

Instructional Activity: Part Two

Use the vocabulary cards – *Colours* (1.6.1) to introduce students to colour vocabulary.

Note: Although you will automatically teach the colour-objects vocabulary (apple, carrot, banana, and so on) through this activity, focus more on the actual colour shown in each card than on the picture representing that colour. Make sure you have coloured the pictures in the appropriate colours on the vocabulary cards.

As you display each card, say the colour word, select a marker or coloured pencil of that colour, then point the marker to the colour of the object on the card. Encourage students to say the colour word for each card, and also to share their first-language translations for the colour word.

Provide students with markers or coloured pencils as well as several small pieces of drawing paper. Have students select a vocabulary card, say the colour word, and find a pencil or marker to match that card. Then, ask students to draw something of that colour on one of the pieces of paper.

Mix up the vocabulary cards with one student's drawings, and have students match the cards to the drawings while saying the colour word.

Instructional Activity: Part Three: Find and Touch

Note: This receptive activity gives students an opportunity to review the target vocabulary through hands-on exploration. Depending on students' confidence with the vocabulary, you may consider using the vocabulary cards with this activity.

Call out a colour, and have students find and touch an object of that colour somewhere in the classroom. Also, have students take turns taking a leadership role and calling out colours for their classmates.

Peer Activities

- Have each ELL student work with a peer helper to create a colour collage or mosaic poster on a large sheet of poster paper. Ask each pair of students to select a colour on which to focus, write the name of the colour at the top of the poster paper, and then collect various art supplies and materials of that colour. Students' collages can include various art materials such as yarn, paper, paint, fabric, magazine pictures, coloured foil, tissue, cellophane, and so on.

- Have ELL student/peer-helper pairs use the vocabulary cards – *Colours* and focus on classroom objects while they play the game I Spy. For example, have one student say: "I spy, with my little eye, something in the classroom that is yellow." Then, have the other student identify the vocabulary card for yellow as well as classroom objects of that colour.

Independent Activity: Part One

Have each ELL student create his or her own set of colour vocabulary cards that reflect his or her country of origin. These can be coloured and then used with the set provided at the end of the lesson (1.6.1) to play games such as Concentration or Go Fish.

Note: A match or pair for one of the preceding games constitutes two cards depicting the same *colour,* not the same picture, since the pictures reflecting students' countries of origin will be different from those found on the vocabulary cards provided with the lesson.

Independent Activity: Part Two: Activity Sheet A

Directions to students:

Complete the chart to show the names, illustrations, and colours of different foods (1.6.2).

Extensions

- Add new vocabulary to the multilingual word wall.

- Have students add new vocabulary to their personal vocabulary folders or personal dictionaries. Encourage students to include pictures of objects from their countries of origin as well as the newly-introduced vocabulary (objects).

Note: Before beginning the following extension activity, copy the Concentration colour cards (1.6.3) onto sturdy tagboard, and cut out the cards. You should have 11 colour-word cards and 11 paint-splotch cards in total. Colour each paint splotch one of the following colours: red, orange, yellow, green, blue, purple, pink, brown, black, grey, and white.

- Have pairs of students use the Concentration colour cards (1.6.3) to play the game Concentration. Ask players to shuffle the cards and spread them out, facedown, in the space between them. Then, have players take turns flipping over two cards, trying to make a match. Each time a card is flipped over, the player must say the colour word. Play continues until all cards are matched.

▶

Note: Please be aware that the competitive aspect of this game is less important than the new vocabulary review opportunities for students.

Assessment of Learning

Shuffle the Concentration colour cards. Ask the ELL student to match up each colour splotch with its corresponding colour word and read the word aloud. Observe and note if students have any difficulties with the target vocabulary. Use the Vocabulary Tracking Checklist (I.9), shown on page 39, to record results.

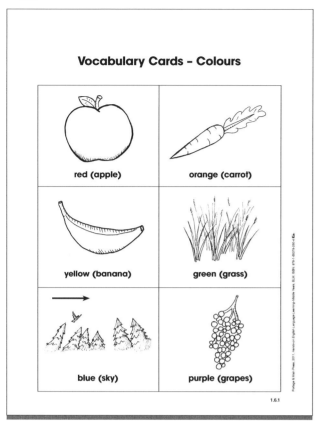

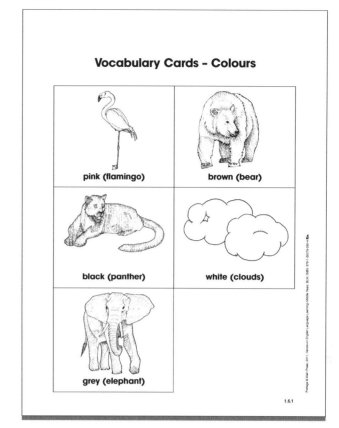

Blackline Masters

The Colour of Food

Food	Illustration	Colour
cherry		
	(carrot)	
		yellow
broccoli		
		black
rice		
		pink
	(cheese)	
		blue
grapes		
		brown

6A   1.6.2

Concentration Colour Cards

red		orange	
yellow		green	
blue		purple	
pink		brown	
black		white	
grey			

Extension   1.6.3

1.6.1 – 1.6.3 – 87

7 Numbers, Counting, and Math

Curricular Connections

- Language Arts: speaking, listening, reading, writing, viewing, representing
- Mathematics: counting, number concepts, calendars, surveys, tallies, graphs
- Science: collecting and displaying data
- Social Studies: collecting and displaying data

Background Information for Teachers

The following activities can be used and modified as appropriate for middle-years learners. Some ELL students will be familiar with concepts involving numbers, counting, and related math skills but may require instruction in the related English vocabulary. Others may have limited exposure to these mathematical concepts and may therefore require instruction in both concepts and related English language. It is therefore important to assess students' entry skills and background knowledge and cater instructional activities accordingly. A math concepts inventory sheet (1.7.1) is included with this lesson. Use this sheet to assess students' entering math skills and background knowledge (as suggested in Instructional Activities: Parts One, Two, and Three).

Vocabulary – Numbers, Counting, and Math

Number Words

- one
- two
- three
- four
- five
- six
- seven
- eight
- nine
- ten
- eleven
- twelve
- thirteen
- fourteen
- fifteen
- sixteen
- seventeen
- eighteen
- nineteen
- twenty
- thirty
- forty
- fifty
- sixty
- seventy
- eighty
- ninety
- hundred
- thousand

Math Concepts

- greater than
- less than
- equal
- not equal
- add
- subtract
- multiply
- divide
- fraction
- one half
- one third
- one fourth/one quarter
- decimal
- one tenth
- one hundredth

Materials

- various sets of counters (for example, bingo chips, buttons, chain links, cubes)

7

- math concepts inventory sheet (included. Make one copy for each student.) (1.7.1)
- small whiteboards
- dry-erase markers and erasers
- numeral cards (included. Photocopy one set onto sturdy tagboard, and cut apart cards.) (1.7.2)
- vocabulary cards – *Number Words* (included. Photocopy one set onto sturdy tagboard, and cut apart cards.) (1.7.3)
- vocabulary cards – *Math Concepts* (included. Photocopy one set onto sturdy tagboard, and cut apart cards.) (1.7.4)
- hundred chart (included. Make one copy for each ELL student.) (1.7.5)
- picture book that focuses on numbers (for example, *One Is a Drummer: A Book of Numbers* by Roseanne Thong)
- place-value counter cards (included. Photocopy one set onto sturdy tagboard, and cut out cards.) (1.7.6)
- Cross Out game sheet *A* (included. Make two copies for each ELL/English-speaking pair of students.) (1.7.7)
- Cross Out game sheet *B* (included. Make two copies for each ELL/English-speaking pair of students.) (1.7.8)
- number cubes (two for each pair of students)
- pencils
- drawing paper
- coloured construction paper
- stapler
- coiled notebooks (optional; one for each ELL student)
- digital camera(s)
- computer
- scissors
- glue
- blank index cards
- classroom calendar

Integrated Class Activities

Activities involving number concepts will benefit all students in terms of related mathematics skills. Number activities can be adapted for any grade level to focus on number recognition, sequencing, counting forward and backward, skip counting, number words, place value, and number patterns. Display vocabulary cards – *Number Words* (1.7.3) during these activities to support ELL students. Also consider using blank index cards to make additional cards as students' number concepts develop:

- As part of your daily classroom routine, have a student-developed "math problem of the day" for the rest of the class to solve. Display the vocabulary cards – *Number Words* (1.7.3) and *Math Concepts* (1.7.4) while students are working on the math problem to support ELL students.

- Routine calendar activities are an excellent way to focus on numbers and counting in context. Use the classroom calendar to review number recognition, sequencing, counting forward and backward, skip counting, number words, place value, and number patterns with students.

- You can also use daily attendance routines to review number concepts with students. Each day, count the number of students present, and challenge them to determine how many of their classmates are absent.

- Collecting, recording, and presenting data are opportunities for all students to use number concepts in context. As a class, create various graphs based on classroom data. For example, have students sort themselves into groups based on
    - gender
    - number of letters in their first names
    - number of siblings
    - mode of transportation to school

▶

For each category, count the number of students in each group, and use this data to create the graphs.

Whole-Class Career Connections

- Discuss the role of mathematics in everyday life. Brainstorm ways that people use math at home, for example:
    - For cooking/baking
    - For building a deck (or other)
    - For creating household budgets
    - For shopping

- Discuss the importance of mathematics in the workplace. Have students select two careers, such as jobs that family members have, and record all the ways that math is used in each of these jobs. Have students share these ideas with the rest of the class.

Note: It is important to be sensitive to students' individual family circumstances regarding employment. Some family members may not be employed or may work several jobs in order to support the family. Keep such issues in mind when having students conduct this activity.

- Have students review the Employability Skills Checklist (1.1.8) included with lesson 1 and identify those skills that require mathematics.

Instructional Activity: Part One: Counting

Use a collection of counters and the numeral cards (1.7.2) to model the process of counting sets for students. Count out loud, and then select the numeral card that matches your set. After doing this a few times, have students count items (counters) in their first languages and try to identify the corresponding numeral card. Repeat this several times with various counters and different numbered sets to determine ELL students' counting skills. Record results on the math concepts inventory sheet (1.7.1), and use this information as the basis for further instruction.

Instructional Activity: Part Two: Number Words

Using the numeral cards, read the numerals 1 to 10 in sequence, pointing to each numeral as you read it. Then, use counters to show each number as well, placing a set of counters to represent the number under each card.

Now, display the vocabulary cards – *Number Words* (1.7.3). Say each number word in sequence as you place the card under the corresponding numeral card and counters. Have students repeat each number word with you and then count from 1 to 10 as they point to the appropriate vocabulary cards.

Increase the number range as appropriate. Practise using the numeral cards, number word vocabulary cards, counters, and spoken language interchangeably. Repeat this in various ways, such as by having students say the number word and point to the appropriate numeral card. Record results on the math concepts inventory sheet, and use this information as the basis for further instruction.

Instructional Activity: Part Three: Place-Value Counter Cards

Introduce the place-value counter cards (1.7.6). First, pair up each numeral card (1 to 10) and number-word vocabulary card with its corresponding counter card. Display the three sets of cards on a table in sequential order. Point to each numeral, read the number word, and then use a counter card to show the same number, placing it directly below the corresponding vocabulary card.

Next, mix up the numeral cards and the vocabulary cards, and have students re-sequence them. Then, mix up the counter cards, and have students match these to the vocabulary cards.

As appropriate, repeat the preceding activities, increasing the number range as students gain confidence and skill. Record results on the math concepts inventory sheet. Use this information as the basis for further instruction.

Instructional Activity: Part Four: Hundred Chart

Provide each student with a hundred chart (1.7.5), and have students count aloud as they point to each number on the chart. As appropriate, based on students' skills, use the hundred chart to explore counting backward and skip counting with students. Record results on the math concepts inventory sheet, and use this information as the basis for further instruction.

Instructional Activity: Part Five: Number Concepts

Use the vocabulary cards – *Math Concepts* (1.7.4) to explore students' understanding of number concepts. For example:

- Count out eight counters, and place them on a whiteboard.
- Record the numeral 8 on the whiteboard below the set.
- Count out three counters, and place them beside the first set.
- Record the numeral 3 on the whiteboard below the set.
- Place the ">" card between the two sets.
- Say, "Eight is greater than three" as you point to each numeral/symbol.

As appropriate, have students use the "<", ">", "=", and "≠" cards to demonstrate this process. Record results on the math concepts inventory sheet, and use this information as the basis for further instruction.

Instructional Activity: Part Five: Number Operations

Use the vocabulary cards – *Math Concepts* to explore students' understanding of number operations. For example, use the "+" card to demonstrate an addition number story, as in the following:

- Record 6 + 2 on a small whiteboard.
- Place six counters and two counters below the numerals (a).
- Have a student combine the counters and move them over to the right.
- Count the total.
- Place the "=" card to the right of the 2.
- Record 8 on the whiteboard to the right of the = to complete the number sentence (b).
- Say the number sentence as you point to each numeral/symbol. Have students repeat the number sentence.

(a) 6 + 2   (b) 6 + 2 = 8

As appropriate, have students demonstrate this process for addition.

Extend the process to explore students' understanding of subtraction, multiplication, and division.

Record results on the math concepts inventory sheet, and use this information as the basis for further instruction.

Instructional Activity: Part Six: Fractions and Decimals

Use the vocabulary cards – *Math Concepts* to explore students' understanding of fractions and decimals. For example, select the "½" card, and carry out the following:

- Say the fraction aloud, and point to the illustration.
- Draw several shapes on the whiteboard.

▶

- Draw a line through each shape, dividing them into equal halves.
- Colour in one half of each shape.
- Record "½" on the uncoloured half of each shape.

As appropriate, have students demonstrate this process to show the fraction ½.

Extend the process to explore students' understanding of each fraction and decimal.

Record results on the math concepts inventory sheet, and use this information as the basis for further instruction.

Peer Activity

Pair up each ELL student with a peer helper to play the game, Cross Out. Provide each pair with two number cubes, two copies of Cross Out game sheet A (1.7.7), and two pencils. Have player A roll both number cubes, count the number of dots shown together on both cubes, and say the total number aloud. Then, tell him or her to cross out the corresponding numeral on his or her game sheet. Next, have player B roll the two number cubes, count the total number of dots shown, say the number aloud, and cross out the corresponding numeral on his or her game sheet. If a student rolls a number that he or she has already crossed out, he or she does nothing, and play moves to the other student. The player who crosses out all 11 numbers on his or her game sheet first wins.

Next Step

Have ELL-student/peer-helper pairs play Cross Out with larger numbers. Provide students with a full set of vocabulary cards – *Number Words* (1.7.3), two copies of Cross Out game sheet B (1.7.8), and two pencils. Display the vocabulary, and ask each student to select 16 of the numbers to record on his or her blank sheet. Tell students to place their vocabulary cards in a pile. Then, have players take turns selecting a vocabulary card, saying the number aloud, and then crossing out the corresponding numeral on his or her game sheet.

Independent Activity

Read a picture book that focuses on numbers, such as *One Is a Drummer: A Book of Numbers*. Then, have students make their own digital photo number booklets. For each ELL student, staple or bind together several sheets of drawing paper into a booklet, adding a piece of coloured construction paper for the front and back covers. As an alternative, you may provide each ELL student with a ready-made coiled notebook.

On each page of his or her booklet or notebook, have each student record a numeral (beginning with 1, continuing in sequential order to 20, and then by 10s from 30 to 100). Also, have students print or write the corresponding number words for each numeral (on each page). Finally, distribute digital cameras to students (or have them take turns using one camera), and have them take pictures to represent each number in their booklets. For example, students can photograph a collection of 20 pencils for that page of the book. Print out all students' pictures, and ask them to glue them into their booklets or notebooks. Have students use the numeral cards, the number-word vocabulary cards, and the counter cards to help them.

Extensions

- Add new vocabulary to the multilingual word wall.
- Have students add new vocabulary to their personal vocabulary folders or personal dictionaries.

Blackline Masters

Math Concepts Inventory

Student Name _____

Concept		Observed (✓)	Comments
Counts sets of objects in first language to _____			
Counts sets of objects in English to _____			
Recognizes written numerals, and makes corresponding sets of objects to _____			
Reads number words to _____			
Recognizes numbers represented by place-value counter cards to _____			
Uses the hundred chart to:	Count forward		
	Count backward		
	Skip count		
Recognizes and uses mathematical symbols:	+		
	−		
	×		
	÷		
	=		
	>		
	<		
	≠		
	$\frac{1}{2}$		
	$\frac{1}{3}$		
	$\frac{1}{4}$		
	0.1		
	0.01		

Comments: _____

Numeral Cards

1	2
3	4
5	6
7	8
9	10

Numeral Cards

11	12
13	14
15	16
17	18
19	20

Numeral Cards

30	40
50	60
70	80
90	100
1000	

Vocabulary Cards - Number Words

one	two
three	four
five	six
seven	eight
nine	ten

Vocabulary Cards - Number Words

eleven	twelve
thirteen	fourteen
fifteen	sixteen
seventeen	eighteen
nineteen	twenty

Vocabulary Cards - Number Words

thirty	forty
fifty	sixty
seventy	eighty
ninety	hundred
thousand	

Vocabulary Cards - Math Concepts

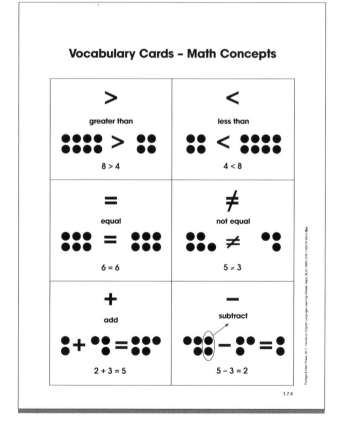

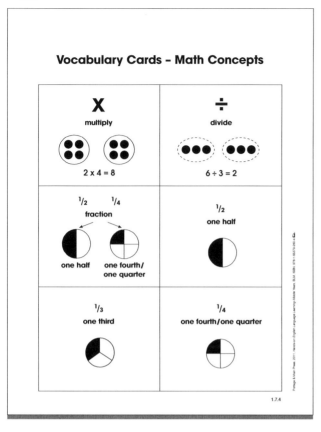

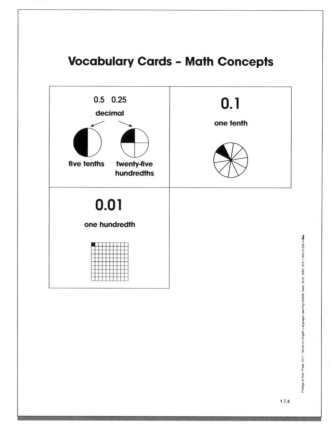

Hundred Chart (1–100)

1	2	3	4	5	6	7	8	9	10
11	12	13	14	15	16	17	18	19	20
21	22	23	24	25	26	27	28	29	30
31	32	33	34	35	36	37	38	39	40
41	42	43	44	45	46	47	48	49	50
51	52	53	54	55	56	57	58	59	60
61	62	63	64	65	66	67	68	69	70
71	72	73	74	75	76	77	78	79	80
81	82	83	84	85	86	87	88	89	90
91	92	93	94	95	96	97	98	99	100

Place-Value Counter Cards

Blackline Masters

1.7.6

Place-Value Counter Cards

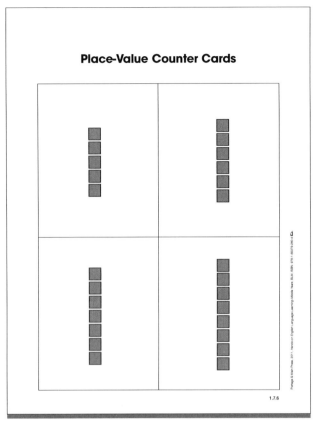

1.7.6

Place-Value Counter Cards

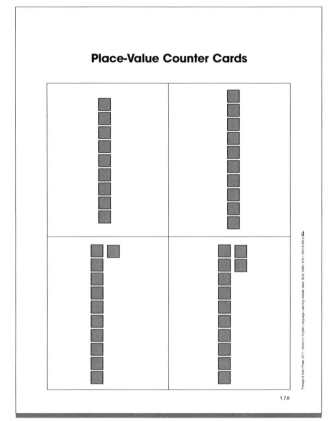

1.7.6

Place-Value Counter Cards

1.7.6

Place-Value Counter Cards

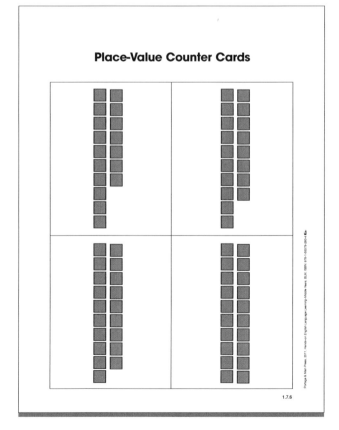

96 – 1.7.6

1.7.6

Place-Value Counter Cards

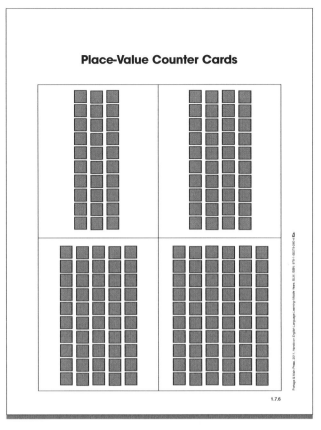

1.7.6

Place-Value Counter Cards

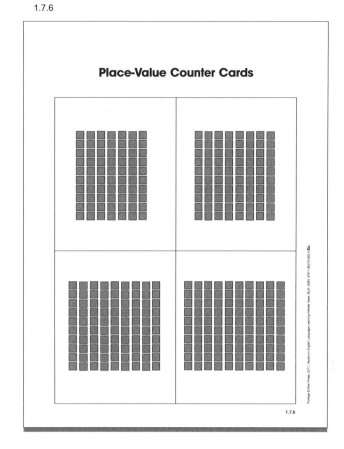

1.7.6

Place-Value Counter Cards

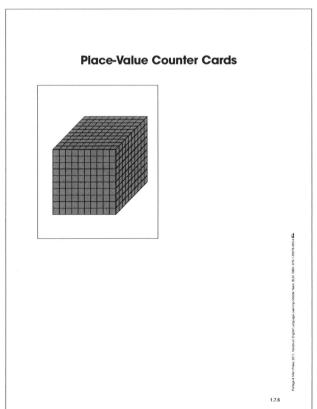

1.7.7

Cross Out Game A (2–12)

4	7	3
10	FREE	9
12	2	11
6	8	5

Peer Activity

Blackline Masters

Blackline Masters

1.7.8

Cross Out Game B

Peer Activity

8 The Calendar – Days of the Week

Curricular Connections

- Language Arts: speaking, listening, reading, writing, viewing, representing
- Mathematics: calendar concepts, surveys, tallies, graphing
- Science: sequencing events
- Social Studies: Cultural diversity
- Art: drawing

Background Information for Teachers

By the time students are ready for this lesson and the following lesson on months of the year, they will most likely have observed several classroom routines and activities that involve the calendar. Some students may not be familiar with the Gregorian calendar system, and they may have many questions about how to organize days and months. Investigate the calendar system with which each ELL student is most familiar in order to determine a starting point for this topic. Be sure to present these other calendar systems to the class to facilitate inclusiveness and to validate ELL students' prior knowledge, languages, and cultures.

Vocabulary – The Calendar – Days of the Week

Days of the Week

- Sunday
- Monday
- Tuesday
- Wednesday
- Thursday
- Friday
- Saturday

Related Concepts

- week
- day
- today
- tomorrow
- yesterday
- weekday
- weekend

Materials

- classroom calendar
- student agendas
- current annual calendars (available free from local banks, real estate agencies, insurance companies, and so on)
- vocabulary cards – *Days of the Week* (included. Photocopy one set onto sturdy tagboard, and cut out cards.) (1.8.1)
- vocabulary cards – *Related Concepts* (included. Photocopy one set onto sturdy tagboard, and cut out cards.) (1.8.2)
- whiteboard and dry-erase markers or chalkboard and chalk
- overhead projector
- pocket chart or chalkboard ledge or other ledge
- scissors
- glue
- chart paper
- student survey (included, two pages. Make a copy of both pages for each ELL student, or several copies if students are surveying multiple classes of students.) (1.8.3)

Integrated Class Activities

- Use daily routines and agenda time to develop all students' calendar skills. Focus on concepts such as saying the date correctly (day, month, date, year), identifying the day and date for yesterday and tomorrow, and counting the number of days and weeks in the current month.

- Have all students in the class complete Activity Sheet A: Days of the Week (1.8.4) to reflect on and record activities in which they participate on a weekly basis.

▶

8

Instructional Activity: Part One

Use the classroom calendar or another calendar to introduce the days of the week. Read aloud the days in order from Sunday to Saturday as you point to the words at the top of the calendar. Next, have students point to the words as you read them in sequence. Encourage them to repeat the words or say them with you as you read.

Introduce the vocabulary cards – *Days of the Week* (1.8.1). Display the cards in sequential order in the pocket chart or on the chalkboard ledge or other ledge.

Read each card aloud while pointing to the word on the card, then point to the day on the actual calendar. At this point, also have students share the names of the days of the week in their first language(s).

Next, spread out the vocabulary cards in sequence. Point to one of the days on the calendar, and have students find the matching card. Mix up the cards, and repeat the activity for each day of the week.

Then, have students practise printing each day of the week on a whiteboard or chalkboard. Display the calendar and the vocabulary cards for students to use as guidance.

Instructional Activity: Part Two

Use the classroom calendar or another calendar to introduce the vocabulary cards – *Related Concepts* (1.8.2). Begin with the words *day* and *week*.

Now, use the calendar to identify one week. Have students say the days of the week in sequence as they point to the words on the calendar. Count the days, and have students repeat the counting. On chart paper, record the following, underlining the words *days* and *week* as shown:

- There are seven <u>days</u> in one <u>week</u>.

Have students examine the calendar month again to determine the number of weeks in the month.

Next, introduce the terms *today, tomorrow*, and *yesterday*. Display those vocabulary cards, and on chart paper, record the following, underlining the word *today* as shown:

- <u>Today</u> is _____.

Have students identify the current day of the week. Model how to record the day and date by completing the sentence as follows, again underlining the word *today*:

- <u>Today</u> is Tuesday, October 3.

Then, use the calendar to introduce and have students practise using the terms *tomorrow* and *yesterday*. Record the following on chart paper:

- <u>Tomorrow</u> will be _____.

Have students identify the current day of the week, and then identify the day after. Model how to record the day and date by completing the sentence as follows:

- <u>Tomorrow</u> will be Wednesday, October 4.

Repeat the same process to introduce the term *yesterday.*

Finally, introduce the terms *weekday* and *weekend*. Explain that we come to school on weekdays. Again, display the vocabulary cards – *Days of the Week* (1.8.1) in sequence. Have students identify the weekdays and the weekend days. Mix up the cards, and have students sort them by weekdays and weekend days.

Have students share what they do on weekends. Record their ideas on chart paper.

100   Hands-On English Language Learning • Middle Years

Peer Activity

Distribute copies of the student survey (1.8.3 – two pages) to ELL students. Have each ELL student work with a peer helper and use the first page of the student survey to survey classmates about their favourite day of the week. Also, have surveyed students explain their reasons for selecting specific days. Tell students to compile their results on the second page of the survey. Use the results to create a bar graph.

To extend this activity, have students survey one or two other classes as well, and use the results to construct a double or triple bar graph.

Independent Activity: Activity Sheet A

Directions to students:

Print or write the days of the week on the cycle chart in the correct order. For each day on the chart, draw a picture of an activity that you do on that day of the week. Describe each activity (1.8.4).

Extensions

- Add new vocabulary to the multilingual word wall.
- Have students add new vocabulary to their personal vocabulary folders or personal dictionaries.

Assessment of Learning

Observe ELL students as they work together with their classmates on the peer activity. Focus on students' abilities to work with others. Use the Cooperative Skills Teacher-Assessment sheet (I.10), shown on page 39, to record results.

Blackline Masters

1.8.1

Vocabulary Cards – Days of the Week

Sunday	Monday
Tuesday	Wednesday
Thursday	Friday
Saturday	

1.8.2

Vocabulary Cards – Related Concepts

week | day

today | tomorrow

yesterday | weekday

1.8.2

Vocabulary Cards – Related Concepts

weekend

1.8.3

Date: _____ Name: _____

Student Survey

Survey Question: Which day is your favourite day of the week? Why?

Name	Favourite Day	Reason

Peer Activity

Date: _____ Name: _____

Survey Results: Students' Favourite Days of the Week

Day	Total
Sunday	
Monday	
Tuesday	
Wednesday	
Thursday	
Friday	
Saturday	

Which day of the week is the favourite day for the most students?
_____

Which day of the week is the favourite day for the least students?
_____

What is your favourite day of the week? Why?
_____
_____

What is your least favourite day of the week? Why?
_____
_____

Peer Activity

Date: _____ Name: _____

Days of the Week

Wednesday   Saturday   Thursday

Monday   Tuesday   Friday

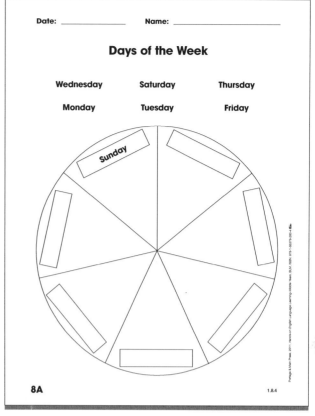

8A

Blackline Masters

9 The Calendar – Months of the Year

Curricular Connections

- Language Arts: speaking, listening, reading, writing, viewing, representing
- Mathematics: calendar concepts, surveys, tallies, graphs
- Science: environmental sustainability, life cycles, living things, seasonal changes
- Social Studies: cultural diversity, celebrations

Background Information for Teachers

As with the preceding lesson, investigate your students' background knowledge of calendars, and determine the calendar system used in their countries of origin. Keep in mind the curriculum guidelines for when students are expected to know and be able to sequence the months of the year. You may choose to teach the vocabulary but not expect sequencing if it is not an outcome or expectation for your grade level.

Vocabulary – The Calendar – Months of the Year

- month
- year
- January
- February
- March
- April
- May
- June
- July
- August
- September
- October
- November
- December

Materials

- *On the Day You Were Born*, a book by Debra Frazier
- *A Birthday Cake Is No Ordinary Cake*, a book by Debra Frazier
- classroom calendar
- current wall calendars (available from local banks, real estate agencies, insurance companies, and so on. Try to obtain calendars with seasonal pictures/photographs.)
- student agendas
- examples of calendars from other countries, and specifically from ELL students' countries of origin
- pictures associated with the various months of the year (for example, seasonal or holiday pictures)
- vocabulary cards – *Months of the Year* (included. Photocopy one set onto sturdy tagboard, colour the pictures, and cut out the cards.) (1.9.1)
- whiteboard and dry-erase markers or chalkboard and chalk
- pocket chart or chalkboard ledge or other ledge
- scissors
- glue
- mural paper
- yarn or string (optional)
- digital camera
- blank index cards

Integrated Class Activities

- To focus on birthdates, read the books *On the Day You Were Born* and *A Birthday Cake Is No Ordinary Cake*, both by Debra Frazier. Both books focus on environmental sustainability, while celebrating children's births.

9

Note: When many of these students arrive in Canada, they don't know their actual birthdates, so they are assigned January 1 as their date of birth and a year of birth based on their size. As well, some families may not celebrate events such as birthdays. It is also important to keep in mind that, depending on past life experiences and schooling, some students may not have a good sense or understanding of time.

- On the classroom calendar record special days (holidays, birthdays, celebrations, festivals, and so on) that students celebrate. Acknowledge these throughout the school year, and have students share how their families celebrate these days.
- Have students use blank index cards to make a new set of vocabulary cards for the months of the year, which reflect their birthdays and special celebrations.
- Each month, have all students complete Activity Sheet B (1.9.3) — a monthly calendar page. On their calendar pages, have students record school and class events, field trips, assignments, and special days.
- Use student agendas to record school and class events, field trips, assignments, and special days.
- Display the vocabulary cards – *Months of the Year* (1.9.1), and invite all students to create their own cards to represent special occasions and celebrations in their own families and cultures.

Instructional Activity

Review the classroom calendar with students, pointing to the month of the year and reading the name. Then, use the wall calendar to introduce students to all months of the year. Point to the current month of the year, and say the name aloud; then, point to the month on the classroom calendar to indicate that the two names (words) are same.

Beginning with the page for January, flip through the generic wall calendar, pointing to and saying the name of each month. Discuss the photograph or picture shown on each page.

Introduce the vocabulary cards – *Months of the Year* (1.9.1); display them in the pocket chart or on the chalkboard ledge or other ledge. Read through the month names in sequential order. For each month/card, point first to the word on the card and then to the month name on the wall calendar.

Next, spread out the vocabulary cards in sequence. Point to one of the months on the calendar, and have students find the corresponding month of the year card. Do the same for each month of the year. Then, mix up the cards, and repeat the activity.

Then, on a whiteboard or chalkboard, have students practise printing or writing each month of the year, using the vocabulary cards and calendar for guidance.

Have students share the names of the months of the year in their first language(s).

Peer Activities

- Have each ELL student work with a peer helper to create a 12-month calendar on mural paper. Divide a long sheet of mural paper into 12 sections, and draw a 7-column by 6-row grid in each section. Have the partners record one month of the year on each grid. Ask them to complete each month by recording the days of the week in the first row and the numerical dates in the other cells. Then, have them ask all their classmates to share their birthdates, and have the partners record these on the calendar.
- As an alternative to the preceding activity, have ELL-student and peer-helper pairs create wall calendars of their classmates'

▶

birthdays. Distribute 12 copies of Activity Sheet B (1.9.3) to each pair, and ask students to complete each page. Then, have them use a digital camera to photograph each student in the class. Ask students to attach each photograph to the calendar on the month of that student's birthday. Have them specify the numerical dates by drawing arrows between the photos and the numerical dates on the calendar or by gluing string or yarn to the calendar to connect the photo and the date.

Independent Activity: Part One: Activity Sheet A

Directions to students:

Print or write the names of the months of the year in sequence. Draw a picture to illustrate each month (1.9.2).

Note: Encourage students to include illustrations that are personally relevant in terms of interests, family, and culture.

Independent Activity: Part Two: Activity Sheet B

Directions to students:

Complete the calendar page for the current month. Use the classroom calendar to help you spell the days of the week and the month (1.9.3).

Extensions

- Add new vocabulary to the multilingual word wall.
- Have students add new vocabulary to their personal vocabulary folders or personal dictionaries.
- Have each student print the first letter of each month vertically on a piece of drawing paper and then record and/or illustrate familiar words that begin with that letter. The following example uses animal names:
    - **J**ackfish
    - **F**ox
    - **M**oose
    - **A**nt
    - **M**ule
    - **J**aguar
    - **J**ellyfish
    - **A**naconda
    - **S**nake
    - **O**ctopus
    - **N**ewt
    - **D**og

1.9.1

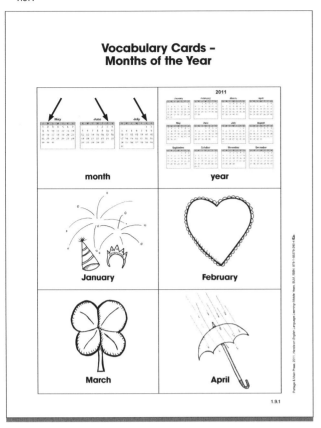

1.9.1

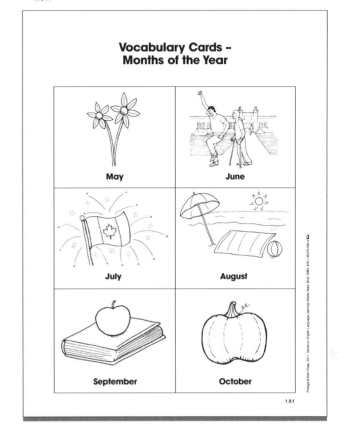

1.9.1

1.9.2

Date: _____   Name: _____

Months of the Year

Blackline Masters

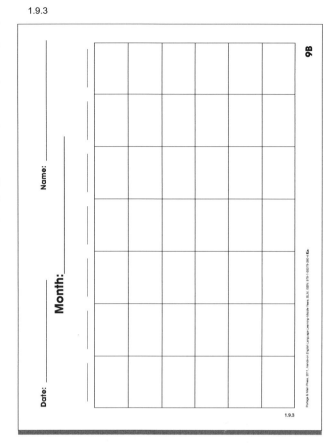

10 Personal Information

Curricular Connections

- Language Arts: speaking, listening, reading, writing, viewing, representing
- Mathematics: number concepts
- Social Studies: community, cultural diversity, mapping skills
- Health: personal safety
- Art: drawing
- Drama: role playing

Background Information for Teachers

Throughout this lesson, it is crucial for students to understand that they should never share their personal information with strangers, unless specific circumstances require this (for example, registering for school), in which case their parents or guardians would be present. Be cautious even in having students write out their addresses and telephone numbers in the classroom. These tasks are best done orally, and teachers can assess students' knowledge of this information through observation.

Note: In this lesson students learn question-and-answer vocabulary including "When is your birthday?"; "My birthday is _____." As described in the note on page 105, however, be aware that some students may not know their actual date of birth.

Vocabulary – Personal Information

Personal Information

- What is your name? My name is _____.
- When is your birthday? My birthday is on _____.
- Where are you from? I am from _____.
- How old are you? I am _____ years old.
- Where do you live? I live _____.
- What is your address? My address is _____.
- What is your phone number? My phone number is _____.
- Who is in your family? In my family there is _____.

School Information

- Which school do you go to? I go to _____ school.
- What room are you in? I am in room _____.
- What grade are you in? I am in grade _____.
- What is your teacher's name? My teacher's name is _____.

Materials

- vocabulary cards – *Personal Information* (included. Make an overhead copy of the cards. Also, photocopy a set of cards onto sturdy tagboard, and cut them out.) (1.10.1)
- vocabulary cards – *School Information* (included. Make an overhead copy of the cards. Also, photocopy a set of cards onto sturdy tagboard, and cut them out.) (1.10.2)
- pocket chart
- overhead projector
- discussion prompts *A, B,* and *C* (included. Make one copy of each prompt for each ELL student.) (1.10.3, 1.10.4, 1.10.5)
- school registration form
- audio recorder
- local telephone book
- supplies for making student address books (paper, markers or coloured pencils, stapler)
- city or community map
- sticky notes or blank index cards
- glue

10

Integrated Class Activities

- Discuss the topics of personal information and minimizing security risks with all students. This discussion provides an opportunity to review personal safety issues, emphasizing that students should never share personal information with strangers personally or over the internet, and they should only share the information with friends or classmates if they have parental permission.

- Teach all students how to use the local telephone book or internet-based Canada-411 service to look up addresses and telephone numbers for the local library, recreation/community centre, museum, and so on. Have students make their own telephone/address books for important people and places in their community.

Note: Inform students and their families about community organizations that can communicate with them in their first language(s), and have students include these in their telephone/address books as well.

- Use a city or community map to identify locations by address. On sticky notes or blank index cards have students record the names and addresses of important places in the community such as libraries, recreation/community centres, stores, and so on. Then, have them attach the notes or index cards to the map (use glue with the index cards).

- Challenge students to locate their street names on a city or community map or on an internet map site such as Google maps. Discuss safe routes to and from school, as well as the routes to favourite places in the local neighbourhood.

Whole-Class Career Connections

- Have students identify careers related to the local telephone company. Invite a guest from the phone company's human resources department to talk to students about these careers and related training programs. Be sure to ask the guest speaker to discuss employability skills related to careers in their field.

- Have students identify careers related to Canada Post. Invite a guest from the local human resources department to talk to students about careers with Canada Post and related training programs. Be sure to ask the guest speaker to discuss employability skills related to careers in their field.

Instructional Activity: Part One

Introduce the new vocabulary – *Personal Information*. Display the overhead of the vocabulary cards (1.10.1), and read the first question aloud, pointing to the words as you read. Conduct a role play with two students by having one student ask the question while another student answers. Repeat this with each question and answer set.

Note: If students are not familiar with or do not know some of their own personal information, provide time for them to gather this information before conducting the next part of the activity. Some students may not have telephones and therefore will not be able to respond to this question. Modify the question accordingly, or eliminate it altogether.

Have the whole class or a group of 10 or more students play the following game together:

Divide the group of students into two equal groups. Have one group form a circle with their backs to the centre and fronts facing outward.

10

Have the second group form a circle around the first group, facing inward. Each student should be facing another student.

Point to a question card on the overhead, and have the students in the inside circle ask this question to the students facing them. Next, point to the answer card, and have the students in the outside circle answer the question, inserting their personal data in the blank.

Now, have the students in the outside circle take one step to the right so that they are facing a new student. Repeat the activity with a new question and answer.

Once all questions have been asked and answered, repeat the activity, but have the students in the two circles reverse roles (students in the outside ask the questions and students in the inside respond). Have students in the inside circle move to the right after each question. To model this process for students, teachers may have students ask them questions and use examples from their own lives.

Note: You can modify this activity for working with smaller groups or with individual students. Place the vocabulary cards in a pile, face down. Have a student pick up one card and read the question, and have a second student (or yourself) answer the question. Repeat this several times, switching roles, as students take turns asking and answering questions.

This is a good time to give students the opportunity to discuss their past experiences. Have them share information about where they lived, and what it was like compared to their current experience.

Note: It is important to be cautious and sensitive when asking students to share information about past experiences. Some ELL students will have gone through traumatic events, and sharing information about these events may be difficult. This is also true when having students share information about their homes. Some ELL students will have lived in refugee camps or other places where homes were less than comfortable. Allow students to choose whether or not to share information. Seek advice from the school guidance counselor about this, and consider the needs and past experiences of each ELL student on an individual basis.

Instructional Activity: Part Two

Note: The focus of the following activity should be dialogue and oral/receptive language.

Review the target vocabulary – *Personal Information* with students.

Distribute discussion prompts A, B, and C (1.10.3, 1.10.4, 1.10.5), and use them to ask students questions that elicit answers. For example, using discussion prompt A, say:

- Teacher: My name is _____. What is your name?

- Student: My name is _____. (Have the student say his or her name.)

- Teacher: I am _____ years old. How old are you?

- Student: I am _____ years old. (Have the student say his or her age.)

- Teacher: In my family there is _____, _____, _____, (identify immediate family members) and me. Who is in your family?

- Student: In my family there is _____, _____, _____, (have the student name immediate family members) and me.

Module 1   111

10

Continue in a similar manner for discussion prompts B and C.

Also, have students share translations for these sentences in their first language(s).

Assessment for Learning

Use the preceding discussion prompts activity to assess students' personal information-related vocabulary. Use copies of the Anecdotal Record sheet (I.3), shown on page 37, to record students' responses to the discussion questions. This will also help you to determine if students are ready for the peer activity.

Instructional Activity: Part Three

Note: The following activity encourages oral and receptive language while targeting specific vocabulary.

Introduce the vocabulary cards – *School Information* (1.10.2). Display the vocabulary cards in the pocket chart, and use the questions to prompt student responses.

This is a good time to give students the opportunity to discuss their past school experiences. Have them share information about where they went to school and what school was like compared to their current experience.

Note: Some students may not have had any school experience prior to coming to Canada, or they may have faced challenges with their school experience; as before, be cautious and sensitive when asking students to share information.

Peer Activity

Note: For this activity students will need to know how to operate an audio recorder.

Provide ELL-student and peer-helper pairs with a full set of vocabulary cards (both *Personal Information* and *School Information* – 1.10.1, 1.10.2). First, have students match each question to its corresponding answer phrase.

Then, have students use the audio recorder to record themselves as they ask each other and respond to the questions. Initially, have the ELL student ask the questions while the peer helper responds; next, have them play back the recorder to listen to the dialogue.

Next Step

If the ELL student is confident asking questions, have the partners switch roles and conduct the activity a second time.

Extend this activity by having ELL students and their peer helpers ask the same questions to other people in the school, and have them record the responses.

Independent Activity: Part One: Activity Sheet A

Directions to students:

Complete the activity sheet to show your school information (1.10.6).

Independent Activity: Part Two: Activity Sheet B

Directions to students:

Complete the activity sheet to tell about your family (1.10.7).

Extensions

- Add new vocabulary to the multilingual word wall.
- Have students add new vocabulary to their personal vocabulary folders or personal dictionaries.

10

- Have students create celebrity profiles. Ask them to conduct some research about their favourite musician, actor, or other public figure. Then, have students use blank index cards to create celebrity profiles that include the following statements:
  - His/her name is _____.
  - His/her birthday is _____.
  - He/she lives in _____ (city).
  - In his/her family there is/are _____.

Also have students include illustrations or photographs of their chosen celebrities on their profile cards.

Blackline Masters

1.10.1

Vocabulary Cards – Personal Information

What is your name?	My name is _____.
When is your birthday?	My birthday is on _____.
Where are you from?	I am from _____.

1.10.1

Vocabulary Cards – Personal Information

How old are you?	I am _____ years old.
Where do you live?	I live _____.
What is your address?	My address is _____ _____.

1.10.2

Vocabulary Cards – Personal Information

What is your phone number?	My phone number is _____.
Who is in your family?	In my family there is _____ _____ _____ _____

1.10.2

Vocabulary Cards – School Information

Which school do you go to?	I go to _____ _____ school.
What room are you in?	I am in room _____.
What grade are you in?	I am in grade _____.

114 – 1.10.1 – 1.10.2

Blackline Masters

Vocabulary Cards – School Information

| What is your teacher's name? | My teacher's name is _____. |

Discussion Prompt A: This Is Me

My name is _____
I am _____ years old.
In my family there is _____
_____.
This is Me!

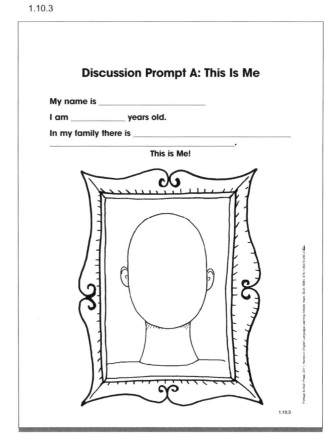

Discussion Prompt B: My Address

My name is
_____.

My address is

Discussion Prompt C: My Telephone Number

My name is _____.

My telphone number is _____.

Blackline Masters

1.10.6

Date: _____ Name: _____

My School

I go to _____ school.

Draw a picture of your school.

[ ]

I am in grade _____.
I am in room _____.
My teacher is _____.

Draw a picture of your teacher.

10A

1.10.7

Date: _____ Name: _____

My Family

There are _____ people in my family.
Their names are:
_____
_____
_____

Here is a picture of my family.

10A

11 | Culminating Activity: Creating A Board Game

Curricular Connections

- Language Arts: speaking, listening, reading, writing, viewing, representing
- Social Studies: community
- Health: personal wellbeing
- Art: drawing

Background Information for Teachers

This culminating activity provides an opportunity for students to review, practise, and apply the vocabulary they have learned in all preceding lessons. It also offers an excellent opportunity to assess student progress.

Materials

- students' personal dictionaries or vocabulary folders and activity sheets from all preceding lessons
- vocabulary cards from all preceding lessons
- board game template (included. Make one copy for each student.) (1.11.1)
- coloured pencils
- various simple board games (for example, Snakes and Ladders, Trouble)
- board game spinner templates (included. Make one copy for each student.) (1.11.2)
- paper clips
- pencils
- large sheets of poster paper or Bristol board (one sheet for each student)
- markers
- coloured pencils
- rulers
- chart paper or whiteboard
- variety of number cubes (dice) and spinners (that is, with varying numbers of sides/sections)

Integrated Class Activities

- Involve the entire class in a project to create board games (see Instructional Activity below for more details). ELL students may focus their games on vocabulary they have learned throughout the module, while other students may select another topic of study, such as the solar system, Canadian explorers, or a novel, and create game cards and a game board related to that theme.
- Explore probability by having students use a variety of number cubes (dice) and spinners with their games.
- Have a family games event. Encourage students to make invitations for family members, and to plan and make refreshments. Then, have students' games on display for everyone to play at the family event.
- Invite family members to teach the class traditional games played in various countries. Discuss the similarities and differences between the various games.

Whole-Class Career Connections

- Have students identify which employability skills they used to create their board games (see Instructional Activity below). Discuss the fact that many of these skills are used not only on the job but also in school, in relationships, and in daily life.
- Have students research game and toy companies and inventors to determine how an idea for a game or toy becomes reality.
- Have a local advertising firm present to the class on how companies use advertising to sell their products to the public.

▶

11

Instructional Activity

Begin by introducing students to some simple children's board games. Have students play these games in small groups. Discuss the process involved in playing many basic board games:

- Players take turns using number cubes or spinners to determine how many spaces to move their game pieces;
- Different challenges on the game board allow players to move forward or cause them to move backward;
- The object of the game is to be the first player to reach the "finish" on the game board.

Now, explain to students that they will have an opportunity to use the English words they have learned throughout this module's lessons to design their own board games. Review the different topics that were covered in the module. Also review the students' activity sheets and personal dictionaries or vocabulary folders, as well as other classroom displays and work related to the module.

Now, provide each student with a copy of the board game template (1.11.1) and two copies of Activity Sheet A (1.11.3). Tell students that they will use these sheets to design their games and then create larger versions of their game boards on poster paper or Bristol board.

Tell students that in each blank square on their game boards, they should draw a picture that represents one new word learned during the module. For example:

- The number 20 represented with place-value counters.
- A pencil
- A water fountain

- The letter *M*, upper and lowercase, in printing and writing (M m; $\mathcal{M}\,m$)

Alternatively, students may also record questions related to the target vocabulary on the blank game-board squares. For example:

- What is your address?
- Which month comes after November?
- How many days are there in a week?

Have students select all of the vocabulary they wish to include on their game boards and record these words onto two copies of Activity Sheet A (1.1.3). They should record 42 vocabulary words in total—21 on each copy of the activity sheet. Also, have them decide on an illustration or a question related to that word and record it on the activity sheet.

Note: Be sure to check students' activity sheets before they proceed to completing the board game template, to ensure that illustrations and questions are adequate for the game.

Once students have completed their activity sheets, have them draw the illustrations or write the questions on their copies of the board game template. Review the various features of the game board with students. Explain that to play the game, players take turns rolling a number cube or spinning the spinner to move their game pieces; if a player can provide the vocabulary word for the picture on which his or her game piece lands, or if he or she correctly answers the question, he or she gets to roll again. Also explain how the "FREE" squares work (the player *does not* have to provide the vocabulary word or answer a question), as well as how the "Go forward" and "Go backward" squares work. Tell students that the object of the game is to be the first player to reach the "FINISH" square.

Note: Consider modelling the game for ELLs first before having them play it themselves.

11

Provide each student with a board game spinner template (1.11.2), a paper clip, and a pencil. Tell them to cut out their spinners and place a paper clip in the centre of the template circle. Then, have them position a pencil point inside the clip, right at the centre point of the circle. The paper clip will then spin freely around the point of the pencil, as in the following diagram:

Provide time for students to review vocabulary and design their games. Have them use the number cubes or spinners to test their games before making their final game boards on poster paper or Bristol board.

Once students have completed their board game templates and you have checked them, have them create larger versions of their games on poster paper or Bristol board. Encourage students to decorate their game boards as well.

When students have finished making their games, have them play the games with classmates. Alternatively, encourage students to set up game stations throughout the classroom to learn about and play one another's games.

Independent Activity: Activity Sheet A

Note: Each student will need two copies of this sheet to record 42 vocabulary words (21 words per sheet).

Directions to students:

Choose 42 words from lessons 1 to 10 to use on your game board. Record these words in the left-hand column of the chart (you will need two copies of the activity sheet to record all 42 words). Choose either an illustration or a question to go with each word. Record your illustrations or questions in the right-hand column of the chart, next to the corresponding word (1.11.3).

Assessment of Learning

- Meet with each student individually, and play his or her board game with him or her. While playing the game, informally assess the student's knowledge of the vocabulary learned throughout the module. Use the Vocabulary Tracking Checklist (I.9), shown on page 39, to record your results.

- Assess students' language and understanding by the degree to which they are successful at teaching their games to others. Look for clarity of instructions.

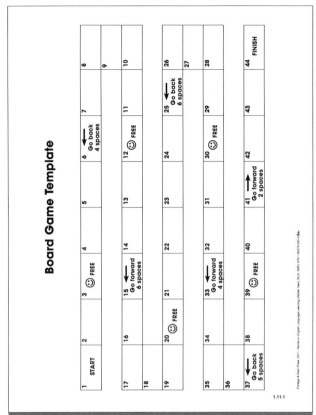

References for Teachers

Almada, Patricia. *English in My Pocket*. Barrington, IL: Rigby, 2000.

Bear, Donald et al. *Words Their Way: Word Study for Phonics, Vocabulary, and Spelling Instruction:* 4th Edition. Toronto: Prentice Hall, 2007.

Brownlie, Faye, Catherine Feniak, and Vicki McCarthy. *Instruction and Assessment of ESL Learners: Promoting Success in Your Classroom*. Winnipeg: Portage & Main Press, 2004.

Coelho, Elizabeth. *Adding English: A Guide to Teaching in Multilingual Classrooms*. Toronto: Pippin, 2003.

Grigsby, Carolyn. *Amazing English! An Integrated ESL Curriculum*. Reading, MA: Addison Wesley, 1996.

Herrell, Adrienne, and Michael Jordan. *Fifty Strategies for Teaching English Language Learners*, 3rd edition. Upper Saddle River, NJ: Pearson/Merrill Prentice Hall, 2008.

Hill, Jane, and Kathleen Flynn. *Classroom Instruction That Works With English Language Learners*. Alexandria, VA: Association for Supervision and Curriculum Development, 2006.

Hill, Jane, Catherine Little, and Jane Sims. *Integrating English Language Learners in the Science Classroom*. Toronto: Trifolium Books, 2003.

Law, Barbara, and Mary Eckes. *Assessment and ESL: An Alternative Approach*, second edition. Winnipeg: Portage & Main Press, 2007.

Law, Barbara, and Mary Eckes. *The More Than Just Surviving Handbook: ESL for Every Classroom Teacher,* second edition. Winnipeg: Portage & Main Press, 2000.

Maitland, Katherine. *Adding English: Helping ESL Learners Succeed*. Grand Rapids, MI: Frank Schaffer Publications, 2001.

Petricic, Gordana. *Play 'n' Talk: Communicative Games for Elementary and Middle School ESL/EFL*. Brattleboro, VT: Pro Lingua Associates, 1997.

Reid, Suzanne. *Book Bridges for ESL Students: Using Young Adult and Children's Literature to Teach ESL*. Lanham, MD: Scarecrow Press, Inc., 2002.

Rojas, Virginia. *Helping Students of Limited English Skills in the Regular Classroom* [videocassette, 30 min.]. LPD Video Journal Education, 2000.

Scott, Deb. *Fifty Reading and Writing Activities*. Toronto: Canadian Resources for ESL, 2004.

_____. *Fifty Speaking and Listening Activities*. Toronto: Canadian Resources for ESL, 2004.

Tompkins, Gail E., and Cathy Blanchfield. *Teaching Vocabulary: 50 Creative Strategies, Grades K–12*. Upper Saddle River, NJ: Pearson/Merrill Prentice Hall, 2004.

Walter, Teresa. *Amazing English! How-To Handbook*. Toronto: Addison-Wesley, 1996.

Middle Years

Module 2

Introduction

This module of **Hands-On English Language Learning** is designed for use with students in grades 5 to 8, who have acquired some basic survival vocabulary and are developing communication skills in the English language (see Stages of Language Acquisition on page 1 of the Introduction to *Hands-On English Language Learning*). These students use English in supported and familiar activities and contexts. They listen with greater understanding and use everyday expressions independently. They demonstrate growing confidence and use personally relevant language appropriately.

The lessons in this module focus on extending students' language and understanding of basic concepts through hands-on activities and real-life applications.

Module Theme: Responsibility for Self

The lessons in this module focus on the theme of personal responsibility, specifically, caring for oneself physically, emotionally, and socially. These concepts and related vocabulary will support students as they transition into a new school, social group, and community.

Effective Teaching Strategies for English Language Learners

While teaching the lessons in this module, be sure to consider the following:

- Students learn language through interaction with others. Create a learning environment that encourages rich dialogue and social communication.
- Use many verbal and non-verbal cues throughout activities. Non-verbal cues include visuals, gestures, and concrete materials.
- Simplify vocabulary and sentence structure to encourage comprehension.
- Give instructions and ask questions in clear, simple English.
- Allow learners sufficient response time for oral responses.
- Provide opportunity for students to use patterned language, in which certain language structures are repeated in various contexts or with different vocabulary.
- Review vocabulary and concepts regularly to check for learner comprehension.
- Encourage, where appropriate, the strategic use of students' first languages and prior knowledge as a bridge to English language learning.

Reinforcing Vocabulary

Students should learn to recognize and understand the vocabulary presented in this module. At the same time, they should be encouraged to make connections between their first languages and the English language. To reinforce vocabulary, consider having either a multilingual word wall for the classroom, or individual vocabulary folders for students.

Multilingual Word Wall

Dedicate a classroom bulletin board to your word wall, and display the letters of the alphabet along the top. Use index cards to record English vocabulary introduced in each lesson, tacking these to the board under the appropriate letter. Also include vocabulary in students' first languages (use students' prior knowledge, bilingual dictionaries, other students, staff, parents, and bilingual members of the community as sources of vocabulary). This contributes to the world/classroom-as-a-global-village message, validates first languages/cultures, and creates an atmosphere of inclusiveness. It also establishes an environment in which knowledge about other languages, and the merits of knowing more than one language, are highlighted and celebrated. Along with vocabulary, also include picture and phrase cues, as appropriate. Encourage students to refer to the word wall during activities and assignments.

Vocabulary Folders

If it is not feasible to dedicate classroom wall space to a word wall, use open legal-size folders to make multilingual vocabulary folders for students. Open each folder, and divide it into 26 sections on the inside, one section for each letter of the alphabet, filling up the entire inside area (as in the illustration below). There are two ways students can collect and record vocabulary—they can glue small envelopes to each lettered section, and then record vocabulary on small cards to be housed in the envelopes, or they can record new vocabulary on sticky notes and attach the notes directly to the appropriate lettered sections. Either way, be sure students also include illustrations, usage examples, as well as related vocabulary from their first language with their recorded English vocabulary. Students can close the folder again for storage (for this reason, do not have letter boxes directly on the folder crease).

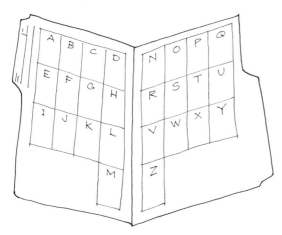

Personal Dictionaries

It can also benefit students to create their own personal English language dictionaries for reference during lessons. Use one of the blackline masters included in module 1 with lesson 1 (1.1.6, 1.1.7). Or, have students use notebooks with sticky notes to indicate alphabetization.

Note: In addition to recording English words in their personal dictionaries, also have students record words in their first languages where appropriate. This helps them make bilingual connections and extend meaning. It will therefore benefit ELL students if bilingual dictionaries are available in English and their first languages (see Books for Students on page 128 and References for Teachers on page 220).

Differentiating Instruction

A number of English language learners will have been in school prior to their arrival at your school and, as a result, will have literacy skills that are on par with their same-age peers. Other students may have little or no previous school experience and may not be literate in their first languages. Consequently, the lessons in this module of **Hands-On English Language Learning** offer many opportunities to help students develop their reading and writing skills while learning English. Visual cues, concrete manipulatives, and cooperative learning are needed to support students as they learn all aspects of the English language.

However, teachers will still need to differentiate instruction and adapt both activities and activity sheets to meet the needs of individual learners. For example, a student with limited reading and writing abilities might work with a peer to complete activity sheets or use drawings instead of words. As another example, personal dictionaries may be essential for ELL students but can be equally beneficial for all students in the class through differentiation. More academically advanced students might collect descriptive words for use in personal writing, while students requiring additional support in spelling might collect challenging words for use in writing activities while, at the same time, ELL students would collect target vocabulary with pictures to reinforce recognition. Suggestions for adaptation are made throughout the module, but teachers are also encouraged to use their own experience, techniques, and personal knowledge of students to differentiate instruction.

Peer Helpers

Many of the lessons presented in this module require the support of peer helpers to work in partnership with ELL students. Developing a classroom culture of inclusion and acceptance will be enhanced by working with the class to develop criteria for helpers, and to discuss why it is important to help one another.

Every student in the class should have the opportunity to help and interact with the ELL students in the class; it is not always necessary to choose the top academic students. Before any peer activity with ELL students, the teacher and peer helpers should discuss the specific task, and the benefits to both the ELL student and the peer helper.

Note: It is important that students working together in a peer-helper setting focus on English language usage. However, it is also helpful for ELL students, when possible, to have access to others who speak the same first language. This allows ELL students access to translation and interpretation, acknowledges their first languages, and builds on their background experiences.

Note: Throughout *Hands-On English Language Learning*, we use the term *English-speaking student* (rather than the more cumbersome *students for whom English is a first language*) to distinguish these students from their English-language-learner classmates. We recognize that the term *English-speaking student* is not completely accurate, since ELL students are also English-speaking students—though their language use is still developing. The rationale for use of this term is simply one of space.

Assessing Students' Prior Knowledge – Assessment for Learning

Before beginning this module, it is beneficial to determine students' prior knowledge of lesson concepts and which of the target vocabulary students already know. This provides information that allows teachers to refine lessons and instructional activities to meet the individual strengths and needs of students. As a pre-module assessment strategy, consider using the Vocabulary Tracking Checklist (I.9; shown on page 39 in the Introduction to *Hands-On English Language Learning*) along with all vocabulary cards provided in the module. Conference with ELL students individually, and review the target vocabulary with them to determine the vocabulary with which they are familiar. Also, discuss concepts related to the vocabulary in order to reveal prior knowledge.

Note: This assessment activity also serves as an activating strategy that introduces students to the language, visuals, and concepts focused on throughout the module.

Career Connections

All modules in the *Hands-On English Language Learning* program for middle years include a focus on career education for students. These activities are intended for use with the whole class, in an integrated setting, since career education is an important topic for all students. For ELL students specifically, such activities will offer them insight into the possibilities for their future, since many of the careers available to them might be quite different from those available in their countries of origin. Learning about careers offers students a closer look at one aspect of Canadian culture, so students acquire essential understanding while developing language skills.

It is important to note that some of the language used during career connection activities might be quite challenging for ELL students. For example, there is a focus on employability skills, and their importance in the workplace. Although some of the vocabulary used in describing these skills is at a more advanced language level, the activities themselves are well-suited to both ELL students and their English-speaking peers. Career connection activities focus on class discussion, guest presentations, role playing, and so on, and ELL students will adapt in this immersive environment.

Books for Students

Aliki. *Feelings.* New York: Greenwillow Books, 1984.

Arnold, Tedd. *Even More Parts: Idioms from Head to Toe.* New York: Dial Books for Young Readers, 2004.

Cox, Judy. *My Family Plays Music.* New York: Holiday House, 2003.

Dunleavy, Deborah. *Jumbo Book of Music.* Toronto: Kids Can Press, 2001.

Herzog, Brad. *E is for Extreme: An Extreme Sports Alphabet.* Chelsea, Ml.: Sleeping Bear Press, 2007.

Heywood, Rosie. *The Great City Search.* London, England. Usborne, 1997.

Moses, Brian. *I Feel Angry* (Kids Corner: Kid-to-Kid Books). Littleton, MA: Sundance, 2000.

_____. *I Feel Frightened* (Kids Corner: Kid-to-Kid Books). Littleton, MA: Sundance, 1999.

_____. *I Feel Sad.* (Kids Corner: Kid-to-Kid Books). Littleton, MA: Sundance, 1999.

Prelutsky, Jack. *Good Sports: Rhymes About Running, Jumping, Throwing, and More.* New York: Knopf Books for Young Readers, 2007.

Spelman, Cornelia M. *When I Feel Sad.* Morton Grove, IL: Albert Whitman & Company, 2002.

Trumbauer, Lisa. *Living in a City.* Mankato, MN: Capstone Press, 2005.

_____. *Living in a Rural Area.* Mankato, MN: Capstone Press, 2005.

_____. *Living in a Small Town.* Mankato, MN: Capstone Press, 2005.

_____. *Living in a Suburb.* Mankato, MN: Capstone Press, 2005.

Waber, Bernard. *Fast Food! Gulp! Gulp!* Boston: Houghton Mifflin, 2001.

Weeks, Sarah. *Two Eggs, Please.* New York: Atheneum Books for Young Readers, 2003.

Multicultural Books

Aliki. *Painted Words; Spoken Memories.* New York: Greenwillow Books, 1998.

Blackstone, Stella. *My Granny Went to Market: A Round-the-World Counting Rhyme.* Cambridge MA: Barefoot Books, 2005.

Dooley, Norah. *Everybody Brings Noodles.* Minneapolis, MN: Carolrhoda Books, 2002.

_____. *Everybody Serves Soup.* Minneapolis: Carolrhoda Books, 2000.

_____. *Everybody Bakes Bread.* Minneapolis, MN: Carolrhoda Books, 1996.

_____. *Everybody Cooks Rice.* Minneapolis: Carolrhoda Books, 1991.

Easterling, Lisa. *Clothing* (Our Global Community series). Chicago: Heinemann, 2007.

_____. *Families.* (Our Global Community series). Chicago: Heinemann, 2007.

_____. *Games.* (Our Global Community series). Chicago: Heinemann, 2007.

_____. *Schools.* (Our Global Community series). Chicago: Heinemann, 2007.

Mayer, Cassie. *Markets.* (Our Global Community Series). Chicago: Heinemann, 2007.

Nishiyama, Akira. *Wonderful Houses Around the World.* Bolinas, CA: Shelter, 2004.

Petty, Kate. *Bicycles* (World Show-and-Tell series). Minnetonka, MN: Two-Can (in association with Oxfam), 2006.

_____. *Hair* (World Show-and-Tell series). Minnetonka, MN: Two-Can (in association with Oxfam), 2006.

_____. *Homes* (World Show-and-Tell series). Minnetonka, MN: Two-Can (in association with Oxfam), 2006.

_____. *Playtime* (World Show-and-Tell series). Minnetonka, MN: Two-Can (in association with Oxfam), 2006.

Ripoll, Oriol. *Play With Us: 100 Games From Around the World*. Chicago: Chicago Review Press, 2005.

Various authors. *Countries of the World series*. Mankato, MN: Capstone Press, 1997–2003 (39 titles).

Language Resources

Adelson-Goldstein, Jayme, and Norma Shapiro. Oxford Picture Dictionary series*, New York: Oxford University Press, 2008.

Cleary, Brian. *Hairy, Scary, Ordinary: What Is an Adjective?* Minneapolis, MN: Carolrhoda Books, 2000.

Hill, L.A., and Charles Innes. *Oxford Children's Picture Dictionary.* London, UK: Oxford University Press, 1997.

Mantra Lingua. *My Talking Dictionary: Book and CD Rom*. London, UK: TalkingPen Publications, 2005 (48 dual-language editions).

Ross Keyes, Joan. *The Oxford Picture Dictionary for Kids*. New York: Oxford University Press, 1998.

Walker, Michael. *Amazing English Buddy Book*. Lebanon, Indiana: Addison-Wesley, 1995.

———. *Amazing English Buddy Book: Newcomer Level*. Lebanon, Indiana: Addison-Wesley, 1995.

*Bilingual versions of the *Oxford Picture Dictionary* are available for English and: Arabic, Brazilian-Portuguese, Chinese, French, Japanese, Korean, Russian, Spanish, Thai, Urdu, and Vietnamese.

Websites

- <http://iteslj.org/questions>

    Conversation Questions for the ESL/ EFL Classroom: This site offers a large collection of questions to help initiate dialogue about a variety of topics in the ELL conversation classroom. Note that some questions will need to be adapted for elementary students.

- <www.intercultures.ca/cil-cai/countryinsights-apercuspays-eng.asp>

    Country Insights: This site provides information about different cultures and includes advice on cultural "do's" and "don'ts.

- <www.eslflow.com>

    ESL flow is a resource for researching ESL/EFL (English as a Foreign Language) ideas and for creating lessons. The site provides a variety of topics at the elementary, pre-intermediate, and intermediate levels. Topics include icebreakers, giving directions, describing people and places, games, and so on. The site also includes current favourite ESL teaching lesson links.

- <www.esl-galaxy.com>

    ESL Galaxy offers numerous printable worksheets for ESL lesson plans and activities, including board games, crosswords, grammar and vocabulary worksheets, theme or topic lesson plans, pronunciation, survival English, song activities, festival and holiday worksheets, conversation and communicative activities, cloze and gap-fill exercises, and more.

- <www.esl-kids.com>

    ESL-Kids.com offers materials for teachers to use with ESL students including flashcards, worksheets, classroom games, and children's song lyrics.

- <www.forefrontpublishers.com/eslmusic>

    ESL Through Music: Focusing on using music to teach English as a second language, this site includes lesson plans, lists of suggested materials to use, and articles on the use of music to teach language, all accompanied by background music to make your visit more enjoyable.

- <www.freethechildren.com>

    Free the Children was founded by 12-year-old Canadian Craig Kielburger in 1995, when he gathered 11 school friends to begin fighting child labour. Today, Free the Children is the world's largest network of children helping children through education, with more than one million young people involved in the organization's programs in 45 countries.

- <http://iteslj.org/c/jokes.html>

    Jokes in English for the ESL/EFL Classroom: Teachers often use jokes in the ESL/EFL classroom to teach culture, grammar and vocabulary. Although many of the jokes and riddles on this site are geared towards older students, there are some simpler ones that are appropriate for younger learners (for example, riddles "in the alphabet").

- <www.gameskidsplay.net>

    Kids Games provides detailed descriptions of classic games that students love to play, including rules for playground games, verses for jump-rope rhymes, ball games, strength games, mental games, and tons more. Many of the games can be adapted to teach particular language structures. Games can be viewed in a number of ways, including a list of "quick favourites," games by category, alphabetically, or you can do a search for a specific game.

- <www.manythings.org>

    Many Things: Interesting Things for ESL Students: This fun study site for ELL students includes word games, puzzles, quizzes, exercises, slang and idioms, proverbs, and much more!

- <http://teach-nology.com/web_tools/rubrics>

    teAchnology: The rubric generators on this site help you to make grading rubrics by filling out a simple form. The materials are created instantly and can be printed directly from your computer.

- <www.tefl.net>

    TFEL.net is a free, independent resource site for anyone involved in teaching English as an additional language. The site offers a range of ESL worksheets, including discussion-based, topic-based, and skill-based ESL worksheets, and more.

1 Emotions

Curricular Connections

- Language Arts: speaking, listening, reading, writing, viewing, representing
- Health: healthy-lifestyle practices, personal wellbeing
- Music: music appreciation
- Art: drawing
- Drama: role playing

Background Information for Teachers

Facial expressions and gestures can be culturally influenced. Consider integrating the cultural aspect of this topic into the learning by asking ELL students how they demonstrate certain feelings without using words (non-verbally) in their first language(s)/home culture(s) and how this compares to the Canadian context. Alternatively, since some ELL students may not yet have the skills to express these ideas, obtain this information from their parents and/or from more advanced ELL students from the same countries of origin.

It is of utmost importance to be sensitive to the personal experiences of ELL students (as with all students) when discussing emotions. Some ELL students may have had experiences with war or other traumatic events that will still affect them. Ensure that care is taken when dealing with students' emotions, and provide necessary supports for helping them to cope with their feelings.

Vocabulary – Emotions

Emotions

- happy
- sad
- angry/mad
- bored
- tired
- great
- excited
- worried
- scared
- shy
- embarrassed
- hurt
- sick
- frustrated
- confused

Emotion Actions

- smile
- laugh
- frown
- cry

Materials

- computer with internet access
- computer printer
- scissors
- Ziploc bags
- vocabulary cards – *Emotions* (included. Photocopy two sets onto sturdy tagboard, and cut apart cards.) (2.1.1)
- vocabulary cards – *Emotion Actions* (included. Photocopy two sets onto sturdy tagboard, and cut apart cards.) (2.1.2)
- student dictionaries
- index cards
- markers or coloured pencils
- magazines, newspapers, and flyers
- glue
- poster paper
- recorded music that reflects various emotions (see third bullet under "Integrated Class Activities")
- MP3 player, CD player, or computer (for playing recorded music)

- songs with lyrics that describe emotions (students will source these songs themselves, either online or from a class or personal music library. See fourth bullet under "Ingrated Class Activities".)
- variety of artwork (see seventh bullet under "Integrated Class Activities")

Integrated Class Activities

- The topic of emotions can lead effectively into discussions about how students deal with their feelings and correlates with the health curriculum in terms of personal wellbeing. For example, how do students solve problems when they are angry, hurt, or worried about something? What are appropriate ways to express anger (with words)? Have students role play scenarios involving circumstances that could trigger anger, hurt, or worry and show ways to solve problems peacefully and effectively. Use the vocabulary cards — Emotions (2.1.1) to support ELL students during these activities.
- Use the vocabulary cards – Emotions (2.1.1) as sentence or story starters for writing. Display the cards, and have students write about personal experiences when they have been happy, bored, excited, shy, confused, and so on.

Note: Approach this topic with sensitivity, as all students will have had experiences that are difficult to share. Consider focusing on the more positive emotions for this writing task. If you observe students having difficulty dealing with emotional experiences, ensure that they are provided with appropriate supports through counseling.

- Work with the music teacher to select recorded music that reflects various emotions. Have students listen to these selections and describe the emotions that the music evokes for them.

- Have students select songs with lyrics that describe emotions. Have the class listen to the songs, discuss the lyrics, and reflect on the emotions that the composer/lyricist was attempting to express.
- Using songs from students' countries of origin, have students act out the storyline or translate it into English.
- Invite musicians from different cultures to play songs from their countries of origin that depict a variety of human emotions.

Note: Teach students appropriate ways to thank guest speakers and other visitors. Have the designated thanker practise the expression of thanks ahead of time.

Note: Before playing students' music selections ensure that they are appropriate for classroom use.

- As a class, examine and discuss a variety of artwork. Have students discuss how each piece of art makes them feel, and why. Also, have students speculate and infer how the artist might have been feeling when creating the artwork. In addition, discuss colour and emotion.

Whole-Class Career Connections

- Discuss ways that various professionals (artists, musicians, authors, poets) portray emotions. For example, examine artwork to determine how facial expressions are used or how colour is used to express emotion. Also, discuss how musicians express emotion through their music and lyrics, and how authors and poets express emotion through writing/poetry.
- Discuss professions related to helping people deal with emotional situations. Have the school guidance counselor talk to students about these professions and how they help support people.

Note: This is an excellent opportunity to provide ELL (and all other middle-years) students with information and access to personal support professionals.

- As a class, have students brainstorm a list of specific people/professionals that they could seek out to help them deal with emotional situations. Each school and community will be unique in this regard, so it is important to be specific. Record this list on chart paper for class display.
- As a class, brainstorm a list of self-help strategies that students can use when they are having emotional difficulties, as well as strategies they can use to help others who are in emotional distress.

Instructional Activity: Part One

Together with ELL students, access a website that depicts emoticons (emotions icons) (for example, <www.myemoticons.com>). Have students select a few sets of emoticons to print off. Cut apart each set of emoticons into cards, and place the sets into separate Ziploc bags.

Note: Be sure that students leave blank space on the cards when they cut them apart for printing the terms for the emotions.

Select one set of emoticons, and display them on a table. Record the word *emotions* on chart paper, and discuss the term. Record students' understanding of the term, and also use student dictionaries to define it. Discuss with students what emotions might be expressed with each card. Challenge students to mimic the expressions displayed on each icon.

Select a second set of emoticons, and display them as a group on a separate part of the table. Challenge students to match emotions between the two sets of icons, for example, finding an icon from each set that depicts "sad".

Instructional Activity: Part Two

Introduce the vocabulary cards – *Emotions* (2.1.1). Place the cards face down on a table. Flip over a card, and have an ELL student read the emotion word (or read it to him or her). Challenge the student to act out the emotion or to show the same facial expression and repeat the word.

Once all the emotion words have been reviewed, turn all the cards face-up on the table. Ask students to identify the emotion words receptively. For example:

- Teacher: I feel sad. Show me sad.
- Student: (points to the card that represents sad).
- Teacher: I feel tired. Show me tired (and so on).

Have small groups of students look through the sets of emoticon cards for illustrations depicting the same emotions as those depicted on the vocabulary cards. Ask them to print the appropriate emotion word on each icon card.

Instructional Activity: Part Three

Introduce the vocabulary cards – *Emotion Actions* (2.1.2), and display them with the vocabulary cards – *Emotions* (2.1.1). Discuss each emotion action in relation to the emotion it conveys. For example, ask:

- What do you do when you are happy?

Have students match *Emotions* vocabulary cards to the related *Emotion actions* cards. Ask questions, and have students respond using vocabulary. For example:

- Teacher: What do you do when you are sad?
- Student: When I am sad, I frown or cry.

Have students suggest emotion actions to represent other emotions, for example:

- bored – yawn
- scared – tremble
- angry (mad) – scowl

Have students make additional vocabulary cards by recording the preceding words on index cards and illustrating them accordingly.

Instructional Activity: Part Four

Have students browse through magazines, flyers, and newspapers to find illustrations and photographs that reflect various emotions. Ask them to cut out the pictures and use them to create a collage on poster paper.

Note: For this activity students may work alone, in pairs, in small groups, or they create a class collage. They may choose to make a collage depicting one emotion or a variety of emotions.

Peer Activities

- Have ELL-student/peer-helper pairs use the vocabulary cards to play a game of Concentration. Ask players to spread out the cards, facedown, between them and then take turns turning over two cards in search of a match. Instruct students to use the vocabulary each time a card is turned over. For example:
  - Student (first card): I feel angry. (Second card): I feel scared.

  If the cards do not match, as in the example above, it is the other player's turn. If the cards do match, the player keeps the cards and takes another turn. The player with the most matches at the end of the game wins.

- Have ELL-student/peer-helper pairs use the vocabulary cards to play charades, acting out the different emotions.

Independent Activity: Part One: Activity Sheet A

Directions to students:

Draw a picture to represent the emotion word found in each box. Use the vocabulary cards and emotion icons to help you (2.1.3).

Independent Activity: Part Two: Activity Sheet B

Directions to students:

Complete the emotions crossword puzzle (2.1.4).

Extensions

- Begin a multilingual word wall for new vocabulary (see page 124). Add new vocabulary – *Emotions/Emotion Actions* to the word wall, as well as illustrations and other visuals related to the vocabulary.

  If it is not feasible to dedicate a bulletin board or classroom wall space to a word wall, make multilingual vocabulary folders for students by dividing legal-size folders into 26 sections, one for each letter of the alphabet (see page 125). Have students add new vocabulary – *Emotions/Emotion Actions* to their vocabulary folders, encouraging them to include illustrations, usage examples, and related vocabulary from their first language(s) with each English term.

- Have students use notebooks, index cards, or the personal dictionary blackline masters included in module 1 (1.1.6, 1.1.7) to create personal dictionaries in which they can record new words and expressions that they learn in each lesson. Ask students to add new vocabulary – *Emotions/Emotion Actions* to their personal dictionaries. Encourage them to use pictures, their emerging English language, and/or their first languages to represent the new terms.

Note: There are two dictionary blackline masters included in module 1—one with columns for English vocabulary and pictures (1.1.6), and a second that encourages bilingual language skills by also providing a column in which students can record vocabulary in their first language(s) (1.1.7). Choose the dictionary template that best suits the individual needs and skills of your ELL students.

- Have students examine anime- and manga-style illustrations. (These are readily available online on various art websites; for example, <http://commons.wikimedia.org/wiki/File:Manga_emotions-EN.jpg>). Use the illustrations to discuss emotions with students, referring to the vocabulary cards and emoticon cards as needed.
- Have students write emails and then adorn them with emotion icons.

Assessment as Learning

Conference with ELL students individually. Provide each student with three or four vocabulary cards depicting emotions, and have him or her discuss or draw pictures to show when he or she has felt that emotion. For example, feeling shy on the first day of school, or feeling happy when it snowed. During discussion, record your observations and conclusions on the Individual Student Observations sheet (I.4), shown on page 37.

2.1.1

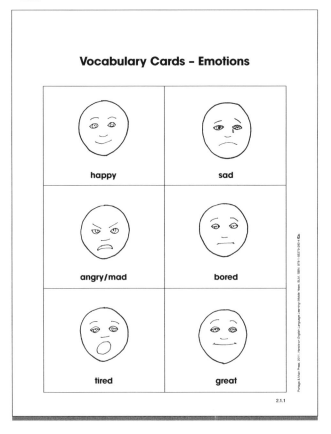

2.1.1

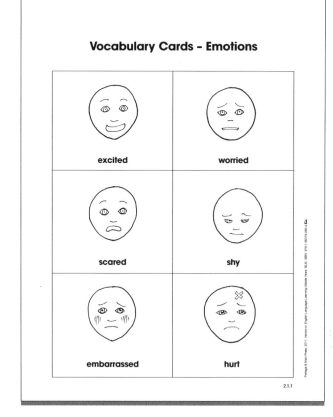

2.1.1

Vocabulary Cards – Emotions

sick	frustrated
confused	

2.1.2

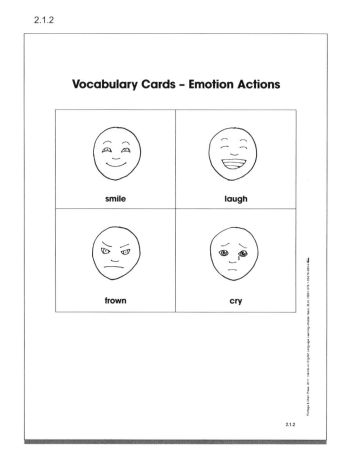

Blackline Masters

2.1.1 – 137

Blackline Masters

2.1.3 — Emotions

happy	worried	tired
scared	shy	bored
hurt	sad	angry/mad
sick	great	excited
confused	frustrated	embarrassed

1A

2.1.4 — Emotions Crossword

Across
1.
3.
8.
9.
10.
12.
13.

Down
2.
4.
5.
6.
7.
10.
11.
13.

1B

138 – 2.1.2 – 2.1.4

2 Clothing

Curricular Connections

- Language Arts: speaking, listening, reading, writing, viewing, representing
- Science: seasonal changes
- Social Studies: cultural diversity, traditions and celebrations
- Health: healthy lifestyle practices
- Art: drawing

Background Information for Teachers

The *present continuous* (also referred to as *present progressive*) expresses an activity that is *in progress at the moment of speaking*. It is a temporary activity that began in the past, is continuing at present, and will probably end at some point in the future.

Teachers should introduce or review with students the use of present continuous prior to beginning the lesson. This will be useful, because phrases like, "I am wearing…" and "She is wearing…" are used frequently throughout the lesson. There is no need to provide a lengthy, detailed explanation to students at this level. Simply provide several examples for students, modeling the phrase with body language. For example:

- I am wear<u>ing</u> jeans and a red sweater. (Point to your clothing.)
- He is wear<u>ing</u> a windbreaker and sweats. (Point to a student's or other person's clothing.)

Record each expression on chart paper, highlighting or underlining the *ing* as shown above.

Vocabulary – Clothing

Clothing

- hat
- cap
- toque
- scarf
- coat
- ski jacket
- parka
- windbreaker
- raincoat/rain slicker
- mitts/mittens
- gloves
- boots
- shirt
- t-shirt
- sweater
- sweatshirt
- hoodie
- jersey
- pants
- sweats/sweatpants
- jeans
- socks
- shoes
- runners
- shorts
- bathing suit
- swimming trunks
- skirt
- dress
- sandals

Accessories

- sunglasses
- belt
- ring
- necklace
- bracelet
- earrings
- watch
- glasses
- hairclip
- neck chain

2

Note: Also include clothing vocabulary that reflects the cultural backgrounds of students in your class, the school, and the community (for example, sari, hijab, chador). Use blank index cards to make vocabulary cards for this vocabulary.

Helpful Verbs/Phrasal Verbs for Use With Clothing Vocabulary

- wear
- try on
- put on
- take off
- change/change out of
- button up
- zip
- tie
- buckle

Materials

- vocabulary cards – *Clothing* (included. Photocopy one set onto sturdy tagboard, and cut apart cards.) (2.2.1)
- vocabulary cards – *Accessories* (included. Photocopy one set onto sturdy tagboard, and cut apart cards.) (2.2.2)
- vocabulary cards – *Helpful Verbs/Phrasal Verbs* (included. Photocopy one set onto sturdy tagboard, and cut apart cards.) (2.2.3)
- vocabulary cards – *Colours*, from module 1, lesson 6 (included) (1.6.1)
- collection of accessories (glasses, watch, sunglasses, ring, bracelet, belt, and so on)
- books about clothing in various cultures (see Books for Students, page 128)
- pocket chart
- drawing paper
- chart paper
- markers
- magazines (fashion, sports, or other magazines with people) and clothing catalogues
- scissors
- glue
- large bag of clothing
- music and player (CD player, MP3 player with speakers, computer, or a radio)
- traditional clothing worn by Canada's Aboriginal* people
- books about traditional clothing from various cultures
- map of the world

*__Note:__ Throughout *Hands-On English Language Learning* we use the term *Aboriginal* to refer collectively to students (or other people) of First Nations, Inuit, and Métis descent.

Integrated Class Activities

- To correlate with the social studies curriculum, have all students discuss clothing that they wear for special occasions and family celebrations.

- Discuss traditional clothing from students' countries of origin or cultural backgrounds, as well as from other countries around the world. If possible, have students, family members, staff, or community members bring in clothing items to show students.

Note: To avoid tokenism, it is important that all types of clothing worn by students in the class are represented. Consider using such headings as *hats/head coverings, shirts, skirts, shoes/footwear,* and so on to categorize clothing, placing the non-Western equivalents under the appropriate headings. Also, seize the opportunity to highlight *why* certain clothing, including the fabrics used, is worn in certain parts of the world—with relation to climate and lifestyle (for example, nomadic people, who live in a hot, dry, desert environment, wear loose-fitting layers of clothing made of lightweight fabric like cotton). It is also important to note that in some countries, certain clothing is worn only during celebrations or ceremonies, while Western-style clothing is worn most often. Where possible, teachers should consult with experts in their communities to ensure that information they present is accurate and respectfully represented.

- As a class, play the game Pass the Bag. Place several pieces of clothing into a large bag. Have students stand in a large circle. Play music as students pass the bag around the circle. When you stop the music, have the student holding the bag pull out an item of clothing and say, "I am wearing (a)..." The game can be particularly amusing if the clothing is interesting or funny. It also adds to the enjoyment if students actually put on the clothing they pull out.

- Have a class dress-up relay race. Divide the class into groups of four. Place a large pile of clothes at one end of the gym or playground. Have the first student in each group run to the pile and put on three items, then run back and tell his or her team members what he or she is wearing, by colour and item. For example, "I am wearing a red shirt, a blue toque, and a brown shoe." The next team member then runs to put on three items. Play continues until all team members have completed the relay.

- Visit a local costume museum to learn more about historical clothing.

- As another excellent connection to the social studies curriculum, read about and/or research traditional clothing worn by Canada's Aboriginal people. Discuss the use of natural materials for this clothing. If possible, invite Aboriginal guest speakers and/or dancers to show the class clothing samples and discuss how they are made.

- Throughout the school year, discuss clothing choices for seasonal and weather conditions (wearing a hat to avoid sunstroke and sunburn, wearing proper winter clothing to avoid frostbite and hypothermia, and so on).

Whole-Class Career Connections

- Have students check the labels on the clothing they are wearing to determine where various items were made. Mark these locations on a map of the world.

- For a social-activism-related activity, discuss the issue of child labour. Have students check out the Kielburger's Free the Children website <www.freethechildren.com>.

- As a class, discuss the process involved in making clothing, from creating fabric, to designing, sewing, shipping to stores, and selling to customers. Make a flowchart to portray this process.

- Using the flowchart (see preceding bullet), brainstorm a list of jobs related to clothing. Try to identify jobs related to each stage in the flowchart process.

- Take students on a fieldtrip to a local garment district or textile museum.

- Visit a local tailor or seamstress.

- Have a community member teach students how to knit or crochet. This can become a valuable social activism project by having students knit or crochet squares that can be made into an afghan and sent to developing countries.

- Invite a local clothing store owner, fashion designer, or manufacturer to share aspects of his or her job with students. Prior to presentations, have students identify questions to ask. Use the Employability Skills Checklist (included in module 1, lesson 1; 1.1.8) to focus questions to guest speakers. Explain to students that the list of skills on the checklist was developed by employers and government representatives, and it is used across Canada to identify the skills needed by employees in all workplaces. Using the checklist for reference, students might ask speakers:

    - What kinds of problems do you have to solve in your job?
    - How do you learn new skills for your job?

- What do you do to help build teamwork with your staff?

Note: Be sure to have students write thank you letters to any guest speaker, reflecting on what they learned from the presentation.

Also note that although it is not appropriate for students to ask about a presenter's salary (this is generally confidential), it is reasonable for them to research this information for themselves (or with your help). The following three websites present average salaries/wages for various jobs in Canada:

- <www.livingin-canada.com/wages-for-social-education-jobs-canada.html>
- <www.payscale.com/research/CA/Employer_Type=School_%2f_School_District/Salary>
- <http://resource.educationcanada.com/salaries.html>

Instructional Activity: Part One

To activate students' prior learning, ask:

- What are you doing right now? (for example, I am sitting, I am looking)

Gauge students' responses to see if they are using the correct verb structure and how much further explanation/support is needed. Use this opportunity to review the present continuous with students.

Now, say:

- Today I am wearing…(point to each item of clothing as you tell students what you are wearing).

Record the clothing vocabulary on chart paper.

Display the vocabulary cards – Clothing (2.2.1), and review the terms and illustrations. Provide students with an opportunity to repeat each word after you say it. Also, have students share clothing vocabulary in their first language(s).

Display the cards in a pocket chart for future reference.

Have students use the phrase, "Today I am wearing…" while they point to and identify each piece of their own clothing. Encourage them to use the vocabulary cards for support.

Instructional Activity: Part Two

Display the vocabulary cards – Colours (1.6.1) in the pocket chart. Have students identify objects in the classroom that represent each colour.

Now, for review purposes, repeat the preceding activity, but include the use of colour words to describe clothing. Say:

- Today I am wearing…(point to each item of clothing as you name it and its colour)

Record the colour and clothing words on chart paper.

Have students use the phrase, "Today I am wearing…" while they point to and identify each piece of their own clothing and its colour. Encourage students to use the vocabulary cards for support.

Instructional Activity: Part Three

Display the vocabulary cards – Accessories (2.2.2). Review each word and illustration. Identify any accessories you and students are wearing. Use the vocabulary cards – Colours to describe the colour of various accessories worn by the group.

Display the collection of accessories, and have students describe and sort them into groups according to the target vocabulary.

Peer Activity

Note: The following activity requires at least four players divided into two even teams.

- This game is similar to Pictionary. Divide the group of students into two even teams. Provide each team with drawing paper and markers, and designate one player on each team as the artist. Have one of the artists select a vocabulary card – *Clothing* from a pile in front of them, look at it, and then pass it to the artist on the other team.

Note: Ensure that the artists conceal the card from the rest of their teammates.

Once both artists have seen the card, have them begin to draw the item of clothing found on the card. The goal is to see which team can identify the clothing item first. Have students take turns being the artist for their team.

Note: Take the opportunity for a teachable moment by reminding your peer helpers about the rules of good gamesmanship and that the game should not become too competitive. The intent is for the ELL students to have fun while practising some of the new clothing vocabulary.

Independent Activity: Part One: Activity Sheet A

Note: This is a two-page activity sheet.

Directions to students:

Find pictures of clothing in catalogues and magazines. Cut out each item of clothing, and glue it onto the chart. Record the name of the item of clothing as well as what colour it is. Use the vocabulary cards – *Clothing* and *Colours* to help you (2.2.4).

Independent Activity: Part Two: Activity Sheet B

Directions to students:

Draw pictures and write about your favourite clothes and accessories for school and for special times such as family celebrations. Explain why these are your favourites (2.2.5).

Extensions

- Add new vocabulary to the multilingual word wall.

- Have students add new vocabulary to their personal vocabulary folders or personal dictionaries.

- Have students organize and present a fashion show. The show could focus on favourite fashions, cultural clothing, or could even be a comedic fashion show depicting costumes and characters from favourite TV shows, bands, and sports from Canadian and American popular culture as well as from students' countries of origin.

- Have students create a poster collage similar to the illustrations in the *Where's Waldo?* books. Encourage them to identify a central character, or even to use a digital photo of themselves and feature it at the top of the poster (as the character to look for within the main poster). Then, to fill the poster, have students use digital photographs or magazine pictures of people wearing similar clothing to the central character, hiding their character within the collage. Challenge other students to find the character.

- Play a version of the game I Spy to describe the colour and names of clothing worn by various students. For example:
    - Student 1: "I spy, with my little eye, someone wearing blue."
    - Student 2: "Is it Chandra, wearing the blue sweater?"

- Read multicultural books (see the Books for Students list on page 128) to explore and discuss clothing from other cultures.

Assessment of Learning

Collect students' completed copies of Activity Sheet A (2.2.4). Conference with students individually to review the lesson's vocabulary orally. This will help to determine students' strengths and any areas of difficulty. Use copies of the Individual Student Observations sheet (I.4), shown on page 37, to record findings.

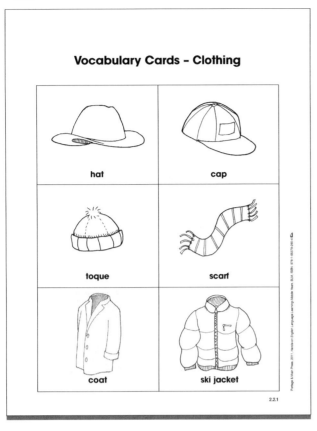
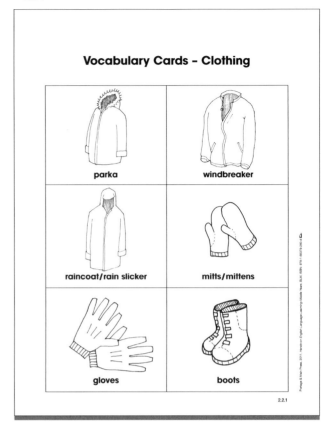
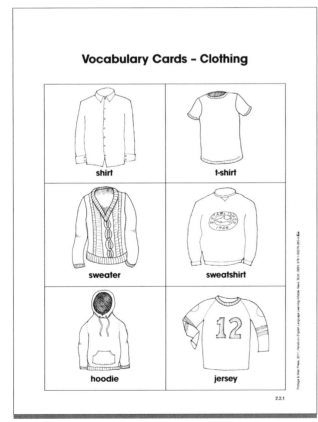
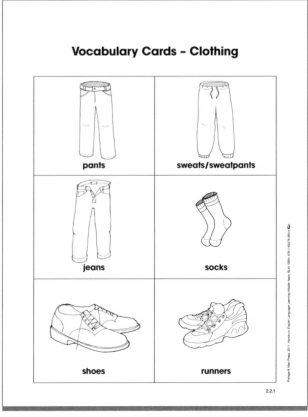

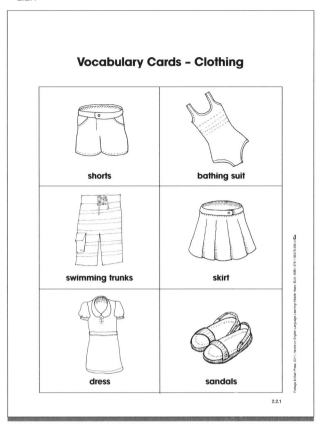
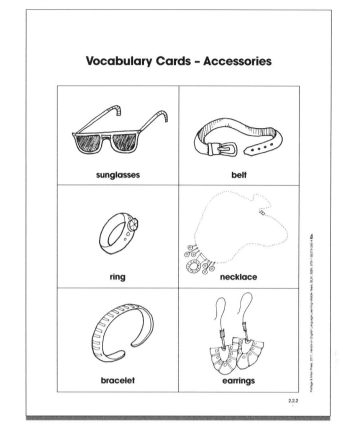
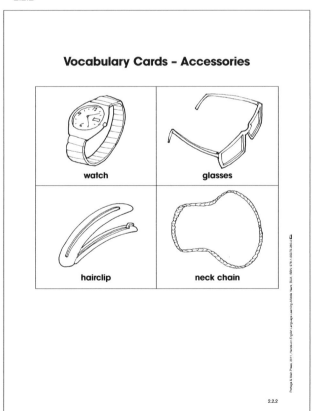
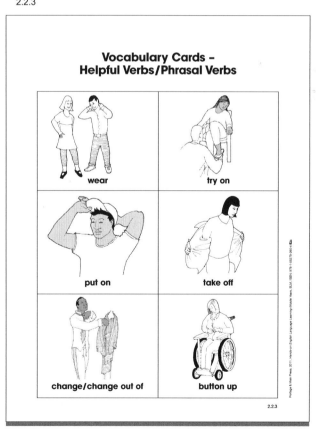

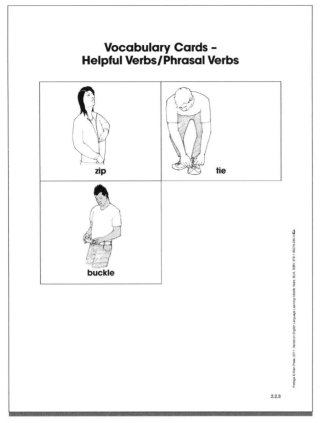

3 Food

Curricular Connections

- Language Arts: speaking, listening, reading, writing, viewing, representing
- Mathematics: surveys, tallies, graphs
- Science: plants, animals, basic human needs
- Social Studies: cultural diversity, basic human needs
- Physical Education: healthy-lifestyle practices
- Health: healthy eating

Background Information for Teachers

In this lesson a great deal of vocabulary is introduced, which may take several sessions to cover, depending on students' existing knowledge of vocabulary and related concepts.

At this stage, many ELL students will be comfortable expressing their likes and dislikes. You may want to review the phrases, "I like…" and "I don't like…" prior to beginning the first activity.

Safety note: Be aware of any student food allergies when conducting the activities in this lesson. Also be aware of any students' cultural or religious food restrictions (for example, pork, beef).

Vocabulary – Food

Vegetables

- onion
- pepper
- mushroom
- lettuce
- broccoli
- potato
- carrot
- bean
- pea
- corn
- cucumber
- spinach
- sweet potato
- squash
- cabbage
- pumpkin

Fruit

- pineapple
- grape
- blueberry
- strawberry
- banana
- orange
- pear
- lemon
- apple
- watermelon
- peach
- cherry
- plum
- kiwi
- grapefruit
- raspberry

Meat and Alternatives

- beef
- chicken
- bacon
- fish
- pork
- beans
- lentils
- tofu
- turkey
- egg

Grain Products

- bread
- bun
- bagel
- pasta

▶

Module 2

- rice
- oatmeal
- couscous
- cereal
- cracker
- pretzel
- pita bread
- tortilla

Milk and Alternatives

- milk
- yogurt
- cheese
- cottage cheese

Oils and Fats

- butter
- margarine
- oil
- salad dressing

Drinks

- water
- milk
- juice
- soft drink/soda/pop
- hot chocolate
- tea
- coffee
- lemonade

Snacks/Desserts

- potato chips
- chocolate bar
- pie
- cake
- donut
- ice cream
- muffin
- cookies
- popcorn

Condiments

- ketchup
- mustard
- relish
- jam/jelly
- peanut butter
- sugar
- pepper
- salt

Other Foods

- soup
- cheeseburger
- hotdog
- pizza
- sandwich
- French fries
- pizza pop
- pancakes

Food-Related Words

- meal
- breakfast
- lunch
- supper
- snack
- plate
- bowl
- spoon
- fork
- knife
- glass
- cup
- mug
- napkin/serviette

Food Actions

- eat
- chew
- drink
- swallow

3

- cook
- bake
- stir/mix
- cut
- peel

Note: Also include vocabulary for foods from the countries of origin of students in the class. Have students use blank index cards to make their own vocabulary cards with labels and pictures of these foods to include with the target vocabulary.

Materials

- copies of *Eating Well With Canada's Food Guide* (available from Health Canada at <www.hc-sc.gc.ca/fn-an/food-guide-aliment/order-commander/index-eng.php>)
- kitchen utensils for making fruit and vegetable salads (knives, cutting boards, serving bowls, forks)
- vocabulary cards – *Food* (included. Photocopy one set onto sturdy tagboard, and cut out.) (2.3.1)
- vocabulary cards – *Food-Related Words* (included. Photocopy one set onto sturdy tagboard, and cut out.) (2.3.2)
- vocabulary cards – *Food Actions* (included. Photocopy one set onto sturdy tagboard, and cut out.) (2.3.3)
- *Everybody Bakes Bread, Everybody Cooks Rice, Everybody Brings Noodles*, and *Everybody Serves Soup,* all books by Norah Dooley (see Books for Students, page 128)
- books about foods from various cultures (see Books for Students, page 128)
- food-bingo game boards (included. Photocopy one board for each student.) (2.3.4)
- bingo chips
- scissors
- glue
- sticky notes
- grocery store flyers

- paper plates (at least six for each student)
- plastic forks
- chopsticks
- blank index cards
- markers
- tape
- string or wool
- wall map of the world
- chart paper
- soap and water (for washing hands) or hand-sanitizer
- variety of food samples from each food group

Note: Be aware of any student food allergies when choosing food samples. Also be aware of any students' cultural or religious food restrictions (for example, pork, beef).

Integrated Class Activities

- The activities presented for Instructional Activity: Part Two (making fruit salad) and Instructional Activity: Part Three (making vegetable salad) can easily be conducted with the whole class. This is an excellent opportunity to introduce students to new varieties of fruits and vegetables and to explore the use of vivid and descriptive adjectives for how the fruits and vegetables look, feel, smell, and taste.

- Have the whole class participate in activities related to the Canada Food Guide (Instructional Activity: Part Four and Instructional Activity: Part Five) to correlate with the health curriculum.

- Have students share family food traditions associated with special occasions.

- To encourage global awareness among students, have a guest teach them how to use chopsticks. Then, ask the guest to prepare a dish together with students, so they can practise using their new skill.

▶

3

- Invite various guests (students' family members or community members) to give cooking demonstrations of foods from other countries/cultures.

- Visit local grocery stores that carry diverse food selections from different countries/cultures.

- Take class fieldtrips to local restaurants that reflect the cultural diversity of the community.

- Conduct research with students to determine which foods are produced in your own community, city/town or province, which foods are produced in Canada (but in other provinces), and which foods are imported from other countries.

- Conduct a class survey to determine students' favourite foods from each food group (favourite fruit, favourite vegetable, favourite dairy product, favourite meat and alternatives, favourite grain product). Use tally charts to record data, and then use the data to create bar graphs.

Note: Following the lesson, and after students have been exposed to new food items, survey the class again, and discuss results to determine if students change their opinions on some foods. Often, opinions are based more on lack of exposure than on experience or preference.

- Conduct research with students to find out from which countries various foods originate. Record the food(s) that originate from each country onto a separate index card. Then, tape one end of a piece of string to each index card, and attach the other end of the string to the specific country on a wall map of the world. Affix the index cards to the wall or bulletin board, around the wall map.

Note: Alternatively, you can use the vocabulary cards – *Food* (2.3.1), rather than the index cards, and use string to attach these to the world map.

Whole-Class Career Connections

- Focus career-connection activities on the agriculture industry. This offers an opportunity to explore food-related careers from an international perspective. Begin by recording the term *Agriculture* in the middle of a sheet of chart paper. Circle the word. Ask students to define this term in their own words (the production of food through farming). Record the class definition on the chart paper, below the title, and circle it. Then, have students identify foods that are produced through agriculture, and record each food on a sticky note. Once you have identified and recorded several foods, sort them according to categories on which students decide (for example, dairy products, plant products, animal products).

- Brainstorm a list of jobs related to agriculture in Canada, as well as in students' countries or origin. Be sure to consider the equipment and services needed by the farmer in order to produce food (machinery, fertilizer, seed, gasoline, veterinarians, and so on).

- Select a local agricultural food item, and create a flow chart to identify the process by which the food is produced. Select other agricultural food items from countries reflecting students' cultural origins. Research how these foods are produced, and compare the process to local agricultural processes.

- Have a farmer or a representative from the provincial department of agriculture speak to students about this career, focusing on the skills needed for this job, as well as the challenges and rewards.

Note: The provincial departments of agriculture offer many valuable resources for classroom use, including educational kits, student booklets, and audio-visual resources. Many of these resources focus specifically on the farming industry and related careers.

- Display a wide variety of foods, and have students display food items from their lunches. Examine labels to determine where foods are produced. Identify locations on a world map.
- Have students record a list of foods produced in their home countries. Display these lists around a wall map of the world, and use string or wool to connect the lists to the appropriate countries.

Instructional Activity: Part One: Fruits

Note: Remember to keep any student allergies in mind for all instructional activities that involve food tasting. Also, have students wash their hands (or use hand-sanitizer) before conducting any of the activities that involve handling of food. This is also an opportunity to discuss food hygiene, which includes the careful washing of produce before eating it.

Display a variety of fruit. Provide plenty of time for students to handle the fruit and discuss their observations. Encourage language through questions such as:

- Which fruit is the biggest?
- Which fruit is the smallest?
- Which fruit are red?
- Which fruit are yellow?
- Which fruit are purple?
- Which fruit are shiny?
- Which fruit are smooth?

Note: If students wish, they may reply in complete sentences. However, this first activity should be primarily a receptive one, and they should not be required to answer in complete sentences.

Cut up several pieces of fruit for students to taste. Mix the fruit together into a fruit salad, and distribute to each student a small amount on a paper plate. Be sure each student receives at least one piece of each type of fruit in the salad.

Ask:

- Which fruit do you like best?
- Which fruit do you not like?

Encourage students to use the phrases *I like...* and *I do not like...* to describe their preferences.

Using the appropriate vocabulary cards – *Food (Fruit)*, have students match each type of fruit to the corresponding card.

Also, use the vocabulary cards – *Food-Related Words (2.3.2)* and *Food Actions (2.3.3)* to discuss utensils and processes used during the making and eating of the fruit salad.

Instructional Activity: Part Two: Vegetables

Repeat the procedure from Instructional Activity: Part One to introduce students to a variety of vegetables. Be sure to give students plenty of opportunities to handle, describe, and taste the various samples. Then, use the vegetables to make a large garden salad for them to sample. Distribute to each ELL student a small amount of salad on a paper plate. Be sure each student receives at least one piece of each type of vegetable in the salad, and have students discuss what they like and dislike.

Using the appropriate vocabulary cards – *Food (Vegetables)*, have students match each vegetable to the corresponding card.

Also, use the vocabulary cards – *Food-Related Words* and *Food Actions* to discuss utensils and processes used during the making and eating of the vegetable salad.

Instructional Activity: Part Three: Grain Products

Read and discuss the picture books *Everybody Bakes Bread, Everybody Cooks Rice, Everybody Brings Noodles,* and *Everybody Serves Soup,* all by Norah Dooley. These books present examples of the similarities and differences in grain products across diverse cultures. Discuss the cultures and foods depicted in the books, and have students discuss the bread, rice, and noodle dishes that are common in their countries of origin.

Display the vocabulary cards – *Food (Grain Products)*, and have students match the foods from the books to the cards.

Note: Provide students with an opportunity to make additional vocabulary cards for foods not depicted in the set of cards.

Instructional Activity: Part Four: Eating Well with Canada's Food Guide

Display a wide variety of foods from the different food groups. Give students plenty of opportunities to handle, describe, and taste the various food samples (as appropriate). Use the vocabulary cards – *Food* to identify each food. Discuss how the different foods are prepared and eaten.

Provide students with copies of *Eating Well with Canada's Food Guide*. Explain that this is a guide to healthy eating. Discuss the importance of eating foods from each group at each meal.

Display several vocabulary cards from the various food groups, and challenge students to use the food guide to help them sort the cards into groups.

Instructional Activity: Part Five: Meals

Discuss the importance of starting the day with a healthy breakfast. Have students use the food samples, the vocabulary cards – *Food,* and the publication, *Eating Well with Canada's Food Guide* to help them identify what they eat for breakfast.

Note: This is an excellent opportunity for students to share foods from their countries of origin. As students suggest cultural foods, discuss the food group(s) to which each one belongs. Also, use multicultural books (see Books for Students, page 128) to discuss foods from other countries.

Have students also use the vocabulary cards to show what they eat for lunch, supper, and snacks.

Note: If some food items that students eat are not represented in the set of vocabulary cards, have them use blank index cards to make additional cards to represent these foods.

As students share their meal routines, take the opportunity to highlight diversity in food choice. Some students and their families may be vegetarian (for religious, cultural, or personal reasons). Others may have specific food and dietary needs as a result of Celiac disease, Crohn's disease, lactose intolerance, food allergies or sensitivities, or other medical conditions. If students are comfortable sharing their special dietary needs, this offers an authentic learning experience for the entire class.

Be sure to also discuss variation in mealtimes in different countries. For example, in Mexico, many people eat their main meal of the day, called *comida*, somewhere between 2 P.M. and 4 P.M.

Peer Activity: Food Bingo

Have each ELL student play this game with three or more peers. Designate one student as the bingo caller, and distribute blank food-bingo game boards (2.3.4) and bingo chips to the other players. Give the caller the collection of vocabulary cards – *Food,* and have him or her spread out the collection face up, for all players to see. Have the players use the vocabulary cards to create their own food bingo game boards by printing their chosen food words and drawing accompanying pictures into each square.

When all students have created their bingo game boards, have the caller shuffle the vocabulary cards and place them in a pile in front of him or her. Ask the caller to take a vocabulary card from the top of the pile and read the card within the context of a sentence, saying either "I like…" or "I do not like…" Tell the players to look for that food on their game boards and use a bingo chip to cover it if they do have the food. Have the first student to make a line of bingo chips on the game board call, "Bingo!"

Then, have students change roles (designating a different student as caller), and play the game again.

Independent Activity: Part One: Healthy Meal and Snack Choices

Provide each student with four paper plates, and have them label the plates "Breakfast," "Lunch," "Supper," and "Snacks."

Distribute grocery store flyers, scissors, and glue, and have students look through the flyers to find healthy items that they might eat at each meal, keeping in mind the Canada Food Guide. Ask students to cut out the pictures that they find and glue them onto each plate. Then, use the plates to create a bulletin board display titled, "Healthy Meal and Snack Choices."

Independent Activity: Part Two: Activity Sheet A

Directions to students:

Draw pictures of the fruit that went into your fruit salad. Label each piece of fruit, as well as each utensil used. Use the vocabulary cards – *Food (Fruit)* and *Food-Related Words* to help you. Describe how you made your fruit salad. Use the vocabulary cards – *Food Actions* to help you (2.3.5).

Independent Activity: Part Three: Activity Sheet B

Directions to students:

Draw pictures of the vegetables that went into your garden salad. Label each vegetable, as well as each utensil used. Use the vocabulary cards – *Food (Vegetables)* and *Food-Related Words* to help you. Describe how you made your vegetable salad. Use the vocabulary cards – *Food Actions* to help you (2.3.6).

Independent Activity: Part Four: Activity Sheet C

Directions to students:

Complete the chart to show the picture and name of each food. Also, complete each sentence to show the foods that you like and do not like (2.3.7).

Extensions

- Add new vocabulary to the multilingual word wall.
- Have students add new vocabulary to their personal vocabulary folders or personal dictionaries.
- Discuss the term *still life picture* with students, and show them some examples. Then, have students use a variety of foods to sketch still-life pictures.
- Have students record their food intake for one week and then assess how well they followed the Canada Food Guide.

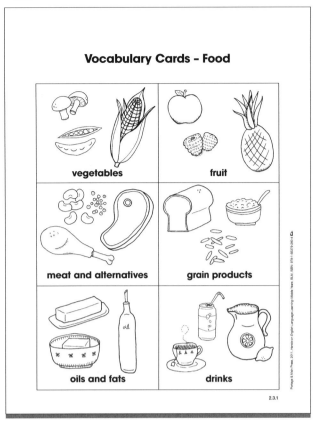

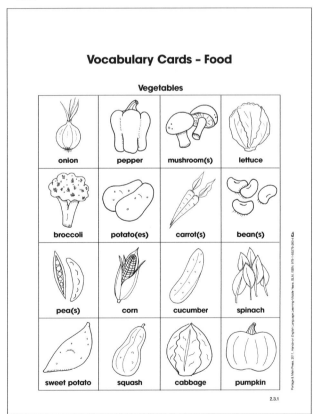

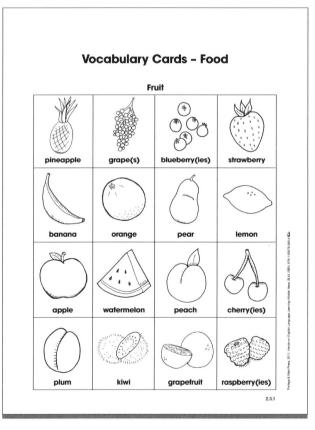

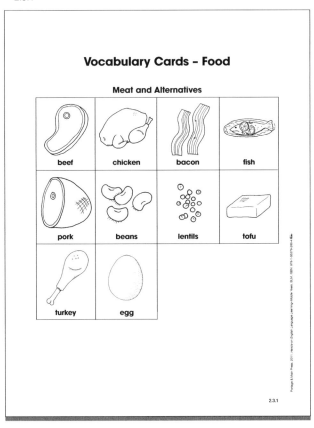

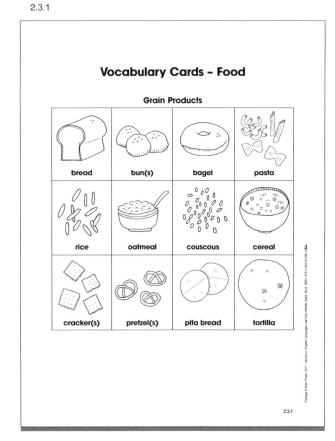

Blackline Masters

2.3.1

Vocabulary Cards - Food
Snacks/Desserts

2.3.1

Vocabulary Cards - Food
Condiments

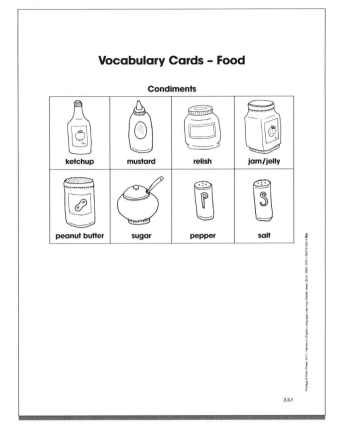

2.3.1

Vocabulary Cards - Food
Other Foods

2.3.2

Vocabulary Cards – Food-Related Words

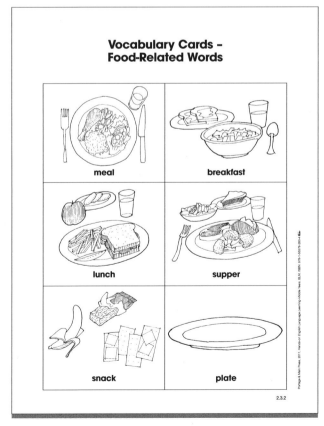

2.3.2

Vocabulary Cards – Food-Related Words

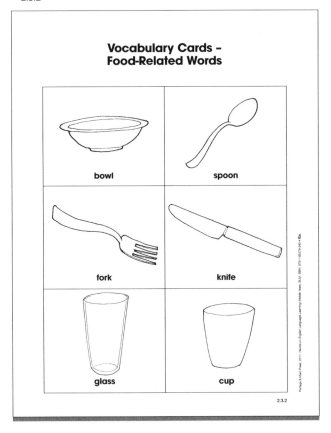

2.3.2

Vocabulary Cards – Food-Related Words

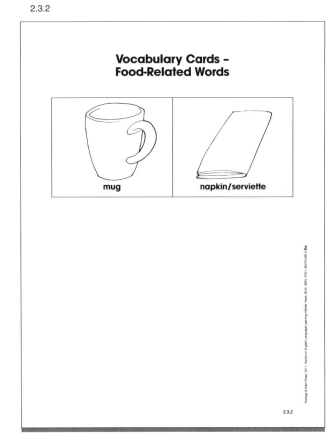

Blackline Masters

2.3.3

Vocabulary Cards – Food Actions

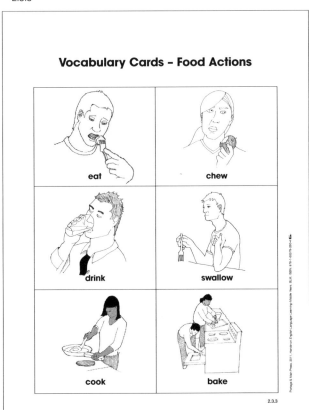

2.3.3

Vocabulary Cards – Food Actions

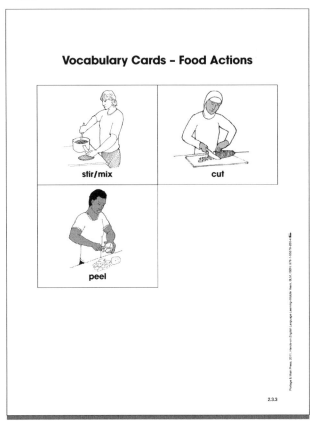

Blackline Masters

2.3.4

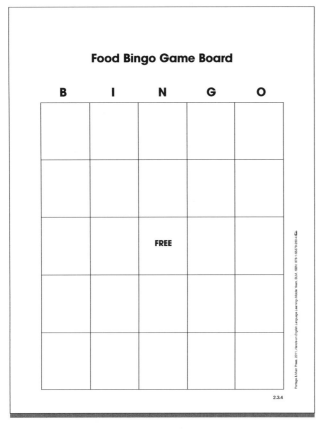

2.3.5

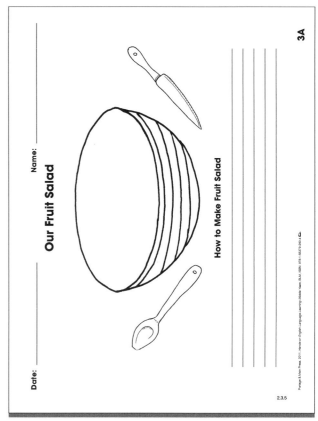

2.3.6

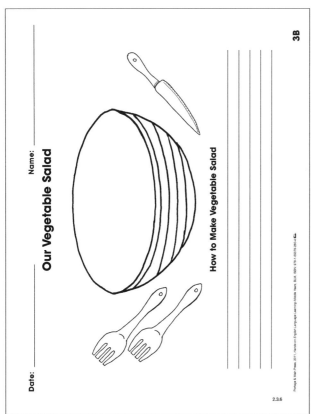

2.3.7

Date: _____   Name: _____

Food to Eat

Food	Illustration	Sentence I like… I do not like…
grapefruit		
	🍌	
	🌽	
potato		
noodles		
	🍋	
tofu		
lemonade		
milk		
	🥪	

3C

158 – 2.3.3 – 2.3.7

4 Body Parts and Health

Curricular Connections

- Language Arts: speaking, listening, reading, writing, viewing, representing
- Mathematics: measuring, symmetry
- Science: living things, animals, life cycles, basic human needs, body systems
- Social Studies: basic human needs
- Physical Education: healthy lifestyle practices
- Health: personal health practices
- Art: drawing

Background Information for Teachers

When learning new vocabulary, students need between 5 and 10 encounters with a word in order to be able to use it in context (Cook 1999). This is why the idea of recycling (bringing back previously learned vocabulary) is so important. For instance, in this lesson, teachers have the opportunity to review clothing words (for example, "On which body part would you put a hat?" Or, "What item of clothing do you wear on your head?"), colour words (for example, "My hair is black"), and number words (for example, "I have 10 toes."). Words can also be recycled in many other different ways, including playing word games, reading books, talking about the words, working the words into warm-up activities, and so on. Remember that research indicates that we can learn only four to seven new words a day; therefore, this lesson will likely take several lessons to complete.

Note: The topic of this lesson lends itself to connections with the physical education/health curriculum. Be sure to inform the phys ed teacher in advance of your students' focus on the concepts in this lesson, so that he or she can consider integrating the topic into the class's physical education and health classes.

Vocabulary – Body Parts and Health

Body Parts

- head
- face
- neck
- hair
- forehead
- eye
- eyebrow
- ear
- nose
- mouth
- lips
- tongue
- tooth/teeth
- cheek
- chin
- arm
- shoulder
- elbow
- wrist
- hand
- finger
- thumb
- leg
- knee
- ankle
- foot
- toe
- stomach
- chest
- back
- bottom

Internal Parts

- brain
- skull
- bone(s)
- heart

▶

4

- lungs
- muscle(s)
- blood

Ailments

- stomachache
- headache
- backache
- toothache
- (I have a) fever
- (I have a) cold
- (I have a) cut
- I hurt my _____/(I have a) hurt _____
- (I feel) sick

Materials

- two traced outlines of the human body (Have a student lie down on a large piece of poster paper or other large paper, and trace the outline of his or her body onto the paper. Onto one of the body outlines, add [draw] the following internal body parts: a brain, a skull, bones, a heart, lungs, muscles, blood [you might also challenge students to help you with these illustrations])
- mural paper
- scissors
- markers or coloured pencils
- glue
- chart paper
- magazines
- mirrors
- vocabulary cards – *Body Parts* (included. Photocopy one set onto sturdy tagboard, and cut out.) (2.4.1)
- vocabulary cards – *Internal Body Parts* (included. Photocopy one set onto sturdy tagboard, and cut out.) (2.4.2)
- vocabulary cards – *Ailments* (included. Photocopy one set onto sturdy tagboard, and cut out.) (2.4.3)
- masking tape
- When You Are Not Feeling Well dialogue cards (included. Photocopy one set onto sturdy tagboard, and cut out.) (2.4.4)
- Career Research template (included. Make one photocopy for each student.) (2.4.5)
- pocket chart
- drawing paper
- string or wool
- rulers or measuring tapes
- blocks (for measuring – see last integrated class activity)

Assessment for Learning

Use Total Physical Response (TPR) to determine students' background knowledge about body parts. Call out various commands (for example, "Point to your arm", "Touch your head"), and note vocabulary that students understand as well as vocabulary that is less familiar.

Note: Please refer to page 60 for a brief description of the Total Physical Response (TPR) strategy.

Integrated Class Activities

- Use this lesson topic to focus on students' health. The previous lesson on food lends itself to discussions about how food provides nutrition and energy for the body. Specifically, discuss nutritional needs for healthy bones and teeth, the importance of dental health, and the importance of personal hygiene to limit the passing of germs.

- To correlate with art, have students find pictures of faces in magazines and cut out the individual features (for example, the nose, the eyes, the chin). Ask them to sort the features they have cut out. Then, have students choose one facial feature from the sorted groups to sketch. For example, students may choose to draw a variety of noses. Following this activity, discuss the

4

vocabulary that can be used to describe facial features.

- For a humorous art activity, have students use the cut-apart facial features from the preceding activity to create new faces, mixing up the features.

- Have students use mirrors to examine their own faces and then sketch self-portraits.

Note: This activity provides an opportunity to discuss and explore symmetry in nature (correlation to math and science), as the human face is an example of a symmetrical life form.

- To connect this lesson to lesson 1 on emotions, have students draw portraits of peers expressing specific emotions (for example, sadness, fear). Discuss how facial features change with emotion.

- As a class, practise healthy hand-washing techniques before all eating or food-preparation activities. Have students wash their hands with soap and water long enough to sing the alphabet song.

- Have students trace one hand and one foot onto paper and then use these to focus on measurement skills. Challenge students to find the length and the width of their foot and hand templates. Also, introduce perimeter, and have students use string or wool to measure the perimeter of their hand and foot templates. They can measure the area by covering the templates with blocks and then counting the blocks.

Note: Before each measuring task, have students estimate the measurement first. Have them record these estimates on the templates and then record their results. Correlate math skills by having students find the difference between their estimation and the actual measurement.

Whole-Class Career Connections

- Brainstorm a list of careers related to maintaining a healthy body. Classify jobs according to categories determined by students, such as careers in the fields of medicine and dentistry, nutrition, health and wellness, and fitness and recreation.

- Survey students to see if any of their family members work within any of the career fields listed above (in the preceding activity), or in any other jobs related to maintaining a healthy body. Invite these individuals to present to the class.

- Have students select one career of interest and research the kind of training required for the career. Ask them to use the Career Research template (included – 2.4.5) to record their findings. Have students present their findings to the class.

Note: If any ELL student requires support for the preceding activity, have him or her work with a peer helper who is interested in the same career.

Instructional Activity: Part One

Display one traced outline of the human body, and use the vocabulary cards – *Body Parts* (2.4.1) and the TPR strategy to review body-parts vocabulary. Hold up each vocabulary card one at a time, and point to the corresponding body part on the body outline, saying the body part as you do so. Use a small, rolled piece of masking tape to attach the card to the body outline in its appropriate location. Give students opportunities to lead the TPR activity by calling out body parts while other students follow the instructions.

Note: Upon completion of the preceding activity, hang the body outline with the attached vocabulary cards somewhere prominent in the classroom. It will remain a useful visual reference for students for future lessons.

▶

4

Instructional Activity: Part Two

Engage students in a discussion about hygiene. As a warm-up activity, act out your morning routine, including brushing teeth, washing face/hands and/or showering, brushing hair, and so on. Ask students:

- What was I doing?

Now, have students act out their own morning routines. As they do this, note some of the important hygiene steps, including washing/having a shower and brushing teeth and hair.

Note: Addressing hygiene issues can be a delicate matter. Teachers should be aware that hygiene can be a culturally-defined practice, and both views and routines may differ from those in our Western society/culture. If you feel you need assistance with this topic, ask the school guidance counselor or health teacher for some advice or direction. It may also be helpful to consult with individuals who have cultural insight or experience.

Instructional Activity Part Three: Internal Body Parts

Display the second traced outline of the human body, and use the vocabulary cards – *Internal Body Parts* (2.4.2) and the TPR strategy to review internal body-parts vocabulary. Hold up each target vocabulary card one at a time, and point to the body part on the body outline, saying the body part as you do so. Use a small, rolled piece of masking tape to attach the card to the body outline in its appropriate location.

Note: Upon completion of the preceding activity, hang the body outline with the attached vocabulary cards somewhere prominent in the classroom. It will remain a useful visual reference for students for future lessons.

Instructional Activity: Part Four

Introduce expressions used to describe when a person is not well (see Vocabulary – *Body Parts and Health* on page 159, and *Ailments* on page 160). Act out different scenarios to engage students, such as:

- (I have a) headache.
- (I have a) toothache.
- (I have a) stomachache.
- (I have a) cold.
- (I have a) hurt (ankle).
- I hurt my (arm)

As you act out each scenario, encourage students to ask, "What is wrong?" or "Are you okay?" Stress for students that it is important to ask for help if they are in pain, sick, or need assistance from an adult. Also, highlight whom they should go to/tell at school if they are not feeling well or need help.

Review with students the expressions on the "When You Are Not Feeling Well" dialogue cards (2.4.4). Display one card for students to examine and discuss. Have them practise using the cards to prompt dialogue such as:

- Student 1: What is wrong?
- Student 2: I have a cold.

Or

- Student 1: What is wrong?
- Student 2: I hurt my finger.

Peer Activities

- Have students work in pairs to trace life-sized body outlines of themselves onto pieces of mural paper. Ask one student in each pair to lie down on the paper while his or her partner traces his or her shape; then, have the partners switch roles. Provide students with markers or coloured pencils, and have them draw clothing onto their body outlines, providing an excellent opportunity to review clothing vocabulary. Tell students to use the human body outline on display to assist them in labeling their own body outlines.

Note: If any student is not comfortable being touched during the tracing activity, teachers can draw a generic body outline similar to the student's size. The student can then use this outline to label body parts.

- Have a small group of both ELL students and peer helpers play the game Simon Says (or use another ethnically diverse name). For example, "Javier says, touch your knee" or, "Marcela says, put your hands on your head." Ask a peer helper to be the first caller and call out commands such as "touch your head," "point to your knee." Explain that all other students must follow the caller's commands, but only if he or she has said "Simon (or Javier) says," first. Students should simply stay as they are if the caller has not said "Simon (or Javier) says," first.

  Consider playing a first round or two of the game with only the peer helpers, to demonstrate for ELL students and make sure they understand how to play.

Next Step

Once ELL students are comfortable with the game, consider having them be the caller by calling out commands.

Independent Activity: Part One: Activity Sheet A

Directions to students:

Print each body-part word in the correct place on the human body picture (2.4.6).

Independent Activity: Part Two: Activity Sheet B

Directions to students:

Print each word in the correct place on the human face (head) picture (2.4.7).

Extensions

- Add new vocabulary to the multilingual word wall.

- Have students add new vocabulary to their personal vocabulary folders or personal dictionaries.

- Have students sort the vocabulary cards – *Clothing* from lesson 2 (2.2.1) by body part. For example, ask:

  - Which clothing item do we wear on our
    - feet?
    - hands?
    - heads?
    - legs?
    - arms?

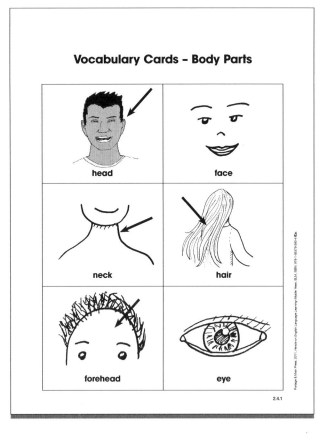
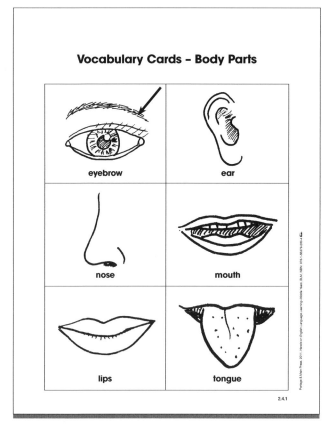
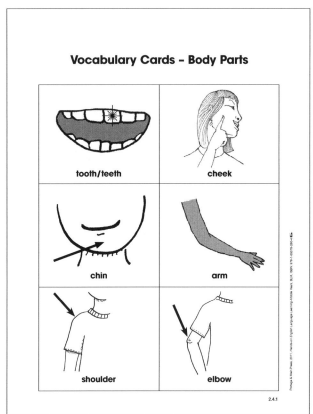
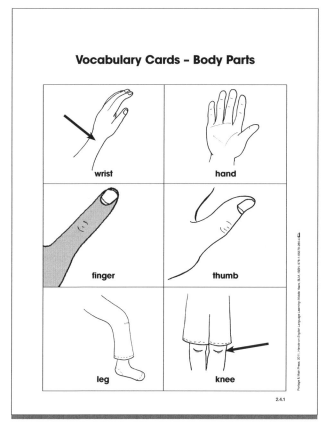

2.4.1

Vocabulary Cards - Body Parts

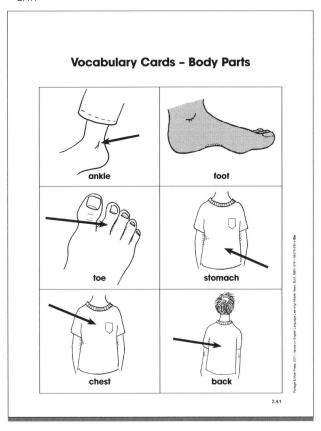

2.4.1

Vocabulary Cards - Body Parts

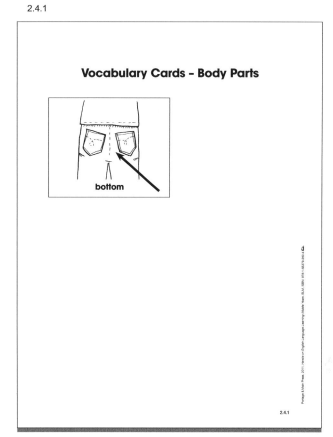

2.4.2

Vocabulary Cards - Internal Body Parts

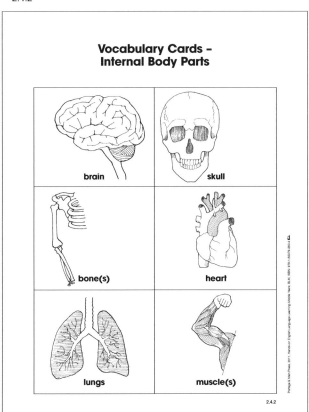

2.4.2

Vocabulary Cards - Internal Body Parts

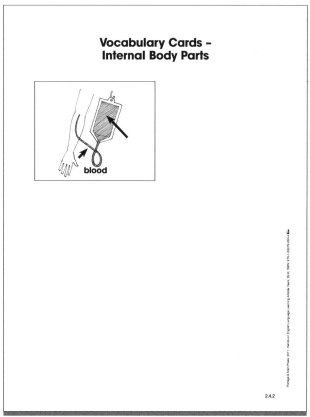

Blackline Masters

2.4.3

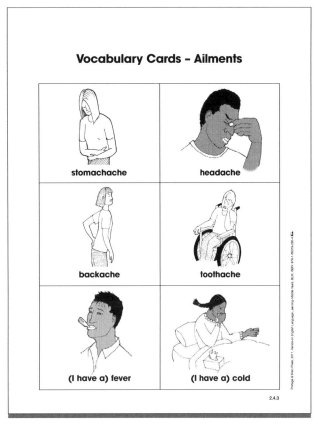

2.4.3

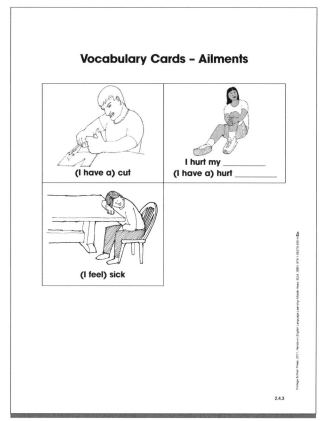

2.4.4

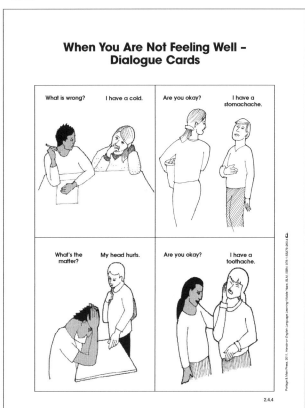

2.4.4

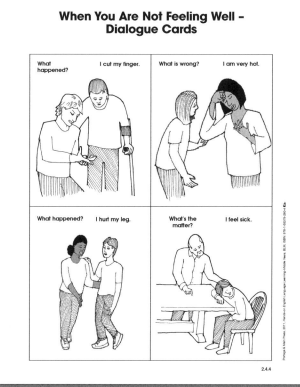

2.4.5

Date: _____ Name: _____

Career Research

Career: _____

Why does this career interest you?
_____
_____
_____

What training would you need for this career?
_____
_____
_____

Where would you get this training?
_____
_____

Describe what you think would be some of the rewards and challenges of this career.
_____
_____
_____
_____

2.4.6

Date: _____ Name: _____

The Human Body

Body Parts

head	chest	thumb	leg
face	elbow	knee	foot
neck	wrist	ankle	arm
shoulder	hand	toe	finger

4A

2.4.7

Date: _____ Name: _____

The Face

Parts of the Face

hair	eye	mouth
forehead	eyebrow	cheek
ear	teeth	chin
nose	lips	

4B

5 Physical Activities

Curricular Connections

- Language Arts: speaking, listening, reading, writing, viewing, representing
- Mathematics: tallies, graphs
- Science: living things, animals, life cycles, basic human needs, human organ systems
- Social Studies: basic human needs
- Physical Education: active living
- Health: personal health practices
- Dance: physical activity

Background Information for Teachers

Although many physical activities necessitate certain types of clothing and equipment, it is important to account for students who wear traditional attire at all times. Keep this in mind throughout the activities of this lesson.

Vocabulary – Physical Activities

- badminton
- baseball
- basketball
- cycling
- football
- golf
- hockey
- jogging/running
- rollerblading/inline skating
- skateboarding
- skiing
- snowboarding
- soccer
- swimming
- tennis
- volleyball
- walking
- hiking
- dancing
- tobogganing
- floor hockey
- wheelchair basketball
- cricket
- curling
- ultimate
- lacrosse
- gymnastics

Materials

- masking tape
- vocabulary cards – *Physical Activities* (included. Photocopy one set onto sturdy tagboard, and cut out.) (2.5.1)
- pocket chart
- chart paper
- markers
- scissors
- Go Fish cards (included. Photocopy two sets, mount onto sturdy tagboard, and cut out.) (2.5.2)
- student journals
- red and green construction paper
- large box of equipment used in any of the physical activities from the target vocabulary (for example, a hockey puck, a basketball, a pair of rollerblades, a tennis racquet)

Integrated Class Activities

- Involve the school's phys ed teacher during instruction of this lesson. Have him or her teach students various skills related to physical activities referred to in the lesson, giving students opportunity to use related English-language vocabulary in a real-life context.

- Play the game Jump the Line with students. Place a long piece of masking tape on the classroom floor. Call one side of the line "true" and one side "false." Using the vocabulary cards – *Physical Activities* as reference, make true-or-false statements that focus on specifics of each physical activity, and have students jump to (or stay on) the appropriate side of the line. For example:

- You hit a baseball with a bat (students jump to "true" side of line).
- In badminton, you hit a ball with a racquet (students jump to "false" side of line).

This activity also gives students an opportunity to discuss the purpose of, rules for, and equipment used for various physical activities.

- Plan fieldtrips to involve students in physical activities they do not do at school. For example, visit a tennis or lawn bowling club, watch a local football or cricket team practise, swim at a local pool, or have students take a golf lesson or a yoga class.

- Promote the benefits of active living and physical fitness for students, and encourage them to increase their activity levels. Consider starting a class or school walking, running, inline-skating, or cycling group.

Note: Be sure to follow safety guidelines, and have students wear required protective clothing/equipment (helmets, knee pads, and so on) during such activities.

- Challenge students to keep journals of their daily physical activities. To track their results have them make tables in their journals like the following:

Date	Physical Activity

After a week, tally the class results, and create a bar graph showing the various physical activities in which students participated.

- Integrate this lesson with an Olympics theme for an excellent opportunity to learn about various countries of the world and the sports in which they participate. Also, consider a parallel study of the Paralympics, to provide students with an opportunity to learn about these sports and athletes as well.

Whole-Class Career Connections

- Have students research the careers of athletes who have participated in the summer and winter Olympics and the Paralympics. Encourage students to select athletes from various countries and who participate in a range of sports. For each athlete, have them complete an index card with the following information:

    1. Name of Olympian/Paralympian
    2. Sport
    3. Country
    4. Awards
    5. Interesting fact

- Invite a sports psychologist to present to the class on the importance of positive thinking for success. Have the speaker refer to the Employability Skills Checklist (included with module 1, lesson 1 – 1.1.8) and discuss how athletes use these skills in their sport.

- Plan a fieldtrip to a local sporting-goods store to investigate various jobs in this field.

Instructional Activity: Part One: Assessment for Learning

Begin by determining the physical activities with which students are already familiar. Distribute scissors as well as red and green construction paper, and have each ELL student cut out one small red card and one small green card from the paper. Explain that students should hold up their green cards when you say something that is true and their red cards when you say

▶

something that is false (or not true). Model the activity first by saying such phrases as:

- I am a teacher (hold up green card for *true*)
- I have two heads (hold up red card for *false*)

Now, hold up various vocabulary cards – *Physical Activities* (2.5.1) for students to examine, and say such phrases as:

- She is playing golf.
- He is cycling.

Have students decide if the statement is true or false and hold up the appropriate card.

Use this activity to identify the physical activities with which students are unfamiliar. Select those vocabulary cards – *Physical Activities*, and use the pictures to highlight features of each activity.

Next, place all vocabulary cards into the pocket chart. Have students use the vocabulary in sentences, and record their sentences on chart paper. For example:

- I like to play football.
- The girl is dancing.
- The boy is curling.

Note: To better ensure that ELL students become familiar with these activities, take every opportunity to have them actually participate in or view the activities (attend school district sporting events, organize activities at lunch hour, have the phys ed teacher introduce new activities, and watch televised sporting events or internet clips).

Instructional Activity: Part Two

Use the vocabulary cards – *Physical Activities* to play a game of charades with students. Shuffle the cards, and place them facedown. One at a time, have an ELL student select a card and act it out while the others try to identify the activity. To ensure students understand the task, model the activity first by acting out one of the activities yourself.

Note: This is an excellent opportunity for ELL students to share physical activities unique to and/or popular in their own cultures.

Instructional Activity: Part Three: Categorizing Physical Activities

Display all the vocabulary cards, and challenge students to sort them in various ways. For example:

- team sports/individual sports
- racquet sports
- field sports
- water sports/land sports
- summer sports/winter sports
- indoor sports/outdoor sports
- sports with a ball
- sports with a stick/bat
- sports for which players wear protective clothing/equipment

Instructional Activity: Part Four

Display the box of equipment used for various physical activities. Have students take turns selecting one item from the box and matching it to the corresponding vocabulary card.

Note: This is an opportunity to extend students' English language vocabulary by learning the words used to describe this equipment (glove, mask, puck, ball, and so on).

Next, encourage students to use action words to describe how equipment is used in a given activity/sport and how the activity is performed. For example:

- In hockey, you hit the puck with the stick.
- In badminton, you use a racquet to hit a birdie over the net.

Peer Activity

Have ELL-student/peer-helper pairs use the Go Fish cards (2.5.2) to play Go Fish. Tell the pairs to deal themselves five cards each and place remaining cards facedown in a pile. Have students take turns asking their partners for a card they need to make a pair. For example:

- Do you have a basketball card?

If the partner has the card, he or she gives it to the asking student. If not, he or she says "Go Fish," and the asking student takes the top card from the pile. The object of the game is for students to match pairs of cards and use up all cards in their hands.

Independent Activity: Part One

Have students survey their classmates to find out about their favourite physical activities.

Review Activity Sheet A (2.5.3) with students as well as the directions to students (see below). Be sure to introduce and practise with students the skill of using tally marks to record (one vertical line for each count of 1 to 4, and a horizontal line for the 5th count).

Activity Sheet A

Note: This is a two-page activity sheet.

Directions to students:

Use the survey sheet to find out which physical activity students in the class like best. Ask each student: Which physical activity do you like best? Use tally marks to record the number of students who like each activity (2.5.3).

Provide an opportunity for students to present their survey findings to the rest of the class.

Note: Since public speaking may be daunting for some students, especially for English language learners, ensure that you give students time and guidance for practising their presentations.

Independent Activity: Part Two: Activity Sheet B

Directions to students:

Draw and write about your own favourite physical activities that you do

- in the summer
- in the winter
- with your family
- at school (2.5.4).

Note: Encourage students to use this activity sheet to expand their vocabulary with regard to their favourite physical activities. For example, challenge them to describe hockey using terms such as *net, goal, referee, centre, defense,* and so on.

Extensions

- Add new vocabulary to the multilingual word wall.
- Have students add new vocabulary to their personal vocabulary folders or personal dictionaries.
- Have students use their survey results from Activity Sheet A to make bar graphs.
- Have students research the origin of various sports (for example, golf originated in Scotland, while basketball originated in Canada). Use the vocabulary cards *Physical Activities* to show this on a map.

Assessment of Learning

While students are presenting their findings from the physical activity survey, assess their progress with English proficiency. Focus on students' efforts to use the new vocabulary while speaking more frequently in complete sentences. Use the Anecdotal Record sheet (I.3), shown on page 37, to record results.

Blackline Masters

Vocabulary Cards - Physical Activies

- badminton
- baseball
- basketball
- cycling
- football
- golf

Vocabulary Cards - Physical Activies

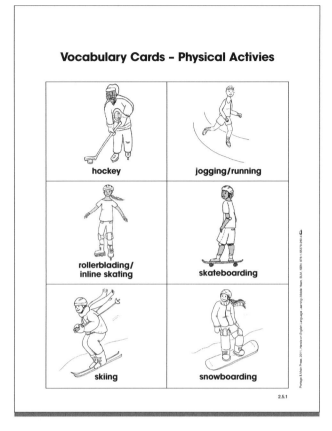

- hockey
- jogging/running
- rollerblading/inline skating
- skateboarding
- skiing
- snowboarding

Vocabulary Cards - Physical Activies

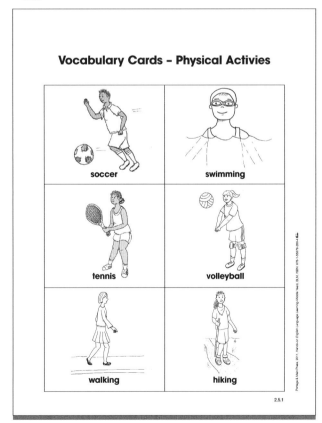

- soccer
- swimming
- tennis
- volleyball
- walking
- hiking

Vocabulary Cards - Physical Activies

- dancing
- tobogganing
- floor hockey
- wheelchair basketball
- cricket
- curling

Blackline Masters

2.5.1

Vocabulary Cards - Physical Activies

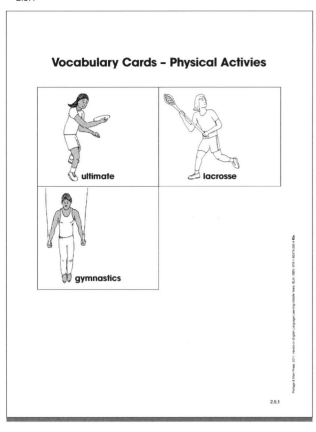

2.5.2

Go Fish Cards

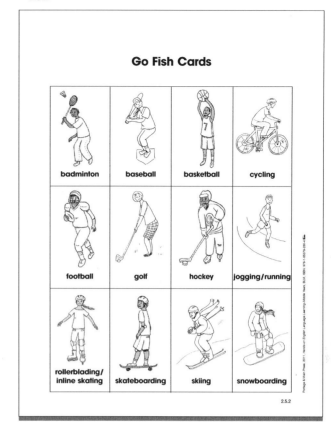

2.5.2

Go Fish Cards

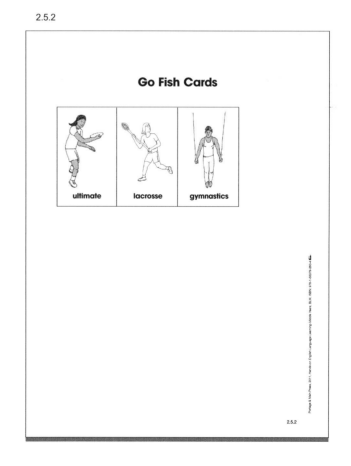

2.5.2

Go Fish Cards

Blackline Masters

2.5.3

Date: _____ Name: _____

Physical Activities Survey
Which activity do you like best?

Activity	Number of Students – Tally	Total
badminton		
baseball		
basketball		
cycling		
football		
golf		
hockey		
jogging/running		
rollerblading/ inline skating		
skateboarding		
skiing		
snowboarding		
soccer		

4A 2.5.3

2.5.3

Date: _____ Name: _____

Activity	Number of Students – Tally	Total
swimming		
tennis		
volleyball		
walking		
hiking		
dancing		
tobogganing		
floor hockey		
wheelchair basketball		
cricket		
curling		
ultimate		
lacrosse		
gymnastics		

4A 2.5.3

2.5.4

Date: _____ Name: _____

My Favourite Physical Activities

My favourite summer activity is _____, because _____.

[picture box]

Description of the activity _____
_____
_____.

My family like to _____, because _____.

[picture box]

Description of the activity _____
_____
_____.

My favourite winter activity is _____, because _____.

[picture box]

Description of the activity _____
_____
_____.

At school I like to _____, because _____.

[picture box]

Description of the activity _____
_____
_____.

5B 2.5.4

6 Hobbies and Interests

Curricular Connections

- Language Arts: speaking, listening, reading, writing, viewing, representing
- Mathematics: measuring time, tallies, graphs
- Science: science-based hobbies
- Social Studies: social-studies-based hobbies
- Music: instruments
- Art: art production

Background Information for Teachers

Cooperative learning activities can help English language learners' language development for a number of reasons:

- The speaking is natural, authentic communication.
- There is a positive interdependence as learners rely on all group members.
- Students work with a group of supportive peers, which makes it feel safer for them to take risks with the language.
- This type of activity maximizes output; output with peers can provide more social inceptive.
- When English-speaking students understand their ELL peers better, they gain an understanding of diverse backgrounds, and they become accustomed to different accents (Coelho 2004).

Vocabulary – Hobbies and Interests

- reading
- painting
- drawing
- crafts
- writing
- listening to music
- playing a musical instrument
- sewing
- knitting
- watching movies/television
- playing board games
- playing card games
- playing video games
- making puzzles
- collecting stamps
- collecting coins
- collecting rocks
- collecting sports cards
- fishing
- computer activities
- watching sports
- theatre/drama
- model building
- jewelry making

Note: Students may have other interests that could be included with the lesson. Use index cards to make additional vocabulary cards for this purpose.

Materials

- vocabulary cards – *Hobbies and Interests* (included. Photocopy one set onto sturdy tagboard, and cut out cards.) (2.6.1)
- time management sheet (included. Make seven photocopies for each student.) (2.6.2)
- index cards
- pocket chart
- chart paper
- markers/coloured pencils
- scissors
- plain, white paper plates
- transparent tape
- poster paper
- sample hobbies (rock, coin, or stamp collections, crafts, artwork, and so on; encourage students to bring in collections/artifacts from their own hobbies).
- art supplies (see fourth integrated class activity)

▶

6

Integrated Class Activities

- Have students, staff, family members, and community members share hobbies and interests with students. Consider having guests present hobbies and interests with which students might be less familiar, such as stamp or coin collecting.

- Have a discussion with students that focuses on why we have hobbies in the first place—what do hobbies give us or do for us? How do they make us feel?

- Begin a class collection with a theme of students' choice. For example, collect coins or stamps from various countries. This will also be an opportunity for students to share details about their countries of origin with their classmates.

- Begin collections that correlate with specific classroom themes and curricular topics. For example, if studying plants in science, collect seeds or potted plants for the classroom. For social studies, collect maps or Aboriginal artifacts.

- Introduce students to new hobbies through art lessons. For example, explore water-colour painting, printmaking, or pottery.

- Introduce students to new hobbies through music. Ask the school music teacher to introduce students to a variety of musical instruments. Or, have guest musicians (or students with musical talents) perform for students.

- To promote reading for interest, begin a book or reading club. Have students log their reading each day, recording the date, book read (be sure to provide books in students' first languages), and amount of time they read. After one month of reading, collect students' results, and create a class tally to show how long students read each day, or how many books they read altogether. Use the data to create bar graphs.

- To promote writing for interest, begin a young authors or poets club.

- This lesson serves as a springboard to discussion on time management, as students need to find a balance between the various aspects of their lives (family, school, peers, sports, hobbies, and so on). Provide students with seven copies of the time management sheet (included, 2.6.2), and have them track and record their activities for a one-week period. Following the recording period, discuss results. Record the amount of time students spend doing tasks such as:

  - physical activities
  - homework
  - watching television
  - playing on computers
  - sleeping
  - reading

This is an excellent opportunity to focus on the pros and cons of various leisure activities, and the importance of finding balance in one's life.

Note: To correlate with mathematics, have students create circle graphs (pie charts) to show how they spend their leisure time.

Instructional Activity: Part One

Display the vocabulary cards – *Hobbies and Interests* (2.6.1) in the pocket chart. Introduce the words *hobby* and *interest*. Ask:

- Do you know what these words mean?

If students are unsure, give an example, such as:

- I like playing the piano and making crafts in my spare time. These are my hobbies and interests.

Display and discuss some of the sample hobbies/interests, such as collections of rocks, stamps and coins, artwork, crafts, and so on.

Have ELL students share some of their own hobbies/interests, as well as those of family members.

Review the new vocabulary, discussing the various hobbies and interests. Also, have students share translations of the lesson's target vocabulary from their first language(s).

Instructional Activity: Part Two

Engage students in a chain drill activity using the vocabulary cards to support the task. Record the first few sentences on chart paper, so that students can see the repetitive pattern. For example:

- Teacher: I like reading. What do you like to do?
- Student 1: I like drawing. What do you like to do?
- Student 2: I like playing the guitar. What do you like to do?

You can vary the sentence pattern to introduce new expressions and ideas such as:

- I would like to learn to sew. What would you like to learn to do?
- Reading helps me relax. What helps you relax?

Students can also include actions with their responses, for example:

- I like playing guitar (student pretends to strum).

Peer Activity

Note: The following activity works best with a small group of ELL students and peer helpers.

- Provide each student with a white paper plate and markers or coloured pencils. Ask each student to use the markers or coloured pencils to draw his or her face on the paper plate. Then, have students flip over their paper plates and use a marker or pencil to divide them into four puzzle pieces. Tell students to record one of their own hobbies or interests onto each piece.

  Distribute scissors, and have students cut apart their puzzles. Next, tell them to turn over the puzzle pieces to show the faces and then mix up all the face pieces together on the table. Now, have students work together as a team to put each puzzle back together. Have them use clear tape to tape the completed puzzles together. Once students have assembled all the puzzles, ask them to flip them over once again and enjoy reading the backs and learning about each other.

- Have ELL students teach their peers about one of their favourite hobbies. This offers an opportunity to engage in experiential learning. ELL students can use hands-on demonstrations to teach the hobby while also developing English-language skills.

Independent Activity: Part One

Have students survey their family members to find out about their favourite hobbies and interests. Review Activity Sheet A (2.6.3) with students, as well as the directions to students (see below). Be sure to review the question on the activity sheet as well as the use of tally marks. Allow time for students to take home the activity sheet to survey family members (as well as extended family or friends, if they choose).

Note: You may wish to decide collectively how many people students should survey.

▶

Activity Sheet A

Note: This is a two-page activity sheet.

Directions to students:

Use the survey sheet to ask family members about their favourite hobbies and interests. Ask each person: What is your favourite hobby or interest? Use tally marks to record the number of people who like each activity (2.6.3).

Once students have completed the activity sheet, have them create posters with drawings and labels representing the diverse interests of their families.

Provide an opportunity for students to present their surveys and posters to the rest of the class.

Note: Since public speaking may be daunting for some students, especially for English language learners, ensure that you give students time and guidance for practising their presentations.

Independent Activity: Part Two: Activity Sheet B

Directions to students:

Draw and write about your own favourite hobby or interest. Describe what materials or equipment you need and how you do it (2.6.4).

Extensions

- Add new vocabulary to the multilingual word wall.
- Have students add new vocabulary to their personal vocabulary folders or personal dictionaries.
- Have students use their survey results from Activity Sheet A (2.6.3) to make bar graphs.

Assessment of Learning

While students are presenting their surveys and posters to the rest of the class, assess their progress. Identify criteria for the task, such as:

1. Accurate recording of survey results
2. Accurate transfer of results to poster
3. Speaking in complete sentences
4. Use of target vocabulary

Record these criteria on the Rubric (I.12), shown on page 39, and record results as students make their presentations.

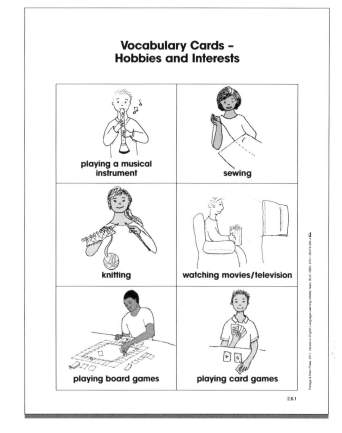

Blackline Masters

2.6.2

Date: _____ Name: _____

Time Management

Time	Activity

2.6.3

Date: _____ Name: _____

Hobbies Survey

What is your favourite hobby/interest?

Activity	Number of Students – Tally	Total
reading		
painting		
drawing		
crafts		
writing		
listening to music		
playing a musical instrument		
sewing		
knitting		
computer activiies		
model building		

6A

2.6.3

Date: _____ Name: _____

Activity	Number of Students – Tally	Total
watching movies		
playing board games		
playing card games		
playing video games		
making puzzles		
collecting stamps		
collecting coins		
collecting rocks		
collecting sports cards		
fishing		
jewelry making		
watching sports		
theatre/drama		

6A

2.6.4

Date: _____ Name: _____

My Favourite Hobby/Interest

I like to (do) _____

because _____

_____

_____

Materials or equipment needed:

_____

_____

What I do:

_____

_____

_____

6B

7 Music and Instruments

Curricular Connections

- Language Arts: speaking, listening, reading, writing, viewing, representing
- Science: sound, designing/making musical instruments
- Social Studies: cultural diversity
- Music: musical instruments

Background Information for Teachers

The first part of this lesson focuses in part on contemporary music. When playing or having students share musical favourites, or when showing music videos, be sure to preview all selections. Some lyrics or video images may not be appropriate for use in a school setting.

The second part of this lesson focuses on musical instruments. This may be of special interest to students in a band program.

Vocabulary – Music and Instruments

General Music Terms

- microphone
- speakers
- singer
- stage
- song
- band
- album
- CD (compact disc)
- radio
- music video
- instrument
- musician
- lyrics

Instruments

- guitar
- drums
- piano
- violin
- flute
- saxophone
- clarinet
- trombone
- trumpet
- tuba
- xylophone
- bongos
- accordion
- banjo
- cymbals
- harmonica
- harp
- recorder
- tambourine

Materials

- chart paper
- markers
- drawing paper
- coloured pencils or markers
- a few current recorded songs and music-video selections of interest to and appropriate for middle-years students
- wide variety of musical instruments
- pocket chart
- vocabulary cards – *General Music Terms* (included. Photocopy one set onto sturdy tagboard, and cut apart cards.) (2.7.1)
- vocabulary cards – *Instruments* (included. Photocopy one set onto sturdy tagboard, and cut apart cards.) (2.7.2)
- Guess My Card Bingo sheet (included. Make three copies for each pair of students.) (2.7.3)
- index cards
- scissors

7

- samples of different genres of music (classical, jazz, country, rock, reggae, and so on)
- samples of music from different countries
- medium for playing music samples (MP3 player, computer, CD player, or cassette player)
- game markers (for example, bingo chips, coins)
- reference material on multicultural music and instruments
- pictures of musical instruments from students' countries of origin
- various print, electronic, or online resources about musical instruments, musicians, and musical groups
- music magazines and/or access to websites with photographs of musicians
- video camera

Integrated Class Activities

- Work with the music teacher to introduce students to a variety of musical genres and instruments.
- Work with the music teacher to explore beatbox* rhythm and percussion with body parts. For example, have students create rhythmic patterns (snap fingers, clap hands, stomp feet, slap knees) to accompany favourite songs.

*Note: The term *beatbox* refers to vocal percussion—using one's mouth, lips, tongue, and voice to produce drum beats, rhythm, and musical sounds.

- Invite guest performers to demonstrate a variety of music genres and instruments. Be sure to include musicians from various cultures who play diverse instruments.
- Have all students conduct research on a musician, musical group, or instrument of their choice. These may include cultural, traditional, or popular contemporary artists and instruments. Provide students with various print, electronic, or online resources as well as a research outline or structure.

Points or topics for researching a musical artist or group might include:

- name of artist/group
- childhood, family, early musical experiences
- career timeline
- musical highlights
- other interesting facts about the artist/group
- photographs

Points or topics for researching a musical instrument might include:

- name of instrument
- country of origin of instrument
- history of instrument
- description of instrument
- labelled illustration of instrument
- how to play instrument
- famous musicians who play instrument
- other interesting facts about instrument

Whole-Class Career Connections

- In general terms, middle-years students are extremely interested in music and will take special interest in careers related to the music industry. However, there are many jobs beyond the role of rock star, and students will benefit from investigating the possibilities. Begin by having the school music, band, or choir teacher speak to the class about his or her job. Prior to the presentation, provide the teacher with a copy of the Employability Skills Checklist (included in module 1, lesson 1 – 1.1.8) so that he or she can speak about the use of these skills in the role of a music educator.

7

- Explore and research other careers in the music industry, such as work in recording, advertising, marketing, disk jockeying, broadcasting, instrument repair, and retail (music stores).
- Have students plan and role play a radio broadcast featuring their favourite music. This can also be recorded or played over the school PA system over the lunch hour or at breaks.

Instructional Activity: Part One

Distribute drawing paper and markers or coloured pencils to students. To introduce various genres of music as well as music from different countries, play a variety of music samples for students. As they listen to the recordings, have students draw pictures that describe how the music makes them feel, which instruments they hear, and so on. Following the listening activity, have students share their pictures with each other. On chart paper, record some of their thoughts and ideas about the various forms of music.

Instructional Activity: Part Two

Display the vocabulary cards – *General Music Terms* (2.7.1) in the pocket chart. Play a few selections of current music and music videos. Discuss the music, using the vocabulary cards as a focus. Ask:

- Do you like this music? Why or why not?
- How does the music make you feel?
- What is the name of the song?
- Who is performing this music?

Record the names of the musicians, bands, and songs on chart paper. Repeat this process using different musical selections.

Have students share the names of popular musicians and songs in their home countries. Record these on chart paper, and encourage students to bring in musical selections to share with classmates (or download these from online music sites). Discuss similarities and differences between various musicians and groups, and the types of music they perform.

Instructional Activity: Part Three

Display various musical instruments for students to examine and discuss. Have them try to play some of the instruments, and ask them to describe how the instruments are played and the sounds that they make. On chart paper, record sentences as students discuss and experiment with the instruments. For example:

- Hit the drum with the drumstick.
- The drum makes a loud bang.
- Shake the tambourine.
- The tambourine jingles.

Next, use the instruments to present vocabulary that describes volume and sound. For example, challenge the students to:

- Make a quiet sound with the triangle.
- Make a loud sound with the drum.
- Tap the bongo softly.
- Strike the cymbal.
- Bang the drum.
- Make a high sound on the xylophone

Note: This interactive task enables students to expand and refine vocabulary through hands-on experience, while providing an opportunity for exposure to new concepts.

Discuss the types of instruments played in students' countries of origin, and have them share their knowledge of these instruments and how they are played. Record the names of these instruments on index cards. Collect pictures of the instruments, and glue them onto the index cards to make additional vocabulary cards.

▶

Instructional Activity: Part Four

Display the vocabulary cards – *Instruments* (2.7.2), and challenge students to match the cards to the instruments on display. Also, have students share translations for this new vocabulary in their first language(s).

Next, engage students in a receptive activity, giving them directions such as:

- Show me the trumpet.
- Point to the guitar.
- Pick up the picture of the banjo.
- Hold up the card with the tuba on it.

Also, have individual students take on a leadership role by giving the commands themselves.

Extend this activity to include more details about how various instruments are played. For example, have individual students select a vocabulary card and act out playing the instrument as they describe what they are doing. For example:

- You blow on a tuba.
- You pull/pluck the strings on a guitar.
- You hit/strike the cymbal.

Finally, challenge students to sort the vocabulary cards in various ways, such as:

- Instruments with strings;
- Instruments made of metal;
- Wind instruments;
- Percussion instruments.

Peer Activities

- Provide small groups of ELL students and peer helpers with a video camera. Have each group select a favourite song and make a music video to share with the class.
- Have ELL-student/peer-helper pairs play Guess My Card Bingo. Provide each pair with scissors, a set of game markers (bingo chips, coins), and three copies of the Guess My Card Bingo sheet (2.7.3). Tell students to cut up one of the sheets to create a set of cards. Ask them to mix up the cards, and place them, facedown, in a pile between them. Have each partner use one of the remaining sheets as a game board.

Ask player A to draw a card from the pile without letting his or her partner see it. Player B has three chances to guess the instrument or music term shown on the card. If he or she guesses the instrument/term within three tries, he or she places a game marker on the appropriate instrument/term on his or her game board. If he or she does not guess the instrument/term, player A places a marker on that instrument/term on his or her game board. Play then shifts to player B, who draws a card; player A has three chances to guess the instrument/term. The first player to fill a complete row or column with game markers calls out BINGO!

Independent Activity: Part One: Activity Sheet A

Directions to students:

Complete the activity sheet to share some of your musical favourites. Collect photographs of your favourite musicians, bands, music videos, and songs to add to the sheet (2.7.4).

Independent Activity: Part Two: Activity Sheet B

Note: This is a two-page activity sheet.

Directions to students:

Make a book to tell about music in your country of origin. Cut out the sheets, and staple them together to make a booklet. Use drawings, online pictures, or digital photographs to illustrate the booklet. Fill in the following information on the book pages:

- On the first page, the title page, record the name of your country of origin and your own name. Include an illustration, photograph, or map on the title page.
- On the second page, illustrate and label some of the instruments played in your country of origin.
- On the third page, illustrate and label some musicians, bands, or singers from your country of origin.
- On the fourth page, write about yourself, and draw your self-portrait, or include a digital photograph (2.7.5).

Have students share their books with their classmates, so they can learn about multicultural music. This also provides English language learners with another venue to practise oral-language skills. On the back of the book (or on an additional sheet of paper), have classmates who have looked at the book provide their signatures and a comment about what they learned or how they enjoyed the book.

Extensions

- Add new vocabulary to the multilingual word wall.
- Have students add new vocabulary to their personal vocabulary folders or personal dictionaries.

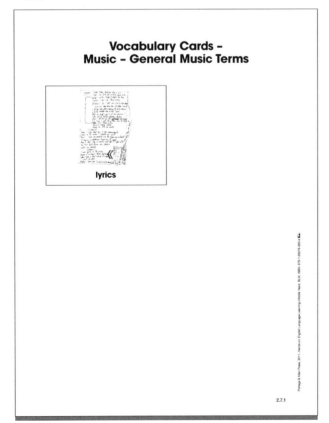
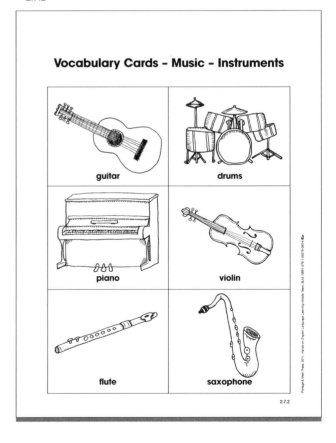

Vocabulary Cards - Music - Instruments

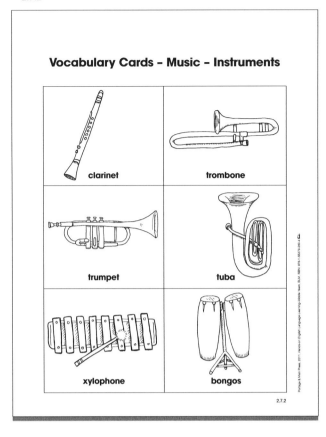

Vocabulary Cards - Music - Instruments

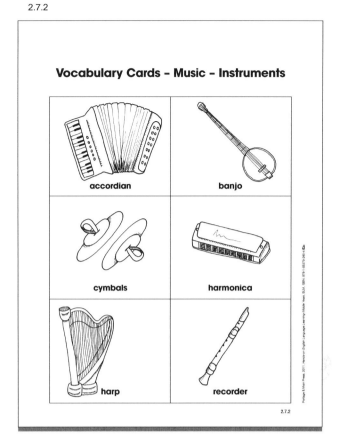

Vocabulary Cards - Music - Instruments

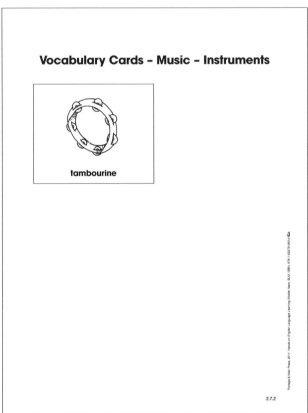

Guess My Card Bingo

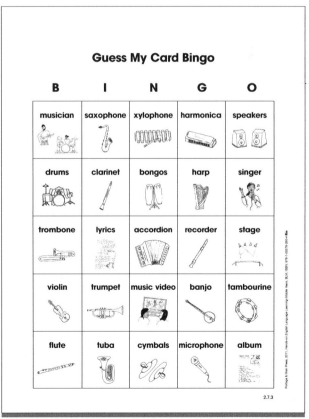

2.7.4

Date: ______________ Name: ______________________

Musical Favourites

My favourite kind of music is ____________________________
because ____ .

My favourite song is ____________________. I like the song because
____ .

My favourite music video is ___________________________ .
I like the video, because ____________________________
____ .

My favourite musician/band is __________________________
because ____
____ .

Here are some photographs of some of my musical favourites.

7A 2.7.4

2.7.5

7B

Musical Instruments:

Music In ____________
(country)

by ____________

date ____________

2.7.5

2.7.5

7B

About the Author

Musicians, Bands, and/or Singers:

2.7.5

8 Homes

Curricular Connections

- Language Arts: speaking, listening, reading, writing, viewing, representing
- Social Studies: basic human needs, cultural diversity, history, mapping skills, community
- Health: healthy living
- Art: drawing, design and colour

Background Information for Teachers

Comparing and contrasting students' homes, or students' homes from recent days and homes from the past, may be a sensitive issue for those students who have been displaced or who come from refugee camps. It is important to be aware of these situations and deal with the topic in a sensitive manner.

Vocabulary – Homes

Types of Homes

- house
- apartment
- duplex
- condominium/condo
- semi-detached home
- mobile home

Rooms and Parts

- kitchen
- refrigerator/fridge
- stove
- counter
- sink
- living room
- bedroom
- bathroom
- basement
- door
- lock
- roof
- window
- chimney
- closet

Furnishings

- table
- chairs
- sofa/couch
- coffee table
- television
- desk
- bed
- dresser

Materials

- clipboards
- paper
- pencils
- digital camera
- vocabulary cards – *Types of Homes* (included. Photocopy one set onto sturdy tagboard, and cut apart cards.) (2.8.1)
- vocabulary cards – *Rooms and Parts* (included. Photocopy one set onto sturdy tagboard, and cut apart cards.) (2.8.2)
- vocabulary cards – *Furnishings* (included. Photocopy one set onto sturdy tagboard, and cut apart cards.) (2.8.3)
- pocket chart
- chart paper
- markers
- catalogues and flyers from furniture stores
- décor/room design magazines
- poster board
- scissors
- glue
- computer with internet access and printer
- drawing paper

▶

Integrated Class Activities

- Have students bring in photographs of their current homes, as well as photos of their homes from their countries or origin, and use them to draw sketches of their homes.

- Discuss the features of *house* versus *home* — what makes a home a home? This is also a good opportunity to discuss homesickness.

- Compare and contrast homes from recent days to homes from the past. This topic will correlate well with social studies units related to local or world history. Create a Venn diagram showing common and unique features, as in the example below:

Homes

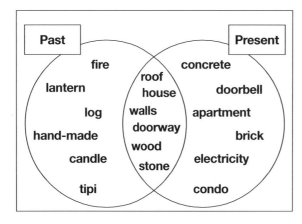

- Conduct research about the homes of Canada's Aboriginal people. Discuss how they used resources from nature, and how they designed and built their homes to protect themselves from weather conditions.

- Invite a guest speaker in to discuss local home construction.

Whole-Class Career Connections

- As a class, brainstorm a list of careers associated with the home-construction industry. List trades people and craftspeople who help to build a house.

- Visit a local community college to investigate training programs offered in various construction-related careers.

- Survey students to determine if any family members work in the construction industry or have special skills in a related field. Have these people present to the class about their jobs, skills, and training. Be sure to have students ask guests about related Employability Skills (see checklist included in module 1, lesson 1 – 1.1.8).

- One of the later activities in this lesson involves students designing and decorating their dream bedrooms (see Instructional Activity: Part Four and Independent Activity: Part Two: Activity Sheet B). Consider having an interior designer or interior decorator speak to the class about the process and provide tips and resources for student use.

Instructional Activity: Part One

Provide students with clipboards, paper, and pencils, and take them for a walk around the local school community. Discuss the different types of homes in the community, and ask students to take digital photographs of some of them. Then, have students use the photos to make sketches of the various homes.

Instructional Activity: Part Two

Following the community walk, have students share their illustrations with each other. Later, display the photos students took in the classroom. On chart paper, record students' ideas and descriptions of homes in the community.

Display the vocabulary cards – *Types of Homes* (2.8.1) in the pocket chart. Have students identify the types of homes they observed on the community walk. Introduce other types of homes as well.

Note: This is an excellent opportunity for ELL students to share information about the common types of homes in their countries of origin.

Use the vocabulary cards – *Rooms and Parts* (2.8.2) and the vocabulary cards – *Furnishings* (2.8.3) to introduce terms for the various rooms, parts, and furnishings in homes.

Instructional Activity: Part Three

Model for students the process of drawing a floor plan. Begin using the classroom as an example. Explain that they should imagine the classroom or school with no roof, and imagine themselves above the classroom, looking down on it. Draw a floor plan of the classroom on chart paper, while encouraging students to suggest features to include, and labeling each object or furnishing.

Next, draw a floor plan of your own home on chart paper. Label the plan with rooms, parts, and furnishings, having students refer to the vocabulary cards.

Have students complete Activity Sheet A, to draw a floor plan of their own homes (2.8.4).

Instructional Activity: Part Four

Have students share ideas about their dream bedrooms. Provide them with copies of Activity Sheet B (2.8.5), and explain that their next assignment will be to design the bedroom of their dreams.

Brainstorm ideas for this first, so that students can envision the wide variety of options available. For example, they might design a thematic room that portrays their favourite sport, hobby, or pastime (martial arts, outer space, dance, football), their secret inner self (superhero, scientist), or a dream for their own future (rock star, firefighter, doctor). Also, have students check out bedroom designs online and in décor magazines.

Ask students to share their ideas for their floor plans as well as furniture, colour schemes, and so on, and record these on chart paper.

Tell students to create their floor plans on Activity Sheet B (2.8.5). Have them use catalogs and internet images to find examples of furniture, carpeting, bedspread, wall colours, and other items they would choose to have in their dream bedroom.

Once they have completed their designs, have students present them to others, and encourage the audience to ask questions. This encourages public speaking and question-answering skills.

Note: An important part of this activity is students sharing their results orally, which will reinforce their learning of English vocabulary while acknowledging each student's unique ideas.

Peer Activity

Have each ELL student work with a peer helper to create a collage depicting homes from around the world. Internet image searches will provide a wide variety of examples for students to include on the collage. For example, have students search any of the following subjects:

- Homes around the world;
- Houses;
- Homes in India;
- Houses in Jamaica.

Have students print the images that they want to include on their posters, cut them out, label them by country, and display them on poster board.

Note: Encourage students to search for pictures of homes that represent the countries of origin of students in the classroom and/or within the school community.

Independent Activity: Part One: Activity Sheet A

Directions to students:

Draw a floor plan for your home. Label all rooms, parts, and furnishings (2.8.4).

Independent Activity: Part Two: Activity Sheet B

Note: This is a two-page activity sheet.

Directions to students:

Design your dream bedroom. On the first page, draw a floor plan for the bedroom. Include parts and furniture, and label them all. Then, find pictures in catalogs and flyers of furniture, carpeting, bedspread, paint colours, and other items you would choose to have in your dream bedroom. Cut out these pictures, and glue them onto the second page of the activity sheet (2.8.5).

Extensions

- Add new vocabulary to the multilingual word wall.
- Have students add new vocabulary to their personal vocabulary folders or personal dictionaries.

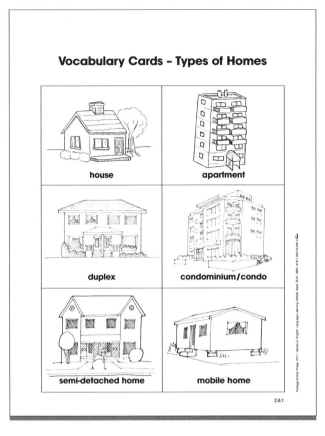
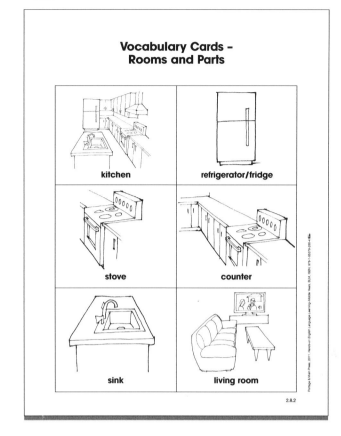
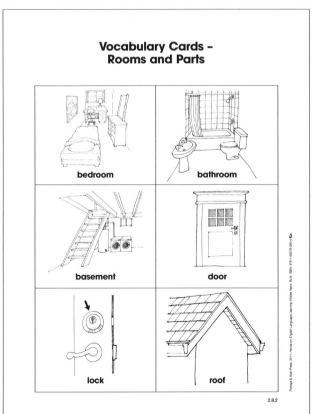
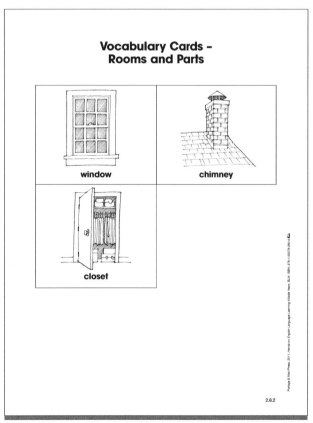

2.8.3

Vocabulary Cards - Furnishings

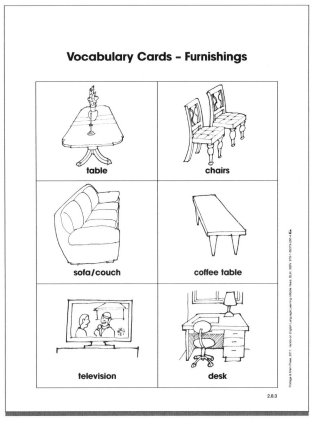

2.8.3

2.8.3

Vocabulary Cards - Furnishings

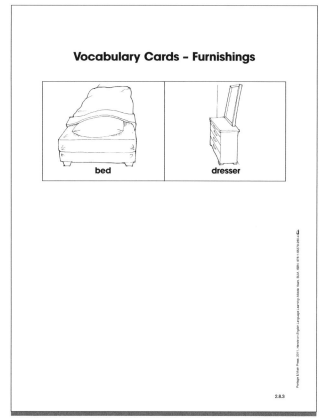

2.8.3

2.8.4

Date: _____ Name: _____

My Home

Draw a floor plan of your home. Use the words below to label the rooms, parts, and furnishings:

kitchen	refrigerator/fridge	stove	sink
living room	bedroom	counter	bathroom
door	lock	window	closet
table	chairs	sofa/couch	coffee table
television	desk	bed	dresser

8A

2.8.4

2.8.5

Date: _____ Name: _____

My Dream Bedroom

Floor Plan
Draw a labeled floor plan of your dream bedroom. Include parts and furniture.

8B

2.8.5

Date: _____ Name: _____

Decorating My Dream Bedroom

Decorate your room! Include colours, furniture, and all details!

8B

9 The Community

Curricular Connections

- Language Arts: speaking, listening, reading, writing, viewing, representing
- Social Studies: basic human needs, mapping skills, community studies
- Health: healthy living
- Art: drawing

Vocabulary – Community

- community
- street/road/avenue
- sidewalk
- highway
- traffic light
- crosswalk/pedestrian crossing
- traffic sign
- stop sign
- street sign
- building
- park
- school
- home
- map
- store
- restaurant
- hospital
- office building
- high rise
- transportation
- bus
- bus stop
- car
- bicycle/bike
- bicycle/bike route
- subway
- taxi (cab)
- route
- trees
- people
- garden

Materials

- clipboards
- paper
- pencils
- digital camera
- chart paper
- markers
- vocabulary cards – *Community* (included. Photocopy one set onto sturdy tagboard, and cut apart cards.) (2.9.1)
- community career interview template (included. Make one copy for each student.) (2.9.2)
- pocket chart
- index cards
- telephone books and/or business directories
- map of local community (wall map or small maps for each student, available online. For example, type the name of your local community/district into the search bar at <http://maps.google.ca>)

Note: This map should show the area immediately surrounding the school.

Integrated Class Activities

- This is an excellent opportunity to review community safety with all students. Discuss the importance of traffic safety, personal safety, and safety related to specific community features (such as water safety if the school is located near a river).

- Discuss ways that students can be positive community citizens through their choices and actions. For example, have a community cleanup event, make posters to discourage graffiti, or raise funds for local park improvement.

- Discuss community governance, local politics, and the election process.

196 Hands-On English Language Learning • Middle Years

9

Whole-Class Career Connections

- Explore the wide variety of service-based careers in your local community, including elected officials, community-service workers, local police, emergency services, utilities workers, recreation staff, as well as store and business owners.

- Have each student select someone from the local community to interview via email or telephone. Distribute copies of the community career interview template (2.9.2), and have students use it to formulate and record their questions. Later, have students share their interview responses with the rest of the class.

Note: Some ELL students may find it less difficult to conduct the interview via email, so they can take time to formulate questions and understand responses.

- Invite local community workers to present to the class, discussing their training and skills as well as the rewards and challenges of the job. Be sure to have students ask guest speakers about how they use Employability Skills in their daily work (see checklist included in module 1, lesson 1 – 1.1.8).

Instructional Activity: Part One

Provide students with clipboards, paper, and pencils, and take a walk around the local school community. Take a digital camera with you. During the walk, have students list all of the things they see in the community (homes, roads, buildings, signs, and so on). Discuss the different features of the community, and take digital photographs of them. Later, have students use the photos to draw sketches that show the various features of the community.

Instructional Activity: Part Two

On chart paper, record the term *Community*. Have students read the word aloud and provide any ideas they have about its meaning. Record students' ideas on the chart paper. Explain that a community is a place where people live and work. Ask:

- What is the name of our community? (record the name on chart paper)

- What different things did you see in our community during our walk?

- How was it different from a walk in the community where you used to live?

Have students review the features and buildings that they observed on the walk. Also display the digital photographs.

Display the vocabulary cards – *Community* (2.9.1) in the pocket chart, and have students match the cards to the features they identified.

Note: Take this opportunity to discuss the local communities in students' home countries from which they came. Record the names and features of these communities, and discuss similarities and differences.

Instructional Activity: Part Three

Display the wall map of the local community, or provide students with individual copies of the map. Ask:

- On which street is our school located?

Record the school's address on chart paper. Challenge students to locate the school on the map.

Have students explain how they get to school. Challenge them to use the map to describe the route they take.

▶

Note: If some students live farther away than the area depicted on the map, provide a map of the larger area.

Instructional Activity: Part Four

Display all vocabulary cards – *Community* in the pocket chart. Use the vocabulary as a springboard to a discussion on safety in the community. Focus on traffic safety, personal safety, and safety related to specific community features (such as water safety around ponds, rivers, and pools).

Create a chart to record safety rules.

Note: If you have already discussed safety issues with the whole class (see first integrated class activity), you may need only to review briefly here, or the preceding activity may not be necessary at all.

Peer Activity

Have ELL students work with peer helpers to explore services that are available in the local community. First, have them brainstorm a list of the businesses found in the community. Encourage them to include restaurants, stores, service stations, health clinics, and any other businesses. Ask them to record the name of each business.

Next, provide students with index cards and local telephone books and/or business directories, and have them write riddles about the various services. Riddles can include hints about location, appearance, and services provided. For example:

Riddle:

- It is located on Perch Street
- It is a red brick building.
- You will notice the smell of cookies when you walk by.

What is it?

Answer: Beto's Bakery

Place the riddles in an envelope, and display them along with the community map. Challenge all students in the class to solve the riddles.

Independent Activity: Part One: Activity Sheet A

Directions to students:

Complete the chart to show different features of your community. Add some of your own ideas as well (2.9.3).

Independent Activity: Part Two: Activity Sheet B

Directions to students:

Draw and write about the route you take to school (2.9.4).

Independent Activity: Part Three: Activity Sheet C

Directions to students:

Record rules that show how to stay safe in the community. Describe a specific example for your community, and include an illustration. For example:

Rule: Cross the street at crosswalks.
Example: Use the crosswalk on Dafoe Street and Peel Avenue (2.9.5).

Extensions

- Add new vocabulary to the multilingual word wall.
- Have students add new vocabulary to their personal dictionaries or personal vocabulary folders.
- Take a fieldtrip on a city bus. As a group, use the following steps to plan the fieldtrip:
    1. Find the final destination on a community map.
    2. Find the bus route online or by using a bus schedule.

3. Decide on time/schedule of departure, arrival, and return.
4. Create a permission note for parents/guardians to fill out.
5. Take a digital camera on the trip, and take photos along the route and at the final destination.
6. When you return, create a photo journal of the trip. Make copies of the photos for each student, and have them write a sentence for each picture that tells something about the trip. This can become part of their personal reading material and something to share with family members.

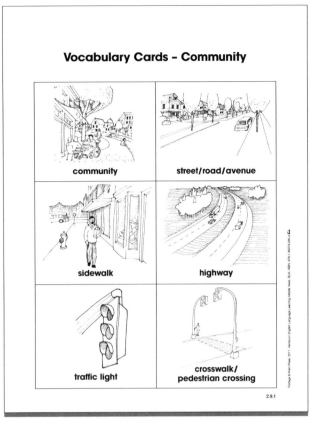
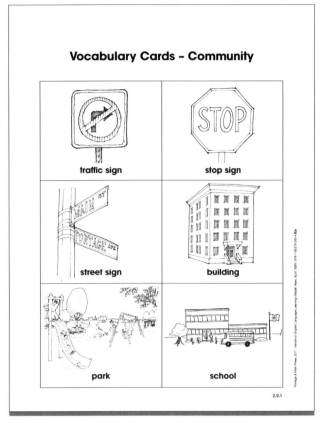

2.9.1

Vocabulary Cards – Community

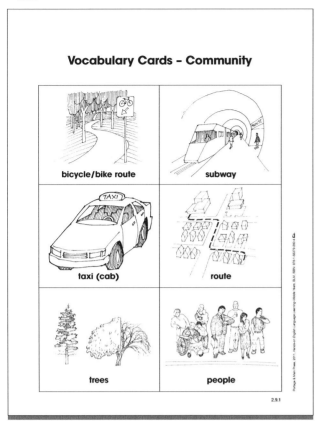

2.9.1

Vocabulary Cards – Community

garden

2.9.2

Date: _____ Name: _____

Community Career Interview

Name of Interviewee: _____ Career: _____
Email address: _____
Work location: _____

Record 5 questions to ask this person about his or her job. Be sure to ask about training, skills, rewards, and challenges of the job. Record your interviewee's answer below each question.

1. _____
Answer: _____

2. _____
Answer: _____

3. _____
Answer: _____

4. _____
Answer: _____

5. _____
Answer: _____

Other interesting facts: _____

2.9.3

Date: _____ Name: _____

My Community

Feature	Local Example (name, location, or description)
Street	
Traffic Light	
Cross Walk/ Pedestrian Crossing	
Park	
Store	
Home	

Describe a store in your local community. Where is it located? What does it look like? What is sold there?

_____
_____
_____
_____

9A

Blackline Masters

2.9.1 – 2.9.3 – 201

Blackline Masters

2.9.4

Date: _____ Name: _____

My Route to School

Describe your route to school. Include street names and community features that you pass along the way.

_____
_____
_____
_____
_____
_____
_____

Draw a map showing your route to school.

9B

2.9.5

Date: _____ Name: _____

Safety in the Community

Rule	Example	Illustration

9C

10 Ordering Food

Curricular Connections

- Language Arts: speaking, listening, reading, writing, viewing, representing
- Mathematics: recognizing and counting money, making change
- Science: basic human needs
- Social Studies: cultural diversity, basic human needs
- Physical Education: healthy lifestyle choices
- Health: Canada Food Guide
- Drama: role playing

Background Information for Teachers

This lesson focuses on ordering food within the local community and the vocabulary students may need to use while doing so. For example, students may need to request milk at a school canteen, ask for ice cream from an ice cream truck, or order a meal at a restaurant. This lesson provides an opportunity for students to enhance their English language skills for practice in a real-life context. Continue to encourage students to make healthy food choices. Consider reviewing lesson 3 about food before beginning this lesson, paying particular attention to activities that focus on the *Canada Food Guide*.

Note: This lesson does not assume that students will be out in the community on their own. It is expected that students will be supervised or monitored by adults during these types of outings.

Vocabulary – Ordering Food

Ordering Food

- milk
- ice cream
- chocolate
- vanilla
- strawberry
- muffin
- butter
- salad
- dressing
- drink
- orange juice
- napkin
- please
- thank you
- change

Helpful Phrases

- May I please have…?
- How much?
- Do you want…?
- Would you like…?
- Here is your change.
- over there

Materials

- dialogue cards 1–4 (included. Photocopy, and cut out cards.) (2.10.1)
- vocabulary cards – *Ordering Food* (included. Photocopy one set onto sturdy tagboard, and cut apart cards.) (2.10.2)
- vocabulary cards – *Helpful Phrases* (included. Photocopy one set onto sturdy tagboard, and cut apart cards.) (2.10.3)

Note: A few of the vocabulary terms in this lesson are abstract and difficult to illustrate. For these vocabulary cards, only the word is included on the card. As teachers and students discover visual examples of each, they are encouraged to add these to the card.

- pocket chart
- menu cards 1–3 (included. Make a copy of each menu for each student.) (2.10.4)
- vocabulary cards – *Food* (included in lesson 3) (2.3.1)
- poster paper
- markers
- grocery-store and restaurant fliers

Module 2

10

- play dishes
- toy food
- toy cash register
- play money
- supplies for food-related fundraisers (for example, popcorn, small bags, table/stand) (see fourth integrated class activity)
- coupons for local restaurants

Integrated Class Activities

- Take fieldtrips to local restaurants that reflect the cultural diversity of the community.
- Have students use menus to create and solve math word problems. For example, have them use menu cards 1–3 (2.10.4), as well as those that they make during the peer activity (see page 205), to write problems such as the following:
  - Mario earned $5 by mowing his neighbour's lawn. He wants to use the money to buy ice cream for himself and his mom. What could he buy at Ike's Ice Cream Shop?
  - How much would it cost to buy a medium mushroom and green pepper pizza at Pappa's Pizza?

  Once they have created their math problems, have students trade them with classmates to solve.
- Have students plan and participate in food-related fundraisers for selected charities or environmental organizations. For example, have a popcorn sale or a watermelon or juice stand on a hot day. This activity encourages development of skills focused on in the lesson, including counting money, making change, and using related vocabulary.

Whole-Class Career Connections

- Take fieldtrips to various local restaurants to observe how this type of business is run and operated. Discuss job descriptions with employees, managers, and owners.

Note: If possible, visit restaurants that reflect students' cultural backgrounds.

- As a class, plan a fundraising project based on selling/ordering food. Choose an issue as a class, considering various fundraising organizations with an environmental or social-justice focus. Students can choose nutritious snacks (for example, popcorn, juice pops, granola bars, fresh fruit, yogurt tubes, or pretzels) to sell during breaks or lunch hour. This is an excellent opportunity to correlate with mathematics in the following ways:
  - Price various potential snack foods in local stores;
  - Determine unit prices;
  - Determine possible selling prices;
  - Choose snacks based on nutrition and profit.

Note: During the planning and implementation of the fundraiser, discuss the Employability Skills Checklist (included in module 1, lesson 1; 1.1.8), reflecting on the types of skills students used.

- Examine coupons for local restaurants. Have students determine the best deals based on nutrition and cost.

Instructional Activity: Part One

Display dialogue card 1 (2.10.1) for students. Ask:

- What is happening in this picture?

Together as a group, read the speech bubbles on the card. Focus on the target vocabulary as it is used.

10

Have two students role play the scene from the card. Or, if you are working with only one ELL student, role play along with the student.

Repeat the process to introduce each of the four dialogue cards.

Discuss students' experiences with each of these types of situations. For example, ask:

- Have you bought ice cream from an ice-cream truck or stand?
- What did you order?
- How much did it cost?
- What is your favourite kind of juice?
- Do you like muffins?
- If so, what kind is your favourite?
- Do you like butter on your muffins?
- Do you like hotdogs?
- Do you like salads?
- Do you like to put dressing on your salad?
- What kind?
- What is your favourite meal to order at a restaurant?

Instructional Activity: Part Two

Display the four dialogue cards in the pocket chart. Describe an item or person in one of the scenes.

For example:

- I am selling muffins. Who am I?

Have a student point to the person working at the muffin shop.

Continue in the same way, but now, have students provide clues or descriptions of things that they see in the dialogue cards, such as:

- I am a frozen treat. What am I?
- I am ordering a salad. Who am I?
- I am made from oranges. What am I?
- I work at a restaurant. Who am I?
- I am made with vegetables. What am I?

Have students identify each item or person as you provide the description.

Instructional Activity: Part Three

Provide students with copies of the three menu cards (2.10.4). Discuss the format of the menus, including headings, foods listed on the left, prices listed on the right.

Have students use the menus to practise dialogue they would use when ordering these foods. Begin with the student acting as the customer and you as the person working in the restaurant/shop, then switch roles.

Note: Be sure to focus on students' pronunciation during the dialogue sessions. Depending on how much pronunciation work you have already done, this activity could easily branch out into one or more separate lessons.

The dialogue activity is also an excellent opportunity to focus on colloquialisms, contractions, and informal language. Try to make your dialogue with students sound as natural and true-to-life as possible. For example, someone whose first language is English might say, "What can I getchya?" rather than "What can I get for you?" Or, he or she might use contractions such as "We don't have any left."

It is important for students to be exposed to this kind of language as well.

Use the vocabulary cards – *Helpful Phrases* (2.10.3) to review all new terminology with students.

Peer Activity

Provide poster paper, markers, and grocery-store and restaurant fliers. Have ELL students work with peer helpers to create menus for a school canteen or a local restaurant. Encourage the inclusion of healthy choices as menu selections.

Note: This is an excellent opportunity to have students create menus with cultural diversity that reflects foods from their countries of origin or other favourites.

Independent Activity: Part One: Activity Sheet A

Directions to students:

Look at each picture. Read the sentences in the speech bubbles at the bottom of the page. For each picture, print the correct sentence in the blank speech bubble. Then, complete the two sentences at the bottom of the page (2.10.5).

Independent Activity: Part Two: Activity Sheet B

Directions to students:

Describe what you think is happening in each picture (2.10.6).

Extensions

- Add new vocabulary to the multilingual word wall.
- Have students add new vocabulary to their personal vocabulary folders or personal dictionaries.
- Create a class cookbook with submissions from each student and family. Include cultural dishes, family favourites, dishes prepared for cultural celebrations, and so on. This is an excellent activity for integrating mathematics skills (measurement) and skills related to sequencing events and following directions. Consider photocopying the cookbook and selling it to raise money for a charitable cause.

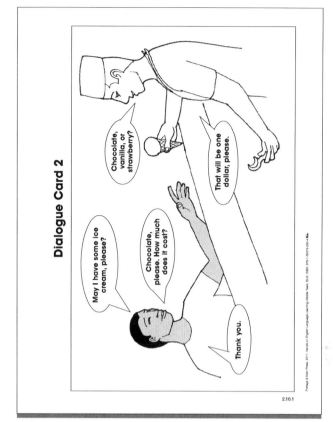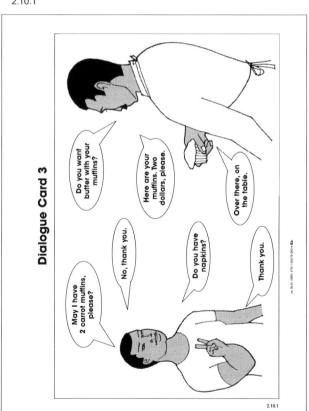

Blackline Masters

2.10.2

Vocabulary Cards – Ordering Food

2.10.2

Vocabulary Cards – Ordering Food

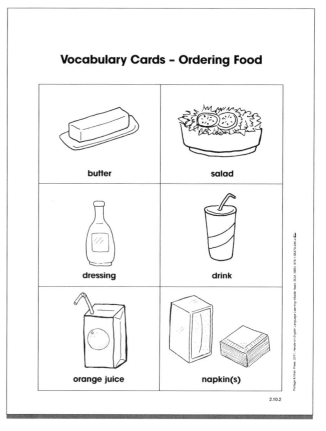

2.10.2

Vocabulary Cards – Ordering Food

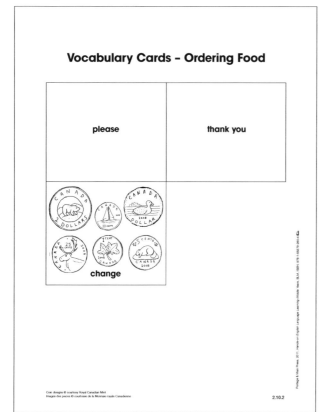

2.10.3

Vocabulary Cards – Helpful Phrases

May I please have…?	How much?
Do you want…?	Would you like…?
Here is your change.	over there

208 – 2.10.2

Menu Card 1

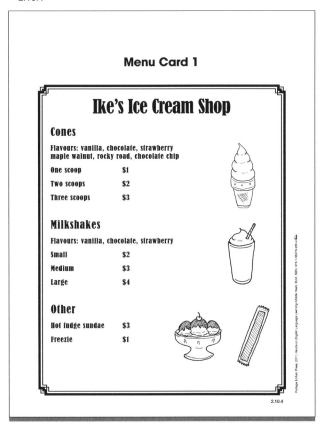

Ike's Ice Cream Shop

Cones
Flavours: vanilla, chocolate, strawberry, maple walnut, rocky road, chocolate chip

One scoop	$1
Two scoops	$2
Three scoops	$3

Milkshakes
Flavours: vanilla, chocolate, strawberry

Small	$2
Medium	$3
Large	$4

Other

Hot fudge sundae	$3
Freezie	$1

Menu Card 2

Pappa's Pizza

Small cheese pizza	$ 5
Medium cheese pizza	$ 7
Large cheese pizza	$10

Toppings: $ 1 each

Pepperoni Green peppers Mushrooms

Onions Ham Olives Pineapple

Menu Card 3

Juan's Place

Sandwiches

Grilled Cheese	$3
Salad Wrap	$3
Chicken burger	$4
Veggie burger	$4

Side Dishes

French fries	$2
Salad	$3
Veggies and dip	$3

Drinks $1
Milk
Chocolate milk
Soft drinks
Lemonade
Iced tea

Ordering Food

Date: _____ Name: _____

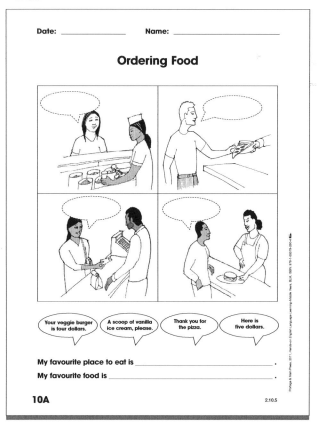

Your veggie burger is four dollars.
A scoop of vanilla ice cream, please.
Thank you for the pizza.
Here is five dollars.

My favourite place to eat is _____ .
My favourite food is _____ .

10A

Blackline Masters

2.10.6

Date: _____ Name: _____

Story Starters

10B

2.10.6

210 – 2.10.5

11 Technology

Curricular Connections

- Language Arts: speaking, listening, reading, writing, media literacy, viewing, representing, critical literacy
- Social Studies: communication, cultural diversity

Background Information for Teachers

Technology-related activities will benefit all middle-years students, including topics related to safety and appropriate use of technology.

Vocabulary – Technology

- computer
- laptop computer
- keyboard
- mouse
- monitor
- printer
- hard drive
- CD (compact disc)
- memory stick
- word processing
- internet
- website
- email
- speakers
- scanner
- webcam
- cell phone
- text message
- online
- URL (address)
- MP3

Materials

- vocabulary cards – *Technology* (included. Photocopy onto sturdy tagboard, and cut apart cards.) (2.11.1)
- access to computer hardware, projector, software, and the internet
- chart paper
- marker
- pocket chart

Integrated Class Activities

- As a class, brainstorm all of the vocabulary that students are familiar with related to computer technology. This may include some of the vocabulary listed at the left, as well as additional vocabulary such as:

  - blog
  - glog
  - social media
  - instant message
  - Facebook
  - Twitter
  - spam
  - iMovie
  - iBook
  - iTunes
  - iPad
  - Comic Life
  - application (app)

  Use hands-on examples to discuss the meaning of this terminology. Have access to a computer and projector or to a computer lab so that students can explore these examples of computer technology. Create class definitions for each term on the list, and record these on chart paper.

- Discuss internet safety issues. Consider bringing in a guest speaker, such as a member of the local police department who has expertise in this area.

- Discuss issues related to online bullying. Present case examples from current events to stress the importance of appropriate use of computer technology.

11

- Create analogies and metaphors related to computer-technology terminology, using the vocabulary cards as reference. For example:
  - A computer is like a house.
  - The hard drive is like a cupboard, because it stores the things we use.
  - The monitor is like a window, because we can see the results of what's happening on the inside.
  - A memory stick is like a book that holds information and can be taken to other places.
- Discuss cell phone rules for school and for personal safety. Be sure to focus on privacy issues when taking photographs, and text-message bullying.

Whole-Class Career Connections

- Have school or school-district/division computer-technology (IT) staff describe their jobs to students. Encourage students to refer to the Employability Skills Checklist (included in module 1, lesson 1; 1.1.8) when formulating questions for guest speakers.
- Explore local career colleges to determine types of careers and training courses available in the computer-technology sector.
- Have students research computer companies such as Microsoft, Dell, Apple, and Hewlett Packard. Encourage them to gather information such as:
  - The full name of the company
  - The name of the President/CEO
  - The type of business
  - The number of employees
  - Profits from last year
  - Stock market information
  - Social action (explore what charities or social issues the company supports)

Instructional Activity: Part One

Display the vocabulary cards – *Technology* (2.11.1). Using a classroom computer, have students match the cards to the parts. During this activity, discuss proper use and care of computers.

Use appropriate software to introduce additional vocabulary such as *word processing, website, email,* and so on.

Provide students with plenty of opportunities to explore computer software and hardware. This hands-on exposure will help to develop their understanding and use of related vocabulary.

Instructional Activity: Part Two

Display all vocabulary cards in the pocket chart. Use the vocabulary as a springboard to a discussion on safety when using technology. Focus on internet safety as well as cell phone safety. Be sure to discuss bullying related to both of these forms of technology.

Create a chart to record safety rules.

Note: If you have already reviewed technology safety issues with the class (see the second, third, and fifth activities from the Integrated Class Activities section), a brief review of these safety issues will suffice here with ELL students.

Peer Activity

Provide opportunities for ELL students to work alongside peers on a variety of computer-related tasks. Have them use selected websites to conduct research, search for images, play educational games, and publish written work.

11

Independent Activity: Part One: Activity Sheet A

Directions to students:

Use the words on the right-hand side of the page to label the computer. Then, record a list of rules or guidelines for proper use and care of a computer (2.11.2).

Independent Activity: Part Two: Activity Sheet B

Directions to students:

Record rules or guidelines for safe and responsible use of computers and cell phones (2.11.3).

Extensions

- Add new vocabulary to the multilingual word wall.
- Have students add new vocabulary to their personal vocabulary folders or personal dictionaries.

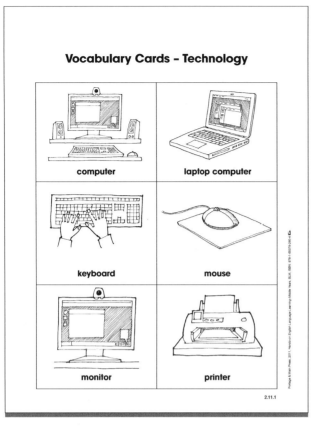
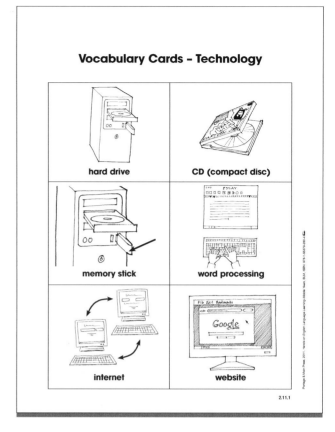
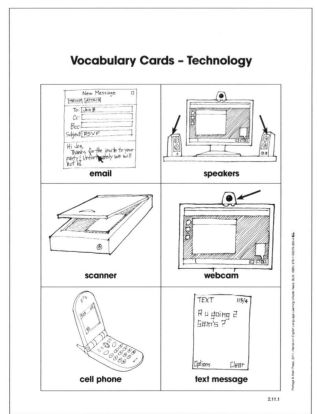
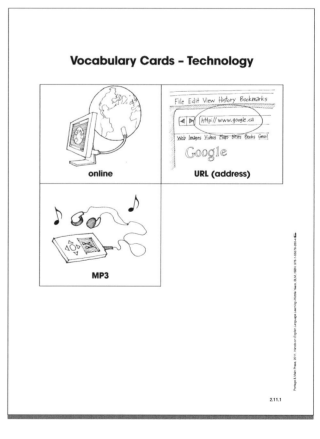

2.11.2

Date: _____ Name: _____

Computer Technology

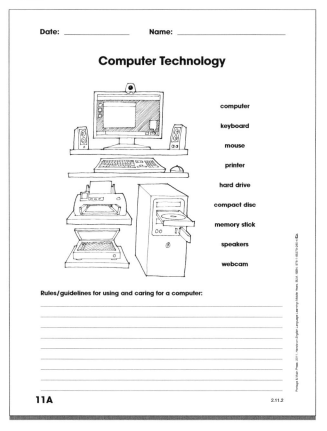

computer
keyboard
mouse
printer
hard drive
compact disc
memory stick
speakers
webcam

Rules/guidelines for using and caring for a computer:
_____
_____
_____
_____
_____
_____

11A

2.11.3

Blackline Masters

11B

Name: _____

Using Technology Safely and Responsibly

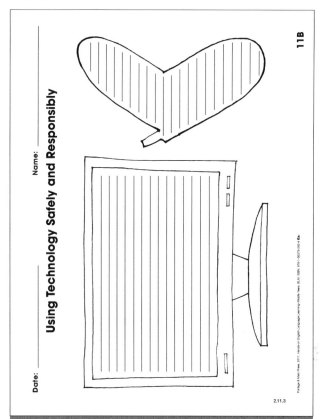

Date: _____

2.11.2 – 2.11.3 – 215

12 | Culminating Activity: Creating an "All About Me" Electronic Portfolio

Curricular Connections

- Language Arts: speaking, listening, reading, writing, viewing, representing
- Social Studies: cultural diversity, personal responsibility
- Health: Healthy lifestyle choices, personal well being
- Music: music appreciation

Background Information for Teachers

This lesson offers students an opportunity to consolidate their learning by developing a personal portfolio related to the topics studied in this module. Tasks included in this culminating activity focus on information and communication technology skills relevant to middle-years learners. These include:

- Communicating electronically, through the use of telecommunication tools and applications such as email, the internet, blogs, tweets, instant messaging, and so on;
- Designing and constructing concept maps using various software programs;
- Using multimedia and integrated software to create presentations that include digital images, graphics, video, and sound;
- Using software to create graphics;
- Using digital and video cameras to make presentations;
- Acquiring information and material from network, electronic, and online resources;
- Demonstrating grade-appropriate keyboarding and desktop-publishing skills (based on local and provincial/territorial guidelines or standards).

– Manitoba Education <www.edu.gov.mb.ca/k12/tech/imym/resources/index.html>

Note: The purpose of the portfolio students create in this lesson is not only to demonstrate their computer skills but also to share what is important about them and to show evidence of their learning in a variety of areas. Give students the freedom to create unique portfolios that reflect themselves and support their learning. Allow them to decide what to include in the portfolio, as long as it relates to the lessons in this module. The independence to choose selections based on their own learning will provide students with a clear purpose, and because they have chosen purposefully, they will be able to speak about the work, and explain how it shows their learning or what it tells about them and their interests. Each student may choose different items to include in his or her portfolio, but the items will be relevant to him or her. This emphasizes respect for individuals and encourages ownership of learning.

Materials

- student vocabulary folders and personal dictionaries
- vocabulary cards and activity sheets from all lessons in this module
- All About Me – Electronic Portfolio template (included. Make a copy for each student.) (2.12.1)
- digital and video cameras
- access to computers and to various software

Note: Students may want to use computers and various programs to create portfolio items (for example, PowerPoint presentations or comic strips using comic life software).

Instructional Activity: Part One

Using the All About Me – Electronic Portfolio template (2.12.1) as a guide, have students review key vocabulary from the previous 12 lessons. Discuss each item on the template, and encourage students to provide ideas about what they might include in their portfolios. Reviewing activity sheets may assist in this task. Also have students use the vocabulary cards and

12

other classroom cues for support during this discussion.

Guide students in planning their "All About Me" electronic portfolios, which should include a variety of work samples showing evidence of their learning in topics focused on in this module. Students do not need to include all topics listed on the template, and they may also provide additional ideas if they wish.

Note: It may be necessary to provide blocks of time for students to develop their portfolios. Consider having peer helpers assist with specific components, as required. For example, ELL students may need someone to help record them if they are including an oral presentation or demonstration.

Instructional Activity: Part Two

Discuss the skills necessary for making a presentation, and record criteria on chart paper. Next, model a presentation for students, and have them identify how you met the criteria in your presentation (eye contact with audience, clear speaking voice, and so on). Then, have students plan and practise presenting their portfolios.

Independent Activity: Activity Sheet A

Directions to students:

Use the Project Tracking sheet to keep track of your progress as you create your electronic portfolio. Record each task (accomplishment) that you complete as well as the date you completed it (2.12.2).

Assessment for Learning

Have students present their "All About Me" electronic portfolios to you as a means of developing presentation skills. This also provides you with an opportunity to assess students' vocabulary development related to specific topics in this module. Following each student's presentation, ask him or her questions that focus on the module's vocabulary, concepts, and the process used to develop the portfolio.

Assessment as Learning

Through discussion, ask students to explain what they like best about their portfolios, and what they would like to change if they could. This offers an opportunity for self-assessment through focused oral responses in a safe and comfortable environment.

Peer Activity

Provide an opportunity for students to share their All About Me portfolios with each other. Begin by having them share their portfolios with one or two peers (it may be intimidating to share in front of a whole group). You may also encourage the audience to ask the presenter one or two simple questions.

Assessment of Learning

Base criteria for All About Me portfolios on each ELL student's individual skills and needs. Work with students to develop these criteria, and create a student checklist for recording self assessment. For example, criteria may include:

- I have included examples that show my learning in English vocabulary, writing, and reading;
- I have included examples from several different lesson topics;
- I have made an interesting display;
- I have used computer technology to demonstrate my skills.

As an alternative, the criteria might focus strictly on oral presentation of the portfolio. In this case, criteria might include:

- I can explain why I chose each piece in my portfolio;

▶

12

- I can select a piece that shows my English learning;
- I have described my personal interests;
- I can describe areas that I need to work on more.

Record criteria on the Rubric (I.12), shown on page 39, and record results for each student.

All About Me – Electronic Portfolio

Date: _____ Name: _____

Topic	Examples	My Ideas
1. Emotions	• Write about a time you felt happy, sad, or shy.	
2. Clothing	• Video fashion show • Design an outfit	
3. Food	• Cooking demonstration • Foods for your family's special occasions	
4. Body Parts and Health	• Self-portrait • Health or exercise plan	
5. Physical Activities	• Graph your exercise • Sports you would like to learn	
6. Hobbies and Interests	• Record yourself doing a hobby or interest • Research a new hobby	
7. Music and Instruments	• Slideshow of favourite bands • Sing a song	
8. Homes	• Home tour (make a narrated digital video or an artistic rendition to describe orally) • Design a new home	
9. The Community	• Tell about another community in which you lived • Describe or tour your favourite place in our community	
10. Ordering Food	• Restaurant critic: Review your favourite restaurant	
11. Technology	• Design a website • Make a slide show	
12. Career Connection	• Reflect on your future • Record a family member at work	
13. Personal Choice	• Anything you want!	

Project Tracking

Date: _____ Name: _____

Your portfolio should include:
1. Title page or opening
2. Scanned copies of selected activity sheets
3. Writing samples
4. Photographs
5. Video
6. Sound effects, speech, and/or music
7. Closing

Remember that this is a personal portfolio, so it should describe YOU!

Start Date: _____ Due Date: _____

Time Management Record

Date	Accomplishment

12A

Blackline Masters

References for Teachers

Almada, Patricia. *English in My Pocket.* Barrington, IL: Rigby, 2000.

Azar, Betty Schrampfer. *Understanding and Using English Grammar,* 4th edition. White Plains, NY: Pearson Education, 2009.

Brown, Susan C., and Marcella Kysilka. *Applying Multicultural and Global Concepts in the Classroom and Beyond.* Boston: Allyn and Bacon, 2002.

Brownlie, Faye, Catherine Feniak, and Vicki McCarthy. *Instruction and Assessment of ESL Learners: Promoting Success in Your Classroom.* Winnipeg: Portage & Main Press, 2004.

Coelho, Elizabeth. *Adding English: A Guide to Teaching in Multilingual Classrooms.* Toronto: Pippin, 2003.

Cook, Vivian. "Going Beyond the Native Speaker in Language Teaching." *TESOL Quarterly,* vol. 33, no. 2 (summer 1999): 185–209.

Grant, Linda. *Well Said: Pronunciation for Clear Communication.* Boston, MA: Heinle & Heinle, 2001.

Grigsby, Carolyn. *Amazing English! An Integrated ESL Curriculum.* Lebanon, Indiana: Addison-Wesley, 1995.

Health Canada. *Eating Well with Canada's Food Guide.* Ottawa: Publications Health Canada, 2007.

Herrell, Adrienne, and Michael Jordan. *Fifty Strategies for Teaching English Language Learners,* 3rd edition. Upper Saddle River, NJ: Pearson/Merrill Prentice Hall, 2008.

High, Julie. *Second Language Learning Through Cooperative Learning.* San Clemente, CA: Kagan Cooperative Learning, 1993.

Hill, Jane, and Kathleen Flynn. *Classroom Instruction That Works With English Language Learners.* Alexandria, VA: Association for Supervision and Curriculum Development, 2006.

Law, Barbara, and Mary Eckes. *Assessment and ESL: An Alternative Approach.* Winnipeg, MB: Portage & Main Press, 2007.

_____. *The More-Than-Just-Surviving Handbook: ESL for Every Classroom Teacher,* 2nd edition. Winnipeg, MB: Portage & Main Press, 2000.

Maitland, Katherine. *Adding English: Helping ESL Learners Succeed.* Grand Rapids, MI: Frank Schaffer Publications, 2001.

Petricic, Gordana. *Play 'n' Talk: Communicative Games for Elementary and Middle School ESL/EFL.* Brattleboro, VT: Pro Lingua Associates, 1997.

Reid, Suzanne. *Book Bridges for ESL Students: Using Young Adult and Children's Literature to Teach ESL.* Lanham, MD: Scarecrow Press, 2002.

Rojas, Virginia. *Helping Students of Limited English Skills in the Regular Classroom* [videocassette, 30 min.]. LPD Video Journal Education, 2000.

Scott, Deb. *Fifty Reading and Writing Activities.* Toronto: Canadian Resources for ESL, 2004.

_____. *Fifty Speaking and Listening Activities.* Toronto: Canadian Resources for ESL, 2004.

Tompkins, Gail E., and Cathy Blanchfield. *Teaching Vocabulary: 50 Creative Strategies, Grades K–12.* Upper Saddle River, NJ: Pearson/Merrill Prentice Hall, 2004.

Walker, Michael. *Amazing English Buddy Book.* Lebanon, Indiana: Addison-Wesley, 1995.

Walker, Michael. *Amazing English Buddy Book: Newcomer Level.* Lebanon, Indiana: Addison-Wesley, 1995.

Walter, Teresa. *Amazing English! How-To-Handbook.* Toronto: Addison-Wesley, 1996.

Middle Years

Module 3

Introduction

This module of **Hands-On English Language Learning** is designed for use with students in grades 5 to 8, who have acquired some basic survival vocabulary and are developing communication skills in the English language (see Stages of Language Acquisition on page 1 of the Introduction to **Hands-On English Language Learning**).These students use English in supported and familiar activities and contexts. They listen with greater understanding and use everyday expressions independently. They demonstrate growing confidence in their use of English, and use personally relevant language appropriately.

The lessons in this module focus on extending students' language and understanding of basic concepts through hands-on activities and real-life applications.

Module Theme: Responsibility for Others

The lessons in this module focus on the theme of responsibility for others, specifically, understanding and respecting diversity. These concepts and related vocabulary will support students as they transition into a new school, community, and country.

There are several valuable resources available from the Government of Canada that relate very well to this unit. These include:

- **Canadian Symbols at Parliament** – This activity resource for teachers and students includes visuals of and information about typical symbols of Canada and Canada's parliament. (Although intended for grades K–3, the visuals and information can be used with all grades.)

- **MPTV** – This educational resource, which includes a video, classroom activities, and supporting teacher materials, is designed to introduce students to the House of Commons and the role of its elected Members of Parliament.

- **Our Country, Our Parliament** – This comprehensive introduction to Canada's Parliament is intended for ELL students in grades 9 to 12, but the content can be easily adapted for use with students in grades 5 to 8 in regular stream social studies classes.

- **Glossary of Parliamentary Terms** – This is a simplified glossary of terms commonly used in Parliament.

All of these resources are free and available from Information Services, Parliament of Canada, Ottawa, ON, K1A 0A9; phone (613) 992-1273; <www.parl.gc.ca/About/Parliament/Education/TeachingTools/index-e.asp>.

Effective Teaching Strategies for English Language Learners

While teaching the lessons in this module, be sure to consider the following:

- Students learn language through interaction with others. Create a learning environment that encourages rich dialogue and social communication.
- Use many verbal and non-verbal cues throughout activities. Non-verbal cues include visuals, gestures, and concrete materials.
- Simplify vocabulary and sentence structure to encourage comprehension.
- Give instructions and ask questions in clear, simple English.
- Allow learners sufficient response time for oral responses.
- Provide opportunity for students to use patterned language, in which certain language structures are repeated in various contexts or with different vocabulary.
- Review vocabulary and concepts regularly to check for learner comprehension.

- Encourage, where appropriate, the strategic use of students' first languages and prior knowledge as a bridge to English language learning.

Reinforcing Vocabulary

Students should learn to recognize and understand the vocabulary presented in this module. At the same time, they should be encouraged to make connections between their first languages and the English language. To reinforce vocabulary, consider having either a multilingual word wall for the classroom, or individual vocabulary folders for students.

Multilingual Word Wall

Dedicate a classroom bulletin board to your word wall, and display the letters of the alphabet along the top. Use index cards to record English vocabulary introduced in each lesson, tacking these to the board under the appropriate letter. Also include vocabulary in students' first languages (use students' prior knowledge, bilingual dictionaries, other students, staff, parents, and bilingual members of the community as sources of vocabulary). This contributes to the world/classroom-as-a-global-village message, validates first languages and cultures, and creates an atmosphere of inclusiveness. It also establishes an environment in which knowledge about other languages, and the merits of knowing more than one language, are highlighted and celebrated. Along with vocabulary, also include picture and phrase cues, as appropriate. Encourage students to refer to the word wall during activities and assignments.

Vocabulary Folders

If it is not feasible to dedicate classroom wall space to a word wall, use open legal-size folders to make multilingual vocabulary folders for students. Open each folder, and divide it into 26 sections on the inside, one section for each letter of the alphabet, filling up the entire inside area (as in the illustration below). There are two ways students can collect and record vocabulary—they can glue small envelopes to each lettered section, and then record vocabulary on small cards to be housed in the envelopes, or they can record new vocabulary on sticky notes and attach the notes directly to the appropriate lettered sections. Either way, be sure students also include illustrations, usage examples, as well as related vocabulary from their first language with their recorded English vocabulary. Students can close the folder again for storage (for this reason, do not have letter boxes directly on the folder crease).

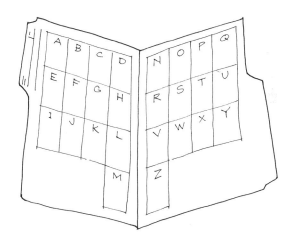

Personal Dictionaries

It can also benefit students to create their own personal English language dictionaries for reference during lessons. Use one of the blackline masters included in module 1 with lesson 1 (1.1.6, 1.1.7). Or, have students use notebooks with sticky notes to indicate alphabetization.

Note: In addition to recording English words in their personal dictionaries, also have students record words in their first languages where appropriate. This helps them make bilingual connections and extends meaning. It will therefore benefit ELL students if bilingual dictionaries are available in English and their first languages (see Books for Students on page 228 and References for Teachers on page 323).

Differentiating Instruction

A number of English language learners will have been in school prior to their arrival at your school and, as a result, will have literacy skills that are on par with their same-age peers. Other students may have little or no previous school experience and may not be literate in their first languages. Consequently, the lessons in this module of *Hands-On English Language Learning* offer many opportunities to help students develop their reading and writing skills while learning English. Visual cues, concrete manipulatives, and cooperative learning are needed to support students as they learn all aspects of the English language.

However, teachers will still need to differentiate instruction and adapt both activities and activity sheets to meet the needs of individual learners. For example, a student with limited reading and writing abilities might work with a peer to complete activity sheets or use drawings instead of words. As another example, personal dictionaries may be essential for ELL students but can be equally beneficial for all students in the class through differentiation. More academically advanced students might collect descriptive words for use in personal writing, while students requiring additional support in spelling might collect challenging words for use in writing activities while, at the same time, ELL students would collect target vocabulary with pictures to reinforce recognition. Suggestions for adaptation are made throughout the module, but teachers are also encouraged to use their own experience, techniques, and personal knowledge of students to differentiate instruction.

Peer Helpers

Many of the lessons presented in this module require the support of peer helpers to work in partnership with ELL students. Developing a classroom culture of inclusion and acceptance will be enhanced by working with the class to develop criteria for helpers, and to discuss why it is important to help one another.

Every student in the class should have the opportunity to help and interact with the ELL students in their class; it is not always necessary to choose the top academic students. Before any peer activity with ELL students, the teacher and peer helpers should discuss the specific task, and the benefits to both the ELL student and the peer helper.

Note: It is important that students working together in a peer-helper setting focus on English language usage. However, it is also helpful for ELL students, when possible, to have access to others who speak the same first language. This allows ELL students access to translation and interpretation, acknowledges their first languages, and builds on their background experiences.

Note: Throughout *Hands-On English Language Learning*, we use the term *English-speaking student* (rather than the more cumbersome *students for whom English is a first language*) to distinguish these students from their English-language-learner classmates. We recognize that the term *English-speaking student* is not completely accurate, since ELL students are also English-speaking students—though their language use is still developing. The rationale for use of this term is simply one of space.

Assessing Students' Prior Knowledge – Assessment for Learning

Before beginning this module, it is beneficial to determine students' prior knowledge of lesson concepts and which of the target vocabulary students already know. This provides information that allows teachers to refine lessons and instructional activities to meet the individual strengths and needs of students. As a pre-module assessment strategy, consider using the Vocabulary Tracking Checklist (I.9) (shown on page 39 in the Introduction to *Hands-On English Language Learning*) along with all vocabulary cards provided in the module. Conference with ELL students individually, and review the target vocabulary with them to determine the vocabulary with which they are familiar. Also, discuss concepts related to the vocabulary in order to reveal prior knowledge.

Note: This assessment activity also serves as an activating strategy that introduces students to the language, visuals, and concepts focused on throughout the module.

Career Connections

All modules in the *Hands On English Language Learning* program for middle years include a focus on career education for students. These activities are intended for use with the whole class, in an integrated setting, since career education is an important topic for all students. For ELL students specifically, such activities will offer them insight into the possibilities for their future, since many of the careers available to them might be quite different from those available in their countries of origin. Learning about careers offers students a closer look at one aspect of Canadian culture, so students acquire essential understanding while developing language skills.

It is important to note that some of the language used during career connection activities might be quite challenging for ELL students. For example, there is a focus on employability skills, and their importance in the workplace. Although some of the vocabulary used in describing these skills is at a more advanced language level, the activities themselves are well-suited to both ELL students and their English-speaking peers. Career connection activities focus on class discussion, guest presentations, role playing, and so on, and ELL students will adapt in this immersive environment.

Books for Students

Aloian, Molly, and Bobbie Kalman. *Explore North America.* New York: Crabtree, 2007.

Bellefontaine, Kim. *ABC of Canada.* Toronto: Kids Can Press, 2006.

Child, Lauren. *What Planet Are You From, Clarice Bean?* Cambridge, MA: Candlewick Press, 2002.

Department of Canadian Heritage. *Symbols of Canada.* Gatineau, QC: Department of Canadian Heritage, 2010.

Ellis, Deborah. *Sacred Leaf.* Toronto: Groundwood, 2007.

_____. *I Am a Taxi.* Toronto: Groundwood, 2006.

_____. *Three Wishes: Palestinian and Israeli Children Speak.* Toronto: Groundwood Books, 2004.

_____. *Mud City.* Toronto: Douglas & McIntyre, 2003.

_____. *Parvana's Journey.* Toronto: Douglas & McIntyre, 2002

_____. *The Breadwinner.* Toronto: Douglas & McIntyre, 2001.

Fitch, Sheree. *If You Could Wear My Sneakers!* Toronto: Doubleday, 1997.

Fleischman, Paul. *Weslandia.* Somerville, MA: Candlewick, 2002.

Harrison, Ted. *Oh Canada.* Toronto: Kids Can Press, 2003.

Major, Kevin. *Eh? to Zed.* A Canadian ABeCedarium. Red Deer Press, 2003

Parry, Caroline. *Let's Celebrate! Canada's Special Days.* Toronto: Kids Can Press, 1987.

Riordon, Rick. *The Lightning Thief* (Percy Jackson and the Olympians series, book 1). Miramax/Hyperion, 2005.

Ulmer, Michael. *M Is for Maple: A Canadian Alphabet.* Chelsea, MI: Sleeping Bear Press, 2004.

Zola, Melanie. *Peanut Butter Is Forever.* Independence, OH: Schoolhouse Press, 1986.

Multicultural Books

Aboff, Marcie. *Guatemala ABCs: A Book About the People and Places of Guatemala.* Minneapolis, MN: Picture Window Books, 2006.

Aliki. *Painted Words and Spoken Memories.* New York: Greenwillow Books, 1998.

Allen, Thomas B. *Where Children Live.* Englewood Cliffs, NJ: Prentice-Hall, 1980.

Berge, Ann. *Russia ABCs: A Book About the People and Places of Russia.* Minneapolis, MN: Picture Window Books, 2004.

Blackstone, Stella. *My Granny Went to Market: A Round-the World Counting Rhyme.* Cambridge, MA: Barefoot Books, 2005.

Cheung, Hyechong, and Prodeepta Das. *K is for Korea.* London, UK: Frances Lincoln Children's Books, 2008.

Cooper, Sharon Katz. *Venezuela ABCs: A Book About the People and Places of Venezuela.* Minneapolis, MN: Picture Window Books, 2007.

_____. *A Book About the People and Places of Italy.* Minneapolis, MN: Picture Window Books, 2006.

Cordero, Flor de Maria. *M is for Mexico.* London, UK: Frances Lincoln Children's Books, 2008.

Das, Prodeepta. *I is for India.* London, UK: Frances Lincoln Children's Books, 2004.

Gorman, Lovenia. *A is for Algonquin: An Ontario Alphabet.* Chelsea, MI: Sleeping Bear Press, 2005.

Heiman, Sarah. *Australia ABCs: A Book About the People and Places of Australia.* Minneapolis, MN: Picture Window Books, 2003.

———. *Egypt ABCs: A Book About the People and Places of Egypt.* Minneapolis, MN: Picture Window Books, 2003.

———. *Germany ABCs: A Book About the People and Places of Germany.* Minneapolis, MN: Picture Window Books, 2003.

———. *Kenya ABCs: A Book About the People and Places of Kenya.* Minneapolis, MN: Picture Window Books, 2003.

Krach, Maywan Shen. *D is for Doufu: An Alphabet Book of Chinese Culture.* Arcadia, CA: Shen's Books, 1997.

Miller, Millie. *Our World: A Country-by-Country Guide.* New York: Scholastic Reference, 2006.

Nishiyama, Akira, and Yoshio Komatsu. *Wonderful Houses Around the World.* Bolinas, CA: Shelter Publications, 2004.

Sanders, Nancy I. *D is for Drinking Gourd: An African American Alphabet.* Chelsea, MI: Sleeping Bear Press, 2007.

Schroeder, Holly. *Israel ABCs: A Book About the People and Places of Israel.* Minneapolis, MN: Picture Window Books, 2004.

———. *New Zealand ABCs: A Book About the People and Places of New Zealand.* Minneapolis, MN: Picture Window Books, 2004.

Seidman, David. *Brazil ABCs: A Book About the People and Places of Brazil.* Minneapolis, MN: Picture Window Books, 2007.

Shoulders, Michael, and Debbie Shoulders. *D is for Drum: A Native American Alphabet.* Chelsea, MI: Sleeping Bear Press, 2006.

Various authors. Countries of the World series. Mankato, MN: Capstone Press, 1997–2003 (39 titles).

Wells, Ruth. *A to Zen: A Book of Japanese Culture.* Saxonville, MA: Picture Books Studio, 1992.

Language Resources

Adelson-Goldstein, Jayme, and Norma Shapiro. Oxford Picture Dictionary series*, New York: Oxford University Press, 2008.

Cleary, Brian P. *Hairy, Scary, Ordinary: What is an Adjective?* Minneapolis: Carolrhoda Books, 2000.

Hill, L.A., and Charles Innes. Oxford Children's Picture Dictionary. London, UK: Oxford University Press, 1997.

Mantra Lingua. *My Talking Dictionary: Book and CD Rom.* London, UK: TalkingPen Publications, 2005 (48 dual-language editions).

Ross Keyes, Joan. *The Oxford Picture Dictionary for Kids.* New York: Oxford University Press, 1998.

Walker, Michael. *Amazing English Buddy Book.* Lebanon, Indiana: Addison-Wesley, 1995.

———. *Amazing English Buddy Book: Newcomer Level.* Lebanon, Indiana: Addison-Wesley, 1995.

---

*Bilingual versions of the *Oxford Picture Dictionary* are available for English and the following: Arabic, Brazilian-Portuguese, Chinese, French, Japanese, Korean, Russian, Spanish, Thai, Urdu, and Vietnamese.

Websites

- <www.intercultures.ca/cil-cai/countryinsights-apercuspays-eng.asp>
  Country Insights: This site provides information about different cultures and includes advice on cultural "do's" and "dont's."

- <www.eslflow.com>
  ESL Flow is a resource for researching ESL/EFL (English as a Foreign Language) ideas and for creating lessons. The site provides a variety of topics at the elementary, pre-intermediate, and intermediate levels. Topics include icebreakers, giving directions, describing people and places, games, and so on. The site also includes current, favourite ESL teaching lesson links.

- <www.esl-galaxy.com>
  ESL Galaxy offers numerous printable worksheets for ESL lesson plans and activities, including board games, crosswords, grammar and vocabulary worksheets, theme or topic lesson plans, pronunciation, survival English, song activities, festival and holiday worksheets, conversation and communicative activities, cloze and gap-fill exercises, and more.

- <www.esl-kids.com>
  ESL-Kids.com offers materials for teachers to use with ESL students including flashcards, worksheets, classroom games, and children's song lyrics.

- <www.jigsawplanet.com>
  Jigsaw Planet: On this site, students can create electronic puzzles of maps (or other pictures) from jpeg files, for online play.

- <www.gameskidsplay.net>
  Kids Games provides detailed descriptions of classic games that students love to play, including rules for playground games, verses for jump-rope rhymes, ball games, strength games, mental games, and more. Many of the games can be adapted to teach particular language structures. Games can be viewed in a number of ways, including a list of "quick favourites," games by category, alphabetically, or you can do a search for a specific game.

- <www.parl.gc.ca/About/Parliament/Education/TeachingTools/index-e.asp>
  Parliament of Canada Classroom Resources: Part of the Parliament of Canada website, this page lists valuable classroom resources available to teachers and students from the Government of Canada, free of charge.

- <www.tefl.net>
  TFEL.net is a free, independent resource site for anyone involved in teaching English as an additional language. The site offers a range of ESL worksheets, including discussion-based, topic-based, and skill-based ESL worksheets, and more.

- <www.unicef.org/voy>
  UNICEF Voices of Youth site: Part of the website for UNICEF (an international organization that advocates for the protection of children's rights), the Voices of Youth site is a forum where youth can explore, discuss, and take action on global problems. The site features interactive games, discussion boards, puzzles, and brain teasers, all based on children's rights.

- <www.worldvision.ca/GetInvolved/
Youth-Action-Zone/Pages/
Youth-Action-Zone.aspx>
World Vision Canada Youth Action Zone site: Part of the website for World Vision Canada (a development, relief, and advocacy organization), the Youth Action Zone site outlines a number of ways youth can take action on global issues, including participating in the 30-Hour-Famine, becoming a World Vision Youth Ambassador, attending the Youth Empowered (YE) leadership event held across Canada every February, or sending a postcard to the Prime Minister to ask for action on the global food crisis.

1 Canadian Geography

Curricular Connections

- Language Arts: speaking, listening, reading, writing, viewing, representing
- Social Studies: Canadian geography, research
- Art: drawing

Background Information for Teachers

There is a great deal of content vocabulary in this lesson, and students should not be expected to master the vocabulary within a certain timeframe. Plan to cover the topic over the course of several sessions, revisiting and recycling vocabulary continually. Be sure to have wall maps of both the world and Canada on display at all times. As in previous lessons, vocabulary cards (3.1.1, 3.1.2) have been included for all terms listed below. Teachers should use these cards in whatever ways they will support students in learning this new terminology.

Vocabulary – Canadian Geography

General Geography Terms

- map
- direction
- North
- South
- East
- West
- urban
- rural
- compass rose
- legend
- scale
- country
- city
- town
- village
- region
- province
- territory
- body of water
- land
- capital
- prairie
- arctic
- mountain
- river
- lake
- island

Canadian Place Names

- British Columbia (BC)
- Alberta (AB)
- Saskatchewan (SK)
- Manitoba (MB)
- Ontario (ON)
- Québec (QC)
- New Brunswick (NB)
- Nova Scotia (NS)
- Prince Edward Island (PE)
- Newfoundland and Labrador (NL)
- Yukon (YK)
- Northwest Territories (NT)
- Nunavut (NU)
- Victoria
- Edmonton
- Regina
- Winnipeg
- Toronto
- Québec city
- Fredericton
- Halifax
- Charlottetown
- St. John's
- Whitehorse
- Yellowknife
- Iqualuit
- Ottawa
- Pacific Ocean

- Atlantic Ocean
- Arctic Ocean
- Hudson Bay

Materials

- vocabulary cards – *General Geography Terms* (Photocopy one set onto sturdy tagboard, and cut out.) (3.1.1)
- vocabulary cards – *Canadian Place Names* (Photocopy one set onto sturdy tagboard, and cut out.) (3.1.2)
- large wall maps of the world and Canada
- globe (optional)
- pocket chart
- visuals of Canada and Canadian landmarks (for example, pictures from calendars, books, and the internet)
- map of Canada puzzle (included. Make one photocopy for each ELL student.) (3.1.3)
- markers or coloured pencils
- white paper
- chart paper
- scissors
- poster paper
- sticky notes
- internet photographs of various Canadian locations (see the second integrated class activity)
- coloured wool
- large and regular-sized index cards

Integrated Class Activities

Note: This lesson on Canadian geography will benefit all students. In addition to the suggested integrated class activities below, all instructional, peer, and independent activities may be done with the whole class.

- As a class, brainstorm Canadian place names (including communities, cities, provinces, countries, bodies of water, and so on). Record these on index cards, and then sort the cards into groups (such as "cities", "provinces", "ocean", "rivers" and so on). Challenge students to see how many of these place names they can locate on a wall map of Canada.

- Have students work in pairs or small groups to research different locations in Canada. These might include communities, parks, bodies of water, or special landforms (such as the Rocky Mountains). Begin with a simple structure, such as the following:

  1. Find the place on the wall map of Canada, and use a sticky note to mark its location.
  2. Record its population (if applicable).
  3. Record five interesting facts about this place.
  4. Find a photograph of this place (the internet will be a good source for this).

  Have the pairs or groups present their research to the rest of the class. Students can place research facts and photographs around the wall map of Canada and use coloured wool to connect them to the specific map locations.

- Invite guests who have lived in or visited other parts of Canada to present to the class.

Note: Teach students appropriate ways to thank guest speakers and other visitors. Have the designated thanker practise the expression of thanks ahead of time.

Whole-Class Career Connections

- Invite a professional in the field of cartography (the study and practice of making maps) to present their skills and experiences to the class.

1

- Research and study early cartographers of Canada, who mapped this vast, wild expanse, including Samuel de Champlain, Joseph Frederick Wallet DesBarres, Joseph-Elzéar Bernier, and Francesco Bressani.

- Have students try their hand at some cartography skills by drawing a map of an area around your school. As a group, decide on the boundaries of the area, and go on a walk to observe features. Then, have students create their maps. Review maps for accuracy and detail.

Instructional Activity: Part One

Display a large wall map of the world. Ask students:

- What is this called?
- What does a map show us?

Use the map to introduce vocabulary such as *compass rose, direction, scale, North, South, East,* and *West.* Display the appropriate vocabulary cards (3.1.1) in the pocket chart as they are introduced. Ask:

- From which part of the world did you come?

Have students point to their countries of origin on the map. Introduce the word *country* by using your finger to trace around the border of one of the countries identified, and saying:

- This is the country of (for example, Argentina).

Continue to focus on countries of origin. Ask:

- In what part of this country did you live?

Introduce terms such as *city, town, village, region, urban, rural,* and so on to describe the specific locations where students lived. Display the appropriate vocabulary cards in the pocket chart as they are introduced.

Note: Also identify local examples of cities, towns, and villages so students can make connections to their own communities. As well, discuss cities, towns, and villages from students' countries of origin.

Have students discuss these terms, define them in their own words, and record their ideas on chart paper. Compare these to dictionary definitions of the terms.

Now, ask:

- Where do you live now?
- What is the name of the country in which you live now?
- Can you show me Canada on the map?

Have students identify Canada, review the spelling and pronunciation of the name, and trace around the borders of the country on the map.

If students are comfortable with the topic, discuss their journeys to Canada from their countries of origin.

Note: Some students may have lived in other countries during their journeys to Canada, so identify these on the world map as well.

Also, discuss features of students' countries of origin as well as their impressions of Canada compared to their countries of origin. Ask:

- What do you miss most about your country?
- Is there anything that you don't miss about your country?
- How is Canada different from your country of origin (in terms of weather, houses, types of stores, and so on)?
- How is Canada the same as your country of origin?

▶

Use a Venn diagram as a graphic organizer to record similarities and differences. For example:

Comparing Canada to _____

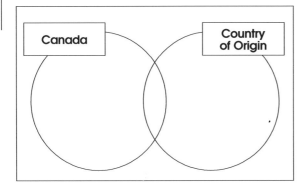

Similarities are recorded in the intersecting area, while differences are recorded in the parts of both circles that don't intersect.

Instructional Activity: Part Two

Focus students' attention on the compass rose on the wall map of Canada. On chart paper, draw a larger version of the compass rose. Ask:

- What do you think the *N* stands for on this picture?

Explain to students that the picture shows a *compass rose.* Record the term on chart paper. Further explain that a compass rose is used on a map to show directions. Ask:

- What are directions?

Record the terms, *North, South, East,* and *West* on chart paper. Also, have students share the vocabulary for these terms from their first languages. Then, record each of the terms on a large index card. Tape the four index cards to the four classroom walls in the appropriate locations.

Have students stand in the centre of the room. Provide instructions, and have students use the cardinal directions to move around the room. For example:

- Face North.
- Take 10 steps North.
- Turn to face East.
- Take 5 steps East.
- Turn to face West.
- Take 12 steps West.
- Turn to face South.
- Take 3 steps South.

Display the vocabulary cards for the compass rose and the cardinal directions in the pocket chart. Review the terms with students, and have them identify and locate each one on a globe or map.

Assessment for Learning

As students follow the directions in the preceding activity, focus on their abilities to use the target vocabulary. This is also an excellent opportunity to review, practise, and assess number vocabulary as well as comprehension of oral instructions.

Instructional Activity: Part Three

Using a large wall map of Canada, show students how Canada is separated into provinces and territories. Introduce the terms *province* and *territory*, and then name each one, using your finger to trace around the area as you name it. Give students opportunities to do the same, tracing around provinces and territories, using the terminology (*province, territory*), and naming them. Ask:

- In which province or territory do we live?
- Do you know about any other provinces or territories in Canada?

Again, point to the different provinces/territories, and say their names. Also, indicate each province's or territory's capital city. Point to the main bodies of water, and say their names.

Note: Some students may have lived in or visited other parts of Canada, so invite them to share their experiences orally, in writing, and/or using pictures.

Finally, review the vocabulary cards – *General Geography Terms* (3.1.1) with students, and have them identify each term on the large wall map of Canada.

Peer Activities

- Have students work in pairs. Distribute copies of the map of Canada puzzle (3.1.3), and have students cut it apart along the dotted borders and then work together to piece the map back together. When each pair is satisfied with their pieced-together map, they can glue down the pieces onto a separate piece of paper. Then, have students colour the map using a different colour for each province and a different shade of blue for each body of water.

- Have students work in pairs and use the website Jigsaw Planet (<www.jigsawplanet.com>) to create an electronic jigsaw puzzle of a map of Canada from a jpeg file.

Independent Activity: Part One: Activity Sheet A

Directions to students:

Use a different colour to shade each of your own country of origin and Canada on the map of the world. Complete the legend (3.1.4).

Independent Activity: Part Two: Activity Sheet B

Directions to students:

Colour the bodies of water blue. Label each province and territory. Use the large map of Canada to help you (3.1.5).

Independent Activity: Part Three: Activity Sheet C

Directions to students:

Look carefully at the shape of each province and territory. Record the name of each. Use the wall map of Canada to help you (3.1.6).

Independent Activity: Part Four: Activity Sheet D

Directions to students:

Draw and write about your favourite place in Canada, as well as your favourite place in another country (3.1.7).

Note: Some ELL students may only have lived in (or visited) the Canadian city/town in which they currently live and should be encouraged to write about that location if this is the case.

Extensions

- Begin a multilingual word wall for new vocabulary (see page 225). Add new vocabulary – *General Geography Terms* and *Canadian Place Names* to the word wall, as well as illustrations and other visuals related to the vocabulary.

  If it is not feasible to dedicate a bulletin board or classroom wall space to a word wall, make multilingual vocabulary folders for students by dividing legal-size folders into 26 sections, one for each letter of the alphabet (see page 225). Have students add new vocabulary – *General Geography Terms* and *Canadian Place Names* to their vocabulary folders, encouraging them to include illustrations, usage examples, and related vocabulary from their first language with each English term.

- Have students use notebooks, index cards, or the personal dictionary blackline masters included in module 1 (1.1.6, 1.1.7) to create personal dictionaries in which they can record new words and expressions that they learn in each lesson. Ask students to add new vocabulary – *General Geography Terms* and *Canadian Place Names* to their personal dictionaries. Encourage them to use pictures, their emerging English language, and/or their first languages to represent the new terms.

    Note: There are two dictionary blackline masters included in module 1—one with columns for English vocabulary and pictures (1.1.6), and a second that encourages bilingual language skills by also providing a column in which students can record vocabulary in their first language(s) (1.1.7). Choose the dictionary template that best suits the individual needs and skills of your ELL students.

- Have students play the computer game *Cross Country Canada*. In the game, the player is a truck driver; the main objective is to travel across the country and drop off packages at specific Canadian locations while learning about provinces, cities, territories. If the player makes sensible choices along the way the trip will be a success.

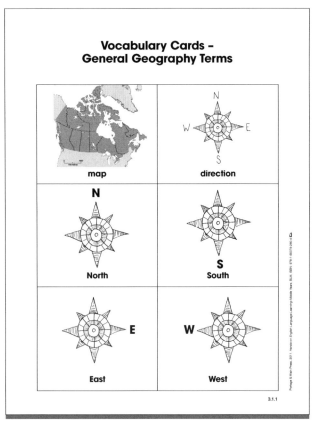
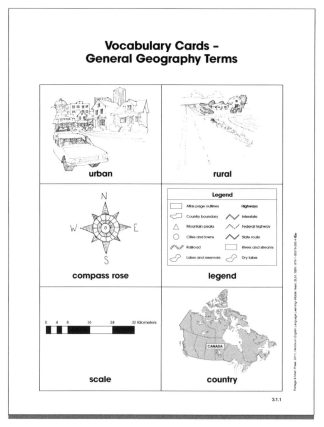
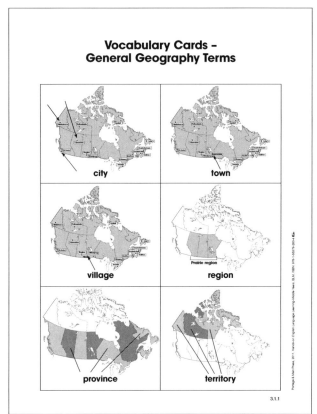
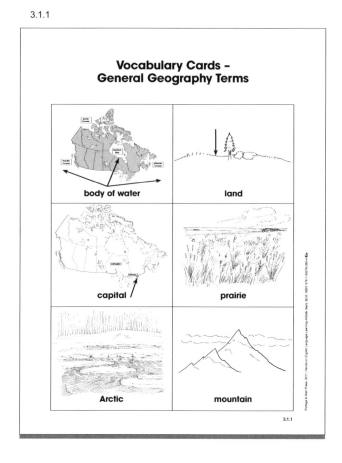

3.1.1

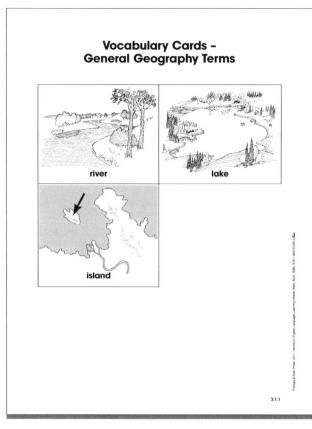

3.1.2

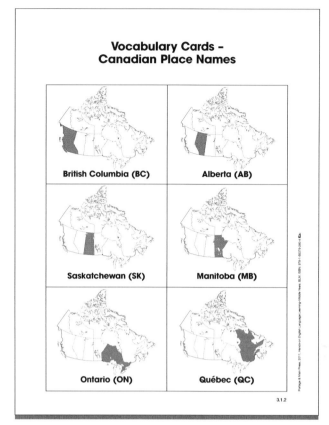

3.1.2

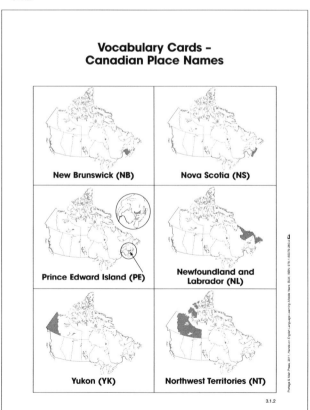

3.1.2

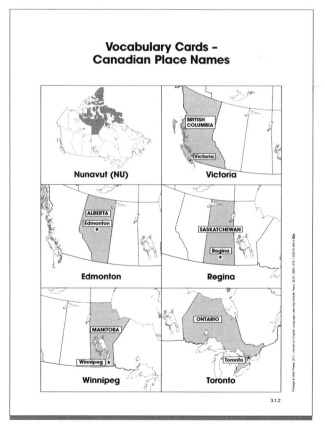

3.1.2

Vocabulary Cards – Canadian Place Names

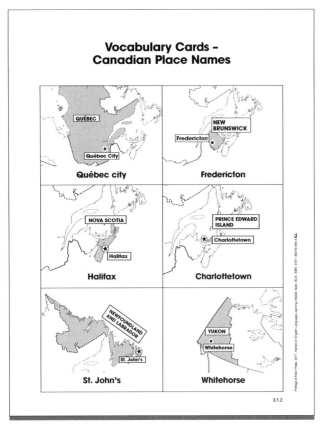

3.1.2

Vocabulary Cards – Canadian Place Names

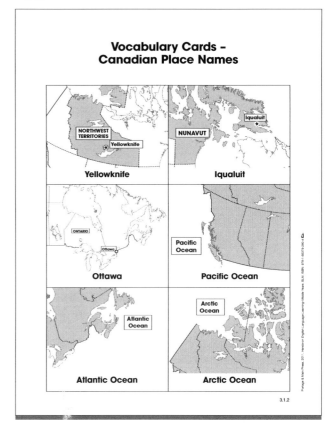

3.1.2

Vocabulary Cards – Canadian Place Names

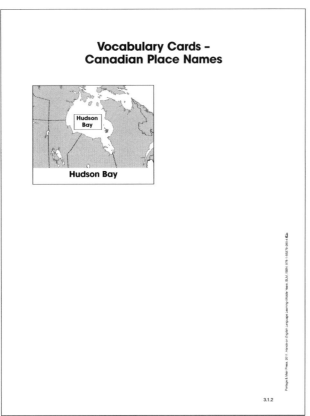

3.1.3

Map of Canada Puzzle

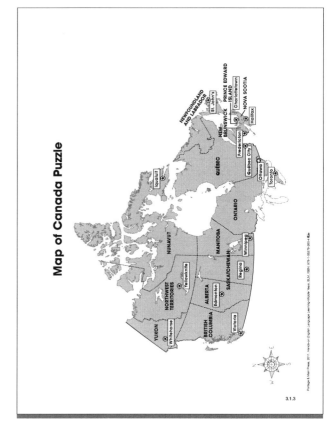

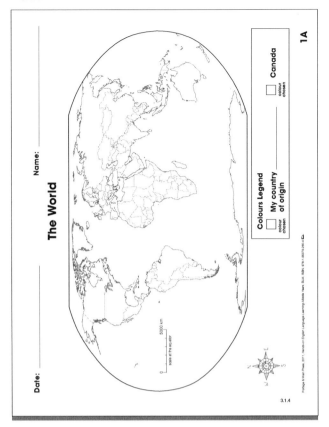

2 Canadian Symbols

Curricular Connections

- Language Arts: speaking, listening, reading, writing, viewing, representing
- Mathematics: money, counting, skip-counting, sorting, tallies, graphs
- Social Studies: Canadian symbols
- Art: drawing, rubbings, illustrations

Vocabulary – Canadian Symbols

Canadian Symbols

- beaver
- Bluenose schooner
- Canada goose
- caribou
- flag
- hockey
- lacrosse
- loon
- maple leaf
- polar bear
- prime minister
- queen
- Royal Canadian Mounted Police (RCMP)
- salmon

Canadian Money

- bills
- coins
- loonie (one-dollar coin)
- toonie (two-dollar coin)
- quarter
- dime
- nickel
- penny
- dollar

Materials

- Canadian flag
- books about or online resources for flags of the world
- drawing paper
- Canadian money (coins and bills. You will need a large collection of Canadian coins.)
- *Eh? to Zed*, a book by Kevin Major, *ABC of Canada*, a book by Kim Bellefontaine, *Oh Canada,* a book by Ted Harrison, or other books for students about Canada and Canadian symbols
- *Symbols of Canada*, a publication of (the Department of) Canadian Heritage
- *Canadian Symbols at Parliament,* a resource available from the Government of Canada (visit <www.parl.gc.ca/About/Parliament/Education/TeachingTools/index-e.asp>)
- vocabulary cards – *Canadian Symbols* (included. Photocopy one set onto sturdy tagboard, cut out, and laminate.) (3.2.1)
- vocabulary cards – *Canadian Money* (included. Photocopy one set onto sturdy tagboard, cut out, and laminate.) (3.2.2)
- pocket chart
- chart paper
- markers
- coins and bills from other countries
- store flyers
- cash register or cash box
- imitation money (templates from vocabulary cards – *Canadian Money* [3.2.2] may also be used)
- calculators
- poster paper
- coloured pencils

Integrated Class Activities

- This lesson on Canadian symbols will benefit all students. In addition to suggested integrated class activities below, all suggested instructional, peer, and independent activities may be done with the whole class.

- Collect coins and bills from other countries. Have students examine and discuss the symbols shown on the coins and bills. Conduct research to find out more about these countries' symbols.
- Have students create a bulletin-board display about symbols of the world. Include Canadian symbols, symbols from students' countries of origin, and those from other countries as well.
- Divide the class into working groups, and provide each group with a large collection of Canadian coins (real ones are required for this activity). Have students sort the coins by year and keep a tally of their results. Then, have them work in groups to create a graph from their data.

Note: Be sure to review criteria for the graph before students begin this task. For example, if groups are constructing a bar graph, it must have:
- a title
- labelled axes
- calibrations to represent tallies
- spaces between the bars

Whole-Class Career Connections

- Research jobs at the Royal Canadian Mint in Winnipeg.
- Write letters to some of the authors who wrote the books used in this lesson (Kevin Major, Kim Bellefontaine, Ted Harrison). Have students ask about their inspiration for writing these books, and about their professions as children's writers.
- Invite members of the RCMP to talk to students about their careers.

Instructional Activity: Part One

Display the Canadian flag for students to see. Ask:

- What is this?
- What is a flag for?
- Where do you see flags?

Discuss the term and the purpose of flags to represent countries or groups of people. Have students examine and describe the features of the Canadian flag. Ask:

- What does the flag for your country of origin look like?

Have students look through books (or at websites) about flags to identify the flags from their own countries of origin. Distribute drawing paper, and have students use markers or coloured pencils to draw replicas of Canada's flag as well as the flags from their countries of origin. Display students' flags in the classroom.

Note: Teachers should be mindful of the fact that, depending on students' backgrounds, flags from different regions may cause some controversy (for example, regions that are in conflict).

Instructional Activity: Part Two

Read aloud one or more books about Canada that show(s) Canadian symbols (for example, *Eh? To Zed, ABC of Canada, Symbols of Canada*). For each symbol found in the book, introduce the term, and record it on chart paper.

Explain that these items are symbols of Canada, or things that are special about Canada and that sometimes represent or stand for Canada. Discuss the symbols with which students are familiar, and have them share their understanding of these items. Also, have ELL students share symbols of their own countries of origin.

2

Display the target vocabulary cards – *Canadian Symbols* (3.2.1) in the pocket chart. Review each symbol of Canada, and have students find the same symbols in the book(s) read.

Instructional Activity: Part Three

Use real Canadian bills and coins to introduce the vocabulary used for Canadian money. Give students plenty of opportunity to handle the money and examine the symbols and identifying features on the coins and bills, and use the vocabulary during this discussion. Have students match the symbols on the bills and coins to those on the target vocabulary cards – *Canadian Money* (3.2.2).

Provide each student with a variety of Canadian coins, and have students examine and discuss the symbols on them. Ask:

- About which of these symbols do you know?

Discuss and record what students know about the symbols on the coins, including

- penny: maple leaf
- nickel: beaver
- dime: Bluenose schooner
- quarter: caribou
- loonie/one-dollar coin: loon
- toonie/two-dollar coin: polar bear
- all coins: queen

Note: There are also several specialty coins in circulation depicting other Canadian symbols, events, and important people. These can be introduced and discussed as they arise.

Instructional Activity: Part Four

Have students use the various Canadian coins and bills to practise counting skills. For example:

- Use pennies or loonies to count forward and backward by ones.
- Use nickels to count by fives.
- Use toonies to count by twos.
- Use dimes to count by tens.

Note: Base implementation of the preceding activity (using money for counting and for development of computational skills) on students' entering skills and grade-level curriculum.

Peer Activity

Provide students with store flyers, imitation money, and calculators. Have ELL-student/peer-helper pairs role play purchasing items and making change. Tell one student to role play a store owner while the other role plays the customer. Have the customer select an item from a flyer and choose bills and coins to purchase the item; then, have the store owner make change if necessary. Tell students to use a calculator to confirm their calculations.

Independent Activity

Distribute a piece of poster paper and some coloured pencils to each student. Have each student fold the paper in half lengthwise to divide it into two parts. Then, tell students to draw a Canadian flag at the top of one side of the poster paper and their country of origin's flag at the top of the other. Ask students to use their new knowledge of Canadian geography and symbols to create a poster comparing the two countries. Be sure they label all figures and symbols on their posters. Students may use wall maps, outline maps of Canada (for example, clean copies of Activity Sheet B from the previous lesson [3.1.5]), the vocabulary cards – *Canadian Symbols* (3.2.1), books, and online resources to help them with ideas and drawings.

Extensions

- Add new vocabulary to the multilingual word wall.
- Have students add new vocabulary to their personal vocabulary folders or personal dictionaries.
- Record each of the 104 words from the book *Eh? to Zed* onto a separate index card. Have students sort the words (places, animals, food, and so on).
- Create an alphabet display of real objects that are Canadian symbols. Record the letters of the alphabet onto individual index cards or onto a strip of cashier tape, and spread out the alphabet letters or strip on a table. Then, place the selected Canadian symbols with their corresponding first letters (for example, a stuffed beaver would be placed with *B*, and a hockey puck would be placed with *H* [or *P*]).
- Have students do coin rubbings of Canadian coins as well as coins from other countries.
- Have pairs of students use two sets of vocabulary cards – *Canadian Symbols* to play the game Concentration.
- Display a collection of Canadian stamps, and have students research and discuss the people and symbols depicted on them.
- Have students create a stamp, coin, flag, or symbol collection to reflect the cultural diversity of the class.
- Research to find out about the Canadian Citizenship test, and the knowledge of Canadian symbols required for this test. Practice tests and study guides are available online at the Citizenship and Immigration Canada website: <www.cic.gc.ca>.

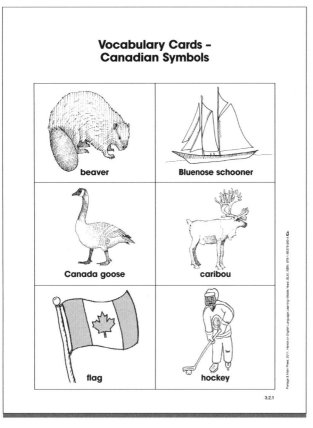
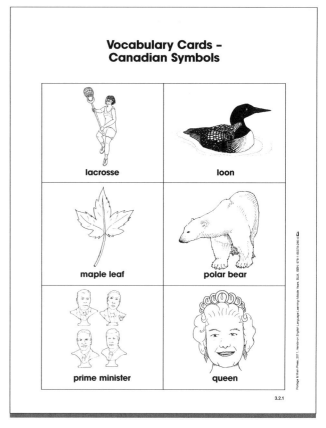
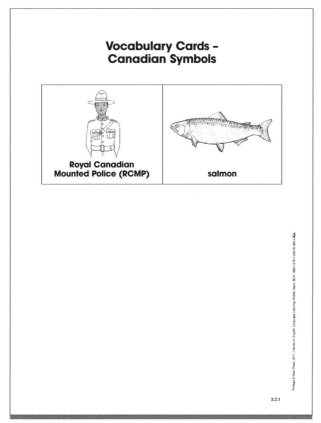
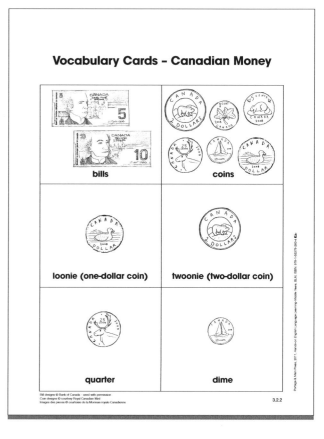

Vocabulary Cards - Canadian Money

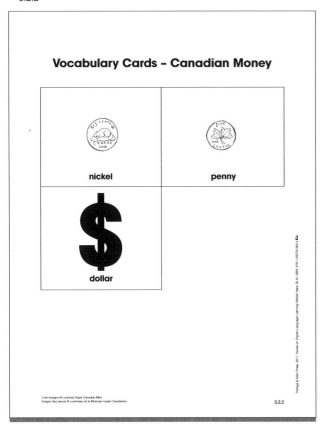

Blackline Masters

3 Celebrations and Holidays

Curricular Connections

- Language Arts: speaking, listening, reading, writing, viewing, representing
- Social Studies: cultural traditions, diversity
- Music: cultural music
- Art: drawing
- Dance: cultural dance

Background Information for Teachers

Have an ongoing discussion about celebrations and holidays throughout the year. Discuss festivals and holidays from a wide range of cultural and religious traditions and beliefs during the appropriate calendar month.

For some ELL students this information will be familiar. For others, however, it will be new. Hence, the lesson will function as a review of the celebrations and holidays about which some students already know, as well as an introduction to some new ones.

Note: Teachers should be aware that some families may not want their children involved in certain holidays or celebrations. Such preferences should be respected, and teachers should ensure that classroom activities are inclusive of all students.

Vocabulary – Celebrations and Holidays

General Celebration and Holiday Terms

- celebration
- holiday
- party
- feast
- candle
- family
- friends
- gift/present
- ceremony
- tradition
- months of the year (recycled from module 1, lesson 9)

Holidays and Celebrations

- April Fools' Day
- Boxing Day
- Calgary Stampede
- Canada Day
- Caribana Festival
- Carnaval de Québec
- Chinese New Year
- Christmas Day
- Christmas Eve
- Civic Holiday
- Diwali
- Easter
- Father's Day
- Folklorama
- Halloween
- Hanukkah
- Kwanzaa
- Labour Day
- Mardi Gras
- May Day
- Mother's Day
- National Aboriginal Day
- National Flag Day
- New Year's Day
- New Year's Eve
- Passover
- Ramadan
- Remembrance Day
- Rosh Hashanah
- Saint-Jean Baptiste Day
- St. Patrick's Day
- Thanksgiving
- Toonik Tyme
- Ukrainian Christmas
- Ukrainian New Year

▶

3

- Valentine's Day/St. Valentine's Day
- Victoria Day
- Yom Kippur

Note: Be sure to include local and provincially-specific holidays and celebrations in your list of vocabulary to target, such as Louis Riel Day, Family Day, Manitoba Day (or the official "birthday" of your province/territory). Make vocabulary cards to reflect these holidays and celebrations.

Materials

- *Let's Celebrate! Canada's Special Days*, a book by Caroline Parry
- vocabulary cards – *Months of the Year* (included in Module 1, Lesson 9) (1.9.1)
- vocabulary cards – *General Celebration and Holiday Terms* (included. Photocopy one set onto sturdy tagboard, and cut out.) (3.3.1)
- vocabulary cards – *Holidays and Celebrations* (included. Photocopy one set onto sturdy tagboard, and cut out.) (3.3.2)
- pocket chart
- Annual Celebrations list (included for teacher reference) (3.3.3)
- Celebrations Information sheet (included for teacher reference) (3.3.4)
- scissors
- tape
- classroom calendar
- index cards

Integrated Class Activities

- All activities in this lesson, including background information on celebrations and holidays and suggestions for a variety of activities, can be done with the entire class. Acknowledging the traditions of students' cultures fosters global citizenship, and all students will benefit from learning more about the celebrations and holidays their classmates observe.

- On the classroom calendar, record upcoming celebrations and holidays. Have students share how their families celebrate these events, and plan classroom celebrations to correspond with these dates.
- Invite students' family members to share traditions with the class.
- Invite local cultural groups to perform music and dance reflective of cultural celebrations and holidays.
- Discuss similarities amongst various celebrations and holidays (family get-togethers, unique foods, special clothing, and so on).

Whole-Class Career Connections

- Visit shops that sell holiday-related merchandise for local celebrations and holidays. These might include specialty food shops, craft stores, dollar stores, cultural stores, gift shops, and card shops. Have employees explain how they create displays to feature items during specific celebrations and holidays.
- Have students role play the job of a greeting-card designer/writer and create cards for special celebrations and holidays complete with illustrations and verses.

Instructional Activity: Part One

Note: The following activity offers an excellent opportunity to share cultural and national traditions with the entire class. This fosters understanding and celebrates diversity.

Read the book, *Let's Celebrate! Canada's Special Days.* While reading aloud, talk about the celebrations discussed and the objects shown in the book.

▶

Assessment for Learning

While you are reading the book, encourage students to identify vocabulary with which they are already familiar, such as letters of the alphabet, colours, and so on.

Instructional Activity: Part Two

Discuss the words *holiday* (a day of celebration, sometimes a day off work) and *celebration* (a day of festivity, but not necessarily a holiday).

Explain that there are many opportunities to celebrate throughout the year, as a family and as a community. Celebrations may include birthdays, anniversaries, special events tied to the seasons, religious holidays, festivals, and so on.

Introduce the vocabulary cards – *General Celebration and Holiday Terms* (3.3.1) as a springboard to a discussion about the features of celebrations. Encourage students to share what they celebrate and the traditions that reflect various celebrations and holidays. As you introduce specific vocabulary (such as *gift/present, candle,* or *feast*), encourage discussion. For example:

- Do you give or receive gifts or presents during any of the holidays that you celebrate? If so, during which holidays/celebrations?
- Do you use candles in any of the celebrations?
- When do you have big meals or feasts?

Talk about how people from different cultures celebrate a variety of special days. Ask:

- Can you tell me about some of the special holidays and celebrations in your culture?

As a student begins to talk about one of the holidays/celebrations from his or her culture, find the appropriate vocabulary card from the vocabulary cards – *Holidays and Celebrations* (3.3.2), and display it in the pocket chart. Give each student a chance to share one or more holidays/celebrations from his or her culture.

Note: Keep some blank index cards handy during the preceding class discussion. If a student mentions a holiday from his or her culture that is not included in the vocabulary cards – *Holidays and Celebrations*, record it on a blank index card, encouraging the student to suggest a simple symbol or picture to help illustrate the card. Later, consult an online source or book/resource of world holidays to confirm English spelling of the holiday.

When students have finished talking about their special holidays/celebrations, place the remaining cards in the pocket chart. Ask:

- Do any of the symbols/pictures on these cards remind you of any other holidays or celebrations?

Review the vocabulary cards, and discuss when and why each holiday is celebrated. Focus a discussion around common features of many celebrations/holidays (family time, special foods, music, and so on).

Note: It is not necessary to use all vocabulary cards. Consider the cultural diversity of the class/school/community when selecting which cards to present.

Peer Activity

Provide ELL-student/peer-helper pairs with the set of vocabulary cards – *Months of the Year* (1.9.1). Have students work together to sequence the cards by placing them on a table, by putting them into the pocket chart, or by taping them to a wall or whiteboard. Have students read the names of the months together and aloud.

Now, have students see how many vocabulary cards – *Holidays and Celebrations* (3.3.2) they can match to the correct month of the year, and place these cards under the appropriate months on the table, in the pocket chart, or on the wall/whiteboard.

Note: You may wish to provide students with copies the Annual Celebrations list (3.3.3) and the Celebrations Information sheet (3.3.4) to assist them with the matching of the vocabulary cards.

Independent Activity: Activity Sheet A

Directions to students:

Choose your favourite celebration or holiday from your country of origin and another favourite celebration or holiday that is celebrated in Canada. Complete the chart (3.3.5).

Extensions

- Add new vocabulary to the multilingual word wall.

- Have students add new vocabulary to their personal vocabulary folders or personal dictionaries.

- Set up a display of books and artifacts about celebrations around the world. Suggest that students bring items from home to include in the display. Encourage students to browse through the books, examine the artifacts, ask questions, and discuss celebrations with their peers.

Blackline Masters

3.3.1

Vocabulary Cards – General Celebration and Holiday Terms

celebration	holiday
party	feast
candle	family

3.3.1

Vocabulary Cards – General Celebration and Holiday Terms

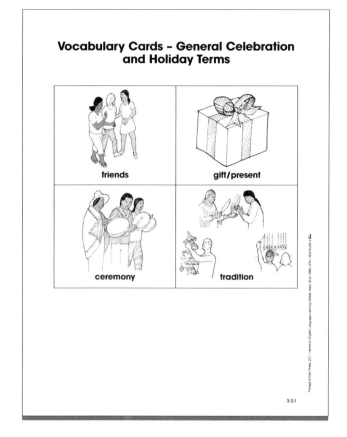

| friends | gift/present |
| ceremony | tradition |

3.3.2

Vocabulary Cards – Holidays and Celebrations

April Fools' Day	Boxing Day
Calgary Stampede	Canada Day
Caribana Festival	Carnaval de Québec

3.3.2

Vocabulary Cards – Holidays and Celebrations

Chinese New Year	Christmas Day
Christmas Eve	Civic Holiday
Diwali	Easter

252 – 3.3.1

Vocabulary Cards – Holidays and Celebrations

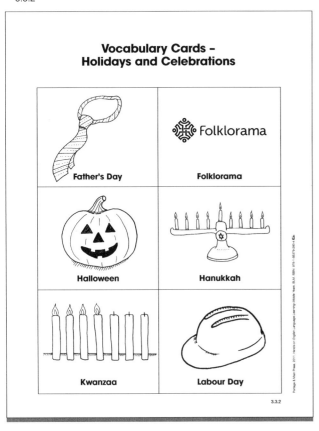

Father's Day	Folklorama
Halloween	Hanukkah
Kwanzaa	Labour Day

Vocabulary Cards – Holidays and Celebrations

Mardi Gras	May Day
Mother's Day	National Aboriginal Day
National Flag Day	New Year's Day

Vocabulary Cards – Holidays and Celebrations

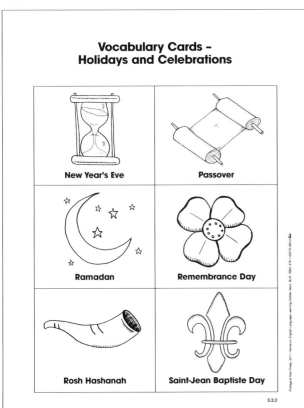

New Year's Eve	Passover
Ramadan	Remembrance Day
Rosh Hashanah	Saint-Jean Baptiste Day

Vocabulary Cards – Holidays and Celebrations

St. Patrick's Day	Thanksgiving
Toonik Tyme	Ukrainian Christmas
Ukrainian New Year	Valentine's Day / St. Valentine's Day

Blackline Masters

Vocabulary Cards – Holidays and Celebrations

Victoria Day

Yom Kippur

Annual Celebrations

January
- 1: New Year's Day
- 6: Epiphany, Festival of the Three Magic Kings (Christian)
- 7: Ukrainian Christmas
- 12, 13: Lohri (Hindu)
- 13, 14: Makar Sankranti (Hindu)
- 14: Ukrainian New Year
- 15, 16: Pongal (Hindu)
- 15: Martin Luther King Jr. Day (United States)
- 26: Republic Day (India)
- 26: Australia Day

January/February
- Tu B'Shevat (Jewish)
- Shab e-Barat (Muslim)
- Basant Panchami (Hindu)
- Chinese New Year (between January 21 and February 20)
- Carnaval de Québec, Canada (17 days)

February
- 2: Candlemas (Christian)
- 3: Setsubun (Japan)
- 6: Waitangi Day (New Zealand)
- 11: National Foundation Day (Japan)
- 14: St. Valentine's Day
- 15: Nehar (Jewish)
- 15: National Flag Day (Canada)

Movable Dates in February
- Argungu Fishing Festival (Nigeria)
- Shrove Tuesday (Christian)
- Mardi Gras (Christian)
- N'cwala Harvest Festival (Zambia)

February/March
- Maghapuja (Buddhist)
- Shivratri (Hindu)

March
- 1: St. David's Day (Wales)
- 3: Matsuri (Japan)
- 6: National Day (Ghana)
- 17: St. Patrick's Day (Ireland)
- 23: National Day (Pakistan)
- 25: National Day (Greece)

Movable Dates in March
- Hola Mohalla (Sikh)
- Holi (Hindu)
- Purim (Jewish)

March/April
- Easter (Christian)

April
- 1: April Fools' Day
- 4, 5: Ch'ing Ming Festival (Hong Kong)
- 13, 14: Baisakhi (Sikh)
- 14, 15: Vishu (Hindu)
- 21: First Day of Ridvan (Baha'i)
- 23: Egemenlik Bayrami (Turkey)
- 23: St. George's Day (England)
- 29: Ninth Day of Ridvan (Baha'i)

Movable Dates in April
- Passover (Jewish)
- Ram Navami (Hindu)
- Toonik Tyme (Canada)

Annual Celebrations

May
- 1: May Day (northern Europe)
- 2: Twelfth Day of Ridvan (Baha'i)
- 3: National Day (Poland)
- 5: Kodomono-hi (Japan)
- 17: National Day (Norway)
- 23: Declaration of the Bab (Baha'i)
- 24: Victoria Day (England)
- 28, 29: Ascension of Baha'u'llah (Baha'i)

Movable Dates in May
- Ascension Day (Christian)
- Visakhapuja (Buddhist)
- Pentecost (Christian)
- Mother's Day (2nd Sunday in May)
- Victoria Day (Canada)

June
- 2: Republic Day (Italy)
- 6: National Day (Sweden)
- 12: Russian Independence Day
- 21: National Aboriginal Day (Canada)
- 23: Midsummer's Eve or St. John's Day (England)
- 24: Saint-Jean-Baptiste Day (Quebec)

Movable Dates in June
- Father's Day (3rd Sunday in June)

July
- 1: Canada Day (Canada)
- 4: Independence Day (United States)
- 9: National Day (Argentina)
- 14: Bastille Day (France)
- 21: National Day (Belgium)

July/August
- O Bon, Family Remembrance Day (Japan)
- Tisha B'Av (Jewish)
- Caribana (first weekend in July or August)

Movable Dates in July
- Calgary Stampede (Alberta, Canada) (10 days)

August
- 1: National Day (Switzerland)
- 6: National Day (Bolivia)
- 17: National Day (Indonesia)

Movable Dates in August
- Civic Holiday (Canada: 1st Monday in August)
- Esala Perahera (Buddhist)
- Raksha Bandhan (India)
- Eisteddfod (Wales)
- Folklorama (Winnipeg, Canada)

August/September
- Janamashtmi (Hindu)
- Onam (Hindu)
- Ganesh Chaturthi (Hindu)

September
- 7: National Day (Brazil)
- 16: National Day (Mexico)
- 18: National Day (Chile)
- 30: National Day (Botswana)

Movable Dates in September
- Rosh Hashanah (Jewish)
- Labour Day (Canada: 1st Monday in September)

Annual Celebrations

September/October
- Yom Kippur (Jewish)
- Succot (Jewish)
- Trung Thu (Vietnam)

October
- 1: National Day (China)
- 9: National Day (Uganda)
- 12: National Day (Spain)
- 12: Columbus Day (United States)
- 24: United Nations Day
- 24: National Day (Zambia)
- 26: National Day (Austria)
- 31: Halloween

Movable Dates in October
- Dussehra (Hindu)
- Simhat Torah (Jewish)
- Thanksgiving (Canada: 2nd Monday in October)

October/November
- Diwali (Hindu)

November
- 1: All Saints' Day (Christian)
- 2: All Souls' Day (Christian)
- 1, 2: Day of the Dead (Christian)
- 5: Guy Fawkes Day (United Kingdom)
- 11: Remembrance Day (Canada)
- 30: St. Andrew's Day (Scotland)

Movable Dates in November
- Thanksgiving (United States: 4th Thursday in November)

December
- 6: National Day (Finland)
- 6: St. Nicholas's Day (Christian)
- 9: National Day (Tanzania)
- 12: National Day (Kenya)
- 13: St. Lucia's Day (Christian)
- 24: Christmas Eve (Christian)
- 25: Christmas Day (Christian)
- 26: Boxing Day (England and Canada)
- 31: New Year's Eve

Movable Dates in December
- Hanukkah (Jewish)
- Kwanzaa (African-American harvest festival)

Celebrations Information

April Fool's Day
- Occurs annually on April 1
- Day is generally observed by playing (a) practical joke(s) on others
- Believed origin involves changes in the calendar (King Charles IX adopted the Gregorian calendar and accepted January 1 as the beginning of the new year. Those who refused or forgot the new date received foolish gifts and invitations to nonexistent parties.)

Boxing Day
- Celebrated on December 26 in Canada, Great Britain, Australia, Bermuda, and some Caribbean Islands
- Originated in Britain long ago; on the day after Christmas the offerings that had been placed in the churches over the holidays were opened and the contents distributed to the poor

Calgary Stampede
- Famous annual event in Alberta
- Formally called the Calgary Exhibition and Stampede
- Held every July for 10 days
- Stampede includes bull riding, barrel racing, and steer wrestling

Canada Day
- Canada's national holiday celebrated on July 1
- Celebrates the first Dominion Day on July 1, 1867 when a vote by the British House of Commons passed legislation to give the Canadian provinces permission to unite and form a confederation
- Celebrated with parades, fireworks, songs, games, dances, crafts, and foods

Caribana
- Based on the Caribbean Carnival
- The largest cultural festival in North America
- Showcases Caribbean music, dance, arts and crafts, fashion, and food
- Highlight of festival in Toronto is the Caribana parade featuring thousands of brilliantly costumed masqueraders and live calypso, soca, steelpan, reggae, and samba bands
- Takes place in August

Carnaval de Québec
- Largest winter carnival in the world
- Takes place in January and February for 17 consecutive days
- Celebrates the magic of winter
- Bonhomme is the renowned key figure of the Carnaval
- Main attractions are located in the heart of Québec City

Chinese New Year
- Takes place between January 21 and February 20 (on the 1st day of the Chinese calendar)
- Lasts for 15 days
- Two celebrations in one: New Year's and a big birthday party; according to Chinese tradition, everyone's birthday is celebrated on New Year's Day
- Time for feasting and visiting family and friends
- Celebrations are based on bringing luck, health, happiness, and wealth for the coming year
- New Year's parade features a large dragon associated with long life and prosperity

---

Celebrations Information

- Families clean their homes thoroughly before the celebrations begin to rid them of last year's bad luck
- All Chinese children, and people who are not married, receive "lucky money" in special red envelopes on New Year's morning

Christmas Eve
- Celebrated on December 24, the eve before Christmas
- Christians often go to church to await the birth day of Jesus
- Children in many countries believe this is the evening Santa Claus delivers gifts to children throughout the world

Christmas Day
- Celebrated on December 25
- Christian holiday that celebrates the birth of Jesus Christ
- The Christian story states that Jesus, the son of Mary and Joseph, was born in a stable in Bethlehem
- A day celebrated with family and friends
- People usually exchange gifts, sing Christmas carols, and enjoy a turkey dinner with family

Civic Holiday
- 1st Monday in August
- Created just so that there is a statutory holiday during August (not in Québec, Newfoundland, or Yukon)

Diwali
- Known as the Festival of Lights
- Popular in India
- Symbolizes the return of Rama (an Indian god who long ago returned from the forest after 14 years and was crowned King of Ayodhya)
- People celebrate by lighting oil lamps to welcome Lakshmi, the goddess of prosperity
- People wear colourful clothes and eat special foods and sweets
- Takes place in October/November

Easter
- Occurs between March 22 and April 20
- It is the Christian holy day when it is said Jesus came back to life after being crucified
- Celebrates the miracle of Jesus rising from the tomb to heaven
- Viewed as a time of new life and rebirth in nature
- Many children associate this day with the Easter bunny, though the Easter bunny has no relation to the Christian Easter story

Father's Day
- Takes place on the 3rd Sunday in June
- Idea first proposed by Mrs. John B. Dodd of Washington in 1909, to honour her father who, as a single parent, raised her
- Proclaimed a national holiday in 1966
- Considered a day to honour fathers and all men who act as father figures

Folklorama
- Celebrated in Winnipeg, Manitoba, during the first two weeks of August
- North America's largest multicultural celebration
- Celebrates diversity and promotes cultural understanding

Celebrations Information

Halloween
- Celebrated annually on the evening of October 31
- Customs include carving a jack-o-lantern, dressing up in costume, trick-or-treating, and bobbing for apples
- Symbolically associated with death and the supernatural
- Falls on the eve of All Saints' Day

Hanukkah
- Also known as the Festival of Lights
- Jewish celebration in December (begins on the eve of the 25th day of the Hebrew month of Kislev)
- Lasts eight days
- Symbolizes the rededication of the Temple of Jerusalem more than 2000 years ago
- When it was time to light the Temple lamp there was only enough oil for the lamp to burn for one day. Miraculously, the lamp burned for eight days.
- Significance of eight days is celebrated by lighting one candle for each of the eight days
- Figure that holds the eight candles is called a menorah

Kwanzaa
- African-American celebration
- Begins on December 26 and lasts for seven days
- Based on seven principles symbolized by candles, which are placed in a candleholder called a kinara—one candle is lit each night
- The seven candles stand for unity, self-determination, collective work and responsibility, cooperative economics, purpose, creativity, and faith
- Families talk about the meaning of each candle the night it is lit
- At the end of the holiday, the community gathers for a feast called a karamu
- A karamu features traditional African food, ceremonies honouring the ancestors, assessment of the old year and commitments for the new, performances, music, and dancing

Labour Day
- Special holiday set aside to honour workers and the contributions they make to their jobs and to society
- Takes place on the 1st Monday in September
- The holiday was born through the activities of the trade unions in the late 1800s
- Some unions still hold annual demonstrations, parades, and picnics on this day

Mardi Gras
- Also known as "Shrove Tuesday" or Carnival
- Annual festival marking the final day before the Christian fast of Lent (a 40-day period)
- Falls between February 3 and March 9
- Term Mardi Gras is French for "Fat Tuesday"
- Carnival season includes spectacular parades featuring pageants, elaborate costumes, masked balls, and dancing in the streets
- Most commonly associated with events in New Orleans

May Day
- Name given to the 1st day of May
- Celebrated mid-way between the long, cold nights of winter and the warm days of summer

---

Celebrations Information

- Celebrated as a festival for children marking the reappearance of flowers during the spring
- Greeted with dancing around a pole covered with garlands, called a maypole (large streamers hanging from the pole are held by the dancers)
- Celebrated in many European countries as a labour day

Mother's Day
- Celebrated on the 2nd Sunday of May
- Origin traced back to spring celebrations in ancient Greece in honour of Rhea, the "mother of gods"
- In 1600s, England celebrated a day called "Mothering Sunday" to honour mothers of England
- Appeared in North America in 1872 when Julia Ward Howe organized a Mother's Day Meeting in Boston
- Time to be thankful for all the things that mothers do for families and others

National Aboriginal Day
- Celebrated June 21 to coincide with the summer solstice
- Officially declared in 1996
- An opportunity for Canadians to recognize the achievements and contributions of Canada's Aboriginal peoples

National Flag Day
- Observed on February 15
- A time to celebrate the importance of our flag as a symbol of Canada's freedom, diversity, and natural beauty

New Year's Eve
- The last night of the year, according to the Gregorian calendar, December 31
- Night of celebration with family and friends
- Lots of feasting, drinking, and dancing

New Year's Day
- First day of the year, January 1, in the Gregorian calendar
- Traditionally observed as a religious feast (believed to be the occasion on which it was revealed that Mary would give birth to the Son of God)
- In modern times has become an occasion for spirited celebration and the making of personal resolutions for the new year

Passover
- Begins on the 15th day of the Hebrew month of Nissan (in April)
- Commemorates the birth of the Jewish nation and the freedom of the Jews
- After 210 years of slavery in Egypt, Moses told Pharaoh, "Let my people go."
- God brought 10 plagues upon the Egyptians (The 10th and final plague was the death of firstborn children.)
- It is believed that God passed through the land of Egypt to execute the plague, but "passed over" Jewish homes, hence the name of the holiday
- There is a special dietary restriction during Passover, specifically no chametz (leavened foods)

Ramadan
- 9th month of the Muslim calendar
- During the month, Muslims fast during daylight hours (called the Fast of Ramadan)
- Time of worship and contemplation
- Time to strengthen family and community ties

Celebrations Information

- Can be celebrated in November, December, January, or February (beginning depends on the sighting of the moon)

Remembrance Day
- November 11
- A day to remember those who fought in the world wars
- Honours more than 1.7 million Canadians who volunteered to fight in major wars and thousands more who have served Canada in pursuit of world peace
- Honours peacekeepers and the promotion of peace
- Commonly associated with the symbol of the poppy

Rosh Hashanah
- Jewish New Year
- Celebrated on the 1st and 2nd days of the Jewish month of Tishri (September or October)
- Begins the observance of the Ten Penitential Days
- In the Bible it is mentioned as a day of remembrance and the sounding of the shofar (ram's horn)

Saint-Jean-Baptiste Day
- Celebrated in Québec on June 24
- Celebrates the birth of St. Jean Baptiste, the patron saint of French Canadians
- There are parades, sports, games, fireworks, and special foods for sale
- The night before the parades, the sky is lit by St. Jean's fires across Québec. A town along the St. Lawrence River lights its fire. The bonfire then becomes a signal for the next town to light its fire, and so on.
- After the rise of the Québec Nationalist movement in the 1970s, June 24 is also called "Fête nationale du Québec"

St. Patrick's Day
- Holiday honouring St. Patrick, the patron saint of Ireland
- Celebrated annually on March 17 (St. Patrick's feast day)
- Saint Patrick was a missionary in the fifth century CE who is credited with converting Ireland to Christianity
- Wearing green clothing on this day is a popular tradition
- The shamrock is the symbol associated with the holiday (has three leaves – used by St. Patrick to explain the Trinity to the Irish people)

St. Valentine's Day
- Celebrated annually on February 14
- Traditions include exchanging of candy, flowers, cards, and gifts between loved ones
- Considered a day of romance
- Truth behind St. Valentine's Day legends is unknown
- Believed to be based on the patron Saint Valentine who performed marriages for young lovers in secret (Emperor Claudius II had outlawed marriage; he had decided that single men made better soldiers than those with families.)

Thanksgiving
- Celebrated on the second Monday of October
- First declared a national holiday in 1879
- A day shared with family and friends to celebrate "the bountiful harvest with which Canada has been blessed"

Celebrations Information

- Associated with turkey, squash, and pumpkin pie
- Holiday believed to have originated in Europe, where farmers would fill a curved goat's horn with fruit and grain to give thanks for the abundance of food at harvest time

Toonik Tyme
- Festival in Iqaluit, Nunavut held the last week in April to celebrate the coming of spring
- Traditional Inuit games, snowmobile and dogteam races, and entertainment
- Festival is named after a legendary Inuk giant called Toonik

Ukrainian Christmas
- Celebrated on January 7 by Ukrainians all over the world
- On Ukrainian Christmas eve (January 6), Ukrainians cook a special dinner of 12 meatless dishes. One of the dishes is called kutia. It is prepared from cooked wheat and a special syrup containing honey, poppy seeds, raisins, and sometimes walnuts.

Ukrainian New Year
- Celebrated on January 14
- On New Year's morning, traditionally, children visited neighbouring homes and scattered wheat in the houses while reciting a verse wishing the neighbours prosperity and health in the new year. In turn, the neighbours offered the children treats or money.

Victoria Day
- Celebrates the birth of Queen Victoria on May 24, 1819
- Often referred to as "Firecracker Day"
- Time of celebration, barbecues, and gatherings with family and friends

Yom Kippur
- Jewish holiday that falls on the 10th day of Tishri (the 7th month of the Jewish calendar)
- Occurs in September or the first half of October
- The most sacred of Jewish holidays
- Considered a day of confession, repentance, and prayers for forgiveness of sins committed during the year
- The day is observed by a rigorous fast and nearly unbroken prayer
- The mood is solemn, but not mournful

My Favourite Celebrations

Name: _____ Date: _____

	Celebration From My Country of Origin	Canadian Celebration
Name of Celebration		
When It Is Celebrated		
Why I Like This Celebration		
Illustration		

3A

4 Relationships

Curricular Connections

- Language Arts: speaking, listening, reading, writing, viewing, representing
- Social Studies: rules and responsibility, citizenship
- Health: Personal relationships
- Art: drawing
- Drama: role playing

Background Information for Teachers

This lesson focuses on cooperation through activities related to interpersonal relationships and interactions with others, particularly friendship.

Vocabulary – Relationships

- friend
- friendship
- personality trait
- positive
- negative
- classmate
- peer
- child
- adult
- neighbour
- stranger

Materials

- vocabulary cards – *Relationships* (included. Photocopy one set onto sturdy tagboard, and cut out.) (3.4.1)
- *Peanut Butter is Forever*, a book by Melanie Zola
- *Percy Jackson and the Olympians: The Lightning Thief*, a book by Rick Riordon
- chart paper
- markers
- relationship scenarios sheet (included. Make one photocopy for each ELL-student/peer-helper pair.) (3.4.4)

Integrated Class Activities

- Peer relationships are an important part of life for middle-years students, and all students will benefit from discussions about friendship. Consider doing all or some of the activities from Instructional Activity: Part Two of this lesson with the whole class.

- To focus on friendship and peer issues, consider reading the following novels to or with the class:
    - *Peanut Butter is Forever*, by Melanie Zola
    - *Percy Jackson and the Olympians: The Lightning Thief*, by Rick Riordon

- All students will benefit from discussion about appropriate social behaviour with others. Consider doing all or some of the activities from Instructional Activity: Part Three of this lesson with the entire class.

Whole-Class Career Connections

- Discuss the various ways that students solve problems with peers at school. Identify the people in the school who can help them resolve problems.

- Have the school counselor present to students on the various aspects of his/her job, and the training required to become a school counselor.

- Discuss other jobs focusing on relationships, such as a mediator or a family or marriage counselor. Discuss the types of skills these people need in order to do their jobs successfully.

▶

Module 3

Instructional Activity: Part One: Friendship

In the middle of a sheet of chart paper, record and circle the term *Friendship*. Ask:

- What is this word?
- What does it mean?
- Are friends important? Why?
- What kinds of things do you do with friends?
- How does a person treat his or her friends?

Use this discussion to create a web about friendship, as in the example below.

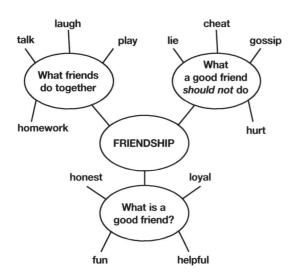

Next, discuss the term *personality trait,* explaining to students that it describes the way a person acts and thinks.

Discuss important traits of a good friend, and encourage students to remember these traits in their daily interactions with peers.

Be sure to discuss negative traits as well, or behaviours that are not as desirable in friendships.

Record positive and negative traits on the web as well.

Independent Activity: Part One: Activity Sheet A

Directions to students:

Complete the herringbone chart by listing positive and negative personality traits (3.4.2).

Instructional Activity: Part Two: Interactions with Others

In follow-up to the discussion on friendship, have students reflect on ways to treat other people outside their circle of friends. Ask:

- Other than your friends, who do you spend time with?

Brainstorm an extensive list, including

- Family (parents/guardians, siblings, grandparents, cousins, aunts, uncles, and so on)
- Neighbours
- Teachers and other school staff
- Friends' families
- Acquaintances at school and in the community
- Strangers

Discuss with students how people should treat others. Use specific examples as a springboard to discussion:

- What would you do if you saw a neighbour at the park?
- How do you act toward a friend's family members when you are in their home?
- What would do if you got the last seat on the bus and an elderly person got on?

Note: Some cultures revere their elderly in a very special way. This may be an opportunity to talk about attitudes toward the elderly and have students share special relationships they have with senior citizens.

Discuss such points as being respectful, polite, and helpful. Have students role play scenarios such as those above, as well as some of their own ideas, to express ways that they would treat others.

Note: Have students share examples of how people interact with others in their home countries. In some cases, expectations for behaviour can differ vastly from culture to culture. It is important for students to learn that one way is not superior to another, but just different, and should be respected as such.

Note: This is also an excellent opportunity to discuss personal safety in terms of addressing strangers and dealing with uncomfortable or unsafe situations.

Independent Activity: Part Two: Activity Sheet B

Directions to students:

Complete the chart to describe the best choices for how to treat friends and other people. Also, complete the writing task. (3.4.3)

Note: Be flexible in terms of how students complete the chart. Their answers can be general or specific, as can their illustrations. For example:

Best Choices	Examples	Illustrations
For How to Treat Friends	■ Help them when they are in trouble ■ Share ■ Be honest ■ Encourage them when they are doing something difficult	
For How to Treat Other People (for example, teachers, neighbours)	■ Say "good morning" or "hello" when you see them ■ Wave when you see them outside ■ Hold the door when someone is carrying a load ■ Admit when you have done something wrong	

Peer Activity

Have ELL-student/peer-helper pairs role play the scenarios on the Relationship Scenarios sheet (3.4.4). Encourage students to discuss together the best choices for how to deal with each situation.

Note: Depending on students' comfort levels, you may choose to have them present a scenario for classmates. This is an excellent springboard for discussion about relationships.

Extensions

- Add new vocabulary to the multilingual word wall.
- Have students add new vocabulary to their personal vocabulary folders or personal dictionaries.
- Discuss cultural sayings or adages related to how we treat others. For example:
    - The Golden Rule: Do unto others as you would have them do unto you, or, treat others the way you like to be treated.
    - Pay it forward: Based on the novel and 2000 movie of the same name, the saying means that when someone does a favour for you, instead of "paying back" the favour to that person, you do something for someone else.

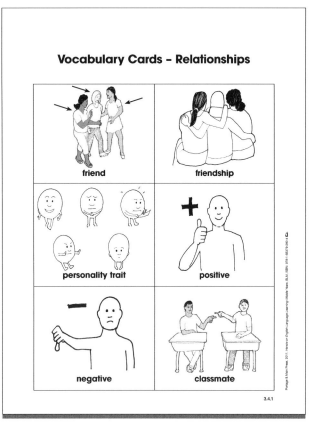
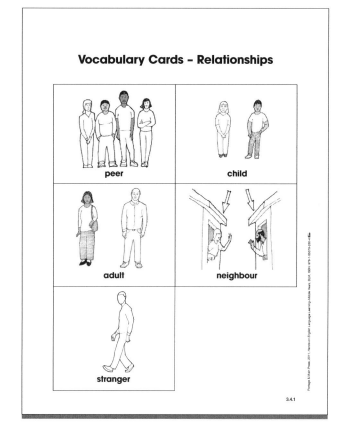

Relationship Scenarios Sheet

You see a classmate being bullied at the shopping mall.	Your mother has a carload of shopping bags filled with groceries.
Your best friend is sick and has missed a week of school.	Your science teacher is away, and there is a substitute teacher in class. Some students are not behaving very well.
There is a new student in your class, who has just moved here from another country. The student is shy and seems very scared in class.	You find an MP3 player in the hallway at school.

Peer Activity

5 Rules, Laws, and Responsibility

Curricular Connections

- Language Arts: speaking, listening, reading, writing, viewing, representing
- Social Studies: rules and responsibility, citizenship
- Health: personal relationships
- Art: drawing
- Drama: role playing

Background Information for Teachers

This lesson focuses on cooperation through activities related to fair play, game rules, and lawmaking.

Vocabulary – Rules, Laws and Responsibility

- board game
- card game
- die/dice
- marker/game piece
- start
- finish
- win
- lose
- tie
- card
- heart
- spade
- diamond
- club
- deal
- deck
- rules
- responsibility
- citizen

Materials

- various board games
- decks of cards
- vocabulary cards – *Rules, Laws, and Responsibility* (included. Photocopy one set onto sturdy tagboard, and cut apart cards.) (3.5.1)
- pocket chart
- markers
- chart paper
- Characteristics of a Good Sport checklist (included. Make a photocopy for each student.) (3.5.2)
- Responsibilities of Canadian Citizens information sheet (included. Make an overhead copy of this sheet, or photocopy for each student.) (3.5.4)
- overhead projector (optional)
- materials for making a class book (paper, binding mechanism, and so on)

Integrated Class Activities

- This lesson provides an excellent opportunity to discuss with students the importance of fair play during games. As a class, brainstorm a list of rules or guidelines for fair play, whether it is for board games, card games, or other types of games. Some ideas to include might be:

  - Play by the rules.
  - Never argue about the game, and discuss differences peacefully.
  - Respect other players.
  - Don't be a show off.
  - Show appreciation for good play/performance by all players, including those on my team and those on the other team.
  - Be a team player.
  - Remember that winning isn't everything, and having fun, improving skills, making friends, and doing your best are just as important.

- Have students conduct a self-assessment of their skills in being a good sport. Use the included "Characteristics of a Good Sport" checklist (3.5.2).

Note: ELL students may require support in understanding and completing this checklist.

- Create a class book of card games. Have each student select a card game, write a description of it, and draw an illustration of the game. Also, include in the book a copy of the class's guidelines for fair play. Bind student's pages together, and place the book in the school library.

Whole-Class Career Connections

- Have (a) member(s) of the local police force talk to students about the training required for their jobs.
- Have students review the Employability Skills Checklist (included in module 1, lesson 1; 1.1.8). Ask (a) member(s) of the local police force about skills related to this list. Also, have them share how they are assessed based on these skills (interviews, written tests, and so on).
- Have students discuss the types of skills required by a sports referee.

Instructional Activity: Part One

Introduce this lesson by asking students to name some of the games they like to play. Record their suggestions on chart paper. Encourage students to think of both outdoor and indoor games, as well as active and quiet/table games.

Use the list to begin a discussion about students' favourite games. Ask:

- What is your favourite game?
- How do you play _____ (name game)?
- What do you need to play the game _____ (name game)?

Introduce the vocabulary cards – *Rules, Laws, and Responsibility* (3.5.1). Use the cards to discuss the procedures, rules, and necessary materials for each game listed.

Now, have students name some of the games played in their countries of origin.

Note: If students are uncomfortable or have difficulty describing the game, encourage them to try a demonstration instead.

Discuss the similarities and differences between the various games. Students may discover that in their home countries, they play a game similar to one played in Canada, but it simply has a different name (for example, soccer versus football).

Next Step

Playing games is an excellent way for students to expand vocabulary and conversational skills. Take this opportunity to have students play several of the games recorded earlier on chart paper. Display the vocabulary cards – *Rules, Laws, and Responsibility* in the pocket chart, and encourage students to use target vocabulary as they play.

After playing several of the games, have students share the challenges experienced while playing various games.

Instructional Activity: Part Two

Discuss with students ways that they are governed in their daily lives. Ask:

- Are you allowed to do whatever you want all the time? Why or why not?
- Who makes rules for you? (parents, teachers, principals, coaches, police, government)
- Why are rules important? (safety, structure, fairness)

5

- What would happen in a soccer game, for example, if there were no rules?
- Who leads a team in a soccer game? (coach)
- What is the coach's job? (to teach the game and lead the team)
- What if there were no coaches?
- What is a referee's job in a soccer game?
- What if there were no referees?

Discuss the game of soccer with students. Ask:

- How is the game of soccer played?
- What are the rules of the game?
- How did you learn the rules for soccer? (taught to me, watched, found out by playing, read)
- What happens if you break a rule in soccer?
- If you were able to make up one new rule for soccer, what would it be? Why?

Have students imagine a game of soccer with no rules. Ask:

- What might happen in this game?
- Would this be a fair and safe way to play? Why not?

Focus now on rules at school. Ask:

- What are the rules in our classroom? (List these on chart paper.)
- Who made up these rules? Why?
- Are the rules exactly the same as those in the classroom next door?
- Are there rules that everyone in the school follows?
- Who made up those rules?
- Are there rules for all schools?
- What might the rules be in other schools?
- Who made up those rules?

Focus now on rules at home. Ask:

- What are your rules at home? (List these on chart paper.)
- Who makes up those rules?

Discuss the fact that different families have different sets of rules. Have students compare and contrast the rules in their homes.

Now, discuss students' understanding of laws. Record the term *Laws* on chart paper. Ask:

- What is a law? (a rule for the people in a community)

Record this definition on the chart paper. Then, ask:

- Who makes laws? (elected governments)
- Who makes sure that these laws are followed? (police, RCMP)
- Why are laws important for communities? (to ensure peoples' safety, to keep peace, to maintain order, and so on)
- What are some of the rules we must follow in our community? (List these on chart paper.)
- What happens if someone does not follow these rules?

This is an excellent opportunity to discuss local current events and community issues as they relate to law-making. For example, discuss:

- Graffiti and tagging
- Cell phone use while driving
- Wearing seatbelts while driving/riding in a car

This is also an opportunity for a discussion about debates and for students to practise their debating skills by arguing on different sides of an issue.

Independent Activity: Activity Sheet A

Directions to students:

Record rules or laws for your classroom, school, home, and community. Illustrate each rule or law, as if you are making a poster to encourage people to follow it. Describe the purpose of each rule or law (3.5.3).

Instructional Activity: Part Three

Discuss the responsibilities of people living in Canada. Ask:

- Aside from following laws, what other things are Canadians and newcomers all supposed to do?

Display the "Responsibilities of Canadian Citizens" information sheet (3.5.4) on the overhead projector (or distribute a copy to each student), and read it aloud together with students. Explain that although some newcomers are not yet Canadian citizens, many of the responsibilities apply to all people living in Canada. Ask:

- Which of these responsibilities are for Canadian citizens only?
- Which ones are meant for all of us?

Discuss voting by citizens who are 18 or older. Also, discuss the importance of recognizing and respecting the freedom and rights of others.

Peer Activity

Have each ELL student work with one or two peer helpers to explain and teach a popular game played in his or her country of origin. (ELL students may request more than one peer helper if the game requires more than two people to play.)

Note: Give ELL students advance notice about this activity, as they may wish to prepare for it. Also, ask students if they will need any help from you (for example, to gather materials needed to play the game).

Extensions

- Add new vocabulary to the multilingual word wall.
- Have students add new vocabulary to their personal vocabulary folders or personal dictionaries.
- Have students play "no rules" games such as bingo or checkers. As a class, discuss the importance of rules for fairness and equity.
- Invite local police officers or lawmakers (government officials) to present to the class.
- If possible, share school district policy manuals, codes of conduct, provincial guidelines, or other documents that govern rules in schools.
- Have students create posters from their illustrations on Activity Sheet A (3.5.3). Display the posters in the classroom, school, and community.

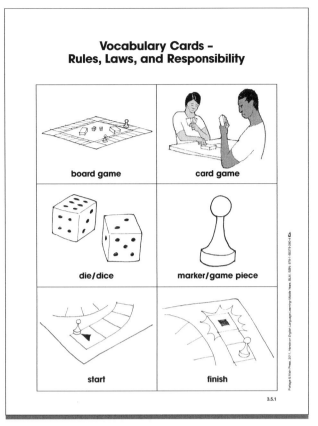
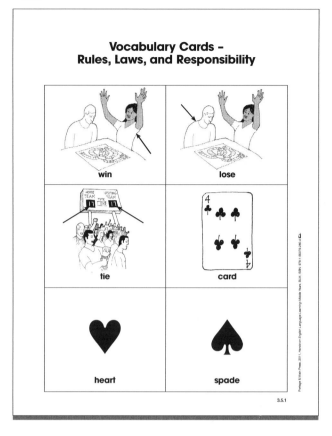

Vocabulary Cards – Rules, Laws, and Responsibility

citizen

Blackline Masters

3.5.2

Date: _____ Name: _____

Characteristics of a Good Sport

	Characteristics	Always	Often	Rarely
	I...			
Fair Play	am a respectful winner			
	don't cheat			
	follow the rules			
	try not to argue			
	accept instruction			
	accept a loss with self respect			
Respect	use materials and equipment properly			
	don't take part in physical violence			
	do not verbally abuse others (e.g., name-calling)			
	admit to my own mistakes			
	control my anger			
	show concern and empathy for the other player or team			
	shake hands at the end of the game			
Teamwork	put team goals ahead of personal goals			
	encourage and include team members			
	don't put down team members			

Modified from Manitoba Education Curriculum for Physical Education and Health

3.5.3

Date: _____ Name: _____

Cooperation

Rule/Law	Purpose (Why is the rule or law important?)	Illustration
Classroom		
School		
Home		
Community		

5A

3.5.4

Responsibilities of Canadian Citizens

- Understand and obey Canadian laws
- Participate in Canada's democratic system
- Vote in elections
- Allow other Canadians to enjoy their rights and freedoms
- Appreciate and help to preserve Canada's multicultural heritage

6 Government

Curricular Connections

- Language Arts: speaking, listening, reading, writing, viewing, representing
- Social Studies: rules and responsibility, citizenship, government
- Mathematics: surveys, tallies, graphing, interpreting data

Background Information for Teachers

This lesson introduces students to the concept of democratic government, levels of government, and the election process in Canada.

The three levels of government—federal, provincial, and municipal—are responsible for different services. Some examples are:

- Federal: citizenship, banks, defence, RCMP
- Provincial: healthcare, childcare, education
- Municipal: public transport, fire department, city police, garbage removal, city streets

The "Levels of Government" information sheet (3.6.1) provides additional information.

Vocabulary – Government

- government
- law
- federal
- leader
- prime minister
- member of parliament (MP)
- provincial
- member of the legislature (MLA)
- territorial
- premier
- municipal
- mayor
- city councilor
- school division/district
- school board
- school trustee
- election
- candidate
- riding
- political party

Materials

- chart paper
- markers
- student dictionaries
- writing paper
- rulers
- several colours of highlighters
- scissors
- masking tape
- map of Canada (included. Make an overhead copy of the map.) (3.6.1)
- map of Canada's Provinces and Territories (included. Make an overhead copy of the map.) (3.6.2)
- map of Communities in Canada (included. Make an overhead copy of the map.) (3.6.3)
- Levels of Government information sheet (included. Make an overhead transparency of this sheet.) (3.6.4)
- dry-erase markers
- overhead projector
- vocabulary cards – *Government* (included. Photocopy onto sturdy tagboard, and cut apart cards.) (3.6.5)
- mural paper
- markers
- current newspapers (local, regional, and national) and news magazines (including ones in different languages and from different cultures)
- newsletters from local school division/ district and minutes from local school board meetings
- access to the internet (for research purposes)

6

Integrated Class Activities

- The study of government will benefit all students in the class, as this topic is integral to the social studies curricular outcomes and expectations. Consider doing any or all of the instructional, peer, or independent activities with the whole class.

- Have a local school trustee talk to the class about this level of government. This is an excellent opportunity for students to share ideas for improving their school. As a form of social action, have students think about issues and concerns related to their school and formulate questions to ask the guest. For example:
  - How would we go about having more trees planted in our field?
  - How does a school decide which courses to offer?
  - Could we have an course in computer electronics?

- Practise the democratic process, and learn about majority rule by voting on regular classroom issues. For example, have students brainstorm ideas for class parties, field trips, research projects, novels to study, and so on. As a class, vote on these issues, and keep tallies to record the decision-making process. Discuss and compare this to the election process in Canada.

- Have the whole class conduct research related to government leaders, both past and present. Students may choose to research a Canadian leader, or a leader in another country. As a class, formulate an outline for the research. For example:
  - Leader's full name
  - His or her personal background (birth date, birthplace, childhood)
  - His or her education
  - His or her career before government
  - His or her positions in government
  - His or her contributions
  - Reflection on why you choose to research this leader, and what you learned

Also, together as a class, identify assessment criteria for this research project, so that students understand what is expected of them. Consider including self, peer, and teacher assessment in this process.

Provide opportunities for students to share their research with the class and others.

Whole-Class Career Connections

- Research the electoral process in terms of the roles and jobs that make the process work. For example, learn about the role of returning officers, polling clerks, security officers, enumerators, and so on.

- Have local elected officials discuss their jobs and the process by which their careers resulted in elected office.

- Research individual politicians who have been forced to leave office as a result of breaching government rules and responsibilities of their office.

Instructional Activity: Part One

Provide students with writing paper. Have them title their sheets "Responsibilities of Family Members", and ask them to list the members of their household across the top of the sheet. Then, have students use their rulers to draw vertical lines between the names to create a chart. Ask:

- What is a responsibility? (something that is your job to do, that you must look after)
- What is each member in your household responsible for?
- Which chores does each person do?

▶

Module 3

On his or her chart, have each student record each family member's responsibilities and chores under that person's name. Suggest responsibilities such as:

- walking the dog
- cleaning bedroom
- laundry
- shovelling snow
- paying bills

Discuss students' responses. Ask:

- Are there any chores that *anyone* in the family could do?
- Are there some jobs that the adults in your house must do?
- Are there any chores that need more than one person to complete?

Explain to students that governing the country is similar to running a household. Everyone must take some responsibilities. In Canada, the responsibilities are divided among three levels of government.

Record the terms *federal, provincial*, and *municipal* on chart paper. As a class, discuss students' prior understanding of these terms.

Note: You may also wish to review students' understanding of a municipality. Discuss the differences between urban and rural communities in terms of size (city, town, village, and so on). Also, have students identify their own community as a city, town, or village. For those living on reserves, highlight the unique characteristics of this type of community as well.

Instructional Activity: Part Two

In the centre of a piece of chart paper, write the word *Government*, and circle it. Ask:

- Have you seen this word before?
- What does it mean?

As students discuss the term, record their ideas to create a concept web. They may be familiar with some people in government or governmental positions that should be included in the concept web.

For example:

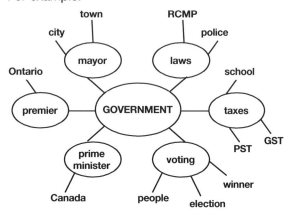

Once students have shared all of their ideas, review and discuss the concept web. Together, determine a definition for the term *government*. Have students check their dictionaries and compare the class definition to the dictionary definition. The class definition can then be modified, extended, or corrected for accuracy.

Explain to students that they are going to learn about the government of Canada. Encourage them to begin collecting newspaper articles and other materials related to the topic. Students may also suggest family members, family friends, and local government officials who could be invited to speak to the class.

Instructional Activity: Part Three

On chart paper list the names of the prime minister, the premier, and the local mayor, reeve, or chief. Ask:

- Who are these people?
- Where have you heard their names?
- What do these people do?

6

Record students' responses on the chart paper, beside each name.

Now, display the copy of the map of Canada on the overhead projector (3.6.1). Read the statement under the map, and complete the sentence.

Repeat using the map of Canada's provinces and territories (3.6.2). Read the statement under the map, and complete the sentence.

Then, repeat using the map of Canada's communities (3.6.3). First, have students locate their community on the map (add a dot in the correct location, and label it), as well as surrounding communities. Read the statement under the map, and complete the sentence.

Note: Encourage students to find pictures of the government leaders to display with the maps.

Next, display the Levels of Government information sheet (3.6.4), and discuss these responsibilities.

For review, display the corresponding overhead map of Canada again (either 3.6.1, 3.6.2, or 3.6.3), and ask the following questions:

- How many prime ministers are there in Canada? (3.6.1)
- How many premiers are there in Canada? (3.6.2)
- How many mayors are there in Ottawa? (3.6.3)
- Do we have a mayor in our community? (3.6.3)
- In which community near us would there be a reeve? A chief? A mayor? (3.6.3)

Instructional Activity: Part Four

Review with students the names of the prime minister, the premier, and the mayor/reeve/chief of your local community. Ask:

- How did these people become government leaders?

Discuss with students their prior knowledge of how elections work in Canada. Ask:

- What is an election?
- Who votes in an election?
- For whom do voters vote?

Model a simple election by having students vote for their favourite pizza toppings. Record this data as a tally on chart paper.

Now, record the term *political party* on chart paper. Explain that in Canada, political parties are groups of people with similar opinions and ideas about issues that affect Canadians. Ask students:

- Do you know the names of any political parties in Canada?

Record students' responses on chart paper.

Review in simple terms the process of elections in Canada. Explain that during an election, each political party has individuals called "candidates" running (competing) in local communities called "ridings", and people vote for one of these candidates. Whichever candidate gets the most votes wins the election in that riding; that individual is *elected* for that riding. Whichever political party elects the most candidates forms the government, and the leader of that party becomes the government leader.

This is an excellent opportunity to have students share their experiences and understanding of government and elections in their countries of origin. Their stories may be vastly different from the Canadian experience, so provide time for discussion.

▶

Note: This topic may be highly sensitive for some students, so be sure to consider students' cultural and political backgrounds during such a discussion.

Finally, introduce and discuss the target vocabulary for this lesson. Display the vocabulary cards – *Government* (3.6.5) in the pocket chart. Have students use the various terms in sentences to demonstrate their understanding.

Note: At this point, omit discussion about (and vocabulary cards for) school division/district, school board, and school trustee.

Instructional Activity: Part Five

Display the vocabulary cards for school division/district, school board, and school trustee. Explain that elected individuals are also responsible for the schools in communities. In each community, called a "school division" or "school district," candidates run in a smaller election to become a "school trustee." The elected trustees form a school board, a team of individuals, which is then responsible for decisions about all the schools in the area (school division or district).

Ask students:

- Do you know the name of our local school division/district?
- Do you know the names of any of the school trustees?
- What responsibilities do you think school trustees would have?
- What kinds of decisions would they have to make?

Record students' ideas on chart paper.

Display local school division/district newsletters and minutes from school-board meetings. Have students look at these and discuss their ideas about the responsibilities of school boards.

Peer Activity

On a large sheet of mural paper, draw an intersecting triple Venn diagram, as in the example below:

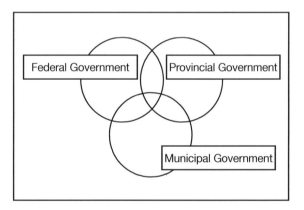

Provide ELL-student/peer-helper pairs with a variety of newspapers and news magazines (including ones written in their first languages and from other cultures) along with highlighters and masking tape. Be sure that each pair has a different colour of highlighter (so their work can be identified on the class Venn). Have students locate articles about services provided by the three levels of government. Encourage them to refer to the overhead maps and to the "Levels of Government" information sheet for assistance. Ask students to use their highlighters to emphasize the "proof" and then cut out the articles and glue them directly onto the Venn diagram in the appropriate circle or section.

Note: More than one pair of students may work on the same Venn diagram at different times. The different coloured highlighters will help students to identify their own work later.

6

Independent Activity: Activity Sheet A

Directions to students:

Complete the sentences at the top of the page. Then, use the chart to record responsibilities of all three levels of government (3.6.6).

Extensions

- Add new vocabulary to the multilingual word wall.
- Have students add new vocabulary to their personal vocabulary folders or personal dictionaries.
- Have students conduct research about the current prime minister, premier, and mayor, reeve, or chief. Students should look for the following information about each one:
  - Full name
  - Birth date
  - Birth place
  - Education
  - Career history
  - Political life
- To further explore the topic of government, introduce students to the various resources and videos available from the Government of Canada (see Parliment of Canada website, referenced on page 230)

Blackline Masters

3.6.1

Canada

The federal government looks after the entire country.

The head of the federal government is the prime minister.

The name of Canada's prime minister is _____.

3.6.2

Canada's Provinces and Territories

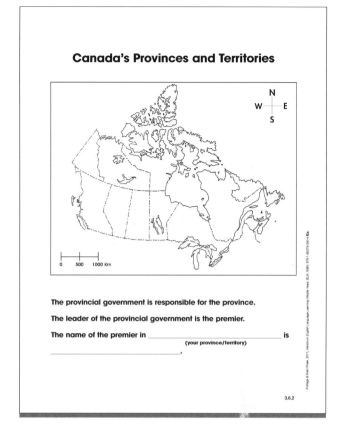

The provincial government is responsible for the province.

The leader of the provincial government is the premier.

The name of the premier in _____ (your province/territory) is

_____.

3.6.3

Communities in Canada

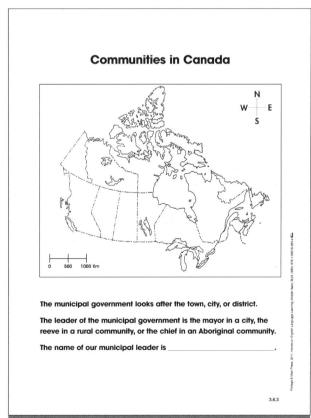

The municipal government looks after the town, city, or district.

The leader of the municipal government is the mayor in a city, the reeve in a rural community, or the chief in an Aboriginal community.

The name of our municipal leader is _____.

3.6.4

Levels of Government

Government of Canada
- Makes laws for all of Canada
- Responsibilities include:
  - Armed forces: soldiers, army, navy, air force
  - Passports
  - Television and radio
  - RCMP
  - Banks and money
  - Fisheries
  - Stamps and postal services
  - National parks

Provincial/Territorial Government
- Makes laws for the province/territory
- Responsibilities include:
  - Driver's licences
  - Healthcare*
  - Education
  - Childcare
  - Birth certificates
  - Provincial parks

Municipal Government
- Makes laws locally
- Responsibilities include:
  - Garbage pick-up and recycling
  - Repairing streets
  - Snow ploughing
  - Local police, fire, and ambulance
  - Public transit

*Note: Administration and delivery of healthcare services in Canada (which include insured primary healthcare such as services provided by physicians and other health professionals and care in hospitals) are the responsibility of each province or territory, guided by the provisions of the Canada Health Act. The provinces and territories fund these services with assistance from the federal government.

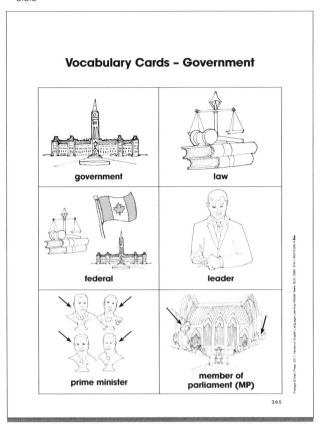
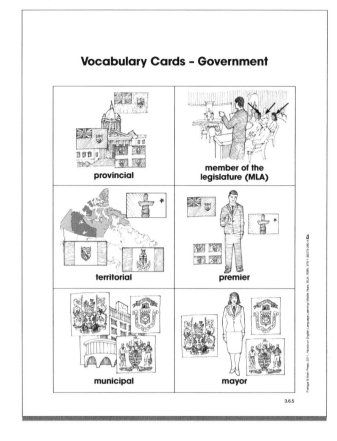
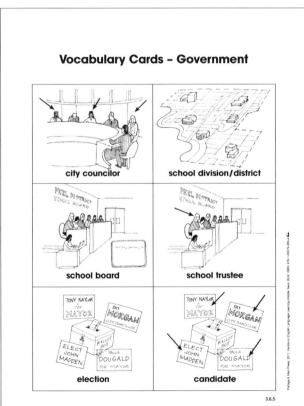
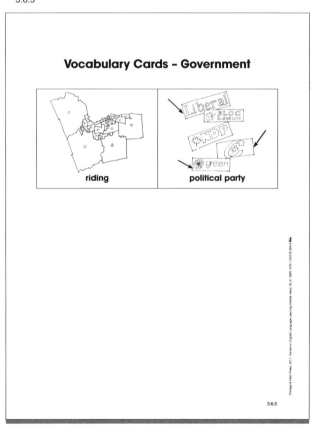

Blackline Masters

Date: _____ Name: _____

Government Leaders

The leader of the federal government is called the _____ .

This leader's name in Canada is _____ .

The leader of the provincial/territorial government is called the _____ .

This leader's name in our province/territory is _____ .

The leader of the municipal government is called the _____ .

This leader's name in our area is _____ .

Government Responsibilities

Federal	Provincial/Territorial	Municipal (Local)

6A

7 World Geography

Curricular Connections

- Language Arts: speaking, listening, reading, writing, viewing, representing
- Mathematics: surveys, graphs
- Science: landforms, graphs
- Social Studies: mapping skills, world geography, landforms
- Health: personal wellbeing
- Art: drawing

Vocabulary – World Geography

World Geography

- Earth
- globe
- atlas
- continent
- ocean/sea
- country
- equator
- prime meridian
- latitude
- longitude
- North Pole
- South Pole

Specific Locations

- North America
- South America
- Europe
- Africa
- Asia
- Australia
- Antarctica
- Pacific Ocean
- Atlantic Ocean
- Arctic Ocean
- Indian Ocean

Note: Depending on students' grade level(s), you may choose to focus on all vocabulary or select those words most appropriate for your students.

Materials

- vocabulary cards – *World Geography* (included. Photocopy one set onto sturdy tagboard, and cut apart cards.) (3.7.1)
- vocabulary cards – *Specific Locations* (included. Photocopy one set onto sturdy tagboard, and cut apart cards.) (3.7.2)
- pocket chart
- world globes (one for each student or pair of students)
- world maps
- maps of Canada
- commercial (store-bought) dictionaries and picture dictionaries
- balloons
- ballpoint pens
- chart paper
- permanent markers
- coloured wool
- markers or coloured pencils
- student atlases
- books that reflect the school's cultural diversity

Integrated Class Activities

- This lesson on world geography will benefit all middle-years students. Consider conducting all or some of the activities with the whole class. Display the vocabulary cards – *World Geography* (3.7.1) and the the vocabulary cards – *Specific Locations* (3.7.2) to support ELL learners during these activities.

- Have students who have originated from different countries trace their routes to Canada. For students born in Canada, have them interview family members to find out how their ancestors came to Canada. Use coloured wool on a map of the world to trace the routes of all students or their ancestors, or draw the routes on a printed or laminated map. This is an excellent opportunity to showcase cultural heritage.

- Take the opportunity to compare the distances travelled by various students. This data can also be used to create a bar graph.
- Have students survey their classmates as well as the rest of their school community to determine how many countries of the world are represented in the school population. Group countries by continent, and have students use the data to create pictographs or bar graphs.
- Create classroom- and school-library book collections (adolescent fiction, non-fiction, and reference books) that reflect the school's cultural diversity based on students' results from the preceding survey.

Whole-Class Career Connections

- As a class, brainstorm a list of jobs related to world geography. These might include (among others) geography teacher, town planner, travel agent, airline staff, air-traffic controller.
- Have a local travel agent present to the class about his or her training and work.
- Plan a fieldtrip to a local airport to observe the careers of airport personnel, air traffic controllers, and airline staff.

Instructional Activity: Part One

Provide students with world globes, and also display a world map. Have students brainstorm a list of words to describe what they see on the globe. Record these words on chart paper. Ask:

- What is a globe?

Explain that a globe is a model of the earth. Ask:

- What do you see on the globe?

Add to the list on chart paper, asking questions to trigger responses. For example, ask:

- What do the blue areas show? (water)
- What are the names of the bodies of water you see on the map? (list the names of the oceans)

Record the term *ocean* on chart paper. Explain that an ocean is an area of salt water surrounding Earth's land. Ask:

- What is salt water?
- Are the lakes and rivers in our community salt water?

Record the term *sea* on chart paper. Explain that sea is another word for ocean.* All of the salt water areas on Earth are called either oceans or seas. Have students identify some of the seas on Earth (Mediterranean, Caribbean, Red).

*Note: Although a sea is often considered to be smaller than an ocean, colloquially, the two terms are used as synonyms.

Now, have students locate the land masses on their globes. Ask

- What colour is the land on the globe? (this may vary on individual globes as well as from globe to globe)
- What large land areas do you see? (list the continents)

Record the term *continent* on chart paper. Explain that a continent is a large area of land. There are seven continents on Earth. Ask:

- Can you locate and name the seven continents?

Record these on chart paper.

Now, focus students' attention on the world map. Explain that a map shows a flat (two-dimensional) picture of the earth rather than the three-dimensional one shown on a globe. Have students identify the oceans and continents on the world map.

Provide students with atlases. Spend time reviewing the format of this resource so that students can find specific maps. Have students explore the atlases and use them to identify the oceans and continents.

Finally, have students share translations from their first language(s) for new vocabulary introduced in this activity.

Assessment for Learning

Have students use the terms recorded on chart paper to identify locations on the world map. For example, point to a word such as *water, ocean, land,* or *continent,* and have students identify an example on the world map.

Instructional Activity: Part Two

Display the world map and a map of Canada. Focus on each of the seven continents. Record the term *country* on chart paper. Explain that a country is part of a continent where a certain nation of people lives. Have students identify some of the countries on each of the seven continents.

Note: Take this opportunity to have students identify their countries of origin, as well as other countries with which they are familiar. Students may have spent time in or lived in several other countries prior to coming to Canada or on their journey here.

Now, review the terms *land, body of water, island, mountain, lake,* and *river* (all introduced in lesson 1 of this module). Have students locate various islands, mountains, lakes, rivers, and other bodies of water on the world map.

Display the vocabulary cards – *World Geography* (3.7.1) and *Specific Locations* (3.7.2) in the pocket chart. Review the terms with students, and have them identify and locate each one on the globe or map.

Instructional Activity: Part Three

Have students use the wall map of the world to share their route from their country of origin to their current Canadian community. Discuss modes of transportation by which they traveled during the journey.

Note: It is important to be especially sensitive to students' background experiences, as some may have lived through traumatic events during their journey to Canada. Be sure that students know to share only what they are comfortable sharing, and ensure that appropriate supports are in place for them to deal with past trauma.

Peer Activities

- For this peer activity, have each ELL student work side-by-side with a peer helper. Give both students a balloon, and have students blow them up. Referring to a world globe, have students use ballpoint pens to make rough sketches of the continents on their balloons. Ask them to label each continent and ocean on their balloons. Have students use permanent markers to colour each continent a different colour.

- Have each ELL student work with a peer helper and use the website Jigsaw Planet (<www.jigsawplanet.com>) to make an electronic puzzle of a map of the world (from a jpeg file).

Independent Activity: Part One: Activity Sheet A

Directions to students:

Print the names of the oceans and continents on the map. Use a globe or a world map to help you locate each continent and ocean (3.7.3).

Independent Activity: Part Two: Activity Sheet B

Directions to students:

Use the illustrations as clues to help you complete the sentences (3.7.4).

Independent Activity: Part Three: Activity Sheet C

Directions to students:

Use a marker or coloured pencil to trace your route from your country of origin to Canada on the map of the world. Use the same colour of marker or coloured pencil to colour the square on the legend. Describe your journey below the map (3.7.5).

Note: Please refer to the note at the end of Instructional Activity: Part Three (page 279), and, again, be cautious and sensitive to students' background experiences.

Extensions

- Add new vocabulary to the multilingual word wall.
- Have students add new vocabulary to their personal vocabulary folders or personal dictionaries.
- Distribute copies of a world map, and have students label, colour, and then cut out each of the seven continents. Then, ask students to order the continents from smallest landmass to largest.
- Have students complete computer-based "drag and drop" maps of the world, such as the one at Visual ESL.com (see <www.visualesl.com/drag/62.htm>).

Assessment of Learning

Use the words recorded on chart paper during the instructional activities to determine students' degree of facility with these terms. Have students select words and use them in sentences. Record results on copies of the Anecdotal Record sheet (I.3), shown on page 37.

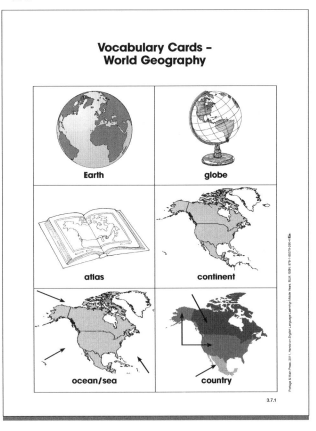
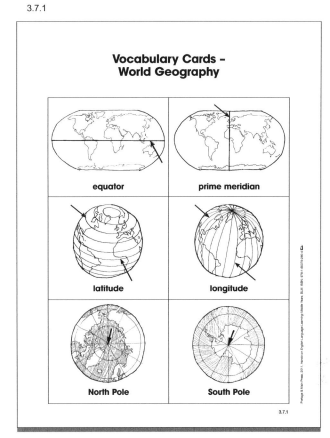
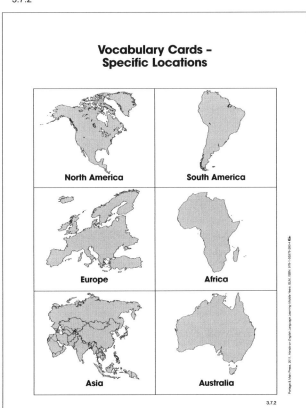
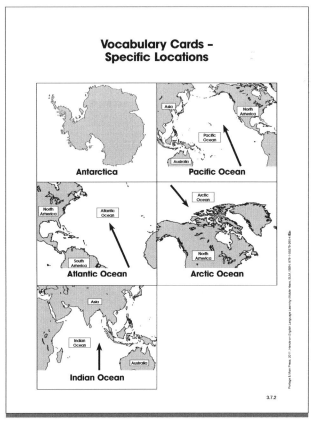

Blackline Masters

3.7.3

Name: _____

The World

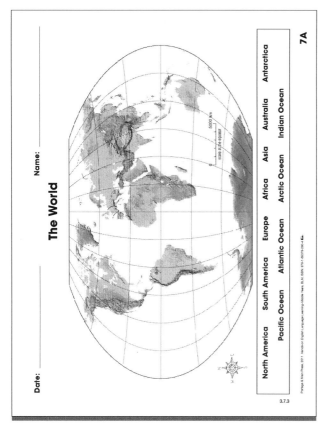

Date: _____

7A

North America · South America · Europe · Africa · Asia · Australia · Antarctica
Pacific Ocean · Atlantic Ocean · Arctic Ocean · Indian Ocean

3.7.4

Date: _____   **Name:** _____

World Words

Part 1:

Earth	globe	atlas	continent
ocean/sea	country	equator	prime meridian
latitude	longitude	North Pole	South Pole

The lines of _____ run vertically (up and down) on the globe.

The lines of _____ run horizontally (sideways) around the globe.

Bodies of salt water are called _____

A _____ is a small model of the Earth.

A _____ is a part of a continent where a nation of people lives.

The _____ is the most northern point on Earth.

Part 2: Use the words from the box at the top of the page that were *not* used in sentences above to write your own sentences.

_____
_____
_____
_____
_____

7B

3.7.5

Date: _____   **Name:** _____

My Journey to Canada

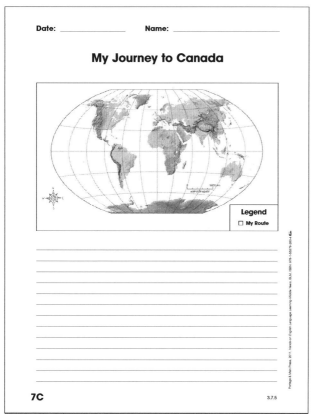

Legend
☐ My Route

_____
_____
_____
_____
_____
_____
_____
_____
_____

7C

8 | North America

Curricular Connections

- Language Arts: speaking, listening, reading, writing, viewing, representing
- Mathematics: cardinal directions, measurement
- Social Studies: mapping skills, cardinal directions, symbols
- Physical Education: orienteering
- Art: drawing, art production, colour, symbols

Vocabulary – North America

- Canada
- United States (of America) (U.S./USA)
- Mexico
- Gulf of Mexico
- border
- state
- scale

Materials

- vocabulary cards – *North America* (included. Photocopy one set onto sturdy tagboard, and cut apart cards.) (3.8.1)
- Survey Sheet (included. Make one copy for each ELL-student/peer-helper pair) (3.8.2)
- pocket chart
- coloured pencils or markers
- large wall map of North America or the world
- large index cards
- markers
- chart paper
- 30-cm ruler
- metre stick
- atlases, or other reference books with country maps and flags
- research materials (books or websites) about flags of students' countries of origin or their ancestors' countries of origin
- poster board
- research materials about flags of Canada, the U.S., Mexico, and other countires

Integrated Class Activities

- This lesson on North America and mapping skills will benefit all middle-years students. Consider conducting all or some of the activities with the whole class. Display vocabulary cards – *North America* (3.8.1) to support ELL learners during these activities.
- Have the physical education teacher introduce the class to orienteering, as a means to using cardinal directions and mapping skills in a real-life context.
- Have students conduct research about the flags of their countries of origin or their ancestors' countries of origin. Then, ask students to recreate the flags on poster board and mount their written research on the poster. Display the posters throughout the school.

Whole-Class Career Connections

- Have students identify the border between Canada and the United States on a large wall map of North America or the world. Then, ask students to share their experiences crossing the border by car. Discuss the role of the customs agents at the border.

Note: Discussing experiences crossing the border by car may be uncomfortable for some students whose families do not own vehicles. As well, other students may have had traumatic experiences when crossing borders in other countries. Be aware of students' circumstances, and handle such discussions with sensitivity and care.

- Have students write letters to local border-crossing staff to ask questions about their training, job descriptions, and work experiences.

Module 3   283

8

Instructional Activity

Display a large wall map of North America or the world, and have students find Canada on it. Record the country name on chart paper. Ask:

- What is a country? (a part of a continent where a nation of people live)
- What is a continent? (a large land mass on Earth)
- Of which continent is Canada a part? (North America)

Have students use their fingers to trace around North America on the map. Ask:

- What other countries are part of North America?

Have students locate, and use their fingers to trace around, the United States and Mexico. Record these names on chart paper.

Note: Also introduce the common abbreviations for the United States (U.S. and USA).

Now, focus on the bodies of water surrounding North America. Ask:

- Which body of water is on the eastern coast of North America?
- Which body of water is on the western coast of North America?
- Which body of water is on the south coast of the US and the east coast of Mexico?

Use the wall map of North America to identify other bodies of water in and around North America.

Introduce the vocabulary cards – *North America* (3.8.1). Have students use the vocabulary cards to identify features and locations on the map of North America. For example:

- Locate the border between the United States and Mexico.
- Which US state is south of British Columbia?
- Which US state is northwest of British Columbia?

Finally, have students focus on the scale on the wall map. Ask:

- What do you think this is?
- What does a scale show?

Explain to students that the scale shows distance on a map in a way that tells us the real distance on the earth or ground.

Use the map scale and a 30-cm ruler and metre stick to determine actual distances on the map. For example, determine the distance between

- San Francisco and Los Angeles
- Vancouver and Winnipeg
- Washington and Boston
- Puerto Vallarta and Mexico City.

Peer Activity

Have ELL-student/peer-helper pairs survey classmates, schoolmates, and school staff about cities they would like to visit in North America. Have the pairs collect their data on the Survey Sheet (3.8.2), and encourage them to use an atlas to help them.

Once the pairs of students have collected their data, they may choose how to display it. For example, they could create a bar graph by city and number of respondents who have visited that city, or they could display the data directly on a wall map by recording, on individual sticky notes, the number of respondents who have visited each city, and attaching each note to the wall map at the corresponding location.

Note: Students may also come up with other ways to present their data and should be encouraged to be creative with this task.

8

Independent Activity Part One: Activity Sheet A

Directions to students:

Colour each of the three countries of North America a different colour, and label each country with its name. Also, label the Atlantic and Pacific oceans. Finally, label the compass rose with the directions North, South, East, and West (3.8.3).

Independent Activity: Part Two: Activity Sheet B

Directions to students:

Use an atlas or another reference book to find the country flag for each of Canada, the United States, and Mexico. On the map of North America, use a different colour of coloured pencil or marker to trace around the borders of each country. Then, label each country, and draw its flag (3.8.4).

Independent Activity: Part Three: Activity Sheet C

Directions to students:

Describe each country's flag. Research the symbols on these flags, and include this in your descriptions (3.8.5).

Extensions

- Add new vocabulary to the multilingual word wall.
- Have students add new vocabulary to their personal vocabulary folders or personal dictionaries.
- Have students conduct research on the flag of their country of origin.

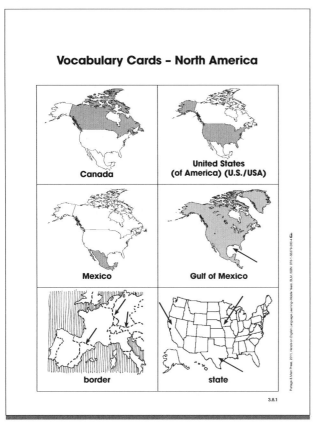
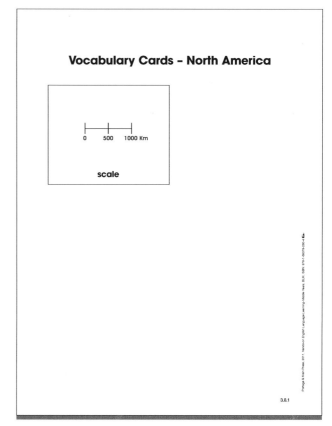
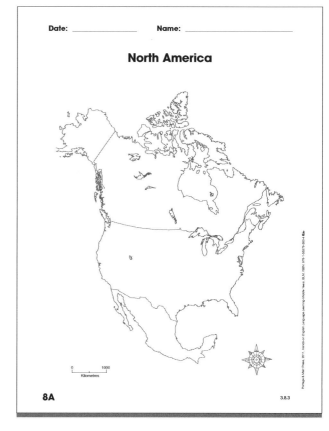

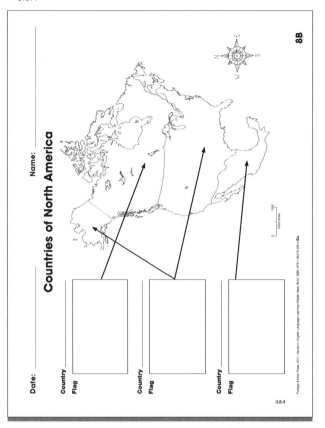

9 Cultural Diversity

Curricular Connections

- Language Arts: speaking, listening, reading, writing, viewing, representing
- Mathematics: surveys
- Social Studies: cultural diversity
- Art: drawing
- Music: cultural songs
- Dance: cultural dances

Background Information for Teachers

Culture refers to the beliefs and distinctive ways of living that a group of people have. Food, clothing, language, religion, art, music, stories, and dance can all be components of a person's or group's culture. Culture may reflect a group of people's community or country, but it also varies from family to family and from person to person.

It is important to discourage creating or perpetuating cultural stereotypes when teaching this topic. Students, families, and guests can share their own experiences and cultural practices, but be cautious of making generalizations.

Keep in mind that many families embrace more than one cultural background and hence bring two (or more) unique perspectives to share.

It is also important to introduce students to the varied meanings of the term *culture*, which cannot be defined simply as originating from a certain country. Students are also part of a school culture, and a local community culture. Those involved in specific sports or hobbies may also be part of a unique culture based on that group's activities. There is also pop culture, which refers to current trends. The emphasis in this lesson is to acknowledge, celebrate, and respect cultural diversity in its many contexts.

Vocabulary – Cultural Diversity

- culture
- food
- clothing
- language
- religion
- art
- music
- stories
- dance
- community
- holiday/celebration

Materials

- chart paper
- markers
- pocket chart
- multicultural books that reflect the cultures represented in the classroom, the school, and the community (see Books for Students, page 228)
- language cards (included. Photocopy one set onto sturdy tagboard, and cut apart cards.) (3.9.1)

Note: The Cree and Ojibwa (also Ojibway or Ojibwe) languages have no word for *goodbye,* which is one of the words included on the language cards. Instead, when parting, they use a phrase similar to *see you again.* The Cree and Ojibwa translations for *see you again* are provided on the language cards. The Hebrew word for hello and goodbye is the same: shalom.

- vocabulary cards – *Cultural Diversity* (included. Photocopy one set onto sturdy tagboard, and cut apart cards.) (3.9.2)

9

Note: Although in most lessons of *Hands-On English Language Learning* pictures are included with the new terms on the vocabulary cards, many of the new terms in this lesson are abstract (for example, *culture, religion*) and difficult to illustrate. For this vocabulary, only the word is included on the card. As teachers and students discover visual examples of each, they are encouraged to add these to the card.

- recording sheets 1 and 2 (included. Make a copy of each sheet for each ELL student.) (3.9.3, 3.9.4)
- photographs and artifacts from various countries

Integrated Class Activities

- The cultural diversity themes presented in this lesson will benefit all students. Consider conducting all instructional, peer, and independent activities with the entire class.

- Create a multicultural display of photos and artifacts from various countries, including those from ELL students' homelands and from other students' ancestral countries of origin, as well as items and photos from travel agencies. If space and time permits, make separate displays for each country or continent. Alternatively, have students work individually or in pairs to create displays for a heritage/cultural fair.

Note: Visit the Canadian Heritage website <www.pch.gc.ca/index-eng.cfm> to find resources, activities, and funding opportunities for school-based heritage projects.

- This lesson presents an excellent opportunity to invite family members to visit the class to share elements of their culture. Have students and their families share information about their culture's music, crafts/art, dance, clothing, food, and so on.

- Visit culturally diverse restaurants and museums to learn more about diversity.
- Collaborate with the school music and phys ed teachers, and have students learn songs and dances from various countries that reflect the school's cultural diversity.

Whole-Class Career Connections

- Invite employees and volunteers from local cultural organizations to discuss their roles and responsibilities.
- Visit various local culturally diverse restaurants. Ask the owners to share the challenges and rewards of their jobs.
- Have students reflect on the role of restaurant owner and which skills (in terms of the Employability Skills Checklist, included in module 1, lesson 1; 1.1.8) would be most useful to develop for this career.

Instructional Activity: Part One

Explain to students that their class, school, and community are made up of many different people, from different families, and from different homes. Ask:

- Which language is spoken most often in our classroom?
- Which languages are spoken in your home?
- Do you think other people in our classroom and school (students, staff, volunteers) speak different languages?

Record the words *hello, goodbye, please,* and *thank you* on chart paper. Have students read and say these words and also say the words in their first language(s).

Display the language cards (3.9.1) in the pocket chart. Say each term, and have students repeat it.

▶

Module 3

Note: If the first language of any ELL student with whom you are working is not represented on the language cards, use the blank cards provided to record the words in the appropriate language.

Once students have had an opportunity to learn some of the words in a variety of languages, ask:

- Why do people speak different languages?

Explain that people come from a variety of different cultures. Print the term *culture* on chart paper. Explain that *culture* means the distinct, unique, or special ways of living that different people have: they may speak different languages, celebrate different holidays, wear different clothing, eat different foods, and listen to different music. Ask:

- What is your culture?
- What are some of the different cultures in our community?

In the centre of the chart paper, record *Cultures in Our Community*, and circle it. Make a concept web to show the different cultures that students suggest.

Display the vocabulary cards – *Cultural Diversity* (3.9.2) in the pocket chart, and review each term with students. Then, use the concept web to springboard a discussion about the term *culture*.

Instructional Activity: Part Two

Use multicultural books to introduce students to the various cultures represented in the class and community. Read the books aloud, and discuss content, pictures, similarities, and differences.

Peer Activity

Have ELL-student/peer helper pairs survey students in the class and people in the school to determine the cultural makeup. First, ask students to use recording sheet 1 (3.9.3) to record the names of students in the class along with their culture and first language. Next, have students use recording sheet 2 (3.9.4) to survey 15 people in the school (outside the class) about their culture and first language.

Later, have students add to the concept web created in Instructional Activity: Part One any new cultures discovered in the class or school, to better represent the school's cultural makeup.

Note that this is a prime opportunity to discuss the challenges of integrating into a new culture while also maintaining one's original culture. Also, discuss immigration and the different reasons people come to a new land. These reasons may be very different for the immigrant who has chosen to leave his or her country and the refugee who may have had no choice at all.

Independent Activity: Activity Sheet A

Directions to students:

On the wheel chart, use words and illustrations to describe your own culture (3.9.5).

Note: Students may wish to take this sheet home and have family members help them to complete it.

Have students share their wheel charts with the rest of the class.

Note: This is an excellent opportunity to discuss similarities and differences of cultural practices, quite possibly even amongst people from the same country of origin. This helps students to better understand diversity without making generalizations.

Extensions

- Add new vocabulary to the multilingual word wall.
- Have students add new vocabulary to their personal vocabulary folders or personal dictionaries.

Language Cards - Hello

Cantonese	Dutch
néih hóu	**goeden dag**
English	French
hello	**bonjour**
German	Cree
guten tag	**tansi**

Language Cards - Hello

Hindi	Hebrew
namasté	**shalom**
Italian	Japanese
ciao	**konnichi wa**
Spanish	Ojibway
hola	**boozhoo**

Language Cards - Goodbye

Cantonese	Dutch
joi gin	**tot ziens**
English	French
goodbye	**au revoir**
German	Cree
auf wiedersehen	**ke ka wa pa mit tin** (see you again)

Language Cards - Goodbye

Hebrew	Hindi
shalom	**alavidha**
Italian	Japanese
arrivederci	**sayonara**
Spanish	Ojibway
adiós	**ke ka wa pa min** (see you again)

Language Cards - Please

Cantonese	Dutch
mm goi	alstublieft

English	French
please	s'il vous plaît

German	Cree
bitte	mahti

Language Cards - Please

Hebrew	Hindi
be'vakasha	krupaya

Italian	Japanese
per favore	dozo

Spanish	Ojibway
por favor	taga

Language Cards - Thank You

Cantonese	Dutch
doh je	dank u

English	French
thank you	merci

German	Cree
danke	ekosi

Language Cards - Thank You

Hebrew	Hindi
toda	dhanyawaad

Italian	Japanese
grazie	arigato

Spanish	Ojibway
gracias	miigwech

3.9.1

Language Cards

3.9.2

Vocabulary Cards – Cultural Diversity

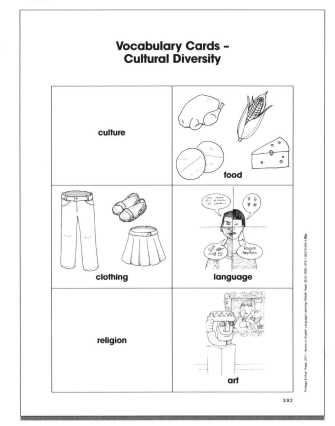

culture | food
clothing | language
religion | art

3.9.2

Vocabulary Cards – Cultural Diversity

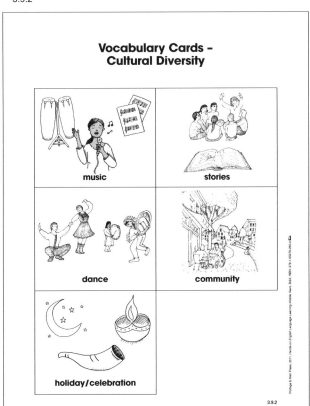

music | stories
dance | community
holiday/celebration |

3.9.3

Date: _____ Name: _____

Recording Sheet 1: A Classroom of Many Cultures

Name	Culture	Language	Birth Place

Peer Activity

Blackline Masters

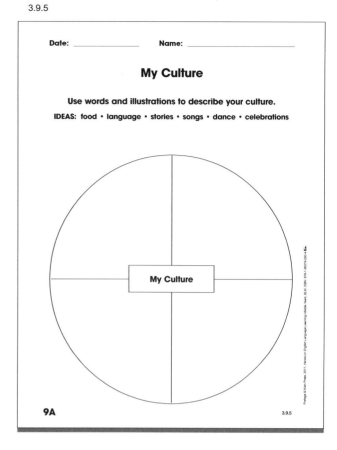

10 Our World Community

Curricular Connections

- Language Arts: speaking, listening, reading, writing, viewing, representing
- Mathematics: graphing
- Science: living things (plants, animals)
- Social Studies: cultural diversity, world geography, mapping skills
- Art: collage

Vocabulary – Our World Community

- world
- community
- same
- different
- compare
- needs

Materials

- students' recording sheets 1 and 2 from previous lesson (3.9.3, 3.9.4)
- chart paper
- markers
- wall map of the world
- books about life in other countries (for example, *Where Children Live*, by Thomas B. Allen. See Books for Students on page 228)
- globe
- pushpins
- sticky notes
- poster paper
- markers or coloured pencils
- scissors
- glue
- computers and access to the internet
- vocabulary cards – *Our World Community* (included. Photocopy one set onto sturdy tagboard, and cut apart cards.) (3.10.1)
- pocket chart
- research materials about various countries
- world map

Integrated Class Activities

- The focus on our world community in this lesson will benefit all students in the class, so consider conducting all instructional, peer, and independent activities with the entire class.
- It is especially valuable to have all students conduct research on a specific country. Have students present their research to the rest of the class. Provide time for students to plan and rehearse their presentations. They may choose to write and recite speeches, make PowerPoint presentations, create a book or a puppet show, or present their findings in another creative way.
- As students share their research from the preceding activity, mark their countries on a world map. Discuss locations in terms of continents and cardinal directions.
- Create a graph that depicts the populations of all countries researched in the preceding activity.
- Discuss similarities and differences among the various countries students researched in the preceding activity. Focus discussions specifically on the topics students researched (for example, land and water, people and cultures, plants, and animals).

Instructional Activity: Part One

Review with students their survey data from the previous lesson (recording sheets 1 and 2 – 3.9.3, 3.9.4). On chart paper, record a list of all the countries of origin represented.

Display the wall map of the world and the globe. Review the map, and have students identify Canada, the compass rose, and various other countries and bodies of water. Have students locate the same items on the globe.

Module 3   295

10

Note: Be sure to make connections between use of the globe and the map. Explain that the map is a flattened-out, two-dimensional version of the globe, showing the entire earth in one view, while the globe is a three-dimensional model of the earth that shows all different views/perspectives.

Have students locate on the map the countries listed on chart paper, and place pushpins in those locations on the map. On a sticky note, record the name of any student(s) or staff member(s) who have come from each of the countries represented by pushpins on the map, and attach the sticky note to the appropriate place on the map. Each of these students or staff members can then act as an "expert" for sharing information about life in that country.

If students have come from other countries of origin, have them share information about those countries. Topics to discuss might include

- Climate
- Land, plants, and animals
- Principal languages
- Currency
- Foods (foods that are local to that country, as well as staple foods)
- Personal knowledge and experiences in terms of schooling, homes, jobs, and so on

Note: As mentioned in the preceding lesson, be careful not to make generalizations or create stereotypes when discussing culture. Emphasize that in the larger context, all humans are individuals; no two humans are the same, and each individual has his or her own unique characteristics.

Examine books about life in other countries of the world. Then, display the vocabulary cards – *Our World Community* (3.10.1) in the pocket chart, and review the terms. Use the books read as a springboard for discussion.

Peer Activity

Have ELL students work with peer helpers to select and research another country. Provide students with poster paper, scissors, glue, drawing paper, and markers or coloured pencils. Tell the pairs to title the sheet of poster paper with the name of the country they are researching. Then, have students review related books to find pictures depicting daily life in that country, which they can reproduce in their own drawings. Or, have them find and print pictures of the same from internet sites like National Geographic Kids <www.nationalgeographic.com/kids>. Finally, ask students to create collage posters by cutting out the pictures they drew or collected and gluing them onto the poster paper.

Note: Students may also include written facts about the country on their posters.

Note: If students are using the National Geographic Kids site for their research, have them click on "People & Places" for information about various places all over the world.

Independent Activity: Part One: Activity Sheet A

Directions to students:

Record details about the country you researched for your peer research poster. Use books and the internet to help you find any more information that you need to complete the activity sheet (3.10.2).

Independent Activity: Part Two: Activity Sheet B

Directions to students:

Use what you learned from your research about another country to compare and contrast that country with Canada. Record the name of the country you researched on the title line.

10

Use sentences and illustrations to describe similarities and differences (3.10.3).

Extensions

- Add new vocabulary to the multilingual word wall.
- Have students add new vocabulary to their personal vocabulary folders or personal dictionaries.

Assessment as Learning

Have students complete copies of the Student Self-Assessment sheet (I.6), shown on page 38, to reflect on their learning about countries of the world.

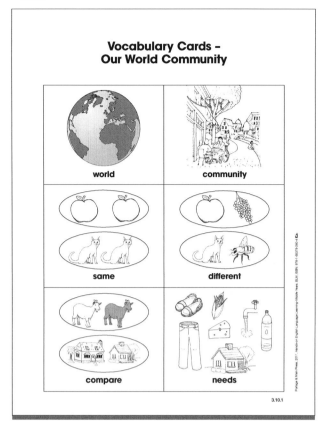

11 Basic Human Needs

Curricular Connections

- Language Arts: speaking, listening, reading, writing, viewing, representing
- Science: living things, sustainable development
- Social Studies: sustainable development, basic human needs
- Health: physical and emotional wellbeing

Background Information for Teachers

Basic human needs can be defined in terms of survival: We need food, water, shelter, clothing, safety, and health to survive.

Note: Students may mention education, love, happiness, and so on as other basic human needs. These can be included during discussions.

Note: It is important to acknowledge that some students may have vivid experience with basic needs *not* being met. Students wishing to share such experiences should be encouraged to do so, but care must be taken to support students' recollections of potentially traumatic circumstances. It is essential for all students to learn that basic needs are not met in the same way for all people around the world and equally important for teachers to be sensitive to students' experiences. This experience may not be limited to ELL students, so consider all students when discussing such topics.

Vocabulary – Basic Human Needs

Basic Human Needs

- food
- water
- shelter
- clothing
- safety
- health

Community Service Workers

- community service worker
- author
- baker
- bus driver
- car mechanic
- carpenter
- childcare worker
- dentist
- doctor
- farmer
- firefighter
- fisher
- garbage collector
- librarian
- logger
- mail carrier
- plumber
- police officer
- RCMP officer
- school secretary
- sewing-machine operator
- shoe salesperson
- snow-plough driver
- store keeper
- teacher

Materials

- chart paper
- markers
- vocabulary cards – *Basic Human Needs* (included. Photocopy one set onto sturdy tagboard, and cut apart cards.) (3.11.1)
- vocabulary cards – *Community-Service Workers* (included. Photocopy two sets onto sturdy tagboard, and cut apart cards.) (3.11.2)
- visualization story (included) (3.11.3)
- pocket chart
- internet access

▶

Module 3

- magazines, flyers, and catalogues
- scissors
- glue

Integrated Class Activities

- This lesson presents an excellent opportunity to discuss the diverse ways that people meet their basic needs. Based on students' personal experiences, as well as research they have done and learning they have gained throughout this module, discuss:
    - Different ways people obtain food (stores, markets, farming, gardens, fishing, hunting)
    - Different water sources (wells, bottled water, taps)
    - Different types of homes (houses, apartment blocks, trailers)
    - Different ways people stay safe (follow laws, listen to parents, lock doors wear seatbelts)
    - Different ways people stay healthy (eat well, sleep, exercise, medical/dental checkups)

Note: This discussion will encourage students to acknowledge and respect the diverse ways that people meet their needs. It may also feature dialogue about ways that people sometimes do not have their basic human needs met. This presents an opportunity to discuss social justice and global citizenship in terms of helping others.

- Consider initiating (a) social justice/global citizenship project(s) to help people meet their basic human needs locally or globally. This topic is focused on more in lesson 12.
- Use the vocabulary cards – *Community Service Workers* (3.11.2) to play a game of charades. Have one student select a card and role play that job, while other students try to guess the identity of the community service worker. Have a second set of vocabulary cards on display for language support for ELL students.
- Have students write riddles for the Community Service Workers. For example:

Riddle:
- I travel in a large truck.
- You will not see me every day on your street.
- I help to keep your community clean.

Who Am I?
Answer: Garbage Collector

Students can record their riddles on index cards and then display them in a pocket chart. They can then attempt to match each riddle to the corresponding vocabulary card.

- To address the basic needs of living beings other than humans, and to integrate environmental concerns into the lesson, discuss ways that animals other than humans meet their needs (or have their needs met). Include pets, farm animals, and wild animals.

Whole-Class Career Connections

- Have students check websites for local colleges to investigate training programs for various community service careers.
- Have students investigate the cost of training programs in fields of individual interest.
- As a class, brainstorm a list of all of the jobs within a hospital. Discuss the importance of each job in terms of patient health.
- Take a fieldtrip to a local hospital, and participate in a guided tour.
- Invite students' family members, staff, and community guests to share information about careers related to helping others in

their community meet basic human needs (for example, counselors, social workers, community-resource/family-support workers).

Instructional Activity: Part One: Basic Human Needs

Begin by asking students what they think they need to stay alive. Record students' suggestions on chart paper.

Have students close their eyes, get comfortable, and listen while you read the visualization story (3.11.3). Ask them to imagine a picture in their minds as you read.

Explain to students that if they do not understand a word in the story, they may raise their hand (while still keeping their head down and eyes closed). Record the unknown words on chart paper as you read. When you have completed reading the story, review the words, and discuss the recorded vocabulary. Share word meanings, usage, and examples. Then, read the story again.

Immediately following the reading of the visualization story, have students discuss what they wished for. Ask:

- What do people need to stay alive?
- What do people need to be healthy and safe?
- What things would we need on Mars in order to stay alive, healthy, and safe?

Record students' suggestions on chart paper.

Now, review the vocabulary cards – *Basic Human Needs* with students. Have students match the terms to the ones you recorded previously on chart paper. Then, have students use each term in a complete sentence, and record students' sentences on the chart paper as well. For example:

- We need food to live.

- People live in different types of shelters, such as houses and apartments.

Instructional Activity: Part Two

Note: Before beginning the next activity, draw the following sorting chart on chart paper:

Food and Water	Shelter	Clothing	Safety	Health

Display the sorting chart, and review with students the terms at the top of each column. Encourage students to use each term in a sentence to ensure understanding. Also, have students share the words in their first language(s). Discuss how students and their families meet their basic needs. Ask:

- Where do you get your food?
- From where does your water come?
- What kind of shelter do you have?
- Where do you get your clothing?
- How do you stay safe?
- How do you stay healthy?

These questions will lead to valuable discussion on the various ways that families meet their needs. For example, while some families may purchase clothing from a store, others may make some of their own clothing, while others may trade clothing with other families or receive hand-me-downs.

11

This is also a good opportunity to discuss circumstances that might make it difficult for families to access food and water, and circumstances that might leave a family without shelter.

Continue with the discussion by asking:

- Which people working in our community help us get our food? (farmers, grocery-store employees, truck drivers, restaurant workers, and so on)
- Which people working in our community build homes for us and others? (loggers, construction workers, electricians, carpenters, bricklayers, and so on)
- Which people working in our community help us get our clothing? (sewing-machine operators, tailors, clothing-store workers, and so on)
- Which people working in our community help to keep us healthy? (doctors, nurses, dentists, ambulance drivers, and so on)
- Which people working in our community help to keep us safe? (police officers, firefighters, and so on)

Note: Some students may have had negative experiences with community helpers (for example, witnessing police not keeping people safe). Once again be sensitive in such circumstances.

Display the vocabulary cards – *Community-Service Workers*. Review the vocabulary with students, and discuss the work that each of these people do in their community. Also, have students share the names of these community helpers in their first language(s).

Note: This is also an excellent opportunity to discuss how both jobs and related vocabulary can vary from country to country. For example, some countries would have no need for a snow plough driver. On the other hand, some jobs are required everywhere, such as farmers.

Peer Activity

Have each ELL student work with a peer helper to create a collage of pictures on the basic needs sorting chart introduced in Instructional Activity: Part Two. Provide students with magazines, catalogues, flyers, scissors, and glue. Have them cut out pictures that reflect food, water, shelter, clothing, health, and safety and glue the pictures onto the chart in the appropriate columns.

Note: If you have only a few ELL students in the class, all ELL-student/peer-helper pairs can make their collages right on the basic needs chart already drawn, which will help them to connect print with visuals. If you have several ELL students, provide each pair with their own sheet of chart paper, and have the pairs work on their own.

Independent Activity: Part One: Activity Sheet A

Directions to students:

Use sentences and illustrations to complete the chart and show how you meet your basic needs in your community (3.11.4).

Independent Activity: Part Two: Activity Sheet B

Directions to students:

Complete the concept map by using sentences and illustrations to describe the jobs that people in your community do to help you meet your basic needs (3.11.5).

Independent Activity: Part Three: Activity Sheet C

Directions to students:

Name a type of job/work you would like to do in the future. Explain why you would like to do this job/work and what you think your workday would be like. Also, name a type of job/work you would *not* want to do, and explain why (3.11.6).

11

Extensions
- Add new vocabulary to the multilingual word wall.
- Have students add new vocabulary to their personal vocabulary folders or personal dictionaries.

Blackline Masters

3.11.1

Vocabulary Cards - Basic Human Needs

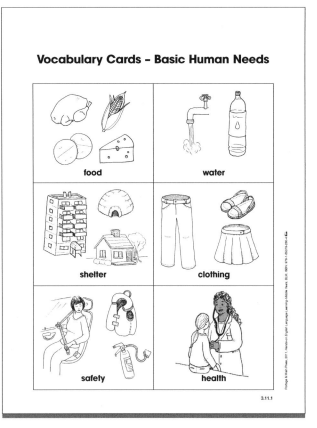

3.11.2

Vocabulary Cards - Community Service Workers

3.11.2

Vocabulary Cards - Community Service Workers

3.11.2

Vocabulary Cards - Community Service Workers

3.11.2

Vocabulary Cards – Community Service Workers

3.11.3

Visualization Story

Close your eyes, relax, and get ready to make a picture in your mind.

Imagine that you are an astronaut about to take off from Earth in your spaceship. The engines roar. 5, 4, 3, 2, 1, BLASTOFF!

You soar through the sky toward outer space. The sky is clear and very dark, and you are surrounded by shining stars and planets.

(Pause here. While students keep their eyes closed, ask them to imagine what outer space looks like, and how they might feel on this journey.)

Your mission is to land on Mars and explore the planet. As you travel toward Mars, you imagine what the planet will be like. Soon, you can see it through the spaceship window, and you head towards it.

Oh no! There is something wrong with the spaceship! The engine stops, and you begin to spin through outer space. The spaceship is headed for Mars, but it will be a crash landing. You close your eyes and hope for the best.

BANG! The spaceship crashes onto the rocky surface of Mars. You look around and see nothing but sand and rock. You quickly get into you spacewalk suit to check out the damage to the spaceship. As you step onto the surface of Mars and look back at the spaceship, you realize that there is no way you will be able to fly home to Earth.

You will need to wait for a long time to be rescued. Can you survive until other astronauts come for you?

Wait! You spot something shiny in the sand. It is a gold lantern! As you rub the lantern, a genie appears. The genie tells you that he has the power to grant you five wishes so that you may stay alive and healthy on Mars. He asks you, "What will your wishes be?"

(Pause again. Have students think about what they would wish for.)

Open your eyes, and get ready to share your wishes.

3.11.4

Date: _____ Name: _____

Meeting Basic Human Needs in the Community

Meeting My Basic Needs

This is how I get food:	
This is how I get water:	
This is how I get clothing:	
This is how I have shelter:	
This is how I have healthcare:	
This is how I stay safe:	

11A

3.11.5

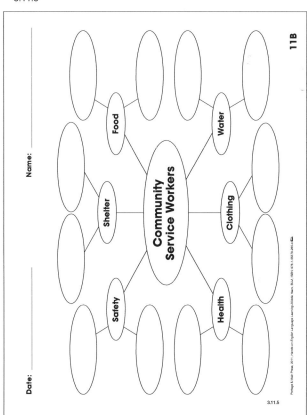

11B

Blackline Masters

Date: _____ Name: _____

In My Future...

The job/work I would like to have is_____.

I would like to do this job/work because_____
_____
_____
_____
_____
_____.

This is what my day at work would be like:

_____
_____
_____
_____
_____
_____
_____

The job/work I would not like to have is_____.

I do not want this job/work because_____
_____
_____
_____
_____.

11C

12 Human Rights

Curricular Connections

- Language Arts: speaking, listening, reading, writing, viewing, representing
- Science: living things, sustainable development
- Social Studies: sustainable development, basic human needs
- Health: physical and emotional wellbeing
- Drama: role playing

Background Information for Teachers

This lesson on human rights and freedoms may be sensitive for some students who have experienced life in countries that do not have these rights and freedoms. Be cautious when dealing with such topics, and focus specifically on the experiences of individual students. Also, be sure that students have support for any emotional issues resulting from personal experiences.

Vocabulary – Human Rights

- human right
- charter
- freedom

Materials

- chart paper
- markers
- wall map of the world
- The Canadian Charter of Rights and Freedoms information sheet (included. Make an overhead transparency of this sheet, as well as a copy for each ELL student.) (3.12.1)
- vocabulary cards – Human Rights (included. Photocopy one set onto sturdy tagboard, and cut apart cards.) (3.12.2)
- seven sheets of chart paper (at the top of each sheet, print one of the rights or freedoms from The Canadian Charter of Rights and Freedoms)
- overhead projector
- highlighters
- student dictionaries
- bilingual dictionaries
- *If You Could Wear My Sneakers*, a book by Sheree Fitch
- *Weslandia*, a book by Paul Fleishman
- The United Nations Convention on the Rights of the Child (UNCRC) information sheet (included. Make an overhead copy of this sheet). (3.12.3)
- Human Rights Action Plan sheet (included. Make one photocopy for each student.) (3.12.4)
- reference material on various social justice issues (for example, hunger/poverty/homelessness; access to clean water; access to education)
- internet access (for research purposes)
- educational materials from non-profit organizations that try to help less fortunate children (UNICEF, The United Way, and so on)
- National Film Board documentary *Hannah's Story* (see sixth integrated class activity)
- books by author Deborah Ellis: *The Breadwinner, Mud City, Parvana's Journey, Three Wishes: Palestinian and Israeli Children Speak,* and *Sacred Leaf*)

Integrated Class Activities

The following series of activities is designed to demonstrate to students that even though they do not have the right to vote, they still have the right for their voices to be heard at the government level. Listed below are some activities that may fit well with current issues in your community. These activities may also offer extension or enrichment opportunities for students.

▶

12

In addition, having the whole class learn about the Canadian Charter of Rights and Freedoms as well as The United Nations Convention on the Rights of the Child will benefit students both in terms of curricular connections and general interest. Any or all of the activities (instructional, peer, independent, whole-class career) in this lesson can be carried out with the whole class.

- Review the basic human needs introduced in lesson 11. Also, review the countries researched in lesson 10. Discuss examples of countries in which people have difficulty meeting their basic needs.

Note: Some students may have emigrated from countries where it was difficult to have their own basic needs met. Again, be sensitive and cautious when discussing such topics.

- Review The United Nations Convention on the Rights of the Child (UNCRC) information sheet (3.12.3). Discuss how some children do not have these basic rights.

- Introduce students to some of the non-profit organizations that try to help less fortunate children, such as UNICEF and World Vision (see list of websites at the beginning of this module). Access educational materials from these organizations, and invite speakers to talk to students. Identify locations where these organizations focus their work, and mark the locations on the wall map of the world. Encourage students to do their part to try to help less fortunate children through classroom fundraising efforts. For example, have a popcorn sale or a read-a-thon, or collect refundable bottles and cans.

- Introduce students to local organizations that try to help less fortunate children or homeless people in their area. These might include a local division of the United Way of Canada or The Salvation Army, a local chapter of Big Brothers Big Sisters of Canada, a soup kitchen, a homeless shelter, and so on. Access educational materials from these organizations, and invite speakers to talk to students. Participate in fundraising activities for such organizations.

- Show students the documentary *Hannah's Story* (National Film Board), the account of a young Winnipeg girl, Hannah Taylor, who has made a difference by founding the Ladybug Foundation and raising money for homeless people.

- Participate in a Town Hall meeting with school board trustees, city councillors, or other members of the government to discuss human-rights issues regarding children.

- Organize a petition that is relevant to students. For example, if students are interested in having a basketball court installed on the school's field, or if they would like a canteen in the lunchroom, they could create related petitions, present the petitions to other students, and circulate them for signatures.

- Read the book, *Weslandia*, by Paul Fleishman. Discuss what rights and responsibilities students think the citizens of Weslandia should have.

- Encourage students to take action on a social issue related to human rights. Have them use the Human Rights Action Plan sheet included (3.12.4) to articulate the issue and the actions they will take.

Whole-Class Career Connections

- Research career organizations dedicated to human rights, such as Doctors Without Borders and Amnesty International.

- Invite visitors who have dedicated their careers to or volunteered for organizations that promote human rights and social justice issues to speak to students.

12

- Read books by author Deborah Ellis including *The Breadwinner, Mud City, Parvana's Journey, Three Wishes: Palestinian and Israeli Children Speak*, and *Sacred Leaf*). These books focus on the lives of children in countries where it can be very challenging to live. Research biographical information about this author, and discuss her reasons for writing about these topics.

Instructional Activity: Part One: Canadian Charter of Rights and Freedoms

Display the overhead of The Canadian Charter of Rights and Freedoms information sheet (3.12.1). Explain that this charter was developed in 1982 by the Canadian government to protect the rights and freedoms of all Canadian citizens. Introduce the target vocabulary cards – *Human Rights* (3.12.2), and discuss these terms in relation to the information sheet.

Provide students with their own copies of the information sheet and highlighters. Focus on and discuss each right separately. Have students work individually or in pairs. Ask them to read one right at a time, and highlight any unfamiliar words. Discuss these new words, and together have students share their ideas about what each right or freedom means. Rewrite these in students' own words, and display them in the classroom. Also, discuss how these rights and freedoms affect their daily lives.

Instructional Activity: Part Two: Rights of the Child

Display the overhead of The United Nations Convention on the Rights of the Child (UNCRC) information sheet (3.12.3). Explain that the United Nations has declared that every child in the world has certain rights. Unfortunately, this does not guarantee that every child *actually* has these rights—the declaration describes a perfect situation. In Canada, we take many of these rights for granted, but in many countries people work tirelessly to improve life for children.

Review and discuss the information sheet. Point out that even having a name is a right. Ask students to imagine how difficult their lives would be without names.

Display the book *If You Could Wear My Sneakers* by Sheree Fitch. Explain that each poem in this book was written to represent one of the rights described in the United Nations Convention on the Rights of the Child (UNCRC) (3.12.3). Select one of the poems, and read it aloud. Discuss which right the poem represents.

Peer Activity

Have each ELL student work with a peer to read, study, and present one of the other poems in the book *If You Could Wear My Sneakers* by Sheree Fitch. Have each pair review the book, select one of the poems, and decide which right it represents. Then, ask the pairs to copy the poem onto chart paper and rehearse reading it aloud. Have each pair present their poem to the rest of the class. Students may also wish to mime the poem by having one student act out the words while the other reads them.

Independent Activity: Activity Sheet A

Directions to students:

Choose three of the rights of the child. Record each right, illustrate it, and describe why it is important for all children (3.12.5).

Extensions

- Add new vocabulary to the multilingual word wall.
- Have students add new vocabulary to their personal vocabulary folders or personal dictionaries.

▶

12

- Have students conduct research on some famous figures who have acted in the name of freedom. Examples may include:
    - Nelson Mandela
    - Ghandi
    - Martin Luther King Jr.
    - Craig Kielburger

- Make a classroom display of universal peace signs and symbols. Some examples include the victory sign made with two fingers, the dove, the olive branch, and the peace sign popularized by the hippie movement. Have students do research to find out if there are other peace signs or symbols specific to their countries of origin or to other countries.

Blackline Masters

3.12.1

The Canadian Charter of Rights and Freedoms

The Canadian Charter of Rights and Freedoms grants Canadians certain rights and freedoms. Here are some of them.

1. **Fundamental Rights:** freedom of conscience and religion; freedom of thought, belief, opinion, and expression; freedom of the press; freedom of peaceful assembly; freedom of association
2. **Democratic Rights:** right to vote
3. **Mobility Rights:** right to enter, remain, and leave Canada or move to other provinces
4. **Legal Rights:** right to life, liberty, and security of the person; right to be secure against unreasonable search or seizure; right not to be detained or imprisoned; right to counsel; right to be presumed innocent until proven guilty
5. **Equality Rights:** right not to be discriminated against based on race, national or ethnic origin, colour, religion, sex, age, or disability
6. **Official Languages of Canada:** English and French are the official languages and will be treated equally
7. **Minority Language Educational Rights:** right to receive instruction in minority language provided out of public funds

3.12.2

Vocabulary Cards – Human Rights

- human right
- charter
- freedom

3.12.3

The United Nations Convention on the Rights of the Child (UNCRC)

The Right to Survive
You have the right to
- Food, water, shelter, and clothing to meet your needs
- Medical services
- Equal opportunities if you have a disability
- Live with your parents or be given good care if this is not possible

The Right to Live in a Safe World
You have the right to
- A clean environment
- Protection from being physically harmed or made to feel badly by what people say
- Special care during times of war and not to be used as a soldier or a hostage (a person who is held captive and whose life is threatened unless certain demands are met)
- Special care if you are a refugee (a person who has to leave his or her country because of war or unfair treatment)
- Fair treatment if you break the law

The Right to Learn and Enjoy Life
You have the right to
- An education that helps you develop to your greatest ability
- Opportunities for recreation and "fun time"
- Freedom to practise your culture
- Freedom to practise your beliefs
- Protection from being forced to work long hours or being sold into slavery

The Right to Be Heard
You have the right to
- A name and a nationality (This gives you the benefits of being a citizen of a country.)
- Have people listen to your opinions, especially about decisions that affect you and your community
- Participate in peaceful gatherings
- Take action to change things for the better (as long as your actions are not illegal)

Note: The United Nations Convention on the Rights of the Child (UNCRC) is an international human rights treaty adopted by the United Nations General Assembly in 1989, which grants all children and young people (aged 17 and under) a wide-ranging set of rights, including civil, political, economic, social, and cultural rights. Nations that endorse this international convention must do everything they can to implement it.

3.12.4

Date: _____ Name: _____

Human Rights Action Plan

You are never too young to make a difference in the world!

The Issue:
_____

My Action Plan:
_____

Declaration: I plan to take action to help improve this issue.
Signature: _____ Date: _____

Integrated Class Activity

Blackline Masters

Date: _____ Name: _____

Rights of the Child

Right	Illustration	Why is this right important for all children?

12A

13 The Media

Curricular Connections
- Language Arts: speaking, listening, reading, writing, media literacy, viewing, representing, critical literacy
- Social Studies: communication, cultural diversity

Background Information for Teachers

In this age of information technology, it is essential that students begin to develop critical literacy skills related to media awareness. It is equally essential that they begin to understand that media can offer a positive means of addressing human rights and social-justice issues. An examination of bias and point of view is an important part of being an informed citizen and consumer.

Vocabulary – The Media
- media (medium)
- newspaper
- headline
- photograph
- cartoon
- comic strip
- advertisement
- flyer
- television (TV)
- commercial
- magazine
- reporter
- interview
- radio
- internet

Materials
- variety of local newspapers
- variety of magazines
- newspapers and magazines from other countries, written in students' first languages (ask students and their family members to provide samples, or access them online or from the library)
- computer with internet access
- flyers
- chart paper
- markers
- vocabulary cards – *The Media* (included. Photocopy onto sturdy tagboard, and cut apart cards.) (3.13.1)
- media interviews (recorded from TV or the radio, downloaded from the internet, or printed in the newspaper or magazines)
- interview guide sheet (included) (3.13.2)
- TV and DVD player/VCR and/or radio (optional)
- student dictionaries
- pocket chart
- bulletin board
- wall map of the world
- coloured wool or string
- materials for making magazines (paper, markers or coloured pencils, coil binding machine or other binding instrument, and so on)

Integrated Class Activities
- Collect copies of newspapers and magazines from other countries. These are available at newspaper and magazine shops/stands and can also be collected from students' families and from other community members. Electronic newspapers are also available online. You can do many activities with these newspapers:
    - Have students compare and contrast various newspapers, identifying similarities and differences in paper size, format, font, photographs, advertisements, and so on.

- Ask students to look in the newspapers or magazines for words they know in the various languages (if you have created a multilingual word wall in the classroom, students will begin to gain familiarity with many different languages).
- Have students who speak languages other than English read or interpret articles or simple advertisements.
- Make a bulletin board display by attaching the various newspapers/magazines around a wall map of the world, and use coloured wool or string to connect the newspapers to their originating countries.
- Have students create their own magazines that focus on favourite hobbies or interests (for example, pets, crafts, music). Students can develop their magazines over time and might include any of the following:
  - Cover page with catchy title, photographs/illustrations, issue date
  - Table of contents
  - Interviews with people related to the topic
  - Advertisements for items related to the topic
  - Puzzle pages related to the topic
  - An advice column related to the topic
  - A fiction story
  - A poetry page

  Magazines can be coil bound and kept in the classroom or school library, or shared with family members at community events.
- Have students design and create advertisements for favourite books. Use features of real magazine and newspaper ads as a springboard for discussion about the characteristics of advertisements.
- Have local media guests speak to students about their jobs and products.
- Have students collect newspaper articles related to basic human needs and human rights. Discuss current social-justice issues related to these articles.
- Have students write letters to the editor of your local newspaper on issues important to them.

Whole-Class Career Connections

- Have students conduct research to write biographies on various well-known people in the media. Include careers in television, radio, newspapers, and magazines.
- Invite members of the media to speak to the class about their careers and training.
- Research and discuss reporters and journalists who have put themselves in danger in order to cover a story.

Instructional Activity: Part One

Provide students with newspapers to examine. Ask:

- What is this called?

Record the word *newspaper* in the middle of a sheet of chart paper. Discuss the newspapers with students, asking them to describe what they see. Record any words associated with the newspaper that students provide. This might include: words, print, photographs, articles, reporter, headline, paper, ink, advertisements, story, report. Ask:

- Why do we read the newspaper?
- What information does the newspaper provide?

Ensure that students explore the various sections of the newspapers. Add more words to the chart paper during this discussion.

Also, have students review newspaper samples from other countries and compare them to the local newspapers, discussing similarities and differences.

Instructional Activity: Part Two

Begin by reviewing the newspaper vocabulary already recorded on chart paper. Ask:

- Are newspapers the only way people get the news?
- How does your family receive the news?

Students may be quite familiar with other forms of media such as TV, magazines, and the internet. They may also be able to share how their families keep in touch with the news in their countries of origin.

Record the term *media* in the centre of a new sheet of chart paper. Ask:

- Do you know what the word *media* means?

Have students share their ideas and look up the word in their student dictionaries. Come up with a class definition in students' own words, and record this definition under the term on the chart paper.

Note: Be sure also to introduce the singular form of the term *media: medium*, and have students use both the singular and the plural form in sentences.

Guide students in a discussion about different kinds of media and, as they share ideas, create a concept map on chart paper. Your concept map may appear something like the following:

```
           Radio
Internet          Newspaper
Website    Media     Headline
         Definition
Magazine          Television
Advertisement      Commercial
```

As you are creating the concept map and introducing new vocabulary, be sure to show as many examples as possible. For example, have students

- Point out a headline in a newspaper
- Find the name of a writer for a magazine article
- Find an advertisement on the internet

Instructional Activity: Part Three

Display the vocabulary cards – *The Media* (3.13.1) in the pocket chart. Have students select a card, read the term, and use the term in a sentence. Also, challenge students to use available media sources to show examples of the vocabulary.

Now, use the vocabulary as a springboard to a discussion on media awareness. Ask students:

- Do you think that everything you see on television is true?
- What about commercials? Do you believe everything you see in them?
- Do you think that everything you read in a newspaper is true?
- What about what you see or read on the internet?

Discuss students' ideas and understanding of these issues.

Note: Media awareness is a rather complex but important concept for middle-years students. It is vital that all students develop critical literacy skills to question, reflect upon, and challenge what they hear, see, and read in the media.

Focus now on issues related to media and social-justice/human-rights issues. Ask:

- Do you think that the media sometimes violates (goes against) peoples' human rights? How?

▶

13

- Do you think that the media sometimes helps support peoples' human rights? How?

Discuss students' ideas in relation to current events. For example, media can have a very positive impact on how the public responds to disasters, such as the tsunami in Thailand (2004) or the earthquake in Haiti (2010). Media coverage spurred people to respond with help and financial support.

Note: This is an excellent opportunity to encourage students to utilize the media to help them in their own social-justice actions. For example, they can write letters to the editor of a newspaper or magazine or contact a journalist to cover specific social-justice events.

Peer Activity

Have each ELL student work with a peer helper to plan a mock interview. For example, the ELL-student interviewer might choose to be a newspaper, TV, or radio reporter. He or she will plan to interview a person in the media, who could be a movie or TV star, a sports star, a politician, or other. Students may make up a person to interview or choose a real person.

Note: Prior to this activity, consider showing students video clips from actual interviews broadcast on TV, radio, or the internet. This is a good way to review students' interview questions as well as any questions they have about the activity itself.

Having students watch or listen to a video- or audio-recording is also a good listening exercise. Be sure to give students a listening task prior to playing the recordings. For example, "I would like you to listen for two different types of questions (including 'who', 'what', 'when', 'where', 'why', and 'how' questions). Record the actual questions that you choose." It is also important to allow students to listen to the recording more than once.

Have the pairs of students use the interview guide sheet (3.13.2) to identify their role as interviewer as well as that of the interviewee and then to prepare a set of questions to ask during the interview. The pairs can also work together to plan answers to the interview questions.

Note: If the interview is with a real person, students may wish to use school library references and/or approved and appropriate websites to conduct research about the person before making up questions for the interview.

Once students have planned their interviews, have them role play with their peer helpers, who will act as the person being interviewed.

Later, have each pair perform their interview for other students or classrooms.

Independent Activity: Activity Sheet A

Directions to students:

Complete the word search activity by finding and circling each media term on the letter grid (3.13.3).

Extensions

- Add new vocabulary to the multilingual word wall.
- Have students add new vocabulary to their personal vocabulary folders or personal dictionaries.
- Have ELL students work alongside their classmates to write and role play news-report skits. Topics can be related to classroom themes of study in core subjects, current events, or issues of interest to students. These can be videotaped and played for the class.
- Have students write and develop newscasts, video clips, or commercials to address a social-justice issue.

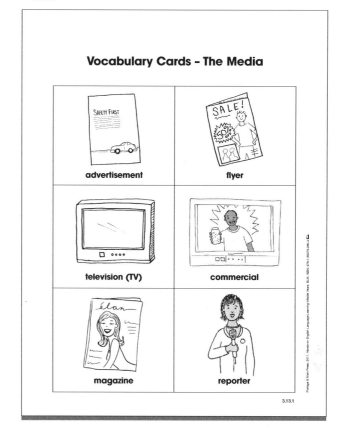

Interview Guide

Date: _____ Name: _____

Interviewer: _____
Person being interviewed: _____
Interview:

Questions	Answers
1.	
2.	
3.	
4.	
5.	

Date: _____   Name: _____

The Media

A	T	E	N	R	E	T	N	I	A	A	Q	C	M	M	O	C
R	H	P	O	O	I	U	U	Y	T	D	R	O	J	E	L	W
E	P	C	A	R	T	O	O	N	C	B	V	M	D	O	M	D
P	A	L	K	J	B	H	G	Y	I	C	F	M	K	I	M	F
O	R	B	T	N	E	M	E	S	I	T	R	E	V	D	A	Y
H	G	T	H	V	H	C	H	X	Z	D	E	R	Q	A	G	E
E	N	E	E	M	Q	C	P	N	A	F	M	C	A	R	A	S
R	F	L	A	F	L	Y	A	W	E	A	E	I	F	D	Z	C
E	Y	L	D	G	T	T	R	R	G	W	E	A	G	V	I	O
T	U	V	Y	U	I	Z	G	N	X	I	S	L	N	U	N	M
R	L	P	P	E	O	N	O	R	E	O	I	P	O	T	E	I
O	M	M	O	C	R	K	T	R	X	W	J	O	A	W	H	C
P	S	D	T	S	U	F	O	E	D	R	S	G	S	P	G	S
E	N	I	L	D	A	E	H	T	R	T	M	P	E	P	E	T
R	V	R	E	T	N	I	P	N	N	V	Q	P	O	R	W	R
A	Z	X	C	V	B	B	J	I	W	E	I	R	Z	B	Q	I
P	O	I	C	A	R	K	U	V	N	Y	H	E	X	T	L	P
T	E	L	E	V	I	S	I	O	N	I	X	W	W	G	H	M

Find each of the following media terms either horizontally (forwards or backwards), vertically (up or down), or diagonally:

- NEWSPAPER
- TELEVISION
- HEADLINE
- TV
- PHOTOGRAPH
- COMMERCIAL
- CARTOON
- MAGAZINE
- COMIC STRIP
- REPORTER
- ADVERTISEMENT
- INTERVIEW
- FLYER
- RADIO
- INTERNET

13A

14 Culminating Activity: Designing a Newspaper

Curricular Connections

- Language Arts: speaking, listening, reading, writing, viewing, representing
- Social Studies: community characteristics, mapping
- Art: drawing, art production, digital photography

Background Information for Teachers

This culminating activity allows students to apply their English skills and background knowledge while applying new concepts about social responsibility to develop a newspaper. It is important that students work in cooperative groups for the activity. If you are working with a small number of English language learners, they could work on this activity in pairs or groups of three along with peer helpers if desired. If you have only one English language learner in your class, it is important to have a peer helper work with him or her on this project. The cooperative-group aspect also allows students to engage in real conversation while negotiating how to plan, design, and write the newspaper.

This activity will take several hours to complete.

Materials

- variety of local, provincial, national, and international newspapers as well as papers from students' countries of origin or in students' first languages
- vocabulary cards from all module 3 lessons
- pocket chart
- activity sheets and other recorded tasks from all module 3 lessons
- scissors
- glue
- markers or coloured pencils
- chart paper
- clipboards
- pencils
- paper
- digital cameras
- access to computers, desktop-publishing software, and digital-photography software

Integrated Class Activities

Consider doing this newspaper project with the whole class. It is an excellent opportunity for students to work cooperatively, develop a variety of research and writing skills, and apply knowledge.

Whole-Class Career Connections

- Have students brainstorm a list of careers related to publishing a newspaper. This might include: reporter, editor, publisher, designer, photographer, and so on.
- Have students email staff from local newspapers and interview them about their jobs.
- Have students send their own newspaper drafts to local newspaper staff to ask for feedback and suggestions.

Instructional Activity: Part One

Have students review various newspapers and identify the types of articles, columns (editorials), advertisements, and sections (or beats) they find. Record their ideas on chart paper. If they do not identify any of the following elements, be sure to include and discuss

- Front-page headline story
- Letters to the editor
- Local stories
- National stories
- International stories
- Advice column
- Sports
- Business

▶

- Arts and entertainment (movies, TV, concerts, book launches)
- Concert reviews
- Book reviews
- Comics
- Family notices
- Classified advertising
- Advertisements
- Weather
- Games/puzzles/crosswords

Have students find examples of each in various newspapers, cut out the examples, and glue them onto the chart paper next to the appropriate heading.

Instructional Activity: Part Two

Explain to students that they will be designing and writing their own newspapers. Provide students with copies of Activity Sheet A (3.14.1). Review the headings and newspaper elements on the chart paper from Instructional Activity: Part One, and explain that students can include these aspects in their newspaper. As a group, decide on the number of stories (articles) students should include in their newspapers as well as the focus of these stories. Consider having students include the following:

- Front-page headline story
- Classroom story
- School story
- Community story
- Provincial story
- National story
- International story
- Cultural event/story/issue
- Human rights/social issue
- Advice column
- Sports story/column
- Business story/column
- Arts and entertainment (movies, TV, concerts, book launches)
- Concert reviews
- Book reviews
- Comics
- Family Notices
- Classified advertising
- Advertisements
- Weather
- Horoscope
- Games/puzzles, crosswords

Note: Some newspapers now include a column on random acts of kindness. Consider having students include this topic, and highlight the acts of classmates, staff, community members, and family in being kind to others.

Have students work with their partners or groups to assign stories and choose their story topics.

Independent Activity: Activity Sheet A

Directions to students:

Decide on the stories/articles you will include in your newspaper, who will report on each one, and the photographs or illustrations you will include. Include all topics decided by the group (3.14.1).

Note: Make additional copies of Activity Sheet A for students, depending on the number of stories/articles they will be including in their newspapers, as determined by the group.

Assessment for Learning

Review students' newspaper planning sheets (Activity Sheet A – 3.14.1), and provide feedback and suggestions for improvement.

Instructional Activity: Part Two

Once students have completed their plans for their newspapers, provide plenty of time for them to complete their research, writing, photography, and illustrations. Be sure to have students do a draft of each story/article and include self editing, peer editing, and teacher editing.

Once students have revised their drafts, have them use desktop-publishing software to complete their newspapers.

When they have completed their newspapers, have each pair or group present theirs to the rest of the class and explain the process that went into planning and designing it. Share the newspapers with other classes, family, and community members.

Assessment as Learning

- Have students complete copies of the Student Self-Assessment sheet (I.6), shown on page 38, to reflect on their learning during this culminating activity.
- Have students complete copies of the Cooperative Skills Self-Assessment sheet (I.7), shown on page 38, to reflect on their ability to work together cooperatively on the newspaper project.

Extension

Have students review newspapers from other countries, including their countries of origin. Discuss the similarities and differences between the newspapers, and have students use the extension activity sheet called "Newspaper Comparisons" (3.14.2) to record their observations.

Assessment of Learning

- Meet with students individually to review their personal dictionaries or vocabulary folders. Discuss the new vocabulary presented throughout the module, and have students explain their illustrations and examples. Also, encourage students to use the vocabulary in sentences. Use the Vocabulary Tracking Checklist (I.9), shown on page 39, to record your results.
- Determine criteria for students' newspaper projects. Criteria should be based on the individual skills and needs of each student. For example, criteria might include
  - All required topics included
  - Accurate spelling and writing
  - Relevant photographs or illustrations
  - Evidence of research

  Record the criteria on the Rubric sheet (I.12), shown on page 39, and record results for each student.

- Assess students on their oral presentation skills as they present their newspapers to others. Determine criteria for students' oral presentations, again based on the individual skills and needs of each student. For example, criteria may include
  - Accurate use of related vocabulary
  - Clear speaking voice
  - Eye contact with audience
  - Makes effort to answer questions

  Record the criteria on the Rubric sheet (I.12), shown on page 39, and record results for each student.

- Complete copies of the Cooperative Skills Teacher-Assessment sheet (I.10), shown on page 39, to reflect on students' abilities to work together in groups for the newspaper project.

Blackline Masters

3.14.1 — Newspaper Planning Sheet

Date: _____ Name: _____

(Four rows of: Reporter → Story → Photo/illustration)

14A

3.14.2 — Newspaper Comparisons

Date: _____ Name: _____

Newspaper 1 title: _____
Origin: _____
Newspaper 2 title: _____
Origin: _____

Compare:
The _____ newspaper (#1) and the _____ newspaper (#2) are similar in these ways:
_____
_____
_____
_____
_____

The newspapers are different in the following ways:

Newspaper 1:	Newspaper 2:

Interesting facts or observations about the newspapers:
_____
_____
_____

Extension

References for Teachers

Brown, Susan, and Marcella Kysilka. *Applying Multicultural and Global Concepts in the Classroom and Beyond.* Boston: Allyn and Bacon, 2002.

Grigsby, Carolyn. *Amazing English! An Integrated ESL Curriculum.* Lebanon, Indiana: Addison Wesley, 1995.

———. *Helping Students of Limited English Skills in the Regular Classroom*, Elementary Edition, prod. Linton, 120 min., Linton Professional Development Corporation, 2000, videocassette.

Law, Barbara, and Mary Eckes. *The More-Than-Just-Surviving Handbook: ESL for Every Classroom Teacher*, 2nd edition. Winnipeg, MB: Portage & Main Press, 2000.

Lawson, Jennifer. *Hands-On Science: Level Four.* Winnipeg: Peguis (Portage & Main Press), 1999.

Walker, Michael. *Amazing English Buddy Book.* Lebanon, Indiana: Addison-Wesley, 1995.

———. *Amazing English Buddy Book: Newcomer Level.* Lebanon, Indiana: Addison-Wesley, 1995.

Middle Years

Module 4

Introduction

This module of **Hands-On English Language Learning** is designed for use with students in grades 5 to 8, who have acquired some basic survival vocabulary and are developing communication skills in the English language (see Stages of Language Acquisition on page 1 of the Introduction to **Hands-On English Language Learning**). These students use English in supported and familiar activities and contexts. They listen with greater understanding and use everyday expressions independently. They demonstrate growing confidence and use personally relevant language appropriately.

The lessons in this module focus on extending students' language and understanding of basic concepts through hands-on activities and real-life applications.

Module Theme: Responsibility for the Earth

The lessons in this module focus on the theme of environmental responsibility, specifically, caring for the earth's land, water, air, and living things. These concepts and related vocabulary will support ELL students as they transition into a new community and country with unique environmental characteristics and needs.

Effective Teaching Strategies for English Language Learners

While teaching the lessons in this module, be sure to consider the following:

- Students learn language through interaction with others. Create a learning environment that encourages rich dialogue and social communication.
- Use many verbal and non-verbal cues throughout activities. Non-verbal cues include visuals, gestures, and concrete materials.
- Simplify vocabulary and sentence structure to encourage comprehension.
- Give instructions and ask questions in clear, simple English.
- Allow learners sufficient response time for oral responses.
- Provide opportunity for students to use patterned language, in which certain language structures are repeated in various contexts or with different vocabulary.
- Review vocabulary and concepts regularly to check for learner comprehension.
- Encourage, where appropriate, the strategic use of students' first languages and prior knowledge as a bridge to English language learning.

Reinforcing Vocabulary

Students should learn to recognize and understand the vocabulary presented in this module. At the same time, they should be encouraged to make connections between their first languages and the English language. To reinforce vocabulary, consider having either a multilingual word wall for the classroom, or individual vocabulary folders for students.

Multilingual Word Wall

Dedicate a classroom bulletin board to your word wall, and display the letters of the alphabet along the top. Use index cards to record English vocabulary introduced in each lesson, tacking these to the board under the appropriate letter. Also include vocabulary in students' first languages (use students' prior knowledge, bilingual dictionaries, other students, staff, parents, and bilingual members of the community as sources of vocabulary). This contributes to the world/classroom-as-a-global-village message, validates first languages/cultures, and creates an atmosphere of inclusiveness. It also establishes an environment in which knowledge about other languages, and the merits of knowing more than one language, are highlighted and celebrated. Along with vocabulary, also include picture and phrase cues, as appropriate. Encourage students to refer to the word wall during activities and assignments.

Vocabulary Folders

If it is not feasible to dedicate classroom wall space to a word wall, use open legal-size folders to make multilingual vocabulary folders for students. Open each folder, and divide it into 26 sections on the inside, one section for each letter of the alphabet, filling up the entire inside area (as in the illustration below). There are two ways students can collect and record vocabulary—they can glue small envelopes to each lettered section, and then record vocabulary on small cards to be housed in the envelopes, or they can record new vocabulary on sticky notes and attach the notes directly to the appropriate lettered sections. Either way, be sure students also include illustrations, usage examples, as well as related vocabulary from their first language with their recorded English vocabulary. Students can close the folder again for storage (for this reason, do not have letter boxes directly on the folder crease).

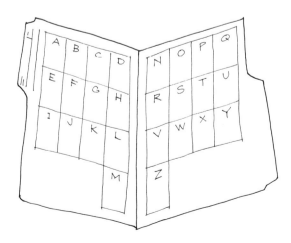

Personal Dictionaries

It can also benefit students to create their own personal English language dictionaries for reference during lessons. Use one of the blackline masters included in module 1 with lesson 1 (1.1.6, 1.1.7). Or, have students use notebooks with sticky notes to indicate alphabetization.

Note: In addition to recording English words in their personal dictionaries, also have students record words in their first languages where appropriate. This helps them make bilingual connections and extends meaning. It will therefore benefit ELL students if bilingual dictionaries are available in English and their first languages (see Books for Students on page 330 and References for Teachers on page 414).

Differentiating Instruction

A number of English language learners will have been in school prior to their arrival at your school and, as a result, will have literacy skills that are on par with their same-age peers. Other students may have little or no previous school experience and may not be literate in their first languages. Consequently, the lessons in this module of **Hands-On English Language Learning** offer many opportunities to help students develop their reading and writing skills while learning English. Visual cues, concrete manipulatives, and cooperative learning are needed to support students as they learn all aspects of the English language.

However, teachers will still need to differentiate instruction and adapt both activities and activity sheets to meet the needs of individual learners. For example, a student with limited reading and writing abilities might work with a peer to complete activity sheets or use drawings instead of words. As another example, personal dictionaries may be essential for ELL students but can be equally beneficial for all students

▶

in the class through differentiation. More academically advanced students might collect descriptive words for use in personal writing, while students requiring additional support in spelling might collect challenging words for use in writing activities while, at the same time, ELL students would collect vocabulary with pictures to reinforce recognition. Suggestions for adaptation are made throughout the module, but teachers are also encouraged to use their own experience, techniques, and personal knowledge of students to differentiate instruction.

Peer Helpers

Many of the lessons presented in this module require the support of peer helpers to work in partnership with ELL students. Developing a classroom culture of inclusion and acceptance will be enhanced by working with the class to develop criteria for helpers, and to discuss why it is important to help one another.

Every student in the class should have the opportunity to help and interact with the ELL students in their class; it is not always necessary to choose the top academic students. Before any peer activity with ELL students, the teacher and peer helpers should discuss the specific task, and the benefits to both the ELL student and the peer helper.

Note: It is important that students working together in a peer-helper setting focus on English language usage. However, it is also helpful for ELL students, when possible, to have access to others who speak the same first language. This allows ELL students access to translation and interpretation, acknowledges their first languages, and builds on their background experiences.

Note: Throughout *Hands-On English Language Learning*, we use the term *English-speaking student* (rather than the more cumbersome *students for whom English is a first language*) to distinguish these students from their English-language-learner classmates. We recognize that the term *English-speaking student* is not completely accurate, since ELL students are also English-speaking students—though their language use is still developing. The rationale for use of this term is simply one of space.

Assessing Students' Prior Knowledge – Assessment for Learning

Before beginning this module, it is beneficial to determine students' prior knowledge of lesson concepts, and which of the vocabulary students already know. This provides information that allows teachers to refine lessons and instructional activities to meet the individual strengths and needs of students. As a pre-module assessment strategy, consider using the Vocabulary Tracking Checklist (I.9) (shown on page 39 in the Introduction to *Hands-On English Language Learning*), along with all vocabulary cards provided in the module. Conference with ELL students individually, and review the vocabulary with them to determine the vocabulary with which students are familiar. Also discuss concepts related to the vocabulary in order to ascertain prior knowledge.

Note: This assessment activity also serves as an activating strategy that introduces students to the language, visuals, and concepts focused on throughout the module.

Career Connections

All modules in the *Hands-On English Language Learning* program for middle years include a focus on career education for students. These activities are intended for use with the whole class, in an integrated setting, since career education is an important topic for all students. For ELL students specifically, such activities will offer them insight into the possibilities for their future, since many of the careers available to them might be quite different from those available in their countries of origin.

Learning about careers offers students a closer look at one aspect of Canadian culture, so students acquire essential understanding while developing language skills.

It is important to note that some of the language used during career connection activities might be quite challenging for ELL students. For example, there is a focus on employability skills, and their importance in the workplace. Although some of the vocabulary used in describing these skills is at a more advanced language level, the activities themselves are well-suited to both ELL students and their English-speaking peers. Career connection activities focus on class discussion, guest presentations, role playing, and so on, and ELL students will adapt in this immersive environment.

Books for Students

Barraclough, Sue. *Weather and Seasons.* Chicago: Heinemann. 2008.

Barwise, Joanne. *Animal Tracks of Western Canada.* Edmonton: Lone Pine 1997.

Bogart, Jo Ellen. *Gifts.* New York: Scholastic, 1995.

Chase, Edith Newlin. *The New Baby Calf.* New York: Scholastic, 1984.

dePaola, Tomie. *Michael Bird-Boy.* Englewood Cliffs, NJ: Prentice-Hall, 1975.

Dr. Seuss. *The Lorax.* New York: Random House, 1971.

Eyvindson, Peter. *Jen and the Great One.* Winnipeg: Pemmican, 1990.

Hickman, Pamela. *The Kids Canadian Plant Book.* Toronto: Kids Can Press, 1996.

Landau, Elaine. *Endangered Plants.* New York: Franklin Watts, 1992.

Peet, Bill. *The Wump World.* Boston: Houghton-Mifflin, 1970.

Rissman, Rebecca, and Adrian Vigliano. *Weather.* Chicago, Il: Heinemann Library, 2008.

Schwartz, David M. *Among the Flowers* (Look Once, Look Again science series). Milwaukee, WI: Gareth Stevens, 1999.

_____. *At the Pond.* (Look Once, Look Again science series). Milwaukee, WI: Gareth Stevens, 1999.

_____. *In a Tree.* (Look Once, Look Again science series). Milwaukee, WI: Gareth Stevens, 1999.

_____. *In the Garden.* (Look Once, Look Again science series). Milwaukee, WI: Gareth Stevens, 1999.

Schwartz, David M. *In the Park.* (Look Once, Look Again science series). Milwaukee, WI: Gareth Stevens, 1999.

_____. *Underfoot.* (Look Once, Look Again science series). Milwaukee, WI: Gareth Stevens, 1999.

_____. *At the Farm.* (Look Once, Look Again science series). Milwaukee, WI: Gareth Stevens, 1998.

_____. *At the Seashore.* (Look Once, Look Again science series). Milwaukee, WI: Gareth Stevens, 1998.

_____. *At the Zoo.* (Look Once, Look Again science series). Milwaukee, WI: Gareth Stevens, 1998.

_____. *In the Desert.* Look Once, (Look Once, Look Again science series). Milwaukee, WI: Gareth Stevens, 1998.

_____. *In the Forest.* (Look Once, Look Again science series). Milwaukee, WI: Gareth Stevens, 1998.

_____. *In the Meadow.* (Look Once, Look Again science series). Milwaukee, WI: Gareth Stevens, 1998.

Sheldon, Ian. *Animal Tracks of the Rockies.* Edmonton: Lone Pine, 1997.

Suzuki, David. *The Tree Suitcase.* Toronto: Somerville House, 1998.

Swanson, Diane. *Coyotes in the Crosswalk: Canadian Wildlife in the City.* Vancouver: Whitecap Books, 1994.

Wright, Alexandra. *Will We Miss Them? Endangered Species.* Watertown, MA: Charlesbridge, 1992.

Wise Brown, Margaret. *The Important Book.* New York: HarperCollins, 1990.

Multicultural Books

Base, Graeme. *The Legend Of The Golden Snail.* New York: Abrams, 2010.

Bruchac, Joseph. *Between Earth & Sky: Legends Of Native American Sacred Places.* San Diego: Harcourt Brace & Co., 1996.

dePaola, Tomie. *Legend Of The Poinsettia.* New York: Putnam, 1994.

Miller, Millie. *Our World: A Country-by-Country Guide.* New York: Scholastic, 2006.

Oughton, Jerrie. *How the Stars Fell into the Sky: A Navajo Legend.* Boston: Houghton Mifflin, 1992.

Page, P.K. *Uirapurú: Based on a Brazilian Legend.* Fernie, BC: Oolichan Books, 2010.

Various authors. Countries of the World series. Mankato, MN: Capstone Press, 1997–2003 (39 titles).

Language Resources

Adelson-Goldstein, Jayme, and Norma Shapiro. *Oxford Picture Dictionary* series*, New York: Oxford University Press, 2008.

Cleary, Brian P. *Hairy, Scary, Ordinary: What Is an Adjective?* Minneapolis: Carolrhoda Books, 2000.

Hill, L.A., and Charles Innes. *Oxford Children's Picture Dictionary.* London, UK: Oxford University Press, 1997.

Mantra Lingua. *My Talking Dictionary: Book and CD Rom.* London, UK: TalkingPen Publications, 2005 (48 dual-language editions).

Ross Keyes, Joan. *The Oxford Picture Dictionary for Kids.* New York: Oxford University Press, 1998.

Walker, Michael. *Amazing English Buddy Book.* Lebanon, IN: Addison-Wesley, 1995.

*Bilingual versions of the *Oxford Picture Dictionary* are available for English and the following: Arabic, Brazilian-Portuguese, Chinese, French, Japanese, Korean, Russian, Spanish, Thai, Urdu, and Vietnamese.

Websites

- <http://aaronburnett.com>
  Aaron Burnett site: Many of the songs written by this Canadian children's musician are about environmental issues.

- <www.saferoutestoschool.ca>
  Active and Safe Routes to School site: A program of Green Communities Canada, this site provides resources, tools, information, and links for schools and communities to create an Active and Safe Routes to School program.

- <www.africanwellfund.org>
  African Well Fund site: This non-profit organization is dedicated to raising money for building and maintaining wells in Africa.

- <www.cmos.ca>
  Canadian Meteorological and Oceanographic Society (CMOS) site: Dedicated to advancing atmospheric and oceanic sciences and related environmental disciplines in Canada, the aim of CMOS is to promote meteorology and oceanography in Canada, serving the interests of meteorologists, climatologists, oceanographers, limnologists, hydrologists, and cryospheric scientists. The site includes resources and links for educators and students related to meteorology and careers in this field.

- <www.eecom.org>
  Canadian Network for Environmental Education and Communication (EECOM) site: This national network for environmental education and communication works to advance environmental learning for Canadians and provides a national medium for people to share ideas, programs, research, resources, events, and services and enhance their professional skills for environmental learning, as well as to nurture environmentally responsible actions.

- <www.cwf-fcf.org>
  Canadian Wildlife Federation (CWF) site. The CWF works to ensure an appreciation of our natural world and a lasting legacy of healthy wildlife and habitat by informing and educating Canadians, advocating responsible human actions, and representing wildlife on conservation issues. The CWF produces various resources, runs a myriad of habitat programs, facilitates financial and in-kind ways of support, and advocates for legislative change to inform, inspire, and educate people about the value of wildlife and healthy habitats.

- <www.intercultures.ca/cil-cai/countryinsights-apercuspays-eng.asp>
  Country Insights site: This site provides information about different cultures and includes advice on cultural "do's" and "don'ts."

- <www.earthday.ca/pub/index.php>
  Earth Day Canada (EDC) site: This national environmental communications organization works to improve the state of the environment by empowering Canadians to achieve local solutions. EDC promotes a peaceful, just, and sustainable world through education, community empowerment, capacity building, campaigns, events, and publications, and has been coordinating Earth Day/Earth Month events and creating successful community programs and artistic and media projects since 1991.

- <www.earthworks-jobs.com/hydro.htm>
  Hydrogeology, Hydrology & Water Resources Jobs page: Part of the EarthWorks website, this page features job postings in the field of water sciences, which can be useful for students' research into various jobs.

- <www.eco.ca>

  Environmental Careers Organization/ECO Canada site: ECO Canada is a non-profit organization that promotes environmental careers. The website offers a wide variety of resources related to specific career choices and training. There is a valuable section on K–12 career awareness that will be useful to educators and students.

- <www.ecokids.ca/pub/index.cfm>

  EcoKids site. EcoKids is an environmental education program that offers curriculum-linked materials and activities for Canadian elementary schools to engage in environmental action. The interactive environmental website offers topical information about the environment through interactive, fun, educational games and activities that utilize participants' willingness to learn.

- <www.ec.gc.ca>

  Environment Canada site: The Environment Canada website offers up-to-date information on weather forecasts, air-quality health index, historical weather, and educational resources for educators and students.

- <www.eslflow.com>

  ESL Flow site: ESL Flow is a resource for researching ESL/EFL (English as a Foreign Language) ideas and for creating lessons. The site provides a variety of topics at the elementary, pre-intermediate, and intermediate levels. Topics include icebreakers, giving directions, describing people and places, games, and so on. The site also includes current, favourite ESL teaching lesson links.

- <www.esl-galaxy.com>

  ESL Galaxy site: ESL Galaxy offers numerous printable worksheets for ESL lesson plans and activities, including board games, crosswords, grammar and vocabulary worksheets, theme or topic lesson plans, pronunciation, survival English, song activities, festival and holiday worksheets, conversation and communicative activities, cloze and gap-fill exercises, and more.

- <www.esl-kids.com>

  ESL-Kids site: ESL Kids offers materials for teachers to use with ESL students including flashcards, worksheets, classroom games, and children's song lyrics.

- <www.evergreen.ca/en>

  Evergreen site: This national, not-for-profit environmental organization works to improve the health of our cities—present and future—by deepening the connection between people and nature, and empowering Canadians to take a hands-on approach to their urban environments. Evergreen tries to motivate people to create and sustain healthy, natural outdoor spaces—including learning (school) grounds, common grounds (publicly accessible land), and home grounds (the home landscape)—and offers practical tools to help people do this successfully.

- <www.green-street.ca/home/index_e.html>

  Green Street site: This national initiative offers environmental learning and sustainability programs that actively engage Canadian elementary and secondary school students to encourage a sense of personal responsibility for the environment; to foster a commitment to sustainable living and promote an enduring dedication to environmental stewardship; and to take action in the school and/or local community, based on issues that are relevant to their concerns.

▶

- <www.members.shaw.ca/kcic1>

    The Flowers of Canada page: Part of the Knight's Canadian Info Collection website, the official flowers of Canada page includes information about flowers for each province and territory as well as the "flower" of Canada, the maple leaf. For each flower, the scientific name (for example, Cypripedium acaule), the common name (for example, Lady's Slipper), a picture, and some brief factual information is provided.

- <www.nationalgeographic.com/kids>

    National Geographic Kids site: Click on "People & Places" for information about various places all over the world.

- <www.seedsfoundation.ca>

    SEEDS Foundation website: SEEDs offers energy and environmental education resources to Canadian students and teachers, and features many exciting programs and challenges including: GREEN Schools Canada – an environmental stewardship program; "Take the Plunge" – a Canadian water conservation challenge; "Write Across Canada" – an environmental writing challenge; Mission CloudWatch – A CloudSat satellite "ground-truth" program; Migration Counts – A SEEDS Canadian bird challenge; the SEEDS Foundation Energy Literacy series; Habitat in the Balance – an online decision-making resource; "Creating a Climate of Change" – a comprehensive package of multimedia instructional resources; and Teaching Activities for Climate Change.

- <www.tefl.net>

    TFEL.net site: TFEL.net is a free, independent resource site for anyone involved in teaching English as an additional language. The site offers a range of ESL worksheets, including discussion-based, topic-based, and skill-based ESL worksheets, and more.

- <www.treecanada.ca/site/?page=home_kids&lang=en>

    TreeCanada website – Kids! (and teachers) section: In the "Kids! (and teachers)" section of this site visitors can access various resources, materials, and programs for teaching children about the benefits of trees, including the Greening Canada's School Grounds program (offers schools the opportunity to create simple, safe, sustainable, and educational landscapes on their grounds); Trees in Canada (provides interactive exploration about the trees that grow in Canada); Canada's Arboreal Emblems (a booklet describing each provincial and territorial tree); the Grow Clean Air Calculator (helps users calculate how much carbon dioxide is produced by common emission sources and how many trees are needed to offset those emissions); Tree Trivia (interesting facts about trees in your neighbourhood); and various other sources for teachers and school boards.

- <www.watercan.com>

    WaterCan website: WaterCan is a Canadian water charity dedicated to fighting global poverty by helping the world's poorest people gain access to clean water, basic sanitation, and hygiene education.

- <http://water.org>

    Water.org website: Water.org is a US-based nonprofit organization committed to providing safe drinking water and sanitation to people in developing countries.

- <www.weather.com>

    The Weather Network site: Visitors to this site will find everything from daily local and international weather conditions and forecasts, to airport and Canadian highway forecasts, to lawn and garden forecasts, to information on air quality.

- <www.wordles.com>

    Wordles site: This website is home to word games, word puzzles, and educational word activities. Teachers can access or make their own word searches, cryptograms, and other word puzzles using specified vocabulary.

- <www.worldwildlife.org>

    World Wildlife Fund (WWF) site: The largest multinational conservation organization in the world, WWF combines global reach with a foundation in science to help preserve the diversity and abundance of life on Earth and the health of ecological systems. WWF focuses on protecting natural areas and wild populations of plants and animals, including endangered species; promoting sustainable approaches to the use of renewable natural resources; and promoting more efficient use of resources and energy and the maximum reduction of pollution.

1 Nature

Curricular Connections

- Language Arts: speaking, listening, reading, writing, viewing, representing
- Science: diversity of living things, adaptations, environmental issues, sustainable development
- Social Studies: geography, environmental issues, sustainable development
- Art: drawing, painting with watercolours

Background Information for Teachers

Many of the suggested vocabulary words and activities for this lesson are based on science content knowledge. The study of life sciences, particularly the plants and animals of the local environment, is a curricular focus at all grade levels. The activities in this lesson will help English language learners to participate more fully in science classes, and will also enhance their basic language skills in order to communicate more fully in subsequent lessons related to environmental issues.

Vocabulary – Nature

- sun
- cloud(s)
- air
- sky
- star(s)
- moon
- tree
- flower
- weed
- grass
- bush
- plant
- seed(s)
- water
- rain
- lake
- river
- stream
- pond
- waterfall
- puddle
- snow
- soil
- rock
- mountain
- hill
- field
- forest
- animal
- bird
- insect
- fish

Materials

- chart paper
- markers
- vocabulary cards – *Nature* (included. Photocopy one set of cards onto sturdy tagboard, and cut cards apart.) (4.1.1)
- small vocabulary cards – *Nature* (included. Photocopy one set for each student.) (4.1.2)
- multicultural books (see Books for Students list on page 330)
- pocket chart
- digital cameras
- drawing paper
- notebooks or poster paper (optional)
- art supplies (paint, paintbrushes, markers, glue, coloured paper)
- landscape pictures (from wall calendars, magazines, or other)
- watercolour paints
- calendar pictures of different landscapes

1

Integrated Class Activities

- As a class, visit a nature reserve, park, or a wildlife sanctuary to observe the natural environment firsthand.

- Encourage students to identify and practise actions that protect the natural environment. These may include raising funds for a local wildlife organization or sanctuary, becoming involved in neighbourhood or habitat cleanups, or starting a classroom recycling program.

- Collect calendar pictures of different landscapes. Have students work in small groups, and provide each group with one calendar picture. Ask each group to discuss their picture and then brainstorm and record words to describe the natural features depicted in it (blue sky, fluffy clouds, rolling hill, lush valley). Next, rotate the pictures among groups, and repeat the process. This activity will encourage the development of students' descriptive vocabulary.

- Have students use watercolour paints to create natural landscapes. Watercolours are particularly effective for creating simple horizon scenes that explore the colours of sky and land.

- On chart paper create a word splash of vocabulary related to nature. Have students quickly brainstorm all the words they associate with the topic. Record the words freely all over the piece of chart paper as in the example below—not in lists or on lines. Then, review the vocabulary with the class by asking individual students to use the words in sentences or to underline words with which they are unfamiliar.

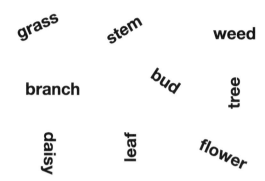

- Using the word splash from the previous activity and their own ideas, have students create haiku poetry about an element of nature (for example, a specific animal, plant, or body of water). A haiku poem consists of three lines and a title: the first line has five syllables, the second line has seven syllables, and the third line has five syllables. For example:

Daffodils
Yellow daffodils
Grow along the garden path
A sure sign of spring.

To enhance student success with this activity, first model the process of writing a haiku poem for students, and have several examples on display as they write their own poems. Also, display the vocabulary cards – Nature (4.1.1) to support ELL students during this activity.

- Invite guests with diverse worldviews about nature into the classroom to speak to students. Examples might include Aboriginal elders, environmentalists, scientists, and staff from local nature facilities.

Note: Teach students appropriate ways to thank guest speakers and other visitors. Have the designated thanker practise the expression of thanks ahead of time.

Whole-Class Career Connections

- As a class, brainstorm careers related to nature. These may include botanist, marine biologist, horticulturalist, zoologist, provincial park ranger, forestry worker. Record these terms on chart paper. Assign to students different careers to research, focusing on the training required and where in Canada students can receive such training.
- Invite a member of a local naturalist society to present to students about the role of the group in protecting nature.
- Have a government representative from a related department, such as natural resource, environment, or sustainable development speak to the class about local, provincial, and national initiatives to protect nature.

Instructional Activity: Part One

On chart paper, record the term *nature*. Have students read and describe the word. Ask:

- What does the word *nature* mean?
- Can you use the word *nature* in a sentence?
- What things are found in nature (i.e., the natural world)?
- What things are *not* found in nature (i.e., human-made things)?

Following this discussion, explain to students that nature is everything around them that is not made by humans. Brainstorm a list of things that are found in nature, and record these on chart paper.

Display the vocabulary cards – Nature (4.1.1) in the pocket chart. Review each word, and have students use the words in sentences.

Also, have students share translations for the new vocabulary from their first language(s).

Instructional Activity: Part Two

Have students share descriptions of nature (plants, animals, landscape, water) found in their countries of origin. Use multicultural books to discuss and compare the natural environment in various countries (see Books for students list on page 330).

Note: Be sure to discuss similarities in nature as well as differences. For example, the sun, the moon, the sky, and the stars are visible no matter where we are on Earth. Some plants, animals, landforms, and bodies of water are also similar in various countries.

Peer Activity

Pair up ELL students with peer helpers, and provide each pair with a set of small vocabulary cards – Nature (4.1.2) and a digital camera. Take students outside. Challenge them to find a real example for each card in their local environment, and have students photograph each example they find. Then, tell them to print their photos, glue them into a notebook, onto a piece of poster paper, or into their personal dictionaries, and label the words. Alternatively, or if cameras are not available, have students record the name of each observed example and draw an illustration of it.

Safety note: It is not advisable for students to take photos of the sun, which can damage the photographer's eyes (as well as the camera). For the preceding activity, *do not* give students the small vocabulary card for "sun", and instruct them *not* to attempt to photograph the sun.

Note: Students will not find examples for all vocabulary words in your local community (for example, *waterfall*). However, this is a good opportunity for students to find out which aspects of nature *are* evident in their own neighborhood. Explore different locales within your school community to observe various forms of nature.

Independent Activity: Part One: Activity Sheet A

Directions to students:

Read each word at the bottom of the page, and write it under the correct picture at the top. For the last row of words, draw your own pictures (4.1.3).

Independent Activity: Part Two: Activity Sheet B

Directions to students:

Look at each picture. Describe how you would spend a day with your family in each place (4.1.4).

Extensions

- Begin a multilingual word wall for new vocabulary (see page 326). Add new vocabulary – *Nature* to the word wall, as well as illustrations and other visuals related to the vocabulary.

    If it is not feasible to dedicate a bulletin board or classroom wall space to a word wall, make multilingual vocabulary folders for students by dividing legal-size folders into 26 sections, one for each letter of the alphabet (see page 327). Have students add new vocabulary – *Nature* to their vocabulary folders, encouraging them to include illustrations, usage examples, and related vocabulary from their first language with each English term.

- Use the templates on the Wordles sight (<www.wordles.com>) to create word searches and other word puzzles that use vocabulary from this lesson as well as upcoming lessons.

- Have students use notebooks, index cards, or the personal dictionary blackline masters included in module 1 (1.1.6, 1.1.7) to create personal dictionaries in which they can record new words and expressions that they learn in each lesson. Ask students to add new vocabulary – *Nature* to their personal dictionaries. Encourage them to use pictures, their emerging English language, and/or their first languages to represent the new terms.

Note: There are two dictionary blackline masters included in module 1 – one with columns for English vocabulary and pictures (1.1.6), and a second that encourages bilingual language skills by also providing a column in which students can record vocabulary in their first language(s) (1.1.7). Choose the dictionary template that best suits the individual needs and skills of your ELL students.

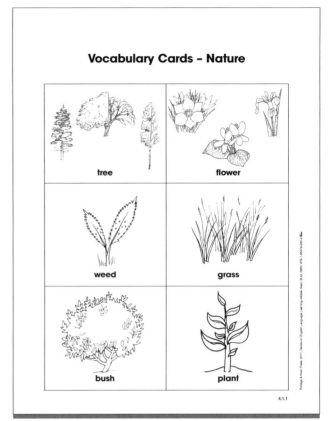
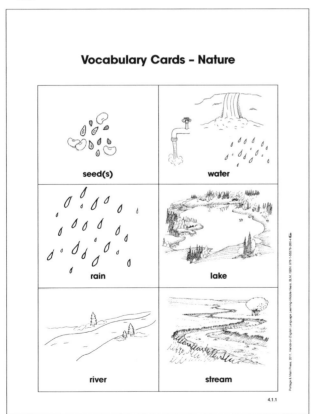
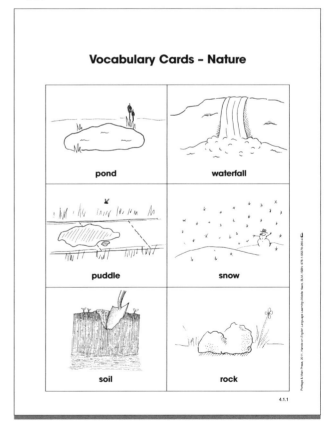

4.1.1

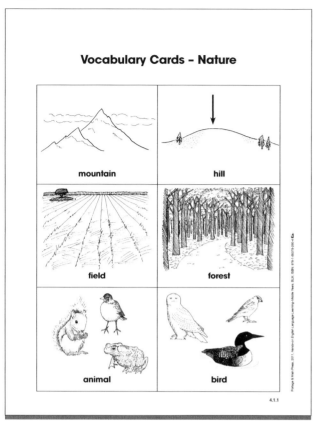

4.1.1

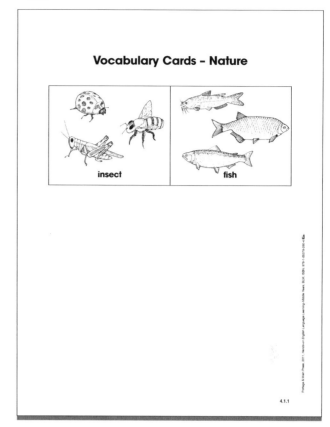

Blackline Masters

4.1.2

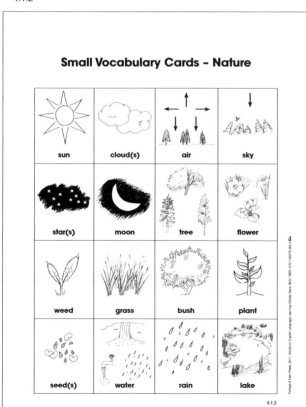

4.1.1 – 4.1.2 – **341**

Blackline Masters

4.13

Identifying Nature Terms

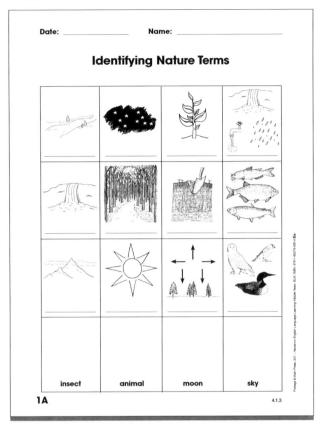

insect | animal | moon | sky

1A

4.1.4

A Day In Nature

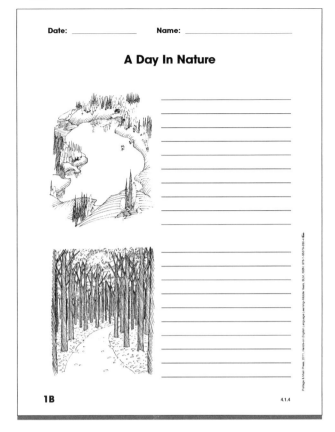

1B

342 – 4.1.3 – 4.1.4

2 Weather and Seasons

Curricular Connections
- Language Arts: speaking, listening, reading, writing, viewing, representing
- Mathematics: measuring weather, calendar
- Science: weather, seasonal changes
- Social Studies: seasonal changes, climate
- Physical Education: active living
- Health: personal health practices

Background Information for Teachers

Discussions of weather should be handled with sensitivity if some ELL students have had traumatic experiences involving extreme weather conditions (for example, being displaced, losing family members and/or homes on account of severe weather).

At the same time, this lesson topic provides a good opportunity to teach about social justice issues and potentially to involve the class in activism to help others (either in their own communities, or elsewhere in the world) who have been seriously affected by weather.

Vocabulary – Weather and Seasons

Weather Terms
- weather
- climate
- cloudy
- cold
- hot
- lightning
- partly cloudy
- rain(ing)
- snow(ing)
- storm
- sunny
- thunder
- windy
- ice
- frost
- blizzard
- fog

Other Useful Vocabulary
- today
- tomorrow
- yesterday
- spring
- summer
- fall/autumn
- winter

Materials
- long strip of paper
- large sticky notes
- access to the internet or newspaper sources for local and world temperatures
- news articles related to local and international weather
- wall map of the world
- *Weather and Seasons*, a book by Sue Barraclough, *Weather*, a book by Rebecca Rissman, or another children's book about weather
- vocabulary cards – *Weather Terms* (included. Photocopy one set onto sturdy tagboard, and cut out.) (4.2.1)
- vocabulary cards – *Other Useful Vocabulary*, (included. Photocopy one set onto sturdy tagboard, and cut out.) (4.2.2)
- pocket chart
- copies of a five-day local newspaper weather forecast which began on the preceding day (preferably one with visual cues)
- weather cards (included. Photocopy one set onto sturdy tagboard, and cut out.) (4.2.3)
- calendar pictures depicting the seasons
- seasonal pictures (included. Photocopy each picture, and colour it appropriately to depict the season.) (4.2.4)

▶

- student dictionaries
- bilingual dictionaries (English and students' first languages)
- vocabulary cards – *Clothing* (from module 2, lesson 2) (2.2.1)
- vocabulary cards – *Physical Activities* (from module 2, lesson 5) (2.5.1)
- chart paper
- markers
- mural paper
- classroom calendar
- wall calendars (available from banks, real estate agencies, and so on)
- catalogues
- magazines
- scissors
- glue
- coloured pencils and/or markers
- sticky tack
- access to a television (for watching a brief report on local weather)

Integrated Class Activities

- As a daily classroom routine, observe, measure, and discuss changes in local weather patterns. Access local daily temperatures, and graph these by the month.
- Collect news articles related to weather in your local community and around the world. Focus on the weather in students' countries of origin.
- Have students design their own class set of weather icons to depict different conditions.
- To assist all students in building vocabulary skills, lay a long strip of paper across the classroom floor, labelled with "cold" near one end and "hot" near the other, as below:

cold	hot

Together with students brainstorm words that describe temperature, such as *warm, cool, frigid, freezing, balmy, tepid,* and so on. Encourage students to use dictionaries and thesauruses to increase the number of words they come up with. Record each word on a large sticky note. Then, challenge students to place the cards on the strip, ordering them from coolest to hottest (for example, freezing, cold, cool, tepid, warm, balmy, hot…).

Note: Some words may go to the left of "cold" (for example, "freezing") and to the right of "hot" (for example, "boiling").

- Have students use internet or newspaper sources to access the temperature in other parts of the world. Ask them to choose a different location each day, find that location on the wall map of the world, and record the day's temperature. Then, have students compare and contrast temperatures (local temperature compared to/contrasted with locations in other parts of the world, as well as two different locations in other parts of the world compared/contrasted).
- Discuss appropriate clothing for weather conditions, and link this to personal health.

Note: Health and safety issues related to seasonal clothing is an important topic for middle-years students, for whom issues of style and social-acceptance are a common focus.

Whole-Class Career Connections

- Brainstorm a list of careers related to weather and seasons. Ideas may include: meteorologist, climatologist, weather reporter, snow-plough operator, beach patrol, and so on. Discuss careers related to specific weather and seasons, and sort the jobs accordingly. For example, springtime may bring risk of flooding, and governments sometimes employ flood experts.

- Watch a brief report on a local weather channel. Then, have students research the role of a meteorologist. Information is easily available on websites such as the Canadian Meteorological and Oceanographic Society (see <www.cmos.ca/carmet.html>) and Environment Canada (see <www.ec.gc.ca/emplois-jobs/default.asp?lang=En&n=39B046ED-1>, <www.ec.gc.ca/EnviroZine/default.asp?lang=En&n=CDF0369F-1>, and <www.ec.gc.ca/EnviroZine/default.asp?lang=En&n=D36C8108-1>).
- Invite a staff member from your school division/district maintenance department to discuss aspects of his or her job related to weather and seasons (snow clearing, air conditioning and heating, and so on).

Instructional Activity: Part One

Read aloud *Weather and Seasons*, by Sue Barraclough, *Weather*, by Rebecca Rissman, or another children's book about weather. While reading, discuss the pictures by pointing to and identifying weather words. Also, encourage students to identify other vocabulary with which they are familiar, such as nature terms and colours.

Instructional Activity: Part Two

Display the vocabulary cards – *Weather Terms* (4.2.1) and *Other Useful Vocabulary* (4.2.2) in the pocket chart. Introduce the term *weather*, as well as the other terms. Ask:

- What is the weather like today?

Record this sentence on chart paper. Have students use the phrase, "Today the weather is _____." to respond to the question. Record their responses on chart paper. Ask:

- How do you know what the weather is like today?

Discuss how we can find out about weather conditions: we can look outside to determine immediate conditions; and we can check weather reports on television, on the radio, in the newspaper, and on the internet to get more detail.

Display the five-day local weather report for students to examine. Ask:

- What was the weather like yesterday?

Point to the correct day on the five-day forecast, and record the sentence on chart paper. Have students use the vocabulary cards to determine an answer, and then record their response(s) in sentence form on the chart paper. For example:

Yesterday it was cloudy.

Now, ask:

- What will the weather be like tomorrow?

Point to the correct day on the five-day forecast, and record the sentence on chart paper. Again, have students use the vocabulary cards to determine an answer, and then record their response in sentence form on the chart. For example:

Tomorrow it will rain.

Continue this process on a daily basis, observing the weather, looking at weather reports, and using the vocabulary cards to identify weather patterns. Use the weather cards (4.2.3) with sticky tack to record this information directly on the classroom calendar.

Also, encourage ELL students to discuss the weather in their countries of origin, and compare it to weather patterns and trends in Canada. Have them share first-language translations for all vocabulary for this lesson as well as new vocabulary that is specific to weather conditions in their countries of origin.

▶

Instructional Activity: Part Three

Display the four seasonal pictures (4.2.4). Discuss the illustrations focusing on weather and changes in the scenes. Use the vocabulary cards – *Other Useful Vocabulary* to introduce the four terms representing the seasons. Ask:

- What is the weather like in summer?
- What is the weather like in winter?
- What is the weather like in spring?
- What is the weather like in fall/autumn?

Now, display only the spring picture. Ask:

- Which season comes after spring?

Display the summer picture along with the spring picture. Ask:

- Which season comes next?

Display the fall/autumn picture with the first two. Ask:

- Which season comes after fall/autumn?

Display the winter picture with the others. Ask:

- Which season comes after winter?

This is an excellent opportunity to review clothing vocabulary with students. Display the vocabulary cards – *Clothing* (2.2.1) in the pocket chart. On the whiteboard or on chart paper, draw a large grid with the headings Winter, Spring, Summer, Fall/Autumn, as below:

WINTER	SPRING
FALL/AUTUMN	SUMMER

Using the vocabulary cards – *Clothing*, ask:

- In what season would you wear _____?

Assist students in organizing the cards on the grid. Some clothing may be worn during more than one season. You may want to make a few copies of the cards, or have students draw arrows or rewrite the word for those clothing terms that repeat.

Instructional Activity: Part Four

Draw the same grid as in the preceding activity, with the season headings, and review the vocabulary cards – *Physical Activities* (2.5.1). Ask:

- Which physical activities do we do in the winter? What about in the spring? In summer? Fall?

Again, have students sort the cards onto the grid. As some activities may be done during more than one (or any) season, consider copying additional cards, using arrows, or rewriting the words for those that repeat.

Peer Activity: Part One

Have groups of ELL students and peer helpers create collages depicting the four seasons. Ask each group to divide a large sheet of mural paper into four sections and label each section with the name of one of the seasons. Then, have students cut out pictures from calendars, catalogues, and magazines and glue them onto the mural paper as well as draw their own illustrations to depict characteristics of the four seasons. Encourage them to include illustrations that depict seasonal weather patterns as well as changes in clothing, activities, plants, and animals during the seasons.

Peer Activity: Part Two

Have ELL-student/peer-helper pairs work together to write weather reports, and then use a video camera to record and present the reports.

Students can imagine working at the weather desk for a local news station.

As an alternative activity, have ELL students create a weather report for a region within their country of origin and present it in their first language. Have the peer helper video record the ELL student's report.

Independent Activity: Part One: Activity Sheet A

Directions to students:

Observe the weather for five days. Using examples from the newspaper, create your own five-day weather report. Use correct weather vocabulary to record your observations of the weather each day. Also, use coloured pencils and/or markers to illustrate your report for each day. You may use the vocabulary cards and your personal dictionary for assistance (4.2.5).

Independent Activity: Part Two: Activity Sheet B

Directions to students:

Write the correct sentence from the bottom of the page under each picture (4.2.6).

Independent Activity: Part Three: Activity Sheet C

Directions to students:

Use pictures and words to show each season, and complete the seasonal cycle (4.2.7).

Extensions

- Add new vocabulary – *Weather and Seasons* to the multilingual word wall or to students' personal vocabulary folders.

- Have students add new vocabulary – *Weather and Seasons* to their personal dictionaries.

- Have students develop a handbook for other newcomer students with advice about Canadian weather, the seasons, what clothing to wear, and for what kinds of activities to wear each type of clothing. Consider making these handbooks bilingual to offer even more support to newcomers.

- Use current events as a springboard to a discussion about how people are affected by severe weather such as recent tsunamis (keeping in mind sensitivity issues noted at the beginning of this lesson). Encourage students to determine ways of helping people who have been affected by severe weather.

- Discuss with students how seasons differ in various parts of the world, including examples such as the rainy season and the monsoons of West Africa and Asia. Also, discuss the fact that in Australia, the seasons are opposite to ours.

Assessment of Learning

Assess students' five-day weather forecast (see Activity Sheet A – 4.2.5). Note such things as correct use of vocabulary, pictures corresponding to expressions, following directions, and so on. Record results on the Individual Student Observations sheet, shown on page 37.

4.2.1

Vocabulary Cards - Weather Terms

4.2.1

Vocabulary Cards - Weather Terms

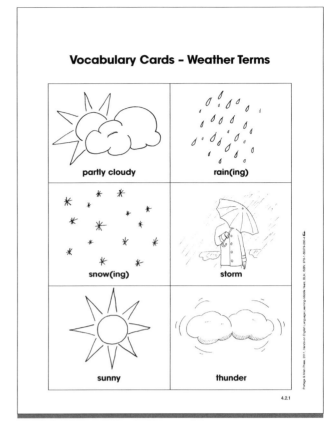

4.2.1

Vocabulary Cards - Weather Terms

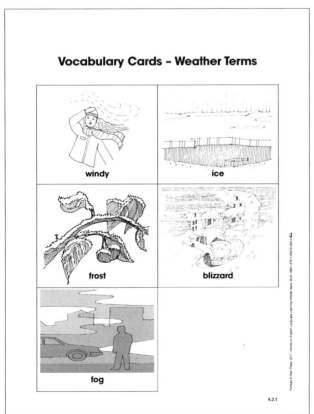

4.2.2

Vocabulary Cards - Other Useful Vocabulary

4.2.2

Vocabulary Cards – Other Useful Vocabulary

winter

4.2.3

Weather Cards

4.2.3

Weather Cards

4.2.4

Seasonal Pictures
Spring

Blackline Masters

Blackline Masters

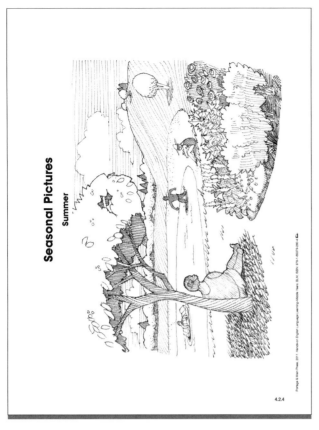

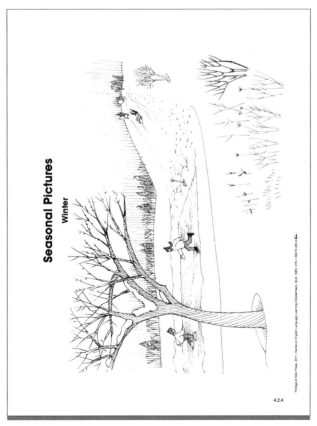

350 – 4.2.3 – 4.2.5

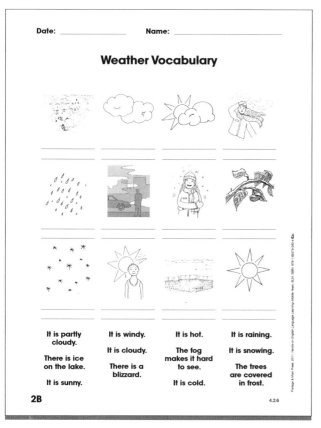
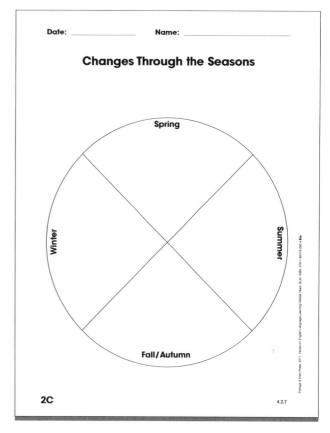

Blackline Masters

3 Animals of Canada

Curricular Connections

- Language Arts: speaking, listening, reading, writing, viewing, representing
- Science: living things, animals, diversity, sustainable development
- Social Studies: environment, sustainability
- Art: drawing
- Drama: role play

Background Information for Teachers

The list of animals is extensive, so this topic will likely take several sessions to cover. Teachers may decide to add to and/or delete from the vocabulary list below and may want to consider topics and themes students are studying in their science and social studies classes, and integrate this animal study into those topics.

It may be beneficial for students to begin with animals found in their own province/territory, as these will become familiar more quickly, and there will be more context for using this vocabulary in daily life. Additional terminology can be added as students gain mastery of initial lists.

This topic lends itself well to cross-curricular connections in science (living things) and social studies (communities, city/country, urban/rural), as well as sustainable development (environmental issues). Specific correlating activities can be planned according to grade-level curriculum topics.

Vocabulary – Animals of Canada

Mammals

- arctic hare
- beluga whale
- beaver
- bison
- black bear
- caribou
- chipmunk
- cougar
- coyote
- deer
- elk
- fox
- gopher
- grizzly bear
- groundhog
- lynx
- mink
- moose
- mountain goat
- mouse
- musk ox
- muskrat
- otter
- polar bear
- porcupine
- prairie dog
- rabbit
- raccoon
- seal
- skunk
- squirrel
- walrus

Birds

- blue jay
- Canada goose
- crow
- duck
- eagle
- hawk
- hummingbird
- loon
- pigeon
- ptarmigan
- robin
- snowy owl

3

- sparrow
- swallow
- woodpecker

Fish

- bass
- catfish
- crayfish
- goldeye
- northern pike
- perch
- pickerel
- salmon
- sturgeon
- trout
- walleye

Insects

- bee
- beetle
- butterfly
- dragonfly
- fly
- grasshopper
- ladybug
- mosquito
- moth
- roach
- wasp

Amphibians

- frog
- salamander
- newt
- toad

Reptiles

- lizard
- snake
- tortoise
- turtle

Farm Animals

- cat
- chicken
- cow
- dog
- goat
- horse
- pig
- rabbit
- rooster
- sheep
- turkey

Materials

- vocabulary cards – *Animals of Canada* (included. Photocopy two sets onto sturdy tagboard, and cut out.) (4.3.1)
- *Animal Tracks of Western Canada*, a book by Joanne Barwise, *Animal Tracks of the Rockies*, a book by Ian Sheldon, or another book about animals.
- animal pictures (from magazines, calendars, and/or internet sites. Have students participate in the collection of pictures.)
- digital camera
- students' personal dictionaries
- clipboards with blank paper
- vocabulary cards – *Farm Animals* (included. Photocopy two sets onto sturdy tagboard, and cut out.) (4.3.2)
- bingo chips
- scissors
- popsicle sticks
- tape
- glue
- markers or coloured pencils
- Bristol board (or other thick paper)
- books or websites about extinct animals and endangered animals in Canada

▶

3

- wall map of your city or town
- bilingual dictionaries (English and students' first languages)

Integrated Class Activities

- Plan a class fieldtrip to the zoo, a farm, or a wildlife sanctuary to provide all students with real-life experiences with animals.
- Mix up the full collection of vocabulary cards – *Animals of Canada* (4.3.1). Divide the class into working groups, and divide the cards evenly among the groups. Challenge the groups to sort their animal cards. Stress that they can sort them any way they like, as long as the rules fit for all animals in each group. Model this activity first for students using a collection of the vocabulary cards, and discuss your sorting rule. Then, have students use different vocabulary cards and a different rule to repeat the activity themselves.
- Have students use the vocabulary cards to play charades. Ask a volunteer to select a card and try to act out that animal for the rest of the class, challenging the other students to guess his or her identity.
- Have students use the vocabulary cards to play Twenty Questions. Ask one student to draw a card from the set; have the other students ask "yes" or "no" questions and try to identify the animal within 20 questions.
- Read about extinct animals and endangered animals in Canada. Brainstorm solutions to help save endangered species.

Whole-Class Career Connections

- Brainstorm a list of careers that involve animals (veterinarian, pet-shop owner, horse breeder, marine biologist, animal farmer, fisher, pet groomer, and so on). Make a community connection by having students identify examples of these services or shops within their community and mark them on a wall map of your city (or town).
- Invite a local animal farmer (cattle, pigs, chickens, bison, and so on) to discuss the rewards and challenges of his or her career.
- Discuss the importance of animals to family survival in some parts of the world. Research programs through which donors can provide a cow, a goat, or another type of farm animal to a family in need, so that they can become more self-sufficient. For example, World Vision distributes a gift catalogue through which donors can purchase a farm animal as a gift to a family or community in need (although the catalogue is distributed during the holiday season, donors are welcome to order items from it all year round). To make specific career connections, research jobs within organizations that offer this kind of program.

Instructional Activity: Part One: Animals of Canada

Read a book about animals, such as *Animal Tracks of Western Canada* by Joanne Barwise, or *Animal Tracks of the Rockies* by Ian Sheldon. Focus on the animals discussed in the book. Discuss the colours and features of the animals shown.

On chart paper, record the term *animal*. Ask:

- What is an animal?

Show three or four of the vocabulary cards – *Animals of Canada*, and say:

- _____ is an animal.
- _____ is an animal.

and so on.

▶

3

Identify some classroom items, and ask:

- Is a desk an animal?
- Is a flower/plant an animal?

Encourage students to provide their own definitions for the term, *animal*. Explain that an animal is a living thing that can move and feel. Also have students check their student dictionaries for a definition of the term.

Give each student a clipboard and some blank paper, and introduce some of the lesson's vocabulary by taking a short walk around the community. Students may be able to spot an assortment of animals outside, such as squirrels, chipmunks, birds, and insects. As they take note of the various animals, have them draw small pictures on their clipboards. While students draw what they observe, take a digital photo of the animal, and record the name of each animal identified by the group.

Back in the classroom, have students record the names of animals they observed on the community walk in their personal dictionaries, including an illustration of each.

Note: Have students use bilingual dictionaries to find the correct spelling for the names of the animals they observed. As well, offer resources with detailed pictures of each animal. Students can also access animal pictures on the internet.

Use the vocabulary cards – *Animals of Canada* to present the remaining vocabulary.

Have ELL students share translations for the animals from their first language(s), as relevant, and discuss which animals are found in their countries of origin.

Note: Some obvious animals of Canada missing from this list are included in the vocabulary cards – *Farm Animals* (4.3.2) (see Instructional Activity: Part Two: Farm Animals).

Encourage students to sort the vocabulary cards by various criteria. For example:

- animals with legs/animals with no legs
- animals that fly/animals that do not fly
- animals with fur/animals without fur

Instructional Activity: Part Two: Farm Animals

Display the vocabulary cards – *Farm Animals* (4.3.2). Ask:

- Where do these animals live?

Identify the picture of the farm. Have students name each farm animal, and help them to describe each animal's characteristics. Also, have students share translations for farm animals from their first language(s), and discuss which ones are also common in their countries of origin. For example:

- This is a horse. A horse has four legs. It has a long tail. It is black. It has fur. It can run fast.

Record these descriptions on chart paper.

Now, have students play the game Who Am I? to review their understanding of farm animals. Ask students to provide clues that will help other students guess the identity of a given farm animal. For example.

- I have wings.
- I have sharp claws to scratch on the ground.
- I lay eggs that you eat at home.
- Who am I?

Discuss the purposes of farming (to provide meat, milk, grains, vegetables, clothing), and compare farming in Canada to farming in students' countries of origin. Identify similarities and differences.

3

Peer Activity: Ognib! (Bingo in Reverse)

Have small groups of students play this variation of the game Bingo. Use two sets of both kinds of vocabulary cards – *Animals of Canada* and *Farm Animals*. Identify one student as the Ognib caller, and provide one full set of vocabulary cards to this student. Have the caller shuffle the cards and place them, facedown, in a pile in front of him or herself. Scatter the second set of cards facedown on a table.

Have each of the other players select five cards from the scattered set and place them, face-up, in front of him or herself. Give each player five bingo chips, and have players place one bingo chip onto each of his or her animal cards.

Tell the caller to draw the top card from his or her set, show players the picture, and call out the name of the animal on the card. If a player has that animal card, have him or her remove the bingo chip from that card. When a player has removed the bingo chips from all his or her cards, he or she shouts out, "OGNIB!"

Independent Activity: Part One: Activity Sheet A

Directions to students:

Draw a picture for each sentence. In the last box, write your own sentence, and draw your own picture of an animal of Canada (4.3.3).

Independent Activity: Part Two: Activity Sheet B

Directions for students:

Write a sentence to describe each picture. In the last box, write your own sentence, and draw your own picture of a farm animal of Canada (4.3.4).

Extensions

- Add new vocabulary – *Animals of Canada* and *Farm Animals* to the multilingual word wall, or have students add it to their personal language folders.

- Have students add new vocabulary – *Animals of Canada* and *Farm Animals* to their personal dictionaries.

- Have students use the vocabulary cards – *Animals of Canada* (4.3.1) and the vocabulary cards – *Farm Animals* (4.3.2) to classify animals by group (birds, fish, mammals, insects, reptiles, amphibians).

- Engage students in a discussion about some of the animals and plants from their home countries. Students may not know the English names, so it may be helpful to find some appropriate library books in advance. Students may then be able to identify certain animals by pointing to a picture. Then, provide the English word for those animals.

Note: The preceding activity will encourage students to see the similarities and differences between the animals of Canada and the animals of their home countries. An intersecting Venn diagram can be used to present this data.

- If students have adequate reading and writing skills in English, distribute the extension activity sheet called "Learning About Animals", and have them record some research about an animal of Canada of their choice. Students do not need to write in complete sentences, but they may use jot notes or even draw pictures and use labels. Preview and model completion of the activity sheet in advance, and provide students with some materials to complete their research (4.3.5).

- Discuss with students characteristics of living things to determine similarities and differences between animals and plants.

3

- Discuss what survival needs animals have, and what people can do to help protect and sustain them.

- Have students use the vocabulary cards – *Animals of Canada* and the vocabulary cards – *Farm Animals* to sort animals according to those that can be found in urban versus rural environments.

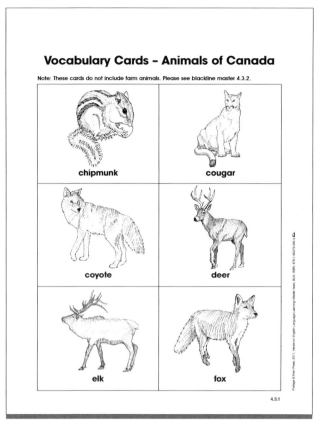

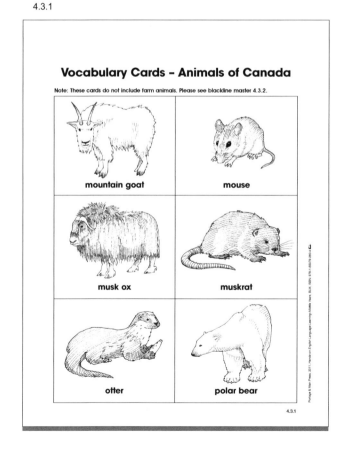

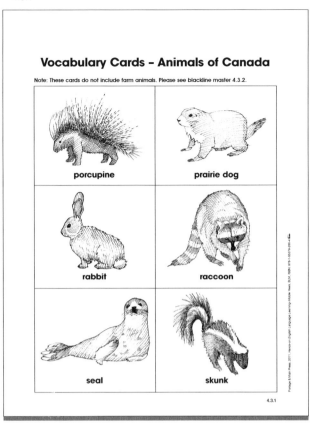
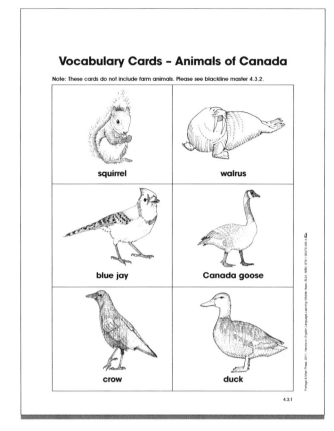
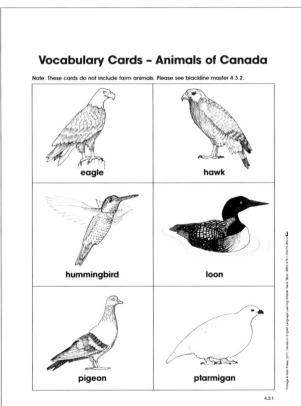
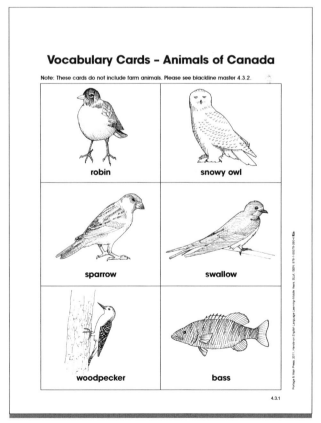

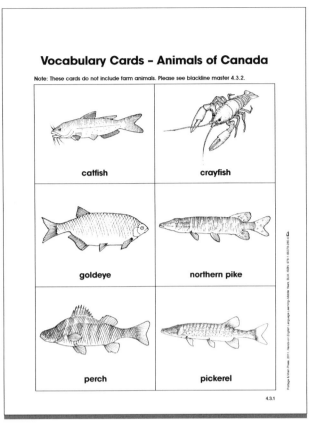

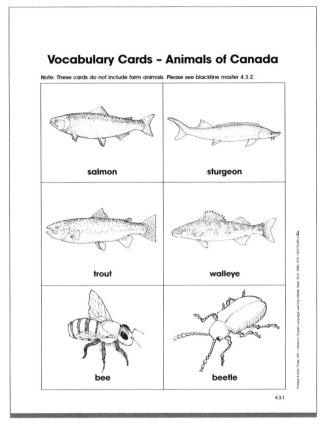

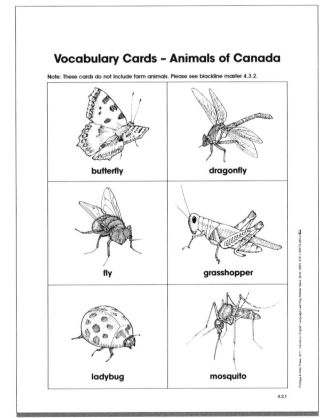

Vocabulary Cards - Animals of Canada

Note: These cards do not include farm animals. Please see blackline master 4.3.2.

moth	roach
wasp	frog
salamander	newt

4.3.1

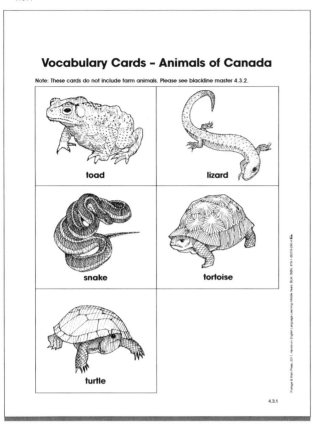

4.3.2

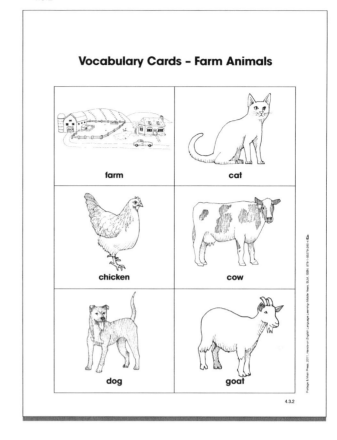

4.3.2

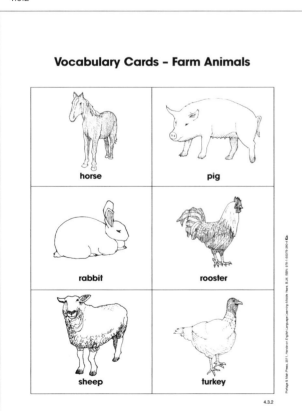

4.3.3

Date: _____ Name: _____

Animals in Canada

Three white polar bears are walking on the ice.	The orange butterfly floats over the flowers.	The green frog is about to catch a fly.
The fish and ducks are swimming in the pond.	The squirrels gather nuts in the fall	Watch out for that skunk!
The robin is feeding her babies in the nest.	These mosquitoes keep biting me!	

3A

Blackline Masters

4.3.1 – 4.3.2 – 361

Blackline Masters

4.3.4

Date: _____ Name: _____

Identifying Farm Animals

3B
4.3.4

4.3.5

Date: _____ Name: _____

Learning About Animals

Animal Name Illustration	What the Animal Eats
Where the Animal Lives	Interesting Facts

Extension
4.3.5

4 Plants of Canada

Curricular Connections

- Language Arts: speaking, listening, reading, writing, viewing, representing
- Mathematics: measurement, sorting, classifying
- Science: living things, plants, environmental issues, sustainable development
- Social Studies: symbols of Canada, environmental issues, sustainable development
- Art: drawing

Background Information for Teachers

In order to provide students with a hands-on experience with plants, it is best if this lesson is conducted during planting/growing season. This will allow students to observe plants in their natural habitats. If this is not possible, have a large collection of houseplants, seeds, and visuals to examine with students. Also, consider field trips to botanical houses, plant conservatories, and nurseries. The following websites offer excellent information, visuals, and resources for students and teachers:

- The Flowers of Canada (Knight's Canadian Info Collection): <www.members.shaw.ca/kcic1>
- TreeCanada – Kids! (and teachers) section: <www.treecanada.ca/site/?page=home_kids&lang=en>

It may be beneficial for students to begin learning about plants found in their own province or territory first, as these will become familiar more quickly and there will be more context for using the vocabulary in daily life.

There is quite an extensive list of vocabulary for this lesson. Teachers should select the vocabulary most suited to their students. For example, you may choose to use only the general terms, such as the parts of plants, *tree, shrub*, and so on. Or, you may choose to have students learn, simply, the difference between *coniferous* trees (mostly needle- and cone-bearing trees) and *deciduous* trees (leaf-bearing trees) as opposed to having them learn the specific names. Alternatively, and depending on students' grade level and background knowledge, you may include more or all of the terms.

Vocabulary – Plants of Canada

Parts of Plants

- plant
- root
- stem
- leaf
- seed
- flower
- fruit

Other Parts of Trees

- tree
- trunk
- branch
- bark

Coniferous Trees

- balsam
- cedar
- pine
- spruce

Deciduous Trees

- ash
- aspen
- elm
- maple
- oak
- willow

▶

4

Shrubs
- lilac

Other Plants
- bullrush
- daffodil
- dandelion
- grass
- tulip
- wild rice
- wheat
- weed

Note: The following vocabulary is for whole-class use.

Provincial and Territorial Flowers
- Pacific dogwood (British Columbia)
- wild rose (Alberta)
- western red lily (Saskatchewan)
- prairie crocus (Manitoba)
- white trillium (Ontario)
- blue flag (Québec)
- mayflower (Nova Scotia)
- pitcher plant (Newfoundland and Labrador)
- purple violet (New Brunswick)
- lady's slipper (Prince Edward Island)
- purple saxifrage (Nunavut)
- mountain avens (Northwest territories)
- fireweed (Yukon)

Materials

- variety of houseplants and outdoor plants
- clipboards
- digital camera
- newspaper
- basin
- magnifying glasses
- pencils
- drawing paper
- collection of leaves (can be collected by students outside of school or during a class community walk)
- collection of seeds and beans
- vocabulary cards – *Parts of Plants* (included. Photocopy onto sturdy tag board, cut out cards, and colour illustrations appropriately. Refer to websites listed on the preceding page or to other sources for accurate colour illustrations.) (4.4.1)
- vocabulary cards – *Other Parts of Trees* (included. Photocopy onto sturdy tag board, cut out cards, and colour illustrations.) (4.4.2)
- vocabulary cards – *Coniferous Trees* (included. Photocopy onto sturdy tag board, cut out cards, and colour illustrations.) (4.4.3)
- vocabulary cards – *Deciduous Trees* (included. Photocopy onto sturdy tag board, cut out cards, and colour illustrations.) (4.4.4)
- vocabulary cards – *Shrubs* (included. Photocopy onto sturdy tag board, cut out cards, and colour illustrations.) (4.4.5)
- vocabulary cards – *Other Plants* (included. Photocopy onto sturdy tag board, cut out cards, and colour illustrations.) (4.4.6)
- vocabulary cards – *Provincial and Territorial Flowers of Canada* (included. Photocopy onto sturdy tag board, cut out cards, and colour illustrations appropriately. Refer to websites listed on the preceding page or to other sources for accurate colour illustrations.) (4.4.7)
- wall map of Canada
- books and other references about plants in Canada
- newsprint
- clipboards
- crayons or coloured pencils
- tree branches
- stapler
- scissors
- tape

4

- Plant Hunt sheet (included. Photocopy for each student.) (4.4.9)
- supplies for school garden or classroom conservatory or terrarium (for example, seeds, gardening tools, terrarium container)
- research materials (books or websites) about caring for plants selected for school garden or classroom conservatory or terrarium
- tape measures or rulers for measuring plant growth
- wall map of Canada
- computer(s), with internet access

Integrated Class Activities

- This lesson on plants of Canada provides ample opportunity for students to conduct in-depth studies of plant life. Consider having the whole class do all instructional, peer, and individual activities for this lesson.
- Start a school garden or classroom conservatory or terrarium. Have students research to determine how to care for selected plants. Measure plant growth over the course of the school year.
- To correlate this lesson with Canadian geography and symbols, conduct a study of Canada's provincial and territorial flowers. Use a wall map of Canada to explain that each province and territory has its own flower, as follows:
   - British Columbia – Pacific dogwood
   - Alberta – wild rose
   - Saskatchewan – western red lily
   - Manitoba – prairie crocus
   - Ontario – white trillium
   - Québec – blue flag
   - Nova Scotia – mayflower
   - Newfoundland and Labrador – pitcher plant
   - New Brunswick – purple violet
   - Prince Edward Island – lady's slipper
   - Nunavut – purple saxifrage
   - Northwest Territories – mountain avens
   - Yukon – fireweed
- Display the vocabulary cards – *Provincial and Territorial Flowers of Canada* (4.4.7), and review the names with students. Have students use internet sites to access colour photos of these flowers. Distribute the integrated class activity sheet called "Flowers of Canada's Provinces and Territories" (4.4.8), and have students complete the map of Canada by drawing, colouring, and labelling the flower for each province and territory.
- Invite guests with diverse world views about the natural environment to speak to the class. This might include an Aboriginal elder to discuss some of the relationships between humans and nature, or a Chinese or other traditional healer who uses herbs and other plants in his or her practice.
- Discuss why plants are important (provide shelter for animals, food, medicine, other products, shade, air quality) and how people should care for them.
- Have students bring to school samples or pictures of indigenous plants from their countries of origin.

Whole-Class Career Connections

- Focus on careers related to plants as food. Invite an organic farmer to present to the class on how he or she is growing plants in a more environmentally friendly way.
- Visit a local greenhouse to see how herbs and vegetables are grown for use in residential gardens.
- Research the process of making bread, from growing the wheat to grinding the flour to baking the bread dough. Visit a local grain farm, granary, grinding mill if accessible, or a bakery.

▶

Instructional Activity: Part One

Display a variety of houseplants and outdoor plants. Allow students time to examine and discuss them. Ask:

- What are these called?
- How are these plants the same?
- How are they different?

On chart paper, record the word *plant*. Ask:

- What is a plant?

Discuss students' understanding of the term, and encourage them to come up with their own definitions.

Show students three or four of the vocabulary cards – *Plants of Canada (Other Plants)* (4.4.1), and say:

- _____ is a plant.
- _____ is a plant.

and so on.

Identify some other items in the classroom. Ask:

- Is a desk a plant?
- Is a person a plant?

Explain that a plant is a living thing that grows in the ground (or, indoors, in a pot of soil), including flowers, bushes, trees, vegetables, and houseplants.

Instructional Activity: Part Two

Cover a work surface with newspaper. Remove one or more houseplants (depending on the number of students) from their pots, shaking the soil into a basin. Place the plants on a table for students to examine. Provide magnifying glasses for close-up observations. Encourage dialogue and inquiry as students examine the plants.

Provide drawing paper and pencils, and have students draw diagrams of the plants. Display the vocabulary cards – *Parts of Plants* (4.4.1) to help students identify the parts of the plants.

Discuss with students what plants need to survive and how people can take care of plants.

Instructional Activity: Part Three

Give each student a clipboard and some blank paper, and introduce some of the lesson vocabulary by taking a short walk around the community. Students may be able to spot various plants in the community. As they notice each plant, have them draw a small picture on their clipboard paper. While students draw what they observe, take digital photos of the plants, and record the names of the plants identified by the group.

Back in the classroom, have students record in their personal dictionaries the names of the plants they observed on the community walk and include a picture of each.

Note: Provide the spelling of difficult words for students, and offer resources for detailed pictures of plants. Students can also access plant pictures on the internet.

Instructional Activity: Part Four

Use the vocabulary cards to present remaining vocabulary. Encourage students to use various criteria to sort the cards. For example:

- plants with bark/plants without bark
- garden plants (or plants we eat)/plants we do not eat

Instructional Activity: Part Five

Display collections of leaves and seeds for students to examine. Encourage open exploration and descriptive discussion. Have students focus on the seeds. Ask:

- What are these called?

4

Have students share their ideas. Explain that a seed is a tiny part of a plant that can grow in the ground to make a new plant. Have students examine the various seeds and describe their features (colour, shape, size). Challenge them to sort the seeds into groups according to their own criteria.

Note: Students may sort seeds by type, or they may sort them into larger groups such as by colour or shape. Both strategies are acceptable, as long as students can articulate their sorting rule.

Now, have students examine the leaves. Ask:

- What are these called?

Have students share their ideas. Explain that leaves are the flat, green parts on a plant that grow from the stem or on branches that grow from the stem. The leaves for different plants are different shapes and sizes.

Have students examine the various leaves and describe their features (colour, shape, size, edges). Challenge them to sort the leaves into groups according to their own criteria.

Peer Activities

- Have students make leaf rubbings by placing a piece of newsprint on top of a leaf and colouring lightly with a crayon or coloured pencil. Ask students to cut out their leaf rubbings, and use the leaves to make "mixed up" trees. Staple a tree branch onto a bulletin board, and have students attach their leaves to the branch.

- Organize the class into groups of ELL students and peer helpers. Provide each group with copies of the Plant Hunt sheet (4.4.9) and clipboards. Have students visit different classrooms and other locations within the school in search of plants. If using digital cameras, ask students to take a picture of each plant they find, record, on the plant hunt sheet, the room number in which it was found, and then print the photos and glue them into the left-hand column of the sheet. If not using digital cameras, have students draw a simple sketch of each plant.

Note: The plant hunt can also be extended to include the school grounds.

Independent Activity: Activity Sheet A

Directions to students:

Draw and label two plants of your choice (this can include trees). Make sure you include the name of the plant at the top, and label all parts of the plant. Describe what you know about each plant (4.4.10).

Extensions

- Add new vocabulary – *Plants of Canada* to the multilingual word wall, or have students add it to their personal vocabulary folders.

- Have students add new vocabulary – *Plants of Canada* to their personal dictionaries.

- Visit a local greenhouse or nursery to examine local plants and trees.

Assessment of Learning

Observe the ELL students as they work together with their English-speaking classmates on the plant hunt peer activity. Focus on their abilities to work with others. Use the Cooperative Skills Teacher-Assessment sheet (I.10), shown on page 39, to record results.

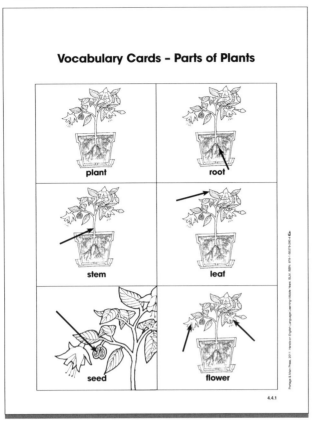

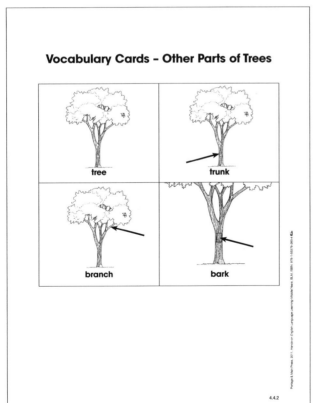
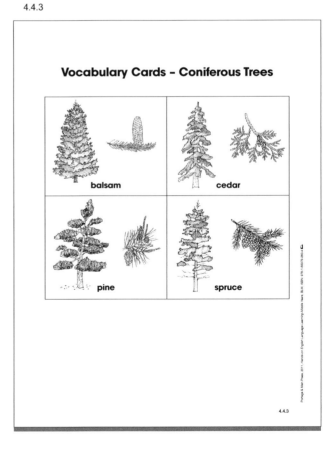

Vocabulary Cards - Deciduous Trees

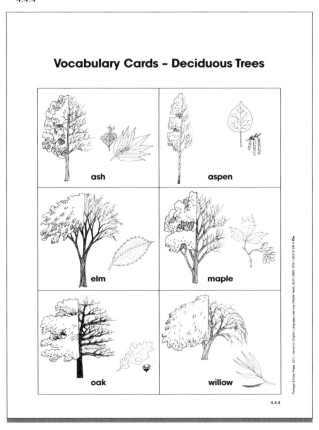

Vocabulary Cards - Shrubs

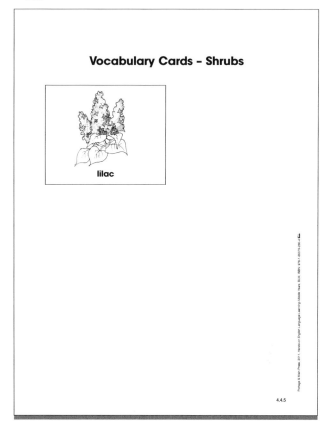

Vocabulary Cards - Other Plants

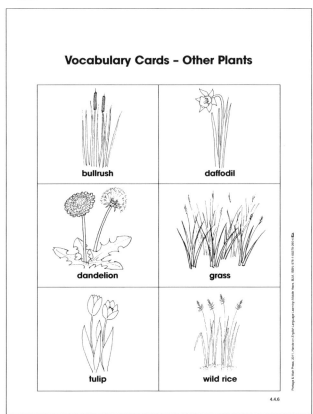

Vocabulary Cards - Other Plants

Blackline Masters

Blackline Masters

4.4.7

Vocabulary Cards – Provincial and Territorial Flowers of Canada

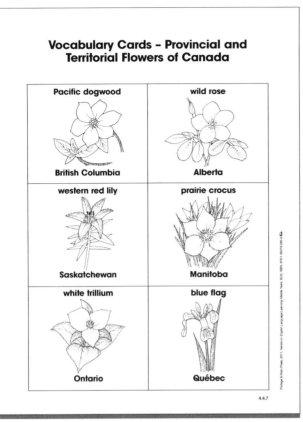

4.4.7

Vocabulary Cards – Provincial and Territorial Flowers of Canada

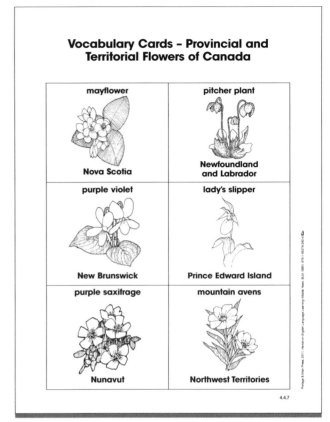

4.4.7

Vocabulary Cards – Provincial and Territorial Flowers of Canada

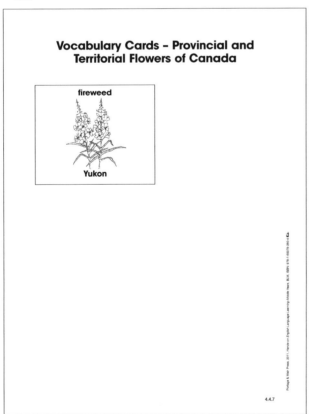

4.4.8

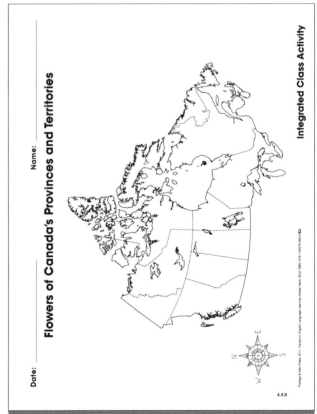

Integrated Class Activity

4.4.9

Date: _____ Name: _____

Plant Hunt

Picture of Plant	Plant Location

Peer Activity

4.4.9

4.4.10

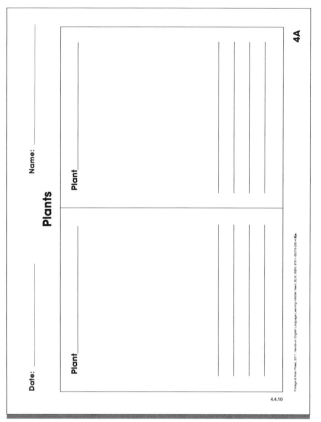

Name: _____

Date: _____

Plants

Plant

Plant

4.4.10

Blackline Masters

4A

4.4.9 – 4.4.10 – 371

5 Natural Habitats

Curricular Connections

- Language Arts: speaking, listening, reading, writing, viewing, representing
- Mathematics: problem solving
- Science: environmental issues, sustainable development, living things (plants, animals)
- Social Studies: environmental issues, sustainable development
- Music: singing, music appreciation, exploring lyrics
- Art: clay modelling, art appreciation

Background Information for Teachers

This lesson helps to develop students' background knowledge of the natural environment and the survival needs of living things, focusing more specifically on the local natural environment and its habitats as well as the plants and animals that live there. To provide students with first-hand opportunities to explore the natural environment, teachers are encouraged to teach this lesson during the spring or early fall when students can comfortably spend time outdoors observing plants and animals.

Many of the vocabulary words and activities suggested in this lesson are based on middle-years science topics. The study of life sciences, particularly the plants and animals of the local environment, is a curricular focus at all grade levels. The activities in this lesson will help students learning English to participate more fully in science classes, and will also enhance their general knowledge of environmental issues.

Vocabulary – Natural Habitats

- animal
- plant
- habitat
- forest
- prairie
- garden
- lake
- river
- stream
- pond
- park
- water
- sun
- air
- soil
- arctic
- tundra
- ocean
- swamp
- marsh
- mountain
- desert
- rainforest
- jungle

Materials

- chart paper
- sticky notes
- scissors
- digital camera
- clipboards
- pencils
- drawing paper
- vocabulary cards – *Natural Habitats* (included. Photocopy one set onto sturdy tagboard, and cut apart cards.) (4.5.1)
- pocket chart
- coloured pictures of various plants and animals (from magazines or websites)
- calendar photographs of different habitats (involve students in collecting these)
- large, blank index cards
- paint and paintbrushes or drawing materials
- multicultural books (see Books for Students, page 330)

- markers or coloured pencils
- poster paper
- Plasticine, play dough, or modelling clay
- access to the internet
- music (CD or MP3) by Canadian children's musician Aaron Burnett
- CD player (or MP3 player/computer) for playing music
- writing paper
- artwork (from books or the internet) of Canadian visual artists who depict the natural environment in their artwork (for example, the Group of Seven, Tom Thomson, Emily Carr, Robert Bateman)
- artwork (from books or the internet) of nature artists from countries other than Canada
- shoeboxes
- art materials for creating habitat dioramas (construction paper, glue, markers or coloured pencils, and so on)
- natural materials for creating habitat dioramas (grass, soil, stones, twigs, sand, and so on)

Integrated Class Activities

- Environmental issues and sustainable development are integral curricular topics at all grade levels, and all students in the class will benefit from exploring these themes. Engage students in the activity "Show That Habitat," which gives them an opportunity to use art to reflect on their knowledge of habitats. Provide students with Plasticine, play dough, or modeling clay. Select one student to call out the name of a habitat (forest, prairie, garden, lake, river, stream, pond, jungle, rainforest, and so on). Challenge students to each sculpt a plant or animal that lives within that habitat. Have the vocabulary cards – Natural Habitats (4.5.1) available for ELL students to use as support during this activity. Once students are finished making their plants/animals, have them share their creations.

- As a class, explore the music and lyrics of Canadian children's musician Aaron Burnett, who focuses many of his songs on environmental issues such as endangered and extinct animals, and care for wildlife. Visit Burnett's website (<http://aaronburnett.com>), read the lyrics for some of his songs, and discuss them with students. Consider also looking for a CD of his music. Then, have students write about the artist's message. As a related activity, have students create their own rap songs or poems to perform.

- Explore the work of Canadian visual artists who depict the natural environment in their artwork. Some examples include the Group of Seven, Tom Thomson, Emily Carr, and Robert Bateman. Also, explore the work of nature artists from other countries, especially from countries of students' origin.

- Collect calendar photographs of different habitats (involve students in collecting these). Have students discuss the various characteristics of these habitats and then draw or paint similar settings on large, blank index cards. These can then be used as postcards for writing activities or displayed in the classroom.

- Have students create mathematical word problems that focus on plants and animals. For example:
  - How many legs are there on 6 squirrels?
  - If there are 24 legs on a group of spiders, how many spiders are in the group?
  - Over the winter there were 240 deer living in Forest Park. In the spring, 28 fawns were born. How many deer live in Forest Park now?

Whole-Class Career Connections

- Brainstorm a list of careers related to specific habitats. For example, oceanographer, marine biologist, coastguard, forest ranger, forest-fire fighter, botanist. Then, have each student select one career to research in terms of training and qualification requirements.
- Visit a zoo to explore how zookeepers design and build animal spaces to replicate animals' natural habitats.
- Visit a local environmental centre, a nature reserve, a park, or a wildlife sanctuary, to explore the careers of people working there.

Instructional Activity: Part One

In the centre of a sheet of chart paper, record the term *animals*. Ask:

- How are all animals alike? (they are living beings, they move, they eat, they need food and water, they need shelter, they have young)
- What different animals can you name?

Have students brainstorm the names of various animals, and record these on sticky notes. Encourage a wide variety of animals by directing questions. Ask:

- Which animals live in water?
- What are the names of some very small animals?
- Which animals live in a garden?
- Which animals fly?

Once students have named a large variety of animals, challenge them to sort the animals into groups. To encourage this process, ask:

- Which animals have fur or hair?
- Which animals can fly?
- Which animals live in water?
- Which animals have six or more legs?
- Which animals have no legs?

Use the sticky notes to create a concept map. Encourage students to organize and label the map. The final product may look something like the following:

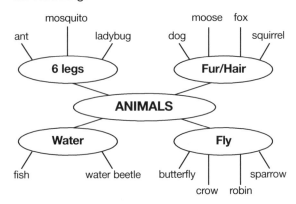

Note: Keep in mind that there are many different formats for concept mapping. Students' final product may look vastly different from the map above and is acceptable if labels and classification are accurate.

Expand the concept map by having students add animal names in their first languages.

Instructional Activity: Part Two

Display coloured pictures of various animals. Have students select an animal and use full sentences and descriptive adjectives to describe its physical features.

Note: Be sure to explain what the term *adjective* means, and give students several examples before having them provide their own sentences. For example:
- The beaver has a large, flat, paddle-shaped tail and webbed feet.
- The Canada goose has a long, black neck and white cheeks.

Then, encourage students to use verbs and adverbs to create sentences that describe the ways animals move.

Note: Again, explain what the terms *verb* and *adverb* mean, and give students examples before having them provide their own sentences. For example:

- The fuzzy, green caterpillar crawls slowly on the ground.
- The colourful butterfly floated quietly in the wind.

Note: This is an excellent opportunity for students to practise English sentence structure and grammar through the use of visual aids. The sentences are made meaningful, because they are not created in isolation but, rather, in context — referring to the topic of study: natural habitats.

Record students' sentences on chart paper. Then, give them an opportunity for dramatic play by having students take turns acting out one of the sentences and playing the role of the animal. Challenge other students to identify which sentence is being acted out.

Instructional Activity: Part Three

In the centre of a sheet of chart paper, record the term *plants*. Ask:

- How are all plants alike?
- What different plants can you name?

Have students brainstorm the names of various plants, and record these on chart paper. Also, have students share the names of these plants in their first language(s), as well as the names of plants that are unique to their countries of origin.

As in Instructional Activity: Part Two, encourage students to describe various plants, using both adjectives and adverbs. For example:

- The huge oak tree stands straight and tall.
- The golden wheat sways gently in the wind.

Instructional Activity: Part Four

Provide students with clipboards, drawing paper, and pencils. Take a walk around your local community to observe animals and plants. Have students keep lists of the animals and plants they see and draw diagrams of their observations.

Note: Use a digital camera to photograph the animals and plants.

During the walk, observe and discuss the habitats in which these plants and animals live. For example:

- Examine the soil and grass in the playground.
- Observe the types of trees in which the birds live.
- Identify a squirrel's home.

Note: Use this community walk as a springboard for discussion of the similarities and differences in the natural environment in various countries. Have students share their background knowledge of plants and animals in other countries. Also, review multicultural books to examine, discuss, compare, and contrast descriptions of local natural environments.

Instructional Activity: Part Five

Display the vocabulary cards – *Natural Habitats* (4.5.1) in the pocket chart. Discuss each term, making connections to the concept map of animals, the brainstormed list of plants, and the observations from the community walk. Ask:

- What do animals need to live? (food, water, air, shelter, space)
- What do plants need to live? (sun, water, air, soil [most plants])

Record the term *habitat* on chart paper. Explain that the place where plants and animals live is called their habitat. An animal finds its food, water, air, shelter, and space in its habitat. Ask:

- What would be a good habitat for a black bear? A polar bear?
- What are some of the features of a polar bear's habit?

▶

- What would be a good habitat for a robin? A fish? A gopher? A butterfly?

Review each vocabulary card that is a natural habitat, including *forest, prairie, garden, lake, river, stream, pond, park, arctic, tundra, ocean, swamp, marsh, mountain, desert, rainforest,* and *jungle,* and have students help to list plants and animals that might live in each habitat.

Discuss the importance of habitats to the survival of plants and animals. Ask:

- What would happen to the animals in a lake if the lake dried up?
- What would happen to the plants and animals in a forest if there was a fire?
- What would happen to the plants and animals in a prairie if houses were built there?

Note: Be sensitive when discussing natural disasters such as droughts or forest fires, since some students may have first-hand experience with such events.

Peer Activities

- Have ELL-student/peer helper pairs use shoeboxes, art materials (for example, construction paper, glue, markers or coloured pencils) and natural materials (for example, grass, soil, stones, twigs, sand) to create habitat dioramas. Ask students to include models of plants and animals that would live in the habitat they have chosen.

- Distribute poster paper and markers or coloured pencils, and have each ELL student work with a peer helper to create a poster of an animal in its habitat. Once students have selected an animal, have them draw it and the habitat, labelling all parts of their posters, and using the vocabulary cards for reference.

- Have each ELL student teach a peer helper about an animal from his or her country of origin. Provide drawing materials so students can draw illustrations of their chosen animals. As an alternative, have pairs of students find information about their animals from books or online.

Assessment for Learning

Have students present their dioramas or posters, describing the habitat, as well as the plants and animals displayed in that habitat. Focus on students' abilities to use vocabulary and appropriate sentence structure. Use the Individual Student Observations sheet (I.4), shown on page 37, to record results.

Independent Activity: Part One: Activity Sheet A

Directions to students:

In the top box, record the name of a habitat, and draw a picture of it. In the middle two boxes, record the name of one animal and one plant that live in that habitat, and draw pictures of each. In the bottom two boxes, record and draw everything that the animal and the plant need in that habitat to live (4.5.2).

Independent Activity: Part Two: Activity Sheet B

Directions to students:

Colour and label the important parts of a pond habitat (pond, marsh, bulrushes, grass, fish, frog, snake, duck, sparrow, dragonfly, shrub, grasshopper, turtle, raccoon) (4.5.3).

Extensions

- Add new vocabulary – *Natural Habitats* to the multilingual word wall or to students' personal language folders.
- Have students add new vocabulary – *Natural Habitats* to their personal dictionaries.
- Plan a field trip to a zoo to see animals in spaces created to replicate their natural habitats.

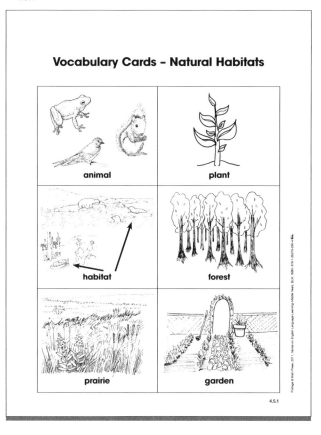
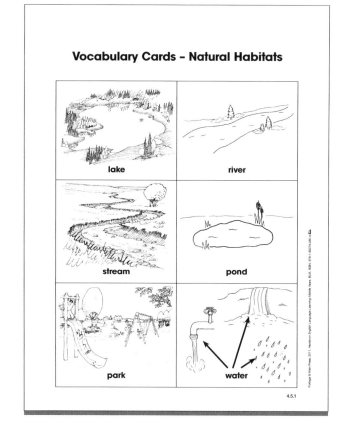
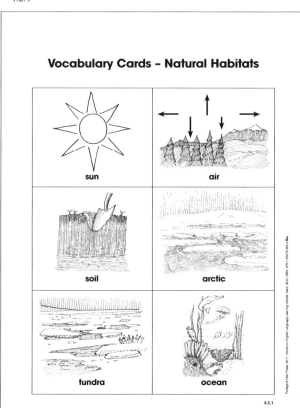
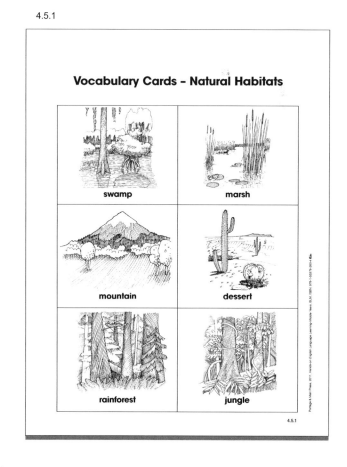

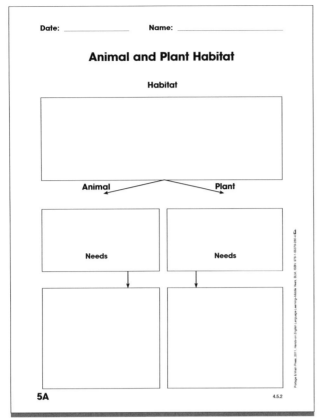
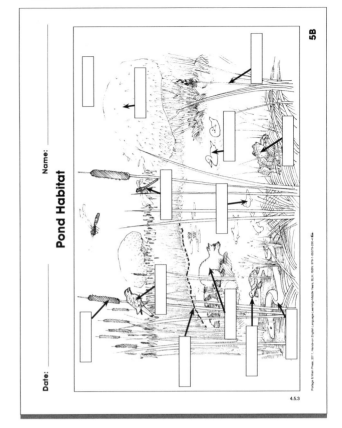

6 Importance of the Environment

Curricular Connections

- Language Arts: speaking, listening, reading, writing, viewing, representing
- Science: environmental issues, sustainable development, living things (plants, animals)
- Social Studies: environmental issues, sustainable development, cultural diversity, legends
- Art: puppet making
- Drama: puppetry

Background Information for Teachers

The *natural environment* is defined as all surroundings not made by humans. In this lesson, students focus on the importance of the natural environment, and how it helps humans, animals, and all other living things in their daily lives.

Vocabulary – Importance of the Environment

- natural environment
- land
- water
- air
- plant
- animal

Materials

- chart paper
- markers
- index cards
- pocket chart
- vocabulary cards – *Importance of the Environment* (included. Photocopy one set onto sturdy tagboard, and cut apart cards.) (4.6.1)
- interview agenda (included. Make one copy for each ELL student.) (4.6.2)
- digital cameras
- audio recorders
- writing paper
- various cultural legends, stories, and folktales (from books or websites) about the natural environment (see Multicultural Books section in Books for Students list on page 330)
- puppet-making materials (paper bags, old socks, sticks, cardboard tubes, material scraps, buttons, sequins, construction paper, glue, markers or coloured pencils, and so on)
- computer with internet access

Integrated Class Activities

- Helping to develop students' understanding of the importance of the environment will provide them with an enhanced purpose for protecting our natural world. As such, all students in the class will benefit from all instructional, peer, and independent activities in this lesson, as well as from the subsequent integrated class activities.

- Visit a local wildlife sanctuary or reserve to see how plants and animals are protected.

- Use the lesson's theme as a springboard for creative writing. Have students select one of the following story titles to write about:
  - If there was no land on earth
  - Where did the water go?
  - A world without air
  - Imagine a world without plants
  - The animals have disappeared!

- Invite guests from various countries to discuss the natural environment in other parts of the world. Take this opportunity to compare and contrast other countries to Canada in terms of the natural environment and the ways that people and other living things rely on it.

▶

- Read books, and have guests share legends and folktales about the natural environment in Canada and other countries. Have students make puppets that reflect characters from the various legends and then recreate these legends for the class or for community performances.

Whole-Class Career Connections

- Invite a career counselor from your school, a post-secondary institution, or an employment service agency to discuss the diversity of careers related to environmental issues.
- Have students explore the website for ECO Canada, the Environmental Careers Organization, at <www.eco.ca>.

Note: This organization's website offers excellent resources for teachers and students alike.

- As a class, explore volunteer organizations and NGOs (non-government organizations) that offer work experiences related to environmental issues.

Instructional Activity: Part One

Display the vocabulary cards – *Importance of the Environment* (4.6.1) in the pocket chart, and review each term with students. Encourage students to describe the illustrations on the cards and use the vocabulary in sentences. Also, have ELL students share translations for these words from their first language(s).

Divide a sheet of chart paper into two columns. At the top of the first column, record "Things in our Community Made by Humans". Ask:

- What things in our community are made by humans?

Discuss features such as buildings, houses, roads, bridges, streetlights, cars, play structures, and so on. Record these on the chart.

At the top of the second column of the chart, record the heading "Our Community's Natural Environment". Explain to students that the community's natural environment includes all things not made by humans. Ask:

- What things in our community are not made by humans?

Brainstorm as many ideas as possible, including examples of land, water, air, plants, and animals. Challenge students to think of a variety of examples, such as:

- Land: soil, rocks, hills, fields, gardens
- Water: rivers, creeks, ponds, rain, puddles, lakes
- Air: wind, sky
- Plants: trees, shrubs, grass, weeds, flowers, vegetables
- Animals: birds, raccoons, squirrels, insects, fish

Record all the examples of land, water, air, plants, and animals on index cards, to be used in the next activity.

Instructional Activity: Part Two

In the pocket chart, display the index cards with examples of land, water, air, plants, and animals. Challenge students to add any new examples, and record these ideas on new index cards. Then, mix up the cards, and challenge students to find a way to sort them.

Note: Students may sort the cards according to the categories already mentioned (land, water, air, plants, and animals), or they may find other ways to sort the cards.

Now, focus on ways that the natural environment is important to people. On chart paper, create a concept web, as in the following example:

6

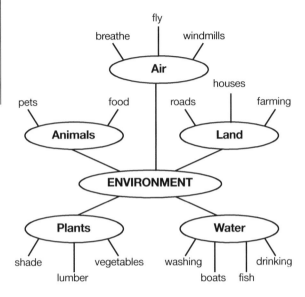

Discuss ways in which people rely on land, water, air, animals, and plants for survival. Record these examples outside the web circles, as in the preceding example. Encourage students to discuss the following ways in which people depend on the natural environment:

- Land: houses, roads, farming, gardening, travel
- Water: drinking, transportation, farming, gardening, fishing, bathing/washing/cleaning
- Air: breathing, air travel, windmills and turbines, sailing
- Plants: food (vegetables and grains), lumber, shade, medicines
- Animals: food, pets, guides (seeing-eye dogs), transportation (horses), milk (cows, goats)

Further discuss how all living things (not just people) depend on the environment for survival. Have students cite examples of how plants and animals rely on land, water, air, and other plants and animals.

Instructional Activity: Part Three

Read various cultural legends, stories, and folktales about the natural environment. Discuss both the descriptions and the illustrations of various natural settings in the books, including habitats, plants, and animals.

Encourage ELL students to share how people and other living things depend on the natural environment in their countries of origin.

Note: This may be an excellent opportunity to invite family members to the school to present to the class on this topic.

Peer Activity

Ask ELL-student/peer-helper pairs to use the included interview agenda (4.6.2) to interview adults in the school about why the natural environment is important. If there are other students or adults in the school that speak the same language as the ELL student, have the student interview someone in his or her first language, record the interview, play it back for the class, and translate the content. Be sure to have students introduce themselves to each adult they approach for an interview and explain what their task is (an introduction is provided on the interview agenda).

Note: Students will ask each interviewee *one* of the six questions.

Have students take photos of the people they interview and use audio recorders to record their interviews.

Note: The audio recording allows students to focus their attention on the interviews and record their ideas on the interview agenda afterward. Be sure students ask permission to record the interview as well as to take interviewees' pictures (the picture-taking part of the activity should be optional).

▶

Independent Activity: Part One: Activity Sheet A

Directions to students:

Use words, phrases, sentences, and illustrations to show examples of the natural environment (4.6.3).

Independent Activity: Part Two: Activity Sheet B

Directions to students:

Use words, phrases, sentences, and illustrations to show why land, water, air, plants, and animals are important to people (4.6.4).

Extensions

- Add new vocabulary – *Importance of the Environment* to the multilingual word wall or to students' personal vocabulary folders.

- Have students add new vocabulary – *Importance of the Environment* to their personal dictionaries.

- Have students write pattern stories about the environment. First, read to students *The Important Book*, by Margaret Wise Brown, discussing the story pattern. Then, have them write their own stories. For example:

*The important thing about the environment
Is that it is the home for all living things.
It is the air and sky
It is the land and water
It is nature
But the important thing about the environment
Is that it is the home for all living things.*

4.6.1

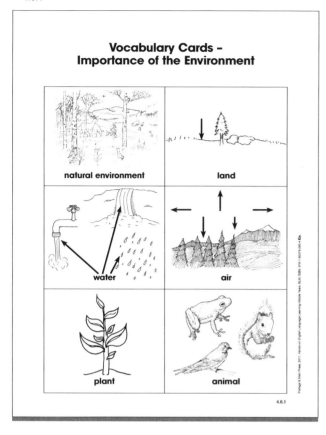

4.6.2

4.6.3

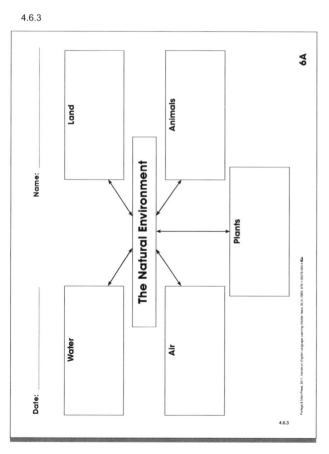

4.6.4

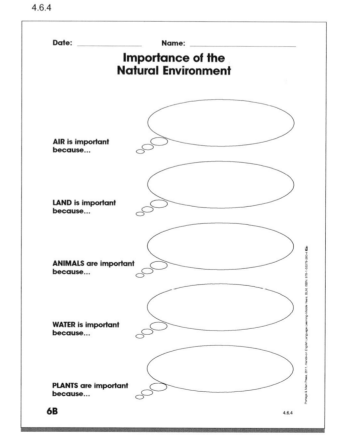

7 Human Impact on the Environment

Curricular Connections

- Language Arts: speaking, listening, reading, writing, viewing, representing
- Science: environmental issues, sustainable development, living things (plants, animals)
- Social Studies: environmental issues, sustainable development
- Art: using clay to illustrate books

Background Information for Teachers

This lesson introduces students to the general ways in which humans impact the natural environment. Lessons 8, 9, 10, and 11 focus on specific environmental issues involving water, air, recycling, and energy.

Note that students should be encouraged to use the terms *human(s)* and *people (person)* interchangeably throughout this lesson. Although *human* is the more academic term, we tend to use *people/person* in conversational contexts, and middle-years students should be aware of both terms.

Vocabulary – Human Impact on the Environment

- harm
- effect
- book review
- title
- author
- illustrator
- characters
- setting
- events
- ending
- favourite
- problem
- solution

Materials

- children's literature focusing on environmental issues, such as *The Lorax*, by Dr. Seuss, *Jen and the Great One*, by Peter Eyvindson, *The Wump World*, by Bill Peet, and *The Tree Suitcase*, by David Suzuki
- bilingual dictionaries (English and students' first languages)
- vocabulary cards – *Human Impact on the Environment* (included. Photocopy one set onto sturdy tagboard, and cut apart cards.) (4.7.1)

Note: Although for most vocabulary cards a picture is included with the new word, some particularly abstract vocabulary, such as *harm, effect(s)*, and *book review*, are difficult to illustrate. For this vocabulary, only the word is included on the card. As teachers and students discover visual examples of each, they are encouraged to add these to the card.

- pocket chart
- chart paper
- markers
- book review sheet (included. Make several copies for each ELL student.) (4.7.3)
- poster paper
- art supplies for making posters
- books illustrated with modelling-clay pictures, such as *Gifts*, by Jo Ellen Bogart and illustrated by Barbara Reid, and *The New Baby Calf*, by Edith Newlin Chase and also illustrated by Barbara Reid
- Plasticine, modelling clay, or play dough
- Styrofoam meat trays, paper plates, or cardboard
- computer with internet access

Integrated Class Activities

- In this lesson, students are introduced to various books with environmental themes. These books will benefit all students in the class, so consider conducting all instructional, peer, and independent activities with the entire class.

- Explore the work of artists who use modelling clay to illustrate books, such as Barbara Reid, who illustrated both *The New Baby Calf*, by Edith Newlin Chase, and *Gifts*, by Jo Ellen Bogart (or visit Barbara Reid's website with students at <www.barbarareid.ca>). Then, have students make Plasticine mosaics similar to those created by Reid to recreate the illustrations in a book such as *The Lorax*, by Dr. Seuss. Provide students with Plasticine (or modelling clay, or play dough), as well as Styrofoam meat trays, paper plates, or cardboard on which they can create their mosaics. Have each student focus on one page of text and the corresponding illustration. Once students have completed their mosaics, sequence the clay illustrations, and have students retell the story.

- Have students conduct research on animals and plants that are endangered and at risk of becoming extinct. To help them select a plant or animal to research further, read books and explore websites that focus on this topic, such as *Will We Miss Them? Endangered Species*, by Alexandra Wright, *Endangered Plants*, by Elaine Landau, or the World Wildlife Fund (WWF) website (<www.worldwildlife.org>). Distribute copies of the Integrated Class Activities sheet called "Researching Endangered Plants and Animals" (4.7.2), and have students use it to help them structure their research. The activity sheets can later be bound together to create a class book about endangered animals and plants.

- Contact the World Wildlife Fund (WWF) (<www.worldwildlife.org>) to find out more about endangered species and what students can do to help.

Whole-Class Career Connections

- Read various books with environmental themes with students, such as those listed in the Materials section on the preceding page. Then, discuss some of the human activities that pose risks to the environment and the jobs related to those activities (for example, logging, mining, hydro dams, fishing, farming, and construction). Have students write letters to related organizations and businesses to ask what they are doing to protect the environment or to reduce the negative impact.

Instructional Activity: Part One

Read various books with environmental themes with students, such as those listed in the Materials section on the preceding page. With each book, use various strategies for language development and comprehension. For example:

- Discuss the front and back covers, focusing on illustrations, the title, the author, and the illustrator.
- Do a "picture walk" of the book, looking through it with students and discussing the picture(s) on each page. Encourage students to predict the events in the story through its pictures.
- Read the book aloud, stopping to discuss the story's events, characters, setting, problems, and solutions.
- Have students complete a book review sheet (4.7.3) for each book. Tell them to use words and pictures to complete the sheet.

Instructional Activity: Part Two

After reading several books on environmental issues, discuss human impact on the environment with students. On chart paper, create a two-column chart. Record the headings "Ways that humans harm the environment" at

▶

the top of one column and "Ways that humans can help the environment" at the top of the other. Focus on each issue separately, asking, first:

- What are parts of the natural environment? (water, land, air, plants, animals)
- From the books we have read, what have you learned about some ways that people sometimes harm the environment?

Record students' ideas in the first column of the chart. Then, ask:

- What could people do instead, so they are helping, not hurting, the environment?

Encourage students to articulate the potential solutions for each environmental issue recorded on the chart. Students may suggest some of the following solutions:

- When trees are cut down for lumber, plant new ones.
- Protect the natural habitats of plants and animals so they can survive.
- Walk, or take a bike more for travelling, and use cars less.
- Recycle.
- Do not litter.

In the pocket chart, display the vocabulary cards – Human Impact on the Environment (4.7.1), and use the information recorded on the chart to discuss the vocabulary. Also, have students discuss human impact on the environment in their countries of origin.

Peer Activity

Have each ELL student work with a peer helper to make a poster encouraging people to take care of the environment. Distribute poster paper, markers, and other art supplies to ELL-student/peer-helper pairs. Later, provide time for students to present their completed posters to the class, and then display the posters throughout the classroom and school.

Note: Before having students begin work on their posters, meet with them individually to identify criteria for assessment (refer to the section below, "Assessment of Learning"). Criteria might include

- neat printing/writing
- correct spelling
- colourful pictures
- important message about the environment

Independent Activity: Activity Sheet A

Directions to students:

Use pictures and words to describe one problem that is caused by humans harming the environment as well as a solution to this problem (4.7.4).

Extensions

- Add new vocabulary – *Human Impact on the Environment* to the multilingual word wall or to students' personal language folders.
- Have students add new vocabulary – *Human Impact on the Environment* to their personal dictionaries.

Assessment of Learning

Review students' environmental posters, focusing on the criteria mentioned above. Record these criteria on copies of the Rubric sheet (I.12), shown on page 39, and record results.

4.7.1

Vocabulary Cards – Human Impact on the Environment

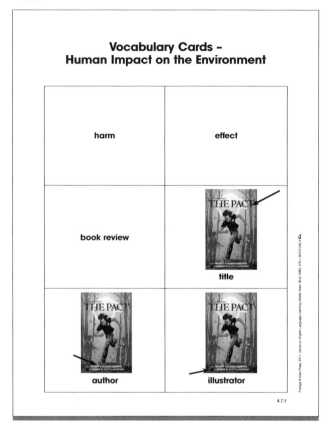

4.7.1

Vocabulary Cards – Human Impact on the Environment

Blackline Masters

4.7.1

Vocabulary Cards – Human Impact on the Environment

4.7.2

Date: _____ Name: _____

Researching Endangered Plants and Animals

Name of plant/animal: _____

What does it look like? _____

Where does it live? _____

Why has it become endangered? _____

What can be done to protect it? _____

Sources used: _____

Integrated Class Activity

4.7.1 – 4.7.2 – 387

Blackline Masters

4.7.3

Date: _____ Name: _____

Book Review

Book Title: _____
Author: _____
Illustrator: _____

Characters	Setting
Events	**Ending**
My Favourite Part	

4.7.4

Name: _____
Date: _____

People and the Environment

People Helping the Environment

People Harming the Environment

7A

8 Air Pollution

Curricular Connections

- Language Arts: speaking, listening, reading, writing, viewing, representing
- Mathematics: using data, making charts
- Science: experimental design, environmental issues, sustainable development, living things (plants, animals), states of matter (solids, liquids, gases)
- Social Studies: environmental issues, sustainable development
- Physical Education: active living
- Health: active living, asthma

Background Information for Teachers

Air pollution is a type of environmental pollution comprised of unwanted and harmful chemical products in the air. These unwanted chemicals are by-products of many of the daily activities of humans.

Clean air is an essential need of all living things. Air pollution is increasingly becoming a problem throughout the world because of a growing number of factories and motorized vehicles, and industrialization in general.

Childhood asthma is an illness that is becoming more and more prevalent, and although the underlying causes aren't fully understood, recent studies have shown a relationship between exposure to air pollutants, specifically "bad" ozone, and this illness (Salam, Islam, and Gilliland 2008; Mi et al 2006). This lesson focuses on the causes of bad ozone and how people can reduce emissions that cause this kind of air pollution.

Vocabulary – Air Pollution

- air pollution
- chemicals
- good ozone
- bad ozone
- ground-level
- asthma
- exhaust
- carbon footprint

Materials

- *Michael Bird-Boy*, a book by Tomie dePaola
- vocabulary cards – Air Pollution (included. Photocopy one set onto sturdy tagboard, and cut apart cards.) (4.8.1)
- pocket chart
- chart paper
- markers
- scissors
- Ozone Information sheet (included. Make a copy for each ELL student.) (4.8.2)
- mural paper
- scissors
- glue
- drawing paper
- magazines and catalogues with pictures of cars, trucks, planes, trains, and factories
- computers with internet access
- local newspapers and newspapers from other countries
- petroleum jelly
- thumbtacks or duct tape (or other utensils for securing paper to an outside location)

Integrated Class Activities

- Discuss the concepts of *carbon footprint* and of individual impact on greenhouse gas emissions. As a class, brainstorm transportation alternatives to single-person motorized vehicles for reducing greenhouse emissions and carbon footprint (for example, walking, cycling, carpooling, public transit). Also, discuss the health benefits of biking or walking, when possible, as opposed to driving. Students can use one of the following websites to calculate and graph their own carbon footprints:

▶

8

- <www.carbonfootprint.com/calculator.aspx>
- <www.nature.org/initiatives/climatechange/calculator/>
- <www.ehow.com/how_2146565_calculate-carbon-footprint.html>

- Initiate a walk-to-school program. Visit the Active & Safe Routes to School website (<www.saferoutestoschool.ca>) for resources, tools, information, and links for creating an Active & Safe Routes to School program.

- Have students or guests who have asthma share their experiences in terms of the effects of air quality on their breathing.

- Use media sources such as local newspapers or online weather sites to track and record the air quality index in your area. The Environment Canada website provides information on air quality and current local AQHI (Air Quality Health Index) conditions for locations across Canada; see <www.ec.gc.ca/cas-aqhi/default.asp?lang=En&n=CB0ADB16-1>.

- Use similar data sources to compare air quality in other countries. Encourage students to infer why some regions would have greater concerns about air pollution than others.

- Conduct a hands-on experiment that allows students to observe air pollutants. Have students spread a thin layer of petroleum jelly onto several sheets of white paper, and tell them to place the sheets in various outdoor locations in order to compare the amount of air pollutants observable. For example, place one sheet close to the site where school buses arrive and depart, another near a high-traffic street, and another in a park or backyard.

Note: Paper should be protected from rain, snow, and wind and should also be secured. If, for example, the paper is on a picnic table, students can use thumbtacks or duct tape to secure it.

After one day, bring the sheets of paper back into the classroom, and have students observe them (pollutants in the air will have stuck to the jelly). Ask them to compare the results, draw conclusions, and record the experiment on the Integrated Class Activities sheet, "Experimental Design" (4.8.3). This sheet uses the standard experimental format, and includes the following components:

- **Purpose**: What you want to find out (in this case, whether there are air pollutants in the air, and how various locations compare in the amount of air pollutants).
- **Hypothesis**: What you think will happen.
- **Materials**: What you need to conduct the experiment.
- **Method**: What you did, including step-by-step procedures.
- **Results**: What happened, including observations, or, sometimes, data recorded on a chart.
- **Conclusion**: What you learned.
- **Application**: How you can use what you learned in your daily life.

Introduce the preceding terms to students as you conduct the experiment, and have them complete the activity sheet during the process.

Note: You can use the same sheet to record any scientific experiment.

▶

8

Whole-Class Career Connections

- Contact local manufacturers to provide information to the class about how they manage air pollutants emitted from their plants. Arrange a field trip to one of these manufacturing plants to observe the plant first-hand.

- Discuss the prevalence of asthma and air-borne allergies in our society. Have students conduct research on these medical conditions, or have afflicted students/family members present on their personal conditions. Invite an allergist to discuss this issue with the class, and to share information on his or her training and career.

- Have students conduct research on how automobile exhaust affects air quality. Also have them research the training required by auto mechanics. Visit an automobile service centre, or have an auto mechanic visit the class to discuss how exhaust systems are designed to reduce this affect.

- As a class, review the employability skills checklist included in module 1, lesson 1 (1.1.8). Have students work in small groups to discuss the careers of some of the guest speakers noted above or of those whom they met on field trips. Ask students to identify significant employability skills for each career. Record discussion points on chart paper, and share these with the class to facilitate discussion.

Instructional Activity: Part One

Read the book *Michael Bird-Boy*, by Tomie dePaola, about a boy who locates a factory that is polluting his community and sets out to find solutions to this problem.

As you read and discuss the story, have students identify sources of air pollution in Michael's community and the solution that Michael finds.

Focus on the main events of the story. Have students retell it in their own words, and record their sentences on chart paper. Next, read through the sentences on the chart paper, and then cut them apart. Challenge students to put the events back in order to tell the story.

Instructional Activity: Part Two

Provide students with copies of the Ozone Information sheet (4.8.2). As a group, read through the sheet, discussing the illustrations and the information provided. Ask:

- What is good ozone?
- Where is good ozone found?
- What is bad ozone?
- Where is ground-level ozone found?
- What causes ground-level ozone?
- How does ground-level ozone affect humans?
- How can people solve the problem of ground-level ozone?

Record students' ideas on chart paper.

In the pocket chart, display and review the vocabulary cards – *Air Pollution* (4.8.1), and use the preceding activities as a springboard to discussion.

Peer Activity

Provide ELL-student/peer-helper pairs with mural paper, scissors, glue, markers, drawing paper, magazines, and catalogues. Ask students to collect pictures of cars, trucks, planes, trains, and factories from magazines, catalogues, and internet sites or draw illustrations themselves. Then, have students use the pictures to create collages titled "What Causes Ground-Level Ozone?"

Assessment for Learning

Have students present their collages to the teacher, then to the rest of the class (and also to other classes if the opportunity arises), describing the causes of ground-level ozone. Focus on students' abilities to accurately use the vocabulary and appropriate sentence structure. Use copies of the Anecdotal Record sheet (I.3), shown on page 37, to record results.

Independent Activity: Activity Sheet A

Directions to students:

Use the words in the box to label the diagram. Draw lines from each word to its location on the diagram (4.8.4).

Extensions

- Add new vocabulary – *Air Pollution* to the multilingual word wall or to students' personal vocabulary folders.
- Have students add new vocabulary – *Air Pollution* to their personal dictionaries.

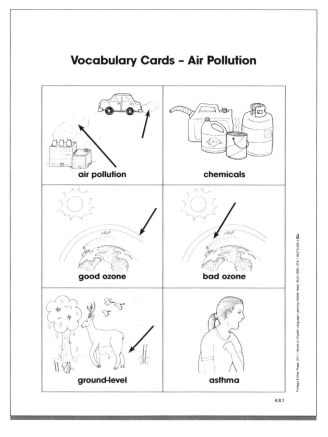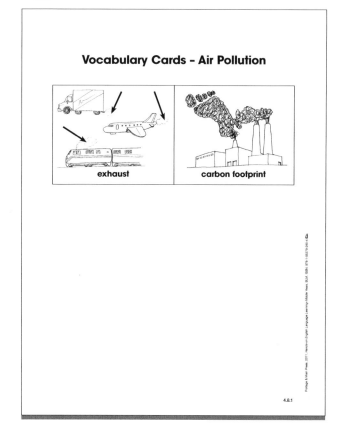

Date: _____ Name: _____

Ozone

| good ozone | earth | sun | ground-level ozone (smog) |
| car | truck | plane | factory |

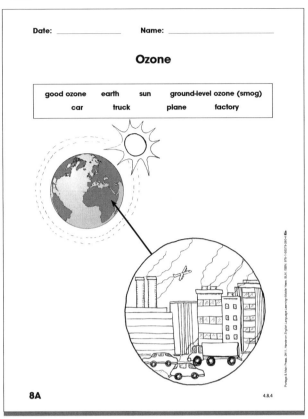

9 Water

Curricular Connections

- Language Arts: speaking, listening, reading, writing, viewing, representing
- Mathematics: measurement (liquids)
- Science: experimental design, environmental issues, sustainable development, living things (plants, animals), states of matter (solids, liquids, and gases)
- Social Studies: environmental issues, sustainable development
- Health: access to clean water

Background Information for Teachers

Water is the most important substance on Earth, because it supports life. All living organisms depend on water to live, but there is only a fixed amount of water on the earth. In this lesson, students learn about the causes of water pollution and how pollution affects the water supply.

Vocabulary – Water

- water pollution
- oil tanker
- oil spill
- acid rain
- water source
- factory
- fertilizer
- garbage
- litter

Materials

- vocabulary cards – *Water* (included. Photocopy one set onto sturdy tagboard, and cut apart cards.) (4.9.1)
- small vocabulary cards – *Water* (included. Photocopy two sets, and cut out cards.) (4.9.2)
- chart paper
- markers
- pictures of water pollution (from books or online sources. Make full-page copies of several images.)
- bowls
- blue food colouring
- cooking oil
- tablespoons
- measuring cup (mL)
- feathers (available at craft stores)
- pieces of faux fur
- plant leaves and flowers
- information about local water sources (available from civic offices)
- pollution scenario cards (4.9.3)
- large, clear basin (a large, glass mixing bowl will work)
- water
- small watering can
- molasses
- vinegar
- salt
- garbage samples (food scraps, plastic wrap [used] or bag, and so on)
- pocket chart
- computer, with internet access

Integrated Class Activities

- The instructional activities included in this lesson are especially effective in demonstrating the need for clean water and the results of water pollution. Consider doing all activities in this lesson with the whole class.

- Have students find out about local initiatives to improve water quality, such as lake, river, and creek cleanups. Invite a guest speaker from the local division of Water Stewardship to present to the class on local issues.

▶

Module 4

- Have ELL students, staff, and guests share information about water availability, water sources, and water pollution in other countries. This offers students an understanding of how water usage can vary around the world.

- Involve students in a project to help provide safe water for communities in need. Check out projects like the African Well Fund (<www.africanwellfund.org>), WaterCan (<www.watercan.com>) and Water.org (<http://water.org>).

- Visit a local water treatment plant to learn about the importance of clean water and the need to control water usage.

Whole-Class Career Connections

- As a class, brainstorm careers related to water. These will include everything from local water company employees, to suppliers of drinking water, to environmentalists, to those who utilize this natural resource in their daily work (fishers; boat manufacturers, sales, and service).

- Discuss the process involved in providing water to homes in your community. Have the local water company present to students, or visit a water treatment plant, and discuss the roles of various employees in the process.

- Have students research careers in water sciences, such as jobs in hydrogeology, hydrology, and water resources. Websites such as Earthworks provide excellent research information; visit <www.earthworks-jobs.com/hydro.htm>.

Instructional Activity: Part One

Discuss the importance of water to all living things. Ask:

- How do humans use water? (drinking, cleaning/bathing, farming, transportation)

- How is water important to other living things? (it nourishes plants and animals; it is a habitat for plants and animals)
- How does water get polluted?
- How does polluted water affect humans?
- How does polluted water affect plants and animals other than people?

Display images of water pollution from books or online sources. Discuss the different forms of pollution.

Explain that oil tankers carry oil for fuel across the oceans to countries all over the world. Ask:

- What do you think would happen if an oil tanker hit a rock or experienced bad weather and spilled oil into the ocean?

Note: Be sure to involve students in the procedures of the following demonstration by having them help add and mix ingredients.

Provide students with bowls, and pour some water into each bowl. Place a drop of blue food colouring into students' bowls to make the water easily distinguishable.

Pour some cooking oil into another bowl. Have students touch the oil and rub it on their fingers. Ask:

- What do you think will happen if some oil is added to the water?

Test students' predictions. Add a few spoonfuls of oil to each student's bowl of water, and have students observe. Ask:

- What happens to the oil?
- Does it mix with the water?
- What would oil look like on the ocean?
- What do you think would happen to animals that lived in the ocean if an oil spill happened?
- What might happen to birds living along the shoreline?

Note: Some students, particularly younger ones, might be quite distressed to realize that oil spills kill wildlife. This topic should be handled with care, to ensure that students get the message about taking greater responsibility and care for the environment, without becoming unduly distraught.

Provide each student with a feather. Ask:

- How are feathers important to a bird?
- What do you think would happen if oil got onto a bird's feathers?

Have students dip their feathers into the bowl and observe what happens. Ask:

- If a bird's feathers were covered with oil, do you think the bird could fly?
- Do you think the bird would survive?

Explain that during an oil spill, oil gets into the eyes and mouths of birds, which can blind and poison them. The oil also soaks into their feathers so the birds cannot fly, and the feathers can no longer provide insulation to keep the bird warm.

Provide students with a small piece of faux fur. Ask:

- How do you think an oil spill would affect animals living near the ocean?

Repeat the investigation with the fur, and have students observe the effects of oil spills on animals.

Explain that the oil affects animals' fur in the same way that it affects birds' feathers. Also, if animals attempt to clean themselves or eat plants or other animals from the ocean, they will be poisoned.

Also repeat this investigation with plant leaves and flowers to see how oil spills might affect shoreline plants.

Note: Oil spills block the sunlight needed by marine plants, and shoreline plants coated with oil cannot respire.

Instructional Activity: Part Two

Discuss local sources of water. Ask:

- From where do we get the water that we use in our community?

Share information about your community's local water source. Ask:

- What do you think would happen if our local water source was polluted?

Note: Again, involve students in the procedures of the following demonstration by having them help add and mix ingredients.

Fill a large, clear basin with water. Add a few drops of blue food colouring to make the water distinguishable. Explain to students that this basin of water represents a community water source.

Use the pollution scenario cards (4.9.3) to demonstrate the impact of water pollution on a community's water source. During the demonstration, discuss the process and effects of water pollution.

Following the demonstration, display the vocabulary cards – *Water* (4.9.1) in the pocket chart. Have students use the vocabulary words in sentences to discuss what they have learned.

Instructional Activity: Part Three

Review with students the information about your community's water source. Ask:

- From where does our water come?
- Is it safe to drink water from lakes and rivers?
- What happens to water before we can drink it?

- Do you think it is important for people to be careful about how much water they use? Why?

Explain that it is important to conserve water. By conserving water, we help to make sure there will be fresh water available in the future. It also helps people to save money. As well, when people conserve water, it means there is more water *now* for other living things.

Title a sheet of chart paper "Conserving Water." Divide the sheet into two columns, and title the columns "At School" and "At Home." Ask:

- How can we save water at school?

Record students' ideas in the first column of the chart. Then, ask:

- How can you and your family conserve water at home?

Record students' ideas in the second column of the chart.

Peer Activity

Have ELL-student/peer-helper pairs use the two sets of small vocabulary cards – *Water* (4.9.2) to play the game Memory. Ask students to shuffle the cards and place them, facedown, in four rows of five cards. Tell player *A* to turn over two cards to see if they match. If they do, have that player use the term in a sentence and then keep the cards. If the cards do not match, tell that player to turn the cards facedown again in the same location. Then, have player *B* turn over two cards and try to find a matching pair. Tell students to continue playing until they have matched all the cards.

Note: When students find a match, have them use the term in a sentence before taking the pair. This supports practice of vocabulary, grammar, sentence structure, and subject-area content.

Independent Activity: Part One: Activity Sheet A

Note: This is a two-page activity sheet. Photocopy the two pages back to back for each student to create a blank brochure template.

Directions to students:

Make a brochure to show people how to reduce water pollution (4.9.4).

Independent Activity: Part Two: Activity Sheet B

Directions to students:

Share this activity sheet with your family. Decide how you can save water at home. Record your ideas (4.9.5).

Extensions

- Add new vocabulary – *Water* to the multilingual word wall or to students' personal vocabulary folders.

- Have students add new vocabulary – *Water* to their personal dictionaries.

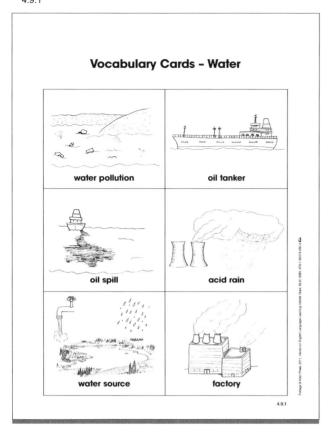
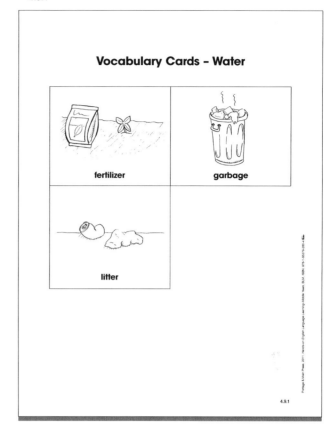

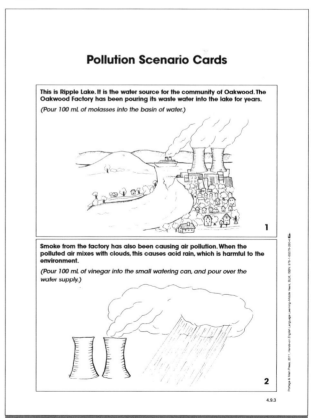

Blackline Masters

4.9.3

Pollution Scenario Cards

Farmer McDonald recently fertilized his field. The fertilizer helps Farmer McDonald to grow better crops. Unfortunately, rain washed the fertilizer into Ripple Lake, and now it is in the water supply.

(Pour 50 mL of salt into the basin of water.)

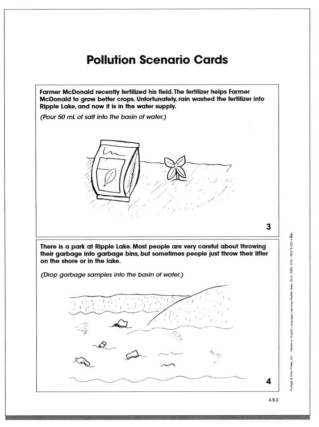

3

There is a park at Ripple Lake. Most people are very careful about throwing their garbage into garbage bins, but sometimes people just throw their litter on the shore or in the lake.

(Drop garbage samples into the basin of water.)

4

4.9.4

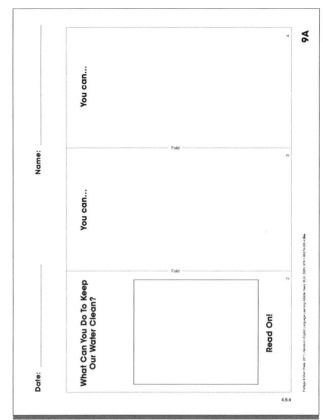

Name: _____ Date: _____

You can...

You can...

What Can You Do To Keep Our Water Clean?

Read On!

9A

4.9.4

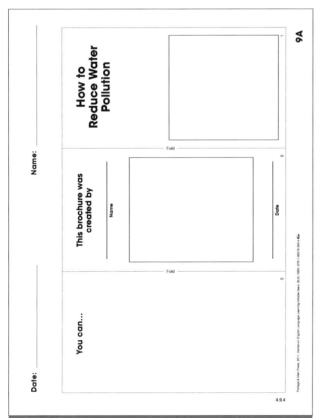

Name: _____ Date: _____

How to Reduce Water Pollution

This brochure was created by

Name _____
Date _____

You can...

9A

4.9.5

Date: _____ Name: _____

Conserving Water at Home

It is important to conserve water for a number of reasons:

1) When we conserve water, we help to make sure there will be fresh water in the future.
2) Conserving water helps people save money.
3) When we conserve water, there is more water for other living things.

Two ways we can try to conserve water at home are:

1

2

9B

400 – 4.9.3 – 4.9.5

10 Reduce, Reuse, Recycle

Curricular Connections

- Language Arts: speaking, listening, reading, writing, viewing, representing
- Mathematics: measurement (volume), collecting data, graphing
- Science: experimental design, environmental issues, sustainable development, living things (plants, animals)
- Social Studies: environmental issues, sustainable development
- Music: song lyrics
- Art: projects with recycled materials

Vocabulary – Reduce, Reuse, Recycle

- reduce
- reuse
- recycle
- recycling bin/blue box
- paper
- aluminum
- plastic
- glass
- landfill

Materials

- recycling bin
- various clean, recyclable items (tin cans, newspaper, glass bottles, plastic containers, and so on)
- scissors
- tape
- glue
- staplers
- markers
- poster paper
- vocabulary cards – *Reduce, Reuse, Recycle* (included. Photocopy one set onto sturdy tagboard, and cut apart cards.) (4.10.1)
- pocket chart
- Did You Know…? information sheet (included. Make an overhead copy of this sheet.) (4.10.2)
- overhead projector
- recycling survey (included. Make a photocopy for each ELL student.) (4.10.3)
- bin for storing recycled, reusable paper
- classroom garbage can
- lyrics and/or recording of Jack Johnson's song "The 3 R's" (see fourth integrated class activity)
- chart paper
- computer with internet access

Integrated Class Activities

- Initiate a garbage-free lunch program in the classroom or school, encouraging students to bring their food in washable, reusable containers or thermoses. Have students take initiative by making posters and announcements about the program and by tracking/tallying success results.

- Recycle paper in the classroom to use for art projects, writing of rough drafts, math calculations, and so on. Have a bin where this paper can be stored and easily accessed.

- Calibrate a classroom garbage can so it can be used to measure the volume, in litres, of garbage collected each day by the class. Ask students to record this data daily and use it to track their progress in reducing, reusing, and recycling. Have students use the data to create pictographs or bar graphs of their results.

- Download the lyrics and/or recording of Jack Johnson's song "The 3 R's" at <www.jackjohnsonmusic.com/music/_detail/curious_george_ost> (on the *Sing-A-Longs and Lullabies for the film Curious George* album), and play the song for (or teach it to) students. This is an excellent song

▶

10

to complement the lesson's theme. Have students create their own rap songs using these lyrics.

- Collect a large selection of recyclable items. Be sure to clean the items well, and ensure cans or containers have no sharp edges. Organize students into groups, and have the recyclables accessible to all groups, along with scissors, glue, tape, staplers, and markers. Have students design and build sculptures and other creations from the recyclable materials. Examples include robots, aliens, puppets, and model buildings and vehicles, but students may choose their own designs.

Assessment as Learning

After students have designed and built items from the recyclable materials, have each student complete a copy of the Cooperative Skills Self-Assessment sheet (I.7), shown on page 38, to reflect on his or her ability to work in a group.

Assessment of Learning

After students have designed and built items from the recyclable materials, use the Cooperative Skills Teacher-Assessment sheet (I.10), shown on page 39, to reflect on students' abilities to work together.

Whole-Class Career Connections

- Have students write letters to the human resources or personnel department of a local recycling company to access information on careers in this field.

- Contact local utility companies (water, hydro, gas) to collect information on jobs related to reducing resource use. Invite any or all of these companies to present to students.

- Together with students, check out websites such as Recycled Art (<www.recycledart.com>), which is devoted to discussing, promoting, and locating art made from recycled materials. Then, invite a local artisan who specializes in reusing materials to present to the class (jewelry makers, sculptors, handbag designers, and so on). Have the artist demonstrate his or her art form and discuss the collection and use of materials. Also ask the artist to discuss the skills he or she uses for his or her art.

Note: Prior to this presentation provide the artist with a copy of the Employability Skills checklist included in module 1, lesson 1 (1.1.8).

Instructional Activity

Place all the clean recyclable items into the recycling bin, and display the bin. Ask students:

- For what is this bin used?
- What kinds of objects do we put into this bin?
- What kinds of objects are *not* recyclable? (plastic bags, light bulbs, actual food, and so on)
- Why do you think we would not recycle these items?

Have students remove the items from the recycling bin, and sort them into paper, aluminum, plastic, and glass items. Ask:

- What happens to the items that we put into the box?
- Why do we recycle?
- Do we recycle at school?
- What kinds of recycling containers (bins) do we use at school?

Display the vocabulary cards – *Reduce, Reuse, Recycle* (4.10.1) in the pocket chart, and review the words with students. Discuss students' background knowledge and experience with recycling. Have students use the new vocabulary in sentences during the discussion.

Display the Did You Know…? information sheet (4.10.2) on the overhead. Read and discuss the ideas presented.

Peer Activity

Have ELL-student/peer-helper pairs use the recycling survey (4.10.3) to survey 10 students and 10 staff in the school about their recycling knowledge and habits. Ask students to record "yes" and "no" responses as tallies, totalling the number for each response and recording it in the "total" blank. Also, have students draw conclusions from their data by responding to the question at the bottom of the sheet. Have students share their results with the class.

Extend this activity by having students represent the results of their surveys in bar graphs.

Independent Activity: Part One: Activity Sheet A

Note: This is a two-page activity sheet.

Directions to students:

Look at the items on the second sheet. Redraw and label each item on the first sheet to show how they would be sorted for recycling. Add four more items (pictures and words) of your choice to the second page, then redraw and label these on the first page as well (4.10.4).

Independent Activity: Part Two: Activity Sheet B

Directions to students:

Describe ways that you can reduce, reuse, and recycle at home and at school (4.10.5).

Extensions

- Add new vocabulary – *Reduce, Reuse, Recycle* to the multilingual word wall or to students' personal vocabulary folders.

- Have students add new vocabulary – *Reduce, Reuse, Recycle* to their personal dictionaries.

- To add to students' knowledge base about recycling, reducing, and reusing check out some of the many programs and challenges found on the SEEDS Foundation website at <www.seedsfoundation.ca>, including: GREEN Schools Canada – an environmental stewardship program; "Take the Plunge" – a Canadian water conservation challenge; "Write Across Canada" – an environmental writing challenge; Mission CloudWatch – A CloudSat satellite "ground-truth" program; Migration Counts – A SEEDS Canadian bird challenge; the SEEDS Foundation Energy Literacy series; Habitat in the Balance – an online decision-making resource; "Creating a Climate of Change" – a comprehensive package of multimedia instructional resources; and Teaching Activities for Climate Change.

4.10.1

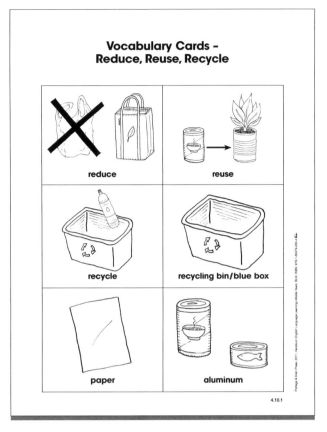

4.10.1

4.10.2

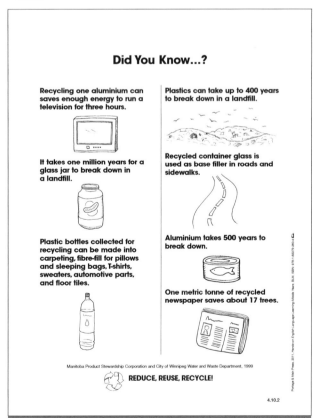

4.10.3

Date: _____   Name: _____

Recycling Survey

1. Do you know the meaning of the word *recycle*?

   Yes _____   Total: _____
   No _____   Total: _____

If the person answered "yes" to question 1, ask the next two questions:

2. Do you recycle at home?

   Yes _____   Total: _____
   No _____   Total: _____

3. Do you recycle at school?

   Yes _____   Total: _____
   No _____   Total: _____

4. Record three things you learned from doing this survey:

   1. _____
   2. _____
   3. _____

Peer Activity

4.10.4

Sorting for Recycling

Date: _____ Name: _____

(Circle divided into 5 sections: Paper, Plastic, Aluminium, Non-Recyclable, Glass)

10A

4.10.4

Items for Sorting

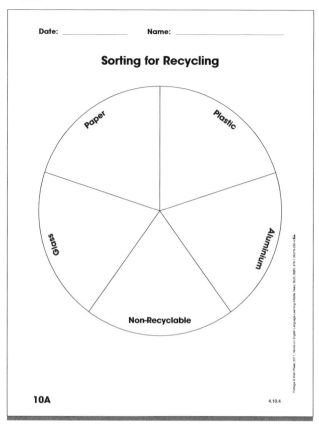

- water bottle
- tuna tin
- flyer
- jam jar
- pickle jar
- pop can
- plastic bag
- milk jug
- margarine tub
- banana
- soup tin
- CFL light-bulb
- milk carton
- juice box
- newspaper

10A

Blackline Masters

4.10.5

Date: _____ Name: _____

The Three Rs for the Environment

At School

Reduce	Reuse	Recycle

At Home

Reduce	Reuse	Recycle

10B

11 Saving Energy

Curricular Connections

- Language Arts: speaking, listening, reading, writing, viewing, representing
- Mathematics: recording data, graphing, operations, money
- Science: environmental issues, sustainable development, experimental design
- Social Studies: environmental issues, sustainable development

Background Information for Teachers

Individual Canadians account for about 28 percent of Canada's greenhouse gas emissions—*almost five tonnes per person annually.* Every time we turn on a computer, a light, or an appliance, drive an automobile, use hot water, or do anything that uses energy, we produce greenhouse gas emissions. Although this issue may be somewhat complex for middle-years students, the idea of saving energy through everyday actions is a valuable lesson for students of any age.

Vocabulary – Saving Energy

- electricity
- car
- gas
- light
- computer
- furnace
- heat
- thermostat
- compact fluorescent lamp (CFL)
- incandescent light bulb
- electric fan
- air conditioner

Materials

- compact fluorescent lamps (CFLs) (also known as a compact fluorescent lights or energy saving lights [or, less commonly, as compact fluorescent tubes or CFTs])
- incandescent light bulbs
- vocabulary cards – *Saving Energy* (included. Photocopy one set onto sturdy tagboard, and cut apart cards.) (4.11.1)
- pocket chart
- chart paper
- markers
- Saving Energy information sheet (included. Make an overhead copy of this sheet.) (4.11.2)
- overhead projector
- switch plate (metal, plastic, or ceramic plate that covers a switch)
- adhesive paper (for example, MACtac)
- scissors
- permanent overhead markers
- resources from local energy companies (brochures, stickers, posters, and information booklets on saving energy are readily available from local electrical and natural gas companies)
- voltmeter
- lamp
- chart paper
- computer with internet access

Integrated Class Activities

- The energy-saving ideas in this lesson will benefit all students in the class, so consider conducting all instructional, peer, and independent activities with the entire class.

- Brainstorm a list of things for which students use electricity (computers, hair dryers, lights, cell phone and iPod rechargers, and so on). Discuss how students would be affected if electrical energy was limited or restricted. The discussion will emphasize the importance of saving energy, while making the topic more personally relevant to students.

- As a class, conduct an experiment to compare how much power is used to light an incandescent light bulb versus a compact fluorescent lamp (CFL). Select one of each type of light bulb, and ensure that the two bulbs are designed to produce equivalent amounts of light (for example, a 13-watt CFL bulb is considered equivalent to a 60-watt incandescent bulb). Use a voltmeter to determine the amount of power used with each light bulb. Plug the voltmeter into a wall socket, insert one bulb into a lamp, and then plug the lamp into the voltmeter. The voltmeter will display or can be used to determine the amount of power used by the bulb. Use the same lamp to repeat the task with the other bulb.
- Have students use the Integrated Class Activity sheet included with lesson 4, "Experimental Design" (4.8.3), to record the results of the preceding experiment.
- Have students graph the results of the light-bulb experiment to visually show the data on how much energy is used by the two different bulbs.
- Contact your local energy supplier to determine the cost of energy in your area. Use the results of the light-bulb experiment to determine how much money could be saved by using compact fluorescent lamps instead of incandescent light bulbs.
- Have students check light fixtures in the school to determine if energy-saving compact fluorescent lamps are being used. If not, have them write a letter to the principal or school board explaining the benefits of using CFLs to save energy and money.

Whole-Class Career Connections

- Have students research the training available locally for becoming an electrician. Also, ask them to research salary range and potential places of employment. Have students use the employability skills checklist included in module 1, lesson 1 (1.1.8) to discuss the key skills needed by electricians.
- To expand students' awareness of other careers involving or related to the electrical field, have them research career information on the EPCOR Science and Safety of Electricity website, "Careers in Electricity" at <www.epcor.ca/sse/more/careers.html> or on the SchoolFinder website at <www.schoolfinder.com/careers/careerindex.asp> (click on "E", and then scroll down to "Electrica…" for various related careers; clicking on one of the careers brings up detailed information about it).
- Contact a secondary school in your area that offers courses in electronics. Have your class visit the school and discuss the program with students and staff. Be sure to discuss how such courses offer students an edge on future careers.

Instructional Activity

Display the compact fluorescent lamps and incandescent light bulbs for students to examine. Ask:

- What are these?
- For what are they used?
- How are they the same?
- How are they different?

Explain to students that the compact fluorescent lamps are being used more and more, because they use much less power than the more traditional incandescent light bulbs do.

Ask:

- Why would people want to save power?

Have students share their ideas, and then display the Saving Energy information sheet (4.11.2) on the overhead projector. Review the sheet with students, and discuss the ideas presented. Ask:

- In what ways might people waste energy?

Display the vocabulary cards – *Saving Energy* (4.11.1) in the pocket chart. Have students use the words to create sentences, and record their sentences on chart paper. Also, have students share these terms in their first language(s).

Peer Activity

Have ELL-student/peer-helper pairs make switch-plate stickers to remind people to turn off the light(s) when they leave a room. Provide each pair of students with a switch plate, a pencil, adhesive paper, and permanent overhead markers. Have them trace the switch-plate cover onto the adhesive paper and cut out the tracing. Then, ask them to use the permanent markers to decorate the tracing with pictures and words to encourage others to turn off lights. The backing can be removed from the adhesive paper and the stickers affixed directly onto switch plates in classrooms and other rooms within the school as well as at home.

Independent Activity: Activity Sheet A

Directions to students:

Use illustrations and descriptive sentences to show examples of saving energy and wasting energy. (For example: The girl has left on lights in three different rooms and has also left the TV and the computer on; with an accompanying picture) (4.11.3).

Extensions

- Add new vocabulary – *Saving Energy* to the multilingual word wall, or have students add the new terms to their personal vocabulary folders.

- Have students add new vocabulary – *Saving Energy* to their personal dictionaries.

Vocabulary Cards - Saving Energy

Vocabulary Cards - Saving Energy

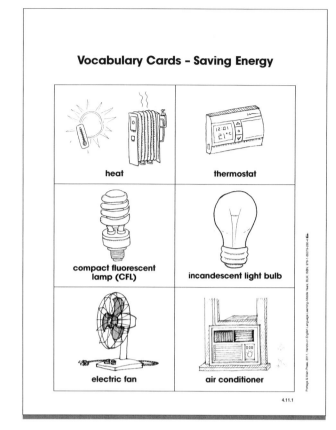

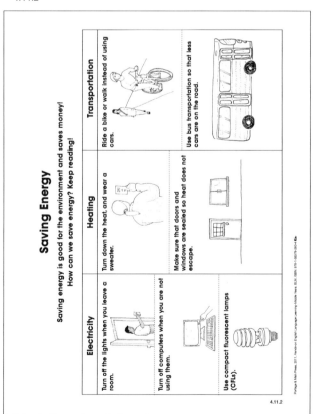

✓ Saving Energy	Wasting Energy ✗

Energy

12 | Culminating Activity: Sustainability Life Practices

Curricular Connections

- Language Arts: speaking, listening, reading, writing, viewing, representing
- Mathematics: collecting, organizing, viewing, interpreting data
- Science: living things, sustainable development, environmental issues
- Social Studies: sustainable development, environmental issues
- Health: physical and emotional wellbeing, basic human needs

Background Information for Teachers

This lesson focuses on making a difference with regard to the environment and the global community; the activities presented in the lesson will help to provide your students with an understanding of global environmental issues. The idea that they can make a difference in the world may seem rather abstract to students, so it is important that issues and potential action plans be relevant to their lives and experiences.

Materials

- overhead projector
- chart paper
- markers
- student dictionaries
- reference material on various sustainable development issues (access to clean water and clean air; environmental issues: pollution, energy use, rainforests, habitat destruction, endangered plants and animals)
- wall map of the world
- charts, posters, and activity sheets from all preceding lessons in this module
- computer with internet access

Integrated Class Activities

This lesson's focus on sustainability life practices will benefit all students in the class, so consider conducting all of the following activities with the entire class.

Whole-Class Career Connection

Have students discuss and research other jobs related to environmental issues. For example:

- Various jobs working for a recycling company
- Various jobs working or volunteering for local or international environmental organizations
- Various jobs working for a company that makes cloth shopping bags

Instructional Activity: Part One

On chart paper, record the term *persuade*. Ask students:

- What does this word mean?

Have students share their ideas and use the word in a sentence to demonstrate understanding. Record their ideas and sentences on chart paper. Also, have students look up the definition of this term in their student dictionaries, and record that definition on the chart paper.

Use Activity Sheet A (4.12.1) to introduce students to the persuasive paragraph. Discuss the purpose of a persuasive paragraph as well as the criteria presented on the activity sheet. Model the process of writing a persuasive paragraph by writing a class one about an environmental issue. As a group, choose a topic of general interest, and work together through the development of a paragraph to persuade others of your collective position. For example:

It is important for all people in our community to recycle. Recyclable materials include paper, plastic, aluminum, and glass. There are many reasons why it is important to recycle. First,

12

recycling cuts down on the amount of garbage we throw out. This means less garbage going into landfills. Secondly, recycling allows materials to be reused. Recycled paper can be made into new paper, instead of cutting down more trees. Third, recycling cuts down on the use of natural resources, such as fossil fuels that are used to make plastic. It is clear that recycling is good for the environment, so be sure to do your part!

Have students select an environmental topic of interest to them, conduct some basic research, and write a persuasive paragraph on the issue. Students can use the activity sheet to guide this process.

Independent Activity: Part One: Activity Sheet A

Directions to students:

Use this sheet as a guide to write a persuasive paragraph on an environmental issue that interests you (4.12.1).

Other Activities That Focus on Environmental Issues

- Have the class participate in Earth Day celebrations.
- Plan an Environmental Fair: Have students select environmental issues of interest to them and then use Activity Sheet B (4.12.2) to make a plan of action that focuses on their chosen topic. Then, have students research their topics with the goal to present to the public for heightened awareness. Students' projects can be displayed much like a science or heritage fair. Invite other classes, students' families, and community members to learn about students' research.
- Brainstorm with students to identify ways that the class and school can help the environment locally; for example, grow potted plants to improve air quality, encourage garbage-free lunches, promote recycling, raise funds for schoolyard trees, and so on.
- Brainstorm with students to identify ways of encouraging their families to help the environment; for example, reduce water usage, walk or use a bike for transportation, and use cars less, use energy-saving light bulbs (compact fluorescent lamps, or CFLs).
- Have students fundraise for local and/or international environmental organizations (for example, Canadian Wildlife Federation, EcoKids, Evergreen, Green Street – see the list of websites on page 332 for URL addresses).
- Show students a recording of *The Girl Who Silenced the World for 5 Minutes*, featuring Severn Cullis-Suzuki speaking at the 1992 UN Earth Summit in Rio de Janeiro (see <www.youtube.com/watch?v=5V7W5-m_ZCE>).
- As a class, design and make your own cloth grocery/shopping bags to replace plastic ones. (For some kid-friendly instructions on how to make one, visit <www.ehow.com/how_5452559_make-own-cloth-grocery-bag.html>).
- Collect used batteries, and dispose of them at an appropriate hazardous waste site in your area.
- Initiate a school- or community-wide fundraiser to sell reusable water bottles to replace plastic ones.

Independent Activity: Part Two: Activity Sheet B

Directions to students:

Record your ideas for a plan of action that will help you contribute towards the solution of a world problem (4.12.2).

▶

12

Assessment of Learning

Use the vocabulary cards from all lessons in this module (4.1.1, 4.2.1, 4.3.1, 4.3.2, 4.4.1, 4.4.2, 4.5.1, 4.6.1, 4.7.1, 4.8.1, 4.9.1, 4.10.1, 4.11.1) to assess students' sentence structure and comprehension skills. Display one card at a time, and have students use each term in a sentence. Use the Vocabulary Tracking Checklist (I.9), shown in the introduction to **Hands-On English Language Learning** on page 39, to record vocabulary that the student knows as well as vocabulary still to be mastered.

Date: _____ Name: _____

Writing a Persuasive Paragraph

In a persuasive paragraph the writer presents his or her opinion on a topic and tries to get the reader to agree with it. The writer includes supporting details in the paragraph, or reasons why the reader should support that opinion.

Topic: Select an environmental issue that interests you. Record your opinion, or what you think, about this issue.

_____
_____
_____

Support: Next, you need reasons for the reader to share your point of view—support for your opinion. This may require some background reading or research. Make some simple jot notes, and add information that may be useful in your persuasive paragraph.

- _____
- _____
- _____
- _____
- _____
- _____

Write: Now, use the following steps to write your persuasive paragraph:

1. Write a topic sentence—a strong statement that clearly states your opinion.

2. Add three or more supporting details or reasons that back up your opinion. Be sure to explain each supporting detail clearly.

3. Add a strong concluding statement at the end of the paragraph that restates your point of view.

4. Edit and proofread your paragraph for spelling, grammar, capitalization, and punctuation.

12A

Date: _____ Name: _____

You Are Never Too Young To Make a Difference!

Here is My Plan to Change the World:

The Problem: _____
_____
_____
_____
_____
_____
_____

My Solution: _____
_____
_____
_____
_____
_____
_____

Declaration:
I plan to take action to help solve this problem.

Signature _____ Date _____

12B

Blackline Masters

References for Teachers

British Columbia Ministry of Education. *Environmental Concepts in the Classroom: A Guide for Teachers.* Victoria, BC: British Columbia Ministry of Education, Legislation & Independent Education Department, 1995.

Government of Canada. *Our Climate is Changing.* Ottawa: Government of Canada, 1999.

Lawson, Jennifer. *Hands-On Science*, grades 1–7 (MB editions). Winnipeg: Portage & Main Press, 1999–2004.

———. *Hands-On Social Studies*, grades 1–4 (MB editions). Winnipeg: Portage & Main Press, 2003.

Manitoba Education and Training. *Education for a Sustainable Future: A Resource for Curriculum Developers, Teachers, and Administrators.* Winnipeg: Manitoba Education and Training, School Programs Division, 2000.

Mi, Y-H. et al. "Current asthma and respiratory symptoms among pupils in Shanghai, China: influence of building ventilation, nitrogen dioxide, ozone, and formaldehyde in classrooms." *Indoor Air.*, v16, i6 (December 2006): 454–464 (<http://onlinelibrary.wiley.com/doi/10.1111/j.1600-0668.2006.00439.x/abstract>)

Salam, Muhammad, Talat Islam, and Frank Gilliland. "Recent evidence for adverse effects of residential proximity to traffic sources on asthma." *Current Opinion in Pulmonary Medicine.*, v14, i1: 3–8 (January 2008). (<http://journals.lww.com/co-pulmonarymedicine/Fulltext/2008/01000/Recent_evidence_for_adverse_effects_of_residential.3.aspx>)

Walker, Michael. *Amazing English Buddy Book.* Lebanon, IN: Addison-Wesley, 1995.

———. *Amazing English Buddy Book: Newcomer Level.* Lebanon, IN: Addison-Wesley, 1995.

Websites

<www.eecom.org>

- **Canadian Network for Environmental Education and Communication (EECOM)** site: This national network for environmental education and communication works to advance environmental learning for Canadians and provides a national medium for people to share ideas, programs, research, resources, events, and services and to enhance their professional skills for environmental learning, as well as to nurture environmentally responsible actions.

<www.cwf-fcf.org>

- **Canadian Wildlife Federation (CWF)** site. The CWF works to ensure an appreciation of our natural world and a lasting legacy of healthy wildlife and habitat by informing and educating Canadians, advocating responsible human actions, and representing wildlife on conservation issues. The CWF produces various resources, runs a myriad of habitat programs, facilitates financial and in-kind methods of support, and advocates for legislative change to inform, inspire, and educate people about the value of wildlife and healthy habitats.

Unit Planning for English Language Learners in an Inclusive Classroom Setting

Module 5

Introduction

The purpose of this module is to provide teachers with guidance in developing their own units of study that address the needs of ELL students within the integrated classroom context. In this environment, ELL students are working alongside their peers on grade-level curriculum material but may require program modifications and accommodations.

Teachers may well find it challenging to plan and implement curricular units to meet the needs of the diversity of learners in their classrooms. The key to doing this successfully is to be knowledgeable of students' strengths, challenges, and experiences and to differentiate instruction and assessment accordingly.

For ELL students in an integrated-classroom setting, language is not learned in isolation, but, rather, in conjunction with new concepts in each subject area. Therefore, it is important that language and subject-specific content be blended together in a holistic approach to teaching and learning. Using this approach, the teacher is responsible for creating a language-rich environment in which learning is accessible to the range of students in the classroom.

The following pages offer a step-by-step universal design template to assist teachers in planning curricular units that will support English language learners in an inclusive, integrated-classroom setting. The approach can be used at any grade level, and for any subject area.

Materials

To follow is a list of materials you might need while using module 5 of **Hands-On English Language Learning** to plan units of study for your students. Note that the blackline masters referred to throughout the module (5.1–5.12) and included at the end of it are not included in the following list:

- chart paper
- markers, pens
- colouring markers or coloured pencils
- highlighters (various colours)
- drawing paper
- writing and scrap paper
- poster paper
- digital camera(s)
- bilingual dictionaries (English and ELL students' first languages)
- picture dictionaries
- clip-art visuals and/or pictures from the internet or magazines (content of visuals will depend on topic being studied)
- any of the vocabulary cards included in modules 1–4 (to be used as a template)
- personal dictionary blackline masters included in module 1 lesson 1 (1.1.6, 1.1.7)
- computers, internet access
- wide variety of language-rich resources at varying reading levels (fiction, non-fiction, reference, music, magazines, newspapers, educational software. Content of resources will depend on topic being studied.)
- wide assortment of poetry (humorous, topical, haiku, nursery rhymes, and so on. Content of poetry will depend on topic being studied.)

Step 1: Assessment for Learning

Before planning a new curricular unit, it is important for teachers to identify the strengths and challenges of all students in the class. For ELL students, this will require a clear understanding of the students' English language skills in reading, writing, speaking, and listening. The educational strengths and needs of English language learners can be identified most effectively by using a variety of assessment tools, such as those presented in the **Hands-On English Language Learning** Assessment Plan (see page 32). Teachers are encouraged to use these assessment strategies along with their own classroom-based assessment tools to identify each student's strengths and challenges. This will help provide teachers with the information they need to determine how to plan a new unit to best meet the needs of ELL learners along with all other students in the class.

A Learner Characteristics template (5.1), onto which teachers can record the learning styles, strengths, needs, and interests of students in the class, is shown on page 427. Completing this chart prior to unit planning ensures a clear focus on supporting individual students through differentiated instruction. When recording observations on the chart consider the following for each student:

- **English language proficiency**: At what stage is the student in developing English language usage in listening, speaking, reading, and writing?
- **Learning style:** Is this student an auditory, visual, tactile, or kinaesthetic learner?
- **Strengths**: In what areas does the student excel? Are there identifiable strengths in specific subjects or in the use of specific skills? Focus not only on academics, but also on other areas such as the arts (for example, knowledge about visual arts, music, dance, drama), practical arts (for example, skills in human ecology [cooking, sewing], woodworking), and physical and social skills.
- **Needs**: In what areas does the student need support? Again, focus not only on academic skills, but also on supports required in other areas such as work habits, monitoring behaviour and social interactions, and fine-/gross-motor skills.

Note: For further information on learning styles, thinking styles, and multiple intelligences, refer to the Manitoba Education *Success for All Learners* document (chapter 4).

- **Interests**: Are there any specific student interests that might be incorporated into a unit of study to enhance student engagement?

By identifying learner characteristics of all students in the class, the teacher is better prepared to examine curricular demands that may require adaptations for English language learners.

Step 2: Curriculum Review

The unit planning process involves an in-depth review of curricular concepts and learning expectations/outcomes. It is essential that teachers carefully explore the curricular guidelines for each unit of study.

Begin by reviewing the introduction to the unit (strand or cluster). Identify main concepts, key vocabulary, and general expectations/outcomes; use the Unit Planning Template (5.2) shown on page 427 to record important information.

Next, identify teaching and learning activities that focus specifically on the expectations/outcomes identified in the curriculum document. Provide details in terms of the kinds of strategies to be used—lectures, demonstrations, role playing, independent research, cooperative learning, performance-based tasks, use of audio-visual resources and technology, and homework expectations. It is important to note that during this planning stage, it is not necessary to provide the specifics of lesson plans but, rather, to identify the kinds of teaching and learning activities that will be conducted in the classroom setting.

▶

Since teaching, learning, and assessment are integral parts of the educational planning process, teachers must consider the kinds of assessment strategies they will use to identify student learning. In keeping with the approach to assessment used in the *Hands-On English Language Learning* program, teachers should be planning assessment *for* learning, assessment *as* learning, and assessment *of* learning (please see pages 35–36 for further information on this approach to assessment). Decisions on assessment strategies to be used should also be recorded on the Unit Planning Template.

The plan articulated thus far is generic in nature, in that it focuses on curricular guidelines and expectations/outcomes. It is now important to determine how this plan matches or does not match the strengths and needs of ELL students in the class. Review the Learner Characteristics chart (5.1) to determine how to adapt teaching/learning and assessment strategies for ELL students. Consider what accommodations might be needed in order for students to participate fully in the unit lessons and acquire related concepts and skills. Record these on the Unit Planning Template under "Adaptations to Teaching/Learning Activities for Individual Students". Similarly, consider the kinds of assessment strategies planned for the unit, and identify how well these strategies match the strengths and needs of ELL students. Determine accommodations needed for the specific assessment strategies planned, and record these under "Adaptations to Assessment Strategies for Individual Students".

Finally, identify any other considerations necessary to support students. For example:

- Will students require any special resources or materials?
- Will students benefit from additional support from other staff, volunteers, or peers?
- Are there opportunities to make connections to the community and to students' families in terms of unit activities (for example, field trips, guest speakers, cultural and language connections)?

Step 3: Instructional Strategies

There is a wide variety of instructional strategies that will prove beneficial to English language learners and, as these are considered best practices in education, they may well benefit all learners in the class. Be sure, therefore, to consider implementing worthwhile strategies with the entire class, or with a variety of students who will benefit specifically from these approaches.

Making Connections to Prior Knowledge

It is important to design all lessons to include a component that activates prior knowledge and language, both in the ELL student's first language and in English. The following are effective activating strategies:

Brainstorming: For each new topic, have students informally reveal what they already know about the subject by sharing ideas orally and recording them. This may be done as a whole-class brainstorm, in small groups, or in pairs.

For a whole-class brainstorm consider using a concept web to record ideas. In the centre of a sheet of chart paper record the topic title, and circle it. Ask students to share their ideas about the topic, and record these in the form of a web (see page 422 for an example of a concept web).

If students are working in small groups or pairs, have each group/pair select one student to be the recorder and take notes. These notes may take the form of a concept web or a simpler format, such as jot notes.

Note: When making connections both to students' prior knowledge and to their first language(s), be aware of students' literacy skills in their first language(s). Depending on past educational experiences, some students may have limited literacy in both English and their first language(s).

KWL chart: The KWL (or Know…Want to Know…Learned) chart is used with small groups, pairs, or by individuals to record knowledge throughout the unit. A KWL Chart template (5.3) is shown on page 427. Before beginning the unit, as a means of activating prior knowledge, have students record, in the first column of the chart, what they already know about the topic. ELL students may write in English, in their first language(s), or they may use illustrations and visuals. In the second column of the chart, have students record what they want to know about the topic. This is usually done in questions. In the third column of the chart, ask students to record what they learn throughout the unit. For this purpose, it is important to revisit the KWL chart frequently.

KWHL chart: The KWHL (Know…Want to Know…How I Can Find Out…Learned) chart is a modification of the KWL activating strategy, which includes a process by which students think about how they can acquire new knowledge. A KWHL Chart template (5.4) is shown on page 427. The first two columns of the KWHL chart are completed just like the KWL chart, with students recording what they know and what they want to know. In the third column, students then record *how* they can answer the questions in the second column. This process encourages students to explore ways of accessing information themselves, rather than assuming that all new knowledge is conveyed by the teacher. The final column is completed throughout the unit, as students learn new information and answer questions recorded in the second column.

Word splash: This strategy is used to explore vocabulary at the beginning of a unit of study. Teachers create a list of vocabulary that is essential to the unit, ensuring that there are several terms with which students are already familiar. These terms may come from curriculum documents, brainstorming activities, or reference material. The vocabulary is recorded on a sheet of paper, usually in a random fashion, as in the following example:

Make a copy of the word splash for each student, and instruct students to

- Circle words with which they are familiar;
- Underline words that they have heard before;
- Put a star beside words that are unfamiliar.

This strategy offers students an opportunity to explore new terms and reflect on their understanding. The word splash can be kept and revisited throughout the unit so students can continue to reflect on their knowledge of vocabulary.

Note: This strategy is also an excellent form of assessment *for* learning (as teachers identify where students are at in terms of vocabulary concepts) and assessment *as* learning (as students reflect on their own skills). The strategy can also be used at the end of a unit as a form of assessment *of* learning, by conferencing one-on-one with students and having them share their understanding of the vocabulary.

Cultural connections: When beginning a new unit, there are often opportunities for students to share cultural connections. For example, if studying musical composers, students might share knowledge of music and musicians from their countries of origin or cultural groups.

First-language connections: The activating strategies listed here also provide opportunities for students to share language connections. For example, when brainstorming or completing a word splash, have students share some of this vocabulary in their first language(s). Record these words on the concept maps and word splash sheets.

Experiential connections: Students will benefit from sharing past experiences related to new topics of study. For example, if the class is studying Canadian geography, ELL students might share experiences related to their travels to Canada. In the same way, if the class is studying water, ELL students might talk about water sources, bodies of water, and precipitation in their country of origin.

Building Vocabulary

Although one of the aims of an inclusive classroom is to enable English language learners to successfully participate in learning activities along with their classmates, it is essential that specific attention be paid to help ELL students build vocabulary necessary for this success. This does not mean that every student in the class needs to master the same vocabulary. Instead, the planning process must consider the need for differentiation of instruction and modifications to vocabulary and related concepts. It is useful for teachers to articulate the vocabulary essential to the unit of study and how this might be modified for ELL students.

The **Language Pyramid** is a useful strategy for representing visually the ideas of differentiation of instruction and modifications to vocabulary.

Use the Language Pyramid template (5.5) shown on page 428 to identify the vocabulary for a given unit. This list may come from curriculum documents, class brainstorming and word-splash activities, or from reference materials used for the unit. Be sure to include general unit vocabulary and concepts. For example, in a novel-study unit, include terms such as *author, illustrator, title, setting, characters*, and so on. In the same way, be sure to include nouns, verbs, adjectives, and adverbs related to the topic of study. Record these in the bottom section of the pyramid.

Next, focus on the ELLs who already have some experience with the English language, and identify the vocabulary that these students should learn during the unit. Begin by reviewing the lower level of the pyramid to determine which of these terms students should be exposed to. Also include any general vocabulary that ELL students may need to use during this unit of study. Record these terms in the middle section of the pyramid.

Finally, consider the beginning English language learners in the class, and identify the vocabulary that these students should learn during the unit. First, review the terms in the bottom and middle sections of the pyramid, and determine which of these beginning ELL students should focus on. Again, remember to consider general vocabulary that these students will need in order to participate in lessons. Record all of these terms in the top section of the pyramid.

To scaffold learning, focus first on the vocabulary listed in the top section of the pyramid, and as ELL students gain mastery, extend this to include vocabulary from the middle and bottom sections. Plan a variety of vocabulary-building activities to support ELL students in the classroom setting. Strategies for building vocabulary include the following:

- Create illustrated vocabulary cards. Use any of the ***Hands-On English Language Learning*** vocabulary cards from modules 1 to 4 as a template to create a vocabulary card for each required word (see page 55 for an example). Small, blank index cards also work well for this purpose. To illustrate the cards use clip art visuals, pictures from the internet or magazines, or hand draw pictures.

- Also consider having students make their own illustrated vocabulary cards—a vocabulary-building activity in itself. Give students digital cameras, and have them take photographs related to unit vocabulary. Also have them use clip art, pictures from the internet or magazines, and their own drawings to illustrate their cards.

- Use the illustrated vocabulary cards made in class to pre-teach key vocabulary in order to enhance student involvement and success in lessons.

- Provide bilingual and picture dictionaries to assist students in creating their own bilingual dictionaries. Have students use the personal dictionary blackline masters included in module 1 lesson 1 (1.1.6, 1.1.7) as templates for creating their personal dictionaries. Then, throughout the unit of study, have them add new terminology to their dictionaries.

Note: Encourage ELL students to include terms from their first language(s) in their personal dictionaries.

- **Three-Point Approach:** This strategy is especially effective for introducing and reviewing more complex terminology. Distribute copies of the Three-Point Approach template (5.6) shown on page 428. Have students record, on the template, a new word or concept as well as a synonym for or an example of that term. Then, have them draw a labelled diagram or an illustration of the term and record a definition for it in their own words. It is often more effective if the teacher models the process first and completes a few examples with a group before students work on this task independently. This strategy is also beneficial as a form of assessment of learning.

- Throughout the unit, assess students' knowledge of related vocabulary. Use the Vocabulary Tracking Checklist (I.9) shown on page 39 of the introduction to ***Hands-On English Language Learning*** to record terms and results.

Conceptual Understanding

During lessons, it is important to support learners as they acquire new information, process ideas, and learn new skills. The following strategies are especially important to use with English language learners:

- Begin each lesson by introducing the topic, the concepts on which you will be focusing, and student expectations. This sets the stage for learning and gives students a clearer sense of what is to come.

- Be sure that lesson introductions include a review of previously taught concepts and vocabulary. This will help all students master learning expectations/outcomes.

- During lessons, use graphic organizers to show how ideas are related. T-charts, Venn diagrams, flow charts, story maps, and timelines are all examples of organizers that do not depend on language knowledge and that promote development of thinking skills, such as classifying, relating cause and effect, comparing and contrasting, or following a sequence.

- Use organizational frames to chart fiction and non-fiction reading. Templates for an Organizational Frame: Fiction Reading (5.7) and an Organizational Frame: Non-Fiction

▶

Reading (5.8) are shown on page 428 for use with fiction and non-fiction reading material. Use these with the whole class, with groups or pairs of students, or with individual students.

Note: Both charts also provide space for ELL students to record new or unfamiliar words to explore and to extend learning.

- Use diverse forms of communication to convey ideas to students. Rather than relying solely on English language to express ideas, also use visuals (illustrations, diagrams, photos), videos, music, art, drama, sketching, mime, role playing, and so on.

- Allow students to show their understanding of a concept in alternative ways (for example, by demonstration, by speaking, with a picture, by writing in their first languages).

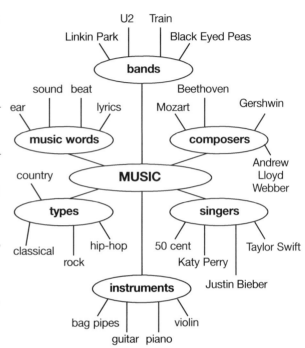

Conducting Research

Many courses in the middle-years curriculum require students to conduct and present independent research. Most students require guidance throughout the research exercise to help make both the process and the product meaningful and educational. It is important, therefore, to ensure that assigned research projects are designed with step-by-step process guidelines and detailed criteria for the product. Consider using the following approach to support students through their research:

1. Choose a Topic: Offer guidance to students in the selection of research topics. If, for example, students are assigned a research project related to a specific subject, such as music, for instance, brainstorm a variety of possible research topics within the realm of music. This may be recorded on a concept web, as in the following example:

If, on the other hand, students are not assigned a specific subject to research, they will still require assistance selecting topics. For example, if they must conduct research for science class and they have full freedom to select their science topics, you may engage students in a "Reflection and Selection" activity. This involves having students reflect on topics of interest within the subject area and on access to resources. See page 429 for a Reflection and Selection template (5.9) to guide this activity.

2. Gather Resources: Assist students in accessing relevant resources, and have them record these on the Research Sources Summary sheet (5.10) shown on page 429. Begin with a visit to the school or local library to access age-appropriate print material. Students may also use this opportunity to review reference material related to their topics. Next, guide students in the selection of relevant websites that are academically sound and geared to students' ages, reading levels, and language levels. Also, be sure students consider newspapers, magazines, and videos as sources of information for their research. Finally, students will benefit greatly if they can access expert knowledge (in-person) related to their research topic. Assist students in connecting with suitable individuals to consult through local schools, organizations, government offices, community colleges, and universities.

3. Record Information: Have students record jot notes—short sentences written in their own words—for each resource they gather. It is important to have ELL students record their jot notes in sentence form, as this helps in the development of English-grammar and sentence-structure skills. A Research Jot Notes template (5.11) is shown on page 429.

Note: It is important that ELL students are offered support during the research process, particularly with any reading and recording. The teacher, an educational assistant, a volunteer, or a peer helper can support ELLs in discussing and processing what they see, read, and record while researching their specific topic.

4. Categorize Information: Once students have recorded information from all their selected sources, and the teacher has reviewed it, they need to organize their data. This process involves reviewing all jot-note sheets and determining categories for sorting the material. For example, if a student is conducting research on Terry Fox, categories might include: personal information (birth date, birthplace), childhood, cancer, becoming a runner, marathon of hope, and long-term impact. As another example, if a student is researching a country, headings might include geography, plants and animals, history, culture, economy, and interesting facts.

To support students in identifying these categories, have them review their jot notes and create a graphic organizer, such as a concept map. Using this kind of visual will help students make connections between the English language, any newly acquired information, and their research categories. A Concept Map template (5.12) is shown on page 429 for students' use to help them categorize their research information.

Once students have identified their categories, have them use the concept map template to expand each one further to include main ideas, headings, or sub-categories. Then, have students review their jot notes and use different coloured highlighters to highlight information related to the various headings. This will provide them with an overall structure for writing and/or presenting the material.

5. Present Research: To help students develop skills in English-language writing, encourage them to transpose their jot notes into written paragraphs, using the categorized format described above to structure their writing.

Students may also create posters, PowerPoint presentations, brochures, and so on for presenting their research. These media offer students the added dimension of visuals—graphics, maps, illustrations, labelled diagrams, and so on—to convey their knowledge. Alternatively, have students expand the research poster idea into a hands-on presentation by creating backboards and displays that include artefacts, models, or demonstrations.

Oral presentation of each student's research is essential regardless of how the research is delivered. Students can share written research papers by reading them orally, or they can present their posters (or other), describing various aspects of it (in the same way, backboards with artefacts can be shared orally by description and through demonstration).

Note: Encourage students to make cue cards to support themselves during oral presentations.

The Language-Rich Classroom

By creating a classroom environment rich in oral and written language, teachers will enhance ELL students' opportunities to acquire and improve their English-language skills. Throughout the *Hands-On English Language Learning* program, many suggestions have been made for designing a language-rich classroom, including

- Development of a multilingual word wall that includes visual representations of new vocabulary and written words in English and students' first language(s).
- Development of personal vocabulary folders for situations where classroom space does not allow for word wall displays.
- Use of personal dictionaries to record new vocabulary.
- Access to a wide variety of language-rich resources, such as fiction, non-fiction, reference, and poetry books, music, magazines and newspapers, educational software, websites, and relevant hardware/technology.

Poetry Workshop

One especially effective strategy for integrating language into several curricular units is to plan and implement a poetry workshop related to the topic of study. The purpose of the poetry workshop is to

- Differentiate reading instruction
- Focus on oral reading and speaking
- Introduce and enhance English vocabulary
- Develop a love of poetry and a feel for the rhythm of language
- Provide a means to accessing a wide variety of language-usage styles

The poetry workshop can be designed to accommodate all learners in the classroom. Consider implementing some of the following ideas for the workshop:

- Gather a wide assortment of poetry of all types—humorous, topical, haiku, nursery rhymes, and so on. Access poems from books and websites.
- Select various poems related to the topic of study. Whether students are studying the human body, weather, Africa, or ancient civilizations, poetry about most topics is likely easy to access online. Involve students in the process of finding poems related to the topic of study.
- Share poems that are special to you, reading them aloud and explaining why they are favourites.
- Have students review the topical poetry. ELL students may buddy-read with peer helpers, since most poems are meant to be read aloud.
- Have ELL students keep track of new words and include them on word walls, in language folders, or in personal dictionaries.
- Have students share their favourite poems, reading them aloud and explaining why and how they are special.
- Create a classroom poetry anthology. Have each student select his or her favourite poem, recopy it onto drawing paper, and then use markers or coloured pencils to illustrate it. Ensure that students also include the poet's name with each poem chosen. Bind together all illustrated poems with a front and back cover.
- Share this anthology with other classes. This offers an excellent opportunity for ELL students to read aloud to others. As a class, you may also set criteria for poetry reading, and use this as a strategy for assessment *as* and assessment *of* learning.

- To extend this into a writing activity, have students use the poetry studied as a springboard for writing their own poetry, and create an anthology of students' poetry.

Other Things to Consider for Unit Planning

Connecting with Parents, Families, and the Community: As part of the planning for a new unit of study, it is beneficial to communicate with parents. This may be done via a class newsletter, a website, or (a) letter(s) written by the teacher or students. Keeping parents informed enables them to better support their children by discussing topics at home, supporting homework completion, and sharing home resources and expertise.

Various factors can make it challenging to connect and engage with some parents/families through class letters, newsletters, and websites. These include varying literacy skills, work constraints, personal difficulties, and differing understandings of the importance of parental/familial involvement in a child's education. Noting these potential challenges, continue with efforts to engage and communicate with families, perhaps utilizing members of the community or cultural liaisons, translators, and family support workers.

In the same way, consider making connections to the local community by inviting guest speakers into the classroom or planning field trips related to the topic of study. This expands students' learning environment and also helps them to develop language skills for daily living.

Books for Students: For each new unit of study, gather a wide variety of books related to the topic, and have them available to students for reference, research, and general enjoyment. Include books at varying reading levels including fiction, non-fiction, and reference books, as well as magazines and poetry. Encourage students to add to the collection with books from home or that they acquire at the library.

Websites: Identify internet sites that are helpful to students and teachers. Be sure to check each site before allowing students access to it (for content, as well as to ensure that it is still accessible).

Materials: Gather all materials required for unit lessons, ensuring that students have opportunities for hands-on experiences and real-life contextual learning. Also, acquire artefacts, models, and visuals related to the unit. For example, if studying a topic such as the solar system, it will be beneficial for students to have access to models, materials for constructing their own models, posters, and other resource materials related to the topic.

Peer Activities: As recommended throughout the *Hands On English Language Learning* program, building relationships among peers is beneficial to all students. For English language learners, working with peer helpers also helps to foster personal connections and language development in a positive environment. Consider planning a wide variety of opportunities for students to work together in partners or small groups as they complete learning activities related to the unit of study.

Activity Sheets: When designing ways for students to record their ideas or learning activities, be sure to consider how activity sheets may be used by various learners. English language learners, for example, may require visual supports on these sheets, or they may need written instructions to be simplified. In the same way, ELL students may benefit from recording their learning through illustrations, labelled diagrams, writing in their first language(s), as well as writing in English. It is important to provide students with many opportunities to hone their writing skills, while at the same time creating learning experiences that promote student success and engagement.

Assessment Strategies: As mentioned in the ***Hands-On English Language Learning*** Assessment Plan (see page 32), as well as earlier in this module, assessment strategies should include:

- Assessment *for* learning: to identify students' entering language skills and conceptual knowledge
- Assessment *as* learning: to encourage independent learning through self-assessment and reflection
- Assessment *of* learning: to identify students' language skills and conceptual knowledge after involvement in one or more learning experiences.

It is important to design and implement assessment strategies for the specific unit of study to ensure that all three of these processes are addressed.

Concluding Note to Teachers

As professionals, the process of unit planning is one that takes a great deal of preparation, thought, and consideration of learners and subject area content. The guidelines provided in this module are intended to assist teachers in accommodating English language learners while planning curriculum-specific units of study for an inclusive classroom. While it is hoped that these guidelines and included templates (5.1–5.12) will benefit teachers, it is important to keep in mind that every classroom environment is unique in nature, and teaching and learning plans must first address the needs, strengths, characteristics, and experiences of students in the classroom.

Blackline Masters

5.1 Learner Characteristics

Date: _____

Student	English Language Proficiency	Learning Style	Strengths	Needs	Interests

5.2 Unit Planning Template

Date: _____

Grade	Subject	Unit Title

Unit Overview

Overall Expectations/General Learning Outcomes

Specific Expectations/Learning Outcomes

Teaching/Learning Activities

Assessment for Learning	Assessment as Learning	Assessment of Learning

Adaptations to Teaching/Learning Activities for Individual Students

Adaptations to Assessment Strategies for Individual Students

Additional Considerations (supports, materials, and so on)

5.3 KWL (Know…Want to Know…Learned)

Name: _____
Date: _____

Know	Want to Know	Learned

5.4 KWHL (Know…Want to Know…How I Can Find Out…Learned)

Name: _____
Date: _____
Topic: _____

What I Know	What I Want to Know	How I Can Find Out	What I Learned

Blackline Masters

5.5 Language Pyramid

Date: _____
Unit: _____

5.6 Three-Point Approach

Date: _____ Name: _____

Definition	Word or Concept	Diagram or Illustration
	Example or Synonym	
Definition	Word or Concept	Diagram or Illustration
	Example or Synonym	
Definition	Word or Concept	Diagram or Illustration
	Example or Synonym	

5.7 Organizational Frame: Fiction Reading

Date: _____ Name: _____

- Title
- Author
- Setting
- Characters
- Problem/Conflict
- Events
- Resolution
- New Words

5.8 Organizational Frame: Non-Fiction Reading

Date: _____ Name: _____

- Title
- Author
- Topic
- Facts
- Diagrams, Illustrations
- Two questions I have about the topic:
- New Words

5.9

Date: _____ Name: _____

Reflection and Selection: Choosing a Research Topic

Research Topic, Subject, or Theme: _____

Topics of interest:
- _____
- _____
- _____

Topics for which I have some background knowledge:
- _____
- _____
- _____

Topics that I find difficult, challenging, or uninteresting:
- _____
- _____
- _____

What resources do I have available to me? (experts, books, websites, organizations)
- _____
- _____
- _____

Think about your responses above. Which is the best research topic for you?
_____

5.10

Name: _____
Date: _____

Research Sources Summary

Research Source (include details of publication and location of source)	Summary of Research

5.11

Date: _____ Name: _____

Research Jot Notes

Source: _____

- _____
- _____
- _____
- _____
- _____
- _____
- _____
- _____

5.12

Name: _____
Date: _____

Concept Map: Categorizing Research Information

Research Topic: → Categories → (six category boxes, each leading to a detail box)

Blackline Masters

References

Manitoba Education. *English as an Additional Language (EAL) and Literacy, Academics, and Language (LAL), Kindergarten to Grade 12, Manitoba Curriculum Framework of Outcomes*. Winnipeg: Manitoba Education, September 2010 (draft).

Manitoba Education (formerly, Manitoba Education and Youth). *Success for All Learners: A Handbook on Differentiating Instruction*. Winnipeg: Manitoba Education and Youth, 1996.

Ontario Ministry of Education. *Supporting English Language Learners: A practical guide for Ontario educators, Grades 1 to 8*. Toronto: Queen's Printer for Ontario, 2008.

Language Resources for Students

Adelson-Goldstein, Jayme, and Norma Shapiro. *Oxford Picture Dictionary* series*, New York: Oxford University Press, 2008.

Cleary, Brian P. *Hairy, Scary, Ordinary: What is an Adjective?* Minneapolis: Carolrhoda Books, 2000.

Hill, L.A., and Charles Innes. *Oxford Children's Picture Dictionary.* London, UK: Oxford University Press, 1997.

Mantra Lingua. *My Talking Dictionary: Book and CD Rom*. London, UK: TalkingPen Publications, 2005 (48 dual-language editions).

Ross Keyes, Joan. *The Oxford Picture Dictionary for Kids.* New York: Oxford University Press, 1998.

Walker, Michael. *Amazing English Buddy Book.* Lebanon, IN: Addison-Wesley, 1995.

---

*Bilingual versions of the *Oxford Picture Dictionary* are available for English and the following: Arabic, Brazilian-Portuguese, Chinese, French, Japanese, Korean, Russian, Spanish, Thai, Urdu, and Vietnamese.